Samuelson
and
Neoclassical Economics

RECENT ECONOMIC THOUGHT

Series Editor:

WARREN J. SAMUELS, *Michigan State University*

This series is devoted to works that present divergent views on the development, prospects, and tensions within some important research areas of international economic thought. Among the fields covered are macro-monetary policy, public finance, labor, and political economy. The emphasis of the series is on providing a critical, constructive view of each of these fields, as well as a forum through which leading scholars of international reputation may voice their perspectives on important related issues. Each volume in the series will be self-contained; together, these volumes will provide dramatic evidence of the variety of economic thought within the scholarly community.

SAMUELSON
AND
NEOCLASSICAL ECONOMICS

EDITED BY

GEORGE R. FEIWEL

KLUWER · NIJHOFF PUBLISHING
BOSTON/THE HAGUE/DORDRECHT/LANCASTER

DISTRIBUTORS FOR NORTH AMERICA:
Kluwer Academic Publishers
190 Old Derby Street
Hingham, Massachusetts 02043, U.S.A.

DISTRIBUTORS OUTSIDE NORTH AMERICA:
Kluwer Academic Publishers Group
Distribution Centre
P.O. Box 322
3300 AH Dordrecht, The Netherlands

Library of Congress Cataloging in Publication Data

Main entry under title:
Samuelson and neoclassical economics.

(Recent economic thought)
   1. Samuelson, Paul Anthony, 1915–   — Addresses,
essays, lectures. 2. Neoclassical school of economics —
Addresses, essays, lectures. I. Feiwel, George R.
II. Series.
HB119.S25S25   330.15′5   81-1211

ISBN 0-89838-069-3   AACR2

CONTENTS

PREFACE

This is not a *festschrift,* but a study of the prodigious Samuelson phenomenon, his history-making contributions to and impact on the economics of our age, and the intricate, often perplexing, and divergent trends in modern economics — all intensely controversial subjects that will be argued, scrutinized, and periodically reassessed by economists of various strands and traditions for years to come, for, as Samuelson wrote of Pigou, "immortality does have its price." A scholar with such an outstanding body of contributions "must expect other men to swarm about it" (1966, p. 1233), subject it to scholarly scrutiny, and challenge it.

Although Paul Samuelson was 65 on May 15, 1980 (and our best wishes go out to him for long life and continued enrichment of economics), this is neither a birthday party nor a gathering of only the Good Fairies, for, as he himself has said of Marx, "a great scholar deserves the compliment of being judged seriously" and critically (1972, p. 268). In accordance with the rule of Roman law, *audiatur et altera pars,* I have invited representative scholars of widely divergent perceptions to offer their critical evaluation of the "age of Samuelson." While the response was by and large gratifying, some scholars were unable to meet the deadline, and with much compunction I have had to expand my own essays to partly fill the gaps.

When I was approached to contribute to and edit this volume, I was already committed to organizing the session on economic theory to honor Samuelson at the 1980 AEA meetings. So whatever merit there is in this volume is largely to the credit of Will Baumol for setting me this happy task. In preparing my introductory comments on Samuelson's place in modern economics, I found myself delving ever deeper into Samuelson's voluminous contributions and growing increasingly more enthusiastic about my subject, so much so that I was seriously contemplating writing a study of Samuelson's influence on modern economics. As I perceived the advantages of division of labor among such highly qualified specialists, I agreed to undertake this volume.

The book was conceived in the form of a few major essays and a number of shorter commentaries on related subjects and from various vantage points, to afford both depth and breadth of coverage. Of course, no single volume can do justice to the multifaceted dimensions of a subject that is so interdependent that even the separation in this volume into four parts is not without its pitfalls.

The introductory essay sets the stage by providing an overview of Samuelson's body of work and reflections on the man and the scholar. Part I opens with Chipman's searching survey of consumption theory, which traces the evolution of Samuelson's thinking and illuminates the professional turnabout in the last four decades, with a commentary on revealed preference after Samuelson by a leading mathematical economist of the younger generation — Andreu Mas-Colell. Negishi (himself a contributor to the subject and author of a well-known survey of stability analysis) extends Samuelson's stability analysis to non-Walrasian economics, while Beach incisively criticizes the entire approach, which is fruitfully extended by Krelle in the Samuelsonian tradition. (The related problem of instability is also treated in some of the papers in Part III.) Lau succinctly traces Samuelson's pervasive influence on production theory, while Joan Robinson reflects on her controversy with Samuelson and provides a succinct statement of her position. Tinbergen concentrates on alternative interpretations of production functions, the phenomenon of counterproduction, and the incomes of the "bearers of competition."

Part II opens with an overview perspective of Samuelson's contributions to trade theory by his distinguished student Wan. Chipman deals with developments in welfare economics, and Kemp and Long revisit the important question of reevaluation of social income in a dynamic system.

In Part III Bronfenbrenner takes up the cudgels for eclecticism in economics. I attempt to depict the Samuelsonian neoclassical synthesis, its major critiques, and the various currents in modern economic theory. The author of the classic *Keynesian Revolution,* Klein, Samuelson's first Ph.D. student — and it is said that MIT has not been able to raise its standards since — extends and generalizes the Keynesian model to cope with today's problems. Wallich reviews expertly the changing scene of monetary economics. In the tension between sophistication and relevance, Kuenne criticizes the modern trends in building very general and elegant models and argues for more relevance to the real world — an argument that is reinforced from a different vantage point by Myrdal, who has long swum against the mainstream. Nell, an established critic of neoclassical economics, takes issue with Samuelson's interpretation of Marx's value theory and provides comparisons of Marxist, neoclassical, and neo-Ricardian analyses. Finally, the paramount problem of making the tradeoff between equality and efficiency operational is ably tackled by yet another Samuelson student, Blinder, who calls for economists' increasing recognition of their proposals' implications for distributive justice and for cooperation between macroeconomists, general equilibrium "practitioners," labor economists, and public finance specialists to solve this onerous problem.

In the concluding part we get further glimpses of the many Samuelsons in Bergson's and Akerlof's profiles of a fellow student and mentor. Intriligator, also a student of Samuelson, uses the revealed preference approach to survey the overall impact of Samuelson's contributions on the profession. Bronfenbrenner also provides insights into the fellow student, the man, and the scholar and speculates on Samuelson's likely place in history.

If we succeeded somewhat in our task, my main feat was in a wise choice of contributors. Working with them was an unforgettable and rewarding experience. I am beholden to them for their interest, cooperation, and commitment and, above all, for putting aside their other pressing work to contribute to this volume. Many scholars who do not appear in the table of contents have left their imprint on it. I must thank them collectively. But I would be remiss not to identify at least some of them. The members of the AEA panel — Kenneth J. Arrow (Stanford University), William J. Baumol (Princeton University and New York University), Lawrence R. Klein (University of Pennsylvania), and Robert M. Solow (MIT) — have provided stimulus, encouragement, and valuable clarifications. In the formative stages I benefited greatly from discussions with Leonid Hurwicz (University of Minnesota), Thomas J. Rothenberg (University of California, Berkeley), and Gerard Debreu (University of

California, Berkeley), who also helped by carefully scrutinizing the introductory essay. Among those who provided some valuable contrasting insights into the Samuelson phenomenon and/or substantive comments on my essays are: Moses Abramovitz, (Stanford University), Earl F. Beach (McGill University), Olivier Blanchard (Harvard University), John S. Chipman (University of Minnesota), Benjamin M. Friedman (Harvard University), Nicholas Georgescu-Roegen (Vanderbilt University), Richard M. Goodwin (Cambridge University), Errol Glustoff (University of Tennessee), Geoffrey C. Harcourt (University of Adelaide), Michael D. Intriligator (U.C.L.A.), Hans E. Jensen (University of Tennessee), Murray C. Kemp (University of New South Wales), Charles P. Kindleberger (MIT), Harvey Leibenstein (Harvard University), Abba P. Lerner (Florida State University), John M. Letiche (University of California, Berkeley), Franco Modigliani (MIT), John R. Moore (University of Tennessee), Takashi Negishi (University of Tokyo), Joan Robinson (Cambridge University), Walter S. Salant (Brookings Institution), Theodore W. Schultz (University of Chicago), Amartya K. Sen (Oxford University), G. L. S. Shackle (University of Liverpool), Wolfgang F. Stolper (University of Michigan), Robert Summers (University of Pennsylvania), Paolo Sylos-Labini (University of Rome), Peter Temin (MIT), and Henry Y. Wan, Jr. (Cornell University). All the above are implicated only in anything that is positive and absolved of any errors of commission or omission.

I would like to express my thanks to Robert Bassett and his assistant, Warner Grenade, of the University of Tennessee library for extraordinary diligence and working in the spirit that the impossible takes just a little bit longer. My thanks also to the staff of the University of California (Berkeley) and Stanford libraries, to Cathy Shires (University of Tennessee) for helping me with some of the correspondence while I was away, and to Paul Samuelson for making available a number of yet-unpublished papers and permission to quote from his letter to William R. Allen.

This undertaking took a high toll willingly paid, particularly by my wife and collaborator, Ida, for she shares the sense of purpose and commitment to what we were doing. One of the greatest benefits that academic life offers is the opportunity to come into contact with great minds. Knowing Paul Samuelson is not only a rare privilege, but also an extraordinary and, at every meeting, a refreshing experience. It is to Paul, the remarkable human being and friend, that this book is affectionately dedicated. Many of the vignettes of Samuelson that I have used here were garnered over several years of contact and discussions when neither of the participants knew to what purpose they would be put, and least of all is Paul responsible for my misinterpretations.

GEORGE R. FEIWEL

REFERENCES

Samuelson, P. A. 1966. *The Collected Scientific Papers of Paul A. Samuelson.* 2 vols. Ed. by J. E. Stiglitz. Cambridge, Mass.: MIT Press.
――――. 1972. *The Collected Scientific Papers of Paul A. Samuelson,* Vol. 3. Ed. by R. C. Merton. Cambridge, Mass.: MIT Press.

1 SAMUELSON AND CONTEMPORARY ECONOMICS: *An Introduction*

George R. Feiwel

Paul Samuelson has made an indelible imprint on modern economics. He ranks among history-making economists for his accomplishments in refining, advancing, and spreading economic knowledge. He has played an outstanding role in the analytical revolution in economic theory. He was the 1970 (first American) recipient of the Nobel Prize in Economic Science (the first prize was awarded in 1969 to Jan Tinbergen and Ragnar Frisch); excerpts from the citation read:

> By his many contributions, Samuelson has done more than any other contemporary economist to raise the level of scientific analysis in economic theory. . . . He has rewritten considerable parts of central economic theory, and has in several areas achieved results which now rank among the classical theorems of economics.

All in all, as Kenneth Arrow put it, "Samuelson is one of the greatest economic theorists of all time" (1967, p. 735).

Samuelson is a major architect of the modern neoclassical conception. His pervasive influence on contemporary economics has also come largely from his role as teacher to generations of economists the world over ever since the first appearance of his masterly and controversial

1

textbook in 1948. Another important role played by Samuelson in the history of economic analysis was that of helping to overcome resistance to the use of mathematics in economics through the authority he had acquired in the profession — a role for which he is praised by one group of economists and criticized by another.

His contributions cover a range of subjects almost as broad as economics itself, from the very esoteric, through questions in the mainstream and issues that have played an important role in the accretion of economic knowledge, to the very relevant modern problems of political economy. As he admitted (with a grain of salt) in his presidential address to the American Economic Association:

> My own scholarship has covered a great variety of fields. And many of them involve questions like welfare economics and factor-price equalization; turnpike theorems and osculating envelopes; nonsubstitutability relations in Minkowski-Ricardo-Leontief-Metzler matrices of Mosak-Hicks type; or balanced-budget multipliers under conditions of balanced uncertainty in locally impacted topological spaces and molar equivalences. My friends warn me that such topics are suitable merely for captive audiences in search of a degree — and even then not after dark. [Samuelson 1966, p. 1499]

Samuelson's steady stream of output is not only astounding in quantity, but also always stimulating and often seminal, if not entirely new. Unlike the output of many of his contemporaries, his contributions are broad and deep enough to have assured him an appreciative audience of his peers, from mathematical theorists to literary economists in almost all fields, including those who differ from him in theory, methodology, ideology, policy, and politics (see Hurwicz 1970, p. 721; Friedman 1970, p. 80). Samuelson's work is spiced with astute observations and analytical pointers that are not always fully integrated with the analytical framework, which decreases his currency among economists whose "revealed preference" is for elegance and enhances it among the rank and file.

THE MAKING OF THE ECONOMIST

In a field as intensely controversial as economics, the work of such a major and wide-ranging contributor as Samuelson has necessarily been subject to clashing perceptions on fundamentals, if not on specific formulations. His general neoclassical approach, if not his macroeconomics and his mathematics, is under strong attack from various quarters.

Neoclassical economics means different things to different people.[1] It can be traced to various streams and traditions in the nineteenth century (primarily to Jevons, Edgeworth, Marshall, Walras, Pareto, Menger, Böhm-Bawerk, J. B. Clark, and Wicksell).[2] Probably a distinction should be made between the broad neoclassical perception of the world and the more narrow economic theories of the neoclassical type. "The twin pillars of neoclassical doctrine are the principle of optimization by economic agents and the coordination of their activities through the market" (Arrow 1975, p. 4). It is commonly believed that the most important criterion for distinguishing the neoclassical economists from their classical (Smith to Mill) precursors is probably the introduction of the subjective theory of value (Samuelson 1947, p. 90). Samuelson perceived that the so-called marginal revolution had in fact little to do with either subjective value and utility or with marginalism; rather, it was concerned with refining the general relations of supply and demand and culminated in Walras's formulation of general equilibrium (Samuelson 1966, p. 1756).

Samuelson perceived Walrasian general equilibrium as the peak of neoclassical economics; he believed that Marshall delayed its understanding. Ironically, some younger general equilibrium theorists perceive Samuelson as too Marshallian. However, the mixture of Walras and Marshall, which manifests itself in varied configurations in time and subjects, and not always as compatible elements, provides one clue to the thinking of this great eclectic.

Samuelson seems to share, albeit with reservations, Schumpeter's evaluation of Walras as "the greatest economist of all time." Samuelson likened Walras to Newton: "For there is but one system of the world and Newton was the one who found it. Similarly, there is but one grand concept of general equilibrium and it was Walras who had the insight (and luck) to find it" (ibid., pp. 1501–02).

Samuelson views Marshall as the most overrated economist, who was so afraid of being unrealistic that he ended up fuzzy, confused, and confusing. He claims that Marshall's ambiguities paralyzed the best economic brains on both sides of the Atlantic for three decades. His contention that the problem of modern economics is to exorcize the Marshallian incubus has hardly endeared him to those who claim that it is all in Marshall[3] (Samuelson 1972, pp. 22–24).

Samuelson recalls that in 1932 Chicago was the best place to study economics, for the subject had not yet been energized by Keynes. While marking time he received a thorough grounding in neoclassical economics and doctrinal history:

Chicago was a better place . . . than would have been Harvard, Columbia, or the London School. Cambridge University was never within my ken, but since economics was also waiting for the invigorating kiss of mathematical methods, it would have been a personal tragedy. . . . (I like to think I might have risen above the tragedy, but as Wellington said of Waterloo, it would have been a "damned close-run thing"). [Samuelson 1977, pp. 885–86]

About his transfer from Chicago to Harvard, Samuelson recollects (ibid., pp. 888–89): "Luck was with me. Harvard was precisely the right place to be in the next half dozen years."[4] And on behalf of his "comrades at arms" he reflects: "Harvard made us. Yes, but we made Harvard."

This transfer placed him in what was then the vanguard of science; "right in the forefront of the three great waves of modern economics: the Keynesian revolution . . . the monopolistic or imperfect-competition revolution, and finally, the fruitful clarification of the analysis of economic reality resulting from the mathematical and econometric handling of the subject. . . ." (ibid., p. 890). By 1950, having heard Frank Knight's diatribe against Keynesians and believers in monopolistic competition, Samuelson was emboldened to egg him on by asking him what he thought of mathematical economists, to which the curt reply was that Knight could not stomach them either. Samuelson came to realize "that the indictment fitted me to a T" (ibid., pp. 886–87).

Samuelson left Harvard, but never the banks of the Charles. He transferred to MIT [where he "made beautiful music together with Robert Solow . . . and even survived collaboration with Franco Modigliani" (1972, p. 684) and *made* its economics department]. About this transfer he said (1977, pp. 890–91): "A better offer came from MIT and when I learned that my departure would not cause irreparable grief, I took the offer." Furthermore, "my parting was eased by the fact that no one, least of all me thought that it was lack of merit that kept me from a chair in economic theory."[5]

Samuelson made the greatest splash in the "third wave" of modern economics:

To a person of analytical ability, perceptive enough to realize that mathematical equipment was a powerful sword in economics, the world of economics was his oyster in 1935. The terrain was strewn with beautiful theorems begging to be picked up and arranged in unified order. [Samuelson 1977, p. 886]

He proceeded to do so in his influential classic, *Foundations of Economic Analysis*. Using his innovative powers and analytical and mathematical skills, he investigated the common elements and aimed at deducing the general principles and unifying the various parts of economic theory. Thus, he concentrated, inter alia, on the nature of the equilibrium system, on the general structure of the problem of maximization under constraints, on the statics and dynamics of nonmaximum systems, and on the relationship between comparative statics and dynamics. The result was a sifting through, a creative reconstruction, and a rigorous formulation of a significant part of received theory with new or refined theorems and novel applications.

Thinking back on his work and thought processes when formulating *Foundations,* Samuelson notes:

> In those days someone once asked me which economic journals I read. I had to reply that I read them all. . . . For myself, it was a matter of pride to try to do justice to the literature. Not only did equity require this, but also the efficiency of building up the edifice of scientific knowledge called for integrating new findings with old. . . . I think it is pride that makes one accept the much, much harder challenge of trying only to produce value-added rather than gross contributions to the body of scientific knowledge. [Samuelson 1972, pp. 687–88]

Twenty years after the original publication of *Foundations,* he confessed (ibid., p. 689) to having become "rather estranged" from his brainchild. In the turbulence engendered by the Keynesian revolution and during the war, "the niceties of pure economics seemed somewhat decadent."

To those who accuse him of the mathematization of economics, Samuelson answers (1977, p. 868): "That is one of the mortal sins for which I shall have to do some explaining when I arrive at heaven's pearly gates."

> What a Daniel-come-to-Judgment I would be, if I, the lamb that strayed fustus' and mustus' from the fold, were to testify before God and this company that mathematics had all been a horrible mistake. . . . I wish I could be obliging. Yet even if my lips could be brought to utter the comforting words, like Galileo I would hear myself whispering inside, "But mathematics does indeed help." [Samuelson 1966, p. 1500]

But in the same breath he warns (ibid., p. 1503) that if economists increasingly concentrate on highly technical economics and statistics, they must expect that the informed citizen will increasingly lose interest in their activities and thus deprive them of a means of influencing public opinion and policy. Beyond Samuelson the superb technician lurks Samuelson the political economist. He speaks of economic theory as "a mistress of even too tempting grace. . . . When man sets himself the challenge to theorize and *yet stay within the constraint of explaining reality,* the task is much the harder — but how much more satisfying the hunt. At night by the fireside let them who will display their easy tiger skins; for man the greatest quarry of all is the study of man. For what do they know of economics, who political economy do not know?'' (ibid., pp. 1680–81).

CONTRIBUTIONS TO THEORETICAL ECONOMICS

In a quest to extricate the theory of demand ''from any vestigial traces of the utility concept'' and to find a consumption theory stripped of nonessentials ''to its bare implications for empirical realism'' (ibid., p. 13; 1972, p. 763), Samuelson pioneered in a 1938 essay the forceful and fruitful revealed preference approach, which not only invigorated consumer's choice theory, but also went beyond it. Samuelson's earliest paper, writes John Chipman in Chapter 2, this volume, ''literally revolutionized the theory of consumer behavior.'' Hendrik Houthakker (1961, p. 706), himself a landmark contributor in this field, called it ''epoch making.'' The perplexing problem of characterizing the economic content of the symmetry of the substitution term in the Slutsky equation, which Samuelson did not solve in that paper, has been cracked after four decades. And, to quote Chipman, ''It must be a very satisfying outcome for the originator of such a fruitful idea; it has in fact been one of the most glorious chapters in the history of economic thought.''

Chipman traces the development in two strands of consumption theory of varied traditions — the revealed preference and the measurement of individual welfare. He argues that Samuelson's achievements have been instrumental in transforming analysis in both strands and have provided the foundations for a synthesis of the two. This has opened the door for building utility functions and welfare measures based on market observations of consumer demand behavior.

One of the major quests of modern mainstream economic theory has been the progressive integration of static and dynamic modes of analysis. In dynamic theory time appears in a most essential way: the system is evolving, and present events, which are the result of preceding developments, contribute in turn to the further development of the system.[6] As Samuelson put it:

> The economist has no choice but to study dynamics; for otherwise there is little possibility of presenting a reasonably realistic description of such phenomena as speculation, cyclical fluctuations, and secular growth. In addition,

dynamic process analysis is an enormously flexible mode of thought, both for pinning down the implications of various hypotheses and for investigating new possibilities. [Samuelson 1966, p. 612]

Although not bereft of certain pitfalls, "dynamic analysis has produced many useful results. In the field of pure theory, the important problem of *stability of equilibrium* is wholly a question of dynamics. For it involves the question of how a system behaves after it has been disturbed into a disequilibrium state" (ibid., p. 613). The problem of stability of equilibrium cannot be meaningfully considered without explicitly specifying the dynamics of the adjustment process. "For the comparative-statics analysis to yield fruitful results we must first develop a theory of dynamics" (Samuelson 1947, pp. 262–63).

Indeed, the genesis of the real dynamic stability analysis can be traced to Samuelson's specification, in his pioneering 1941 work on the relevance of dynamics for statics, of the necessary and sufficient conditions for stability.[7] To him the stability hypothesis has no normative significance, "for the stable equilibrium might be at fifty percent unemployment" (ibid., p. 5).

A spinoff of the stability analysis was the famous correspondence principle (ibid., pp. 258, 284, 350, etc.), whose generality and unambiguity have been questioned by some economists. They have suggested that "in fact, very few useful propositions are derivable from this principle" (Arrow and Hahn 1971, p. 12). However, with suitably restrictive assumptions (notably, nonexistence of inferior goods), the correspondence principle can be made precise and correct. Indeed, Samuelson's contribution to the transfer problem (mentioned later) is a good example of this. Basically, the correspondence principle states (in complete generality) that in problems of comparative statics, the information that the economy moves from one *stable* equilibrium to another conveys information about the parameters of the system that in general provides a clearer a priori picture about the derivatives of the state variables with respect to the exogenous shift variables than without this information. To be sure, this is a weaker statement than Samuelson's original one (to the effect that one could unambiguously determine the signs of these derivatives) but it is far from being an empty statement.

In the early postwar period, with the pathbreaking achievements by Arrow, Debreu, and others (dealing with questions of the existence of equilibrium and the like), the emphasis in general equilibrium analysis shifted primarily to the static aspects of competitive equilibrium and away from Samuelson's, Hicks's, and others' concern with the principles

of operation of a general equilibrium system.[8] The theme of dynamic
stability seems to have a cyclical appeal. It was once again revived at
the threshold of the 1960s by Arrow, Hurwicz, and others (including our
contributor Negishi). But nowadays, as Franklin Fisher suggests (1976,
p. 3), "the subject, if not actually disreputable, is at least not very
fashionable."

Although Samuelson's work was largely influential in stimulating the
tendency of modern theorists toward abstract and rigorously formulated
theorems, neither the questions posed and solutions propounded by Samuelson, nor his predilection for a somewhat cavalier approach to elegance
and his "engineering" mathematics, have always been popular with successive generations of mathematical economists. Toward the close of the
1960s, Samuelson admitted (1972, pp. 42–43) that the mathematization of
economic theory in which he himself participated has been subject to
sharply decreasing returns. "Inequalities, convex sets, and the theories
of cones have made modern formulations more elegant and easier." In
deploring this state of affairs, he pointed to modern treatises (such as his
own, co-authored with Solow and Dorfman, influential *Linear Programming and Economic Analysis* and Debreu's classic *Theory of Value*),
which often "score easy victories and represent a retrogression where
realism in dealing with market imperfections is concerned" (ibid., p. 43).

Looking back on his contributions in *Foundations,* Samuelson noted
that he was fortunate to have stressed the inequalities implied by the
process of maximization (which emerged from his earlier work on revealed preference). He wrote before the ascendence of linear programming and of von Neumann game theory and could not have known that
inequalities would come to play such an important role in economic
theory. But a reader of *Foundations* was prepared to appreciate the new
formulations in activity analysis and the infiltration of convex-set theory,
topology, and probability. Indeed, as he pointed out (ibid., p. 691; see
also pp. 688–89), "in a sense my *Foundations* approach was more general
than many of the modern formulations that posit more convexity than I
was assuming."

He reflected that he was also fortunate to have at times deviated from
his aim of deriving operationally meaningful theorems, for this allowed
him to include such subjects as welfare and dynamics. One concrete
example is Samuelson's celebrated 1939 paper on the interaction of the
accelerator and the multiplier (which, incidentally, he considers to have
brought him more fame than he deserved), which is a good example of
a dynamic system that cannot usefully be analyzed in terms of any
maximum problem (ibid., pp. 2–17). And he muses:

> Were the book being written today with knowledge of the revival of interest in Ramsey growth models, I would certainly have added a chapter on optimal-control theory and similar dynamic maximization matters. And then instead of being preoccupied with the problem of damped stability of dynamic motions, I would have been interested as well in stationary points which are saddle-points, surrounded by dynamic motions of the catenary type that we associate with modern turnpike theory. [Samuelson 1972, p. 691]

Samuelson extended and particularized the general equilibrium framework, specifically making it more suitable for analyzing questions of allocation and interdependence. More concretely, in 1951 he independently formulated and proved the far-reaching nonsubstitutability theorem of modern input-output, which ensures that even though technological substitutions of input proportions are possible, they need, in fact, never be made in a single-primary-input economy where technology exhibits constant returns to scale and joint products are ruled out. This is a remarkable result that revives the classical value theory, in which long-run price ratios are determined purely by production (supply) conditions and thus are completely independent of demand. This formulation is in sharp contrast to the neoclassical model, which assigns an explicit role to demand conditions in price formation.

> After such a theorem has been stated it may indeed seem obvious; but this is the fate of all truth and one has to keep reminding oneself that *ex ante* isn't *ex post*. As Maugham said about an unforgettable Mondrian painting: "It looks as though you had only to take a ruler, a tube of black paint and a tube of red, and you could do the thing yourself. Try!" [Samuelson 1966, p. 521]

Ten years later he came to grips with the problem of time and generalized the nonsubstitution theorem involving heterogeneous durable capital goods (ibid., pp. 515–19; 520–36; see also 373–92). Without anticipating the capital controversy here, Samuelson's provoking claim is of interest:

> In a quasi-realistic world of many different physical capital goods, a proper description of its operations must be in terms of its technological properties. For this reason modern theorists — or perhaps I had better merely speak of one member of the so-called "MIT school" — insist upon working with "capital models" that involve detailed vectors of capital goods, in which there is any finite number of different capital goods (each defined in terms of its *physical* properties) or even an infinite number of such goods. Then any resulting pattern of interest rates and other equilibrium magnitudes will work themselves out. For those with the appropriate mathematical technique or imagination, the result is not only manageable but in addition all its general properties can be inferred. (Sraffa's belatedly published book on commodity production, which eschews use of all magnitudes that cannot be invariantly

defined prior to any confrontation with market forces, is thus completely
within the MIT tradition — or, more fairly, some of us have been Sraffian
without realizing it.)[9] [Samuelson 1966, pp. 524–25]

Samuelson's name figures prominently among the major original contributors to the pure theory of international trade and public expenditure.[10] His contributions include the rigorous presentation and proof of
the factor price equalization theorem; the elucidation (with Stolper) of
the effects of trade restrictions on real wages; the pioneering modern
demonstration of gains from trade; definite clarification of the transfer
problem; and analysis of the time-phased models of trade and of the
continuum of goods model. Samuelson's role in trade theory is illuminated by Wan, Chapter 10, this volume (see Bhagwati 1965). He formulated a pure theory of (important special-type) public goods and had a
remarkable impact on public finance (particularly on the fairly neglected
theory of public expenditure), as indicated by Intriligator, Chapter 23,
this volume (see Burkhead and Miner 1971, pp. 25–96; Arrow 1967, p.
732; Samuelson 1966, pp. 1224–31).

Samuelson's innovations and approach to trade theory are usually
rooted in policy; his model is invariably formulated as general equilibrium
and makes special assumptions to obtain sharp conclusions. But, as his
most steadfast critic, Joan Robinson, has pointed out, this approach is
not without its pitfalls. In fact, to her (1977, pp. 213, xxii), "there is no
branch of economics in which there is a wider gap between orthodox
doctrine and actual problems than in the theory of trade." She recalls
that when Samuelson "visited Cambridge in 1947 with his factor-price-
equalization theorem I was baffled by it and tried to refute it, but I was
caught in the mine-field of assumptions that make it tautological. With
the dissolution of the neoclassical production function after 1953, the
very concept of 'factor prices' came into question."

Be that as it may, it needs to be emphasized that Samuelson played
a major role in elucidating the properties of the standard (2x2x2)
Heckscher-Ohlin model of production. So important has his contribution
been that the model is often called the Heckscher-Ohlin-(Lerner)-Sam-
uelson model. Of course, that model is fundamental to almost all of
"middlebrow" theory, not just trade theory (see Kemp 1969).

Wolfgang Stolper recollects (in a personal letter to me, dated October
28, 1980) that when he showed the first draft of his (yet untitled) paper
to Paul, the latter pointed out to him that he had found a fundamental
point but did not know it. With true scholarly humility Stolper admits:

It was true, I didn't know it. In fact, I believe the most interesting part of what became a joint article is not the analysis of protection, but rather the first clear statement of the relation of prices of goods and factors, the proof that (within limits) an infinity of factor proportions in individual industries is compatible with fixed factor proportions in an economy, and the derivation of the transformation curve from isoquants. . . . In the meantime the box diagram has become so much part of elementary wisdom that people don't realize that it was new in 1941. In the joint article it was entirely due to Paul.

In the postwar period many of Samuelson's contributions centered on neoclassical dynamics and the surrounding debates: the ideologically sensitive and intensely controversial pure theory of capital and growth and the conditions for efficient or optimal intertemporal allocation in the "good society," with the notable implications for macroeconomic policy, capital formation, and social security.

Not all of this was a new theme with him. An early paper (1937) developed rigorously the equilibrium conditions for a consumer's lifetime consumption-saving pattern. His famous 1958 pure consumption-loan model provides a major, if controversial, effort to provide a complete general equilibrium solution to the determination of the time shape of interest rates (or intertemporal terms of trade) and clarifies the perplexing analytical problem introduced by the infinity of the time horizon foreseen with certainty (see Cass and Yaari 1976). Here, inter alia, there is no presumption that in the absence of an appropriate mix of monetary and fiscal policies, laissez-faire will lead society to or near an "optimum." Notably, and somewhat ironically, in monetary economics the consumption-loan model has become the principal vehicle for Robert Lucas — the leading exponent of the rational expectations school — to argue the neutrality of money and to derive completely divergent policy implications (as noted in the Feiwel and Klein essays, Chapters 14 and 15, this volume). The impact of this model is now at its peak (Kareken and Wallace 1980).

A 1953 paper (jointly with Solow) relates the requisites of dynamic efficiency or optimal growth to the balanced growth properties of a von Neumann-type expanding economy. A number of major contributions followed.

The striking production turnpike theorem, thereafter generalized in different variants, shows that "to develop a country most efficiently, under certain circumstances it should proceed rather quickly toward the configuration of maximum balanced growth . . . and then at the end of the twenty year plan move off to its final goal" (Samuelson 1972, p. 15).

The essence of the theorem is the catenary property of efficient paths in closed von Neumann or neoclassical models.[11]

The notorious, often recondite, and ongoing Cambridge-Cambridge controversy transcends the theory of capital and involves the whole corpus of economic theory and underlying ideologies. "It is understandable that strong convictions should lead to strong language, as any reader of the 'capital controversies' can document in quantitative detail, author by author" (Samuelson 1977, p. 141). The last word has not been said on what the shouting is all about, what are the principal issues of controversy and central questions of theory, and what is the appropriate methodology. Clearly the personalities of the chief combatants — the so-called Anglo-Italian offense (led by Joan Robinson, Kaldor, and Pasinetti, and inspired by Sraffa) and the MIT Institute Professors (Samuelson, Solow, and Modigliani, but also including "residents" of Cambridge-on-the-Cam Hahn and Meade) — matter,[12] but much more is at stake. As Samuelson acknowledged:

> Behind an esoteric dispute over "reswitching" or heterogeneity of capital there often lurk contrasting views about fruitful ways of understanding distributional analysis and affecting its content by alternative policy measures. [Samuelson 1977, p. 113]

In a standard survey of the controversies, Harcourt (with strong affinities for Cambridge-on-the-Cam) sees the main issues under discussion as those that preoccupied Ricardo and Marx: the relations between accumulation and income distribution and the origins of profits, their absolute and relative size at any point of time and intertemporally, and similar questions about wages. The debate revolves around value, capital, growth, and distribution theory. The Anglo-Italian criticism is directed against the neoclassical "apologetic" conception loosely identified under the heading of marginal productivity theory and the neoclassical approach to growth theory, including the neglect of effective demand[13] (Harcourt 1972). Solow considers that the main battle is over the theory of profits and capital. He argues (1975, p. 277) that the Anglo-Italians have "gone after peripheral aspects of the profit-cum-interest story, and left its center untouched." In a review article of Harcourt, Stiglitz (1974, pp. 901, 902) (another partisan of MIT) focuses on what he considers to be the three major issues — the determination of savings and the interest rate, reswitching of techniques, and aggregate capital — on which the Anglo-Italians have "gone astray." He argues, inter alia, that ideology plays a far less important role than Harcourt suggests. He claims that "there is a well-known propensity of individuals to dislike what they don't or can't understand," implying that his opponents "do not understand neoclass-ical capital theory." To him it appears that "it is the confused attempt to discredit the marginal-productivity interpretation of the interest rate which imbues the topics of capital theory with their ideological interest to the devotees of Cambridge (U.K.) doctrine."

Samuelson vacillates somewhat in his stance toward the competitive model with respect to its usefulness for approximating essential reality, its predictive power, and its welfare implications. He views (1972, p. 22) the theoretical refinements on the competitive model as a major advance in logical clarity but as something of a retreat in evaluating actual market structures: "We theorists, quite removed from Cook county, have retro-gressed in the last quarter century, taking the coward's way of avoiding the important questions thrown up by the real economic world and fob-bing off in their place nice answers to less interesting easy questions."

One of Samuelson's enduring concerns has been distributional justice and welfare economics, which, Chipman claims in Chapter 11, this vol-ume, has been largely formed in its modern version, by Samuelson's contributions. Samuelson sifted through theoretical welfare economics and made many contributions in this field. Inter alia, he forged ahead on Bergson's social welfare function and developed the concept of "utility possibility frontier." In his classic 1950 paper on the welfare evaluation of real national income (Samuelson 1966, pp. 1044–72), he demonstrated that, despite recent accomplishments in the improved measurement of national income, very little could be inferred from national income com-parisons. Though his proofs were incomplete, he showed that maximi-zation of a separable social welfare function would lead to a situation in which the community acted as if it maximized a single community utility function and that such maximization could be accomplished in a decen-tralized fashion by merely distributing incomes optimally (in lump-sum fashion) and allowing consumers to pursue their individual maximizing behavior.

MARKET, WELFARE, AND FREEDOM

Samuelson has made a relentless effort to understand what it is that the invisible hand is supposed to be maximizing and why it is that the invisible hand itself needs a helping hand. Neoclassical economists have often been accused of perceiving competitive equilibrium allocation as desirable, just, or even socially optimal. Even Samuelson, who has been a standard-bearer in combating this heresy, has been under attack for

propagating it (see Hahn 1973, p. 4). Samuelson has cogently argued
(1977, p. 864) that "competitive equilibrium does not represent the best
state of the world." The concept of the social welfare function

> enabled one to understand for the first time the germ of truth in Adam Smith's
> paradigm of the Invisible Hand: namely, that when conditions of returns and
> tastes, non-externalities, and non-monopolies are right, the algorithm of Wal-
> rasian competition can be combined with the device of ideal lump-sum trans-
> fers to achieve the maximum of a prescribed well-behaved individualistic
> social welfare function. . . .
>
> The Invisible Hand doctrine cannot cogently be used to deduce the opti-
> mality of laissez faire, although many have fallen into this confusion. What is
> saying the same thing, the Pareto optimality property of competitive equilib-
> rium is no theoretical argument for laissez faire, and is in many situations no
> cogent practical argument for favoring the use of competition.[14] [Samuelson
> 1981b, pp. 4 and 7]

Many of Smith's modern followers interpret the invisible hand doctrine
to mean that (1) it creates maximum feasible total satisfaction and (2) all
results of the voluntary agreement of individuals must improve their lot.
Both of these are misinterpretations, for they "neglect the axiom concerning the ethical merits of the preexisting distribution" (Samuelson
1972, p. 624). Samuelson perceives (ibid., pp. 625–26) the importance of
the doctrine to lie in "the system of checks and balances that prevails
under perfect competition, and its measure of validity is at the techno-
cratic level of efficiency, not at the ethical level of freedom and
individualism."

The anonymity of market relations is an attractive feature of competitive capitalism, "as was brought home to many 'liberals' in the McCarthy
era. . . . Many of the people who were unjustly dropped by the federal
government in that era were able to land jobs in small-scale private
industry" (Samuelson 1966, p. 1412). Yet, "a mixed economy in a society
where people are by custom *tolerant* of differences in opinion may provide greater personal freedom and security of expression than does a
purer price economy where people are less tolerant" (Samuelson 1972,
p. 628). Samuelson proffers the examples of Scandinavia and the United
Kingdom for the first and the United States for the second. He goes on
to say (ibid.) that the first countries may enjoy fewer business freedoms,
"but an excommunist probably meets with more tolerance from employers there." And, tracing the history of the United States, he states that
"the days of most rugged individualism — the Gilded Age and the 1920s
— seem to have been the ages least tolerant of dissenting opinion" (ibid.).

Libertarians equate market with freedom, but they "fail to realize that the price system is, and ought to be, a method of coercion":

Anatole France said epigrammatically all that needs to be said about the coercion implicit in the libertarian economics of *laissez-faire*. "How majestic is the equality of the Law, which permits both rich and poor alike to sleep under the bridges at night." I believe no satisfactory answer has yet been given to this. [Samuelson 1966, pp. 1415–16]

Economists are fond of the expression "rationing by the purse." "What a welter of human misery those innocent words can cover" (Samuelson 1973, p. 107).

Following Beveridge, Samuelson makes the interesting distinction between (1) individual human civil liberties and freedoms and (2) ethical judgments of property rights and business activity. This distinction would dissatisfy both the extreme right and left, but for different reasons. And what about the economic libertarians' affirmation that human rights can be preserved and flourish only in a "free private enterprise" society? To Samuelson (1972, pp. 632–33) "this is a conservative's variant of the strong Marxian doctrine that economic relationships allegedly determine political relationships."

Forty years after Friedrich Hayek wrote down his nightmare of the welfare state leading remorselessly to the totalitarian murder of freedom, Scandinavians enjoy freedom second to none that the world has ever seen; and, contrary to the logic of *The Road to Serfdom* societies such as Chile and Singapore with maximal market freedoms live under dictatorships that suppress civil liberties. [Samuelson 1980b, p. 3]

Samuelson recalls (1977, p. 892) that "the great romance in the life of any economist" of his generation was the Keynesian revolution. "It is quite impossible for those who did not live in the *ancien regime* to realize how great were the impacts of Keynes' *General Theory*" (ibid., p. 866). And when asked by a journalist in the 1970s: "Is Keynes dead?", Samuelson retorted: "Yes. And so are Newton and Einstein" (ibid., p. 874).

In 1943 Samuelson wrote (1966, p. 1432) that "bitter experience of the last dozen years, if not of the last century and a half, shows that there is no invisible hand guaranteeing" full use of potential resources. "Whether or not we should prefer it that way, the only alternative is deliberate, purposive, intelligent social action on whatever scale is necessary to ensure continuing full employment." One of his major preoccupations was and is the philosophy, dynamism, modus operandi, and feasibility constraints of the mixed economy, perceived broadly as one

in which a democratic government regulates the market economy and
keeps it prosperous:

> In the mixed economy many of the decision processes determining how society
> is to use its material resources are to be performed by the mechanism of
> markets and prices. But government is to set the rules of the game and to
> have a vital function in providing for the ever-more-important collective needs
> of an interdependent populace. By use of scientific macroeconomic policies
> . . . the mixed economy was believed to be capable of ending for all time mass
> unemployment and chronic depressions. Keynesian policies to stimulate total
> spending could banish once and for all the fear of underconsumption that was
> ever present in a laissez-faire world made up of the thrifty rich and the eager-
> to-spend poor. Thus, one no longer had to be fearful that automation and
> labor-displacing technological invention would cause total unemployment to
> grow. . . . Most important of all, according to the neoclassicists of the mixed
> economy who synthesized the doctrines of Keynes and such microeconomists
> as Alfred Marshall and Leon Walras, the new ability to control the supply of
> domestic purchasing power at will has made obsolete the neo-Marxian view
> . . . that prosperity and full employment . . . is absolutely impossible without
> exploitation of colonial peoples and recourse to foreign investments in outside
> markets. [Samuelson 1972, p. 706]

And he considers that, on balance, the welfare state has done more for
the underprivileged than have the militant socialist programs:

> Redistributive taxation at graduated rates; welfare transfer expenditures to the
> unemployed, the old, the handicapped and the unlucky; and public regulation
> against monopoly and excessive monopoly profits — all these appear to have
> done more for the workers and low-income classes in the Western World than
> the more traditional programs of socialism. [Samuelson 1966, p. 1683]

He has also tried to tackle the riddle of inflation; he has stressed its
multifaceted varieties and sources and the fallacy of single cause or cure.
In another context he said (1966, p. 1325) that "economics does not
provide simple answers to complex social problems," and "the more
assuredly a man asserts the direction along which salvation is alone to
be found, the more patently he advertises himself as an incompetent or
a charlatan." His thesis is that stagflation is now an intrinsic feature of
the advanced mixed economy. It is here to stay for the most affluent
nations. The problem is complex, and the solutions continue to elude
us.[15] The following half-jest, made by Samuelson in connection with
understanding the behavior of the mixed economies, intimates his reso-
lution and earnestness as a scholar:

If it is necessary to learn mathematics to help explain them, I steel myself to this task. If it were necessary to learn Sanskrit, I would grudgingly do so. If to predict the pattern of future events an economist had to spend his middle years hanging by his heels from the ceiling, I would perforce make the sacrifice. And if my reading of Marxian economists generated fruitful hypotheses concerning realistic economic behavior, I would unhesitatingly put in the effort. My only sticking point would come if Dr. Faust's devil required my immortal soul in exchange for understanding of political economy; and even here, so great is my zeal for scientific objectivity, I would certainly feel tempted. [Samuelson 1972, pp. 728–29]

THE WORLDLY PHILOSOPHER

In drawing up the prerequisites for a "master-economist," Keynes suggested (1951, p. 141) that "he must be mathematician, historian, statesman, philosopher — in some degree." This remarkable combination fits Samuelson particularly well. He is a man of intense and sparkling intellect, passion for his chosen field, scholarly versatility and eclecticism, concern for the improvement of economic welfare, and preference for the middle road. He does not take fools gladly and is known for his wit and abrasive sense of humor. Yet he has an enormous capacity for friendship and loyalty. He is a devoted teacher who might not be really successful with the "standard" students, but he is a font of wisdom and inspiration for those special ones able to appreciate the riddles in which he speaks, as Akerlof so vividly illustrates in Chapter 22, this volume. He is a living annal of our profession by virtue of his astounding memory and interest in his fellow economists and their foibles. He is one of the few landmark economists (like Ricardo and Keynes) with a canny ability to make money. Yet his wants have remained modest, and his living standards blend well with the rest of academia. He is one of those rare birds in the economics profession — a technically sophisticated economist who is also erudite and a master of the written language. He is a devoted family man. Like anyone else he has been affected and molded by the landmark events in his life. To mention just a few: His marriage to Marion Crawford was a happy one and by all accounts she had a salutary effect on his character. Such events as his "departure" from Harvard and the McCarthy years had a lasting negative imprint. On the other hand, his association with the Kennedys and the Nobel Prize have had a very favorable impact, contributing to his increasing demonstration of the characteristics of an elder statesman. The tragic and untimely death of his wife Marion has been shattering; it was good that he had his children, Bob Solow, and other friends to sustain him.

Samuelson is no shrinking violet. He is quite aware of his extraordinary intellectual powers:

> I was for a time given some medication that excellently treated the symptoms for which it was prescribed. But during that period, I felt that it took the fine edge off my mind. Suddenly I realized how the other half lives! [Samuelson 1977, p. 883]

Reflecting on his early choice of economics as a career he mused:

> Possibly, I would have done well in any field of applied science or as a writer, but certainly the blend in economics of analytical hardness and humane relevance was tailor made for me or I for it. [Samuelson 1977, p. 895]

But there is yet another ingredient needed for a "master economist" — and Samuelson, like Marshall, has spent a lifetime cultivating the reputation for having a cool head combined with a warm heart.

Whatever truth there is to the legend of the brash and arrogant young Samuelson, the Samuelson of later vintage that I know does not demonstrate these "qualities." There is an endearing quality of diffidence in his often-repeated appreciation for what he calls his luck and good fortune:

> Mine has been a happy life as a scholar. I have had good teachers and good students. I have been paid to do what I like to do, and can take some satisfaction in the good work of my hands. . . . When I think of Wicksell, who was almost my present age before he received his first professorial chair; when I think of the lonely figure of Stanley Jevons, walking on the Australian shore and vowing to make his scholarly mark; when I think of Karl Marx sitting painfully in the British Museum; and when I think of Leon Walras writing all over the globe for some pitiful sign of professional recognition. When I think of all these things, I know how to measure out the consumer's surplus which I have enjoyed. [Samuelson 1972, p. 684]

He reveals sensitivity, self-questioning, and a touching facet of his character when he speaks of his aroused emotions at the picture of a condescending, young, and brash Maynard Keynes according only a few minutes of his time to a grateful sexagenarian Wicksell. "The image of that plump little man nipping along in the wake of unconscious youth is to me a haunting one that makes me whisper 'There, but for the grace . . .' and yet not know to which I am pointing" (Samuelson 1966, p. 1690).

Good fortune also smiled on him with the publication of his famous textbook, which appeared a year after *Foundations*. This led George

Stigler to remark (Samuelson 1972, p. 689): "Professor Samuelson, having achieved fame, now seeks fortune." Reflecting on the essence of the textbook and the real motivation for writing it, Samuelson explained:

> So to speak, I embalmed Keynesianism and the general equilibrium approach, packaged and sold it. I was well rewarded for my efforts from the beginning, but the coin for which any ambitious scholar works is not that of money itself, for otherwise he would have become a plumber or a brewer in the first place. The coin for which he works is influencing the mind of a generation. [Samuelson 1977, p. 870]

Samuelson is proverbially cautious (but considerably less so in recent years), and not without good reason. The early editions of his textbook were subjected to considerable ideological assault. As he recalls (ibid., pp. 870–71), "if you were a teacher at many a school around the country and the Board of Regents of your university was on your neck for using subversive textbooks, it was no laughing matter." He admits that the criticism and resultant cautiousness did stifle his formulations:

> My last wish was to have an intransigent formulation that would be read by no one. But at the same time there was no point in keeping an audience by giving up the substance of the economic understanding I was trying to impart. . . . As a result I followed an Aesopian policy of paying careful attention to every criticism of every line and word of my text. . . . In a sense this careful wording achieved its purpose: at least some of my critics were reduced to complaining that I played peek-a-boo with the reader and didn't come out and declare my true meaning.
>
> Nevertheless, such defensive writing weakens the élan of a book. And I reread today, say the fifth edition of the book, with certain irritation for the care with which many matters are formulated. [Samuelson 1977, pp. 871–72]

Samuelson often stresses that economics is an inexact science. He once remarked (1966, p. 1678) that he wishes he were as sure of anything as X (substituted here to protect the "guilty") is of everything. "I am the contrary of the New England judge who reprimanded counsel with: 'Sir, this Court is often in error but never in doubt.' While I sometimes escape error, I always profess doubt." The economist's "Hippocratic Oath" should read: "An economist, other things equal, should do no harm; in formulating the odds and stating the main reasons behind them, he should come clean on the uncertainties." And to illustrate this point Samuelson recalls (1978c) that "when asked for an off-the-record comment on one of the brilliant economists of our time, I said about my friend: 'The gods gave him every talent — except the gift of maybe.'"
In a eulogy of Okun, Samuelson noted:

Harry Truman is sometimes quoted as saying, "What I want is a one-armed economist, who won't pussyfoot with 'on the one hand this, on the other hand that.'" With respect, this is foolish. What he'd have is a cripple. For one-armed economists come in two dogmatic varieties, those with a right arm only and those with only a left. And *then* you need a two-armed eclectic to adjudicate between them. [Samuelson 1980a]

So, if the late President Truman had asked five economists for an opinion he would have gotten six answers — at least two from the eclectic Samuelson — and perhaps more if he had had the good fortune of having more economists of Samuelson's stamp in that group.

Samuelson believes that in the history of analysis the great eclectics, such as Mill, Smith, and Wicksell, were underrated. His statement about Wicksell is revealing:

Because Wicksell read the works of his predecessors and contemporaries, and acknowledged the fact; because he was eclectic; because he regarded all his own ideas as merely tentative hypotheses; . . . for all these reasons Wicksell is sometimes regarded as not having been a truly original and creative economist. I am convinced this appraisal is quite wrong. [Samuelson 1966, pp. 1687–88]

Also revealing are his evaluations of and comments on some other great minds in the history of science and economics. For instance, he described (ibid., p. 422) Ricardo as vastly overrated as a theorist, but he admitted that Ricardo's logical skills were so considerable that he "would have made a most excellent modern economist." He once referred tongue in cheek to Marx, the analytical economist, as a "minor post Ricardian," and a rather interesting "precursor of Leontief," but even those who sharply disagree with Samuelson on Marx (as does the noted scholar Nell in Chapter 18, this volume) consider Samuelson's substantial analysis as a "milestone in serious evaluation of Marx."

Samuelson considers Jacob Viner as one of the greatest neoclassical economists — and also as a great eclectic, which characteristic particularly endeared him to Samuelson.

I now realize in retrospect that the subject of economics gained from having Viner concentrate upon those areas of wisdom and erudition for which he had a unique comparative advantage, and that more mathematical facility might merely have diverted him from his appointed task. [Samuelson 1977, p. 911]

How many economists, university administrators, and research fund distributors forget or are innocent of the real understanding of comparative advantage!

And as an illustration of "unscholarly" behavior and defense of vested interests, Samuelson offers the following anecdote about Gustav Cassel, who, when asked what he was going to do about an error in his findings, apparently retorted:

> "I have a son-in-law whom I have been helping to finance through Divinity School. Just as he was hoving in sight of graduation he came to me and said he had lost his faith. My advice to him was, 'Just go on as if nothing had happened.' And that suggests my answer to you." [Samuelson 1966, p. 1687]

More recently Samuelson has often been critical of forecasting. He admitted, again tongue in cheek, that fairly rarely does he get contaminated by data. Yet he calls ours "the age of Klein" (1977, pp. 857, 859).

> I suspect it is yet the case that the best judgmental forecasts are still about as good or as bad as the best computer forecasts. Indeed, something like this must be at the heart of the fact that, with the exception of a few, almost all model builders adjust their constants by various quasi-judgmental procedures and believe that this does improve their batting averages. There used to be a marvelous chess machine that could beat all comers. But alas it turned out that curled inside the machine was an actual man. It would be ironic if, inside the Wharton model, we found in the end, Lawrence Klein. [Samuelson 1977, p. 859]

As a political economist, Samuelson feels that he has to be on the firing line, not only to influence the course of events, or to mold public opinion as in his famous *Newsweek* columns, but also to shoulder the burden of anxiety. "When my descendants gather about my knee and say, 'Grandpa, what did you do to add to the gross national product?' my reply will have to be, 'I worried'" (Samuelson 1972, p. 715).

Writing these words in the early 1960s, Samuelson (ibid., pp. 715–17) catalogued with some prescience the *hard* economic problems to worry about and the relatively easier ones. In the first category he put excessive unemployment, creeping cost-push inflation, chronic international balance of payments deficits, and growth potential. In the second he placed federal deficits and rising public debt, automation, disarmament's economic impact, and inability to forecast the future. In almost twenty years it seems that the hard problems have not changed much, but have only increased in acuteness, even if the easy ones have altered. And an older Samuelson (1978b) admitted that he has to ration his "24 hours a day and concentrate on worries that genuinely matter, dispensing with false concerns and relegating minor anxieties to amateurs with excess capacity."

A recurrent theme with Samuelson is that the economic scholar works for the only coin worth having: the applause of his peers. But this is not a plea for logical elegance for the sake of elegance. Neither is it a plea for leaving real-world economic problems to noneconomists. "Rather it is a plea for calling shots as they really appear to be . . . even when this means losing popularity with the great audience of men and running against 'the spirit of the times'" (Samuelson 1966, p. 1516). And, if we work for our own applause, the corollary is "that the most useful criticism of a subject must often bore from within" (Samuelson 1977, p. 858).

In the late 1950s Samuelson (1966, p. 1629) deplored the lack of basic disagreement on fundamentals among American economists. "Today, surveying leading graduate schools, one finds them competing for the same men, teaching the same basic economic doctrines and methods." And in the early 1960s, he rather complacently but facetiously affirmed the superiority of the United States in the development of economics:

> When I state that the *quantity* of economic thought in Cambridge, Massachusetts, is second to none anywhere in the world, I might be able to back this up by a count of the pages of articles published in learned journals, by measurement of the total inches of our theoretical and statistical curves, by the decibel count of the seminars at Harvard and further down the river. But when I go on to state that the *quality* of this thought is second to none, you must make allowance for the fact that Cambridge is where I sip my morning coffee. [Samuelson 1966, pp. 1739–40]

With considerable prescience of things to come on the scene of American economics, he wrote more than three decades ago:

> Fashion always plays an important role in economic science; new concepts become the mode and then are passé. A cynic might even be tempted to speculate as to whether academic discussion is itself equilibrating: whether assertion, reply, and rejoinder do not represent an oscillating divergent series, in which . . . "bad talk drives out good." [Samuelson 1966, p. 1518]

The real world always presents economists with their greatest challenges. The more unsolved problems, the greater is the number of sprouting fads and fashions. Economists are lucky, for "a discipline lives on its unsolved problems; and so, for better or worse, economics is likely to be a lively subject for as many years ahead as man can see" (ibid., p. 1648).

Samuelson is well known for his liberal views (in the modern American sense of the word). He is a great propagator of the so-called new economics, which he has called a good idea whose time has come, has gone, but will come again. To dispel misapprehensions, he has pointed out (ibid., p. 1592) that "despite Mussolini's decorating of Pareto, the old canard that 'a reactionary is a man who believes in equilibrium' is not sustained by the history of mathematical economists." And, at the conclusion of his Nobel Lecture, (1972, p. 16) he quoted H. J. Davenport, who once said: "There is no reason why theoretical economics should be a monopoly of the reactionaries." Samuelson added "All my life I have tried to take this warning to heart, and I dare call it to your favorable attention."

The new conservative trend is a subject of considerable disquietude for Samuelson. Almost twenty years ago he said to a group of bankers (and could easily repeat it today):

> I wish I could have come here and promised that balancing the budget, preserving monetary discipline, reducing Government expenditures and busting the monopoly powers of labor unions would usher in an era of prosperity and growth without inflation or tears. It was not my heart that kept me from doing so; it was my head, and my fear of being in violation of the laws of fraud, that compelled me to say less agreeable words. [Samuelson 1966, p. 1403]

And of the present trend he said in a lighthearted mood (1978a): "Middle-class backlash and taxpayer revolts will not achieve restoration of Herbert Spencer's laissez faire. There is a science fiction of the right as well as of the left and center. Read it and enjoy. But don't bet your nest egg on wishful fantasies." However, in a lecture given to the International Economic Association in September 1980 in Mexico City, he warned of the threat of the appeal of fascism as an "economically workable and efficient" system. And early in 1981 he said to the American Academy:

> If capitalism is efficient and is not politically stable, then one must contemplate a temptation toward an imposed capitalism. . . . If democracy cannot be trusted, write once and forever into the constitution that capitalism must be the law of the land — that's where conservatives are now trying to go." [Samuelson 1981a, pp. 14–15]

But what of himself?

> Personally, I must agree with Winston Churchill when he said that although democracy is not a very good system, it is nevertheless better than any other system. My dream is to make the mixed economy work better. [Samuelson 1980b, p. 35]

In a letter to Bill Allen of U.C.L.A. (dated November 17, 1980) he affirmed:

> Our discipline of economics averages out to a "more conservative ideology" than, say, in 1945. Reflecting as well as helping shape the *Zeitgeist,* my own work would probably reflect some systematic shifts in emphasis. While it

would be ungracious to deny that some of my third thoughts (remember, my *first* thoughts were Knight-Simonian at Chicago before 1935) came under the influence of researches by scholars to the right of me, it would be only honest to report that most of my changes in viewpoint have come from changed perceptions concerning feasibility. (As an example, money plays a more strategic role in my synthesis of post-Keynesian macroeconomics than it did in 1939.) But the net effect on me of Milton's work on money was factually insignificant, and I had to struggle to keep it from being negative — being helped in this struggle by the changing characteristics of the post-1950 liquidity-preference schedules and by the researches of Modigliani and Tobin. So, as I shave each morning, I see in the mirror a Keynesian liberal who has spent the best decades of his life critically reformulating Keynes and the neoclassical mainstream.

Whatever their persuasions and dissensions, most economists will agree that Samuelson has made a real difference to the economics of our age and has vastly contributed to raising the level of economic intelligence almost the world over. It is easy to criticize, but clearly more difficult to build. Samuelson's work — as Arrow wrote — "is a mirror for all of us":

A great leader of his field is not typical of his day; but neither is he outside it. Rather he is like a magnifying glass; not only are the accomplishments the best that the period can produce, but also the underlying conflicts and contradictions are brought out more sharply and separated from the mass of elementary error and shortsightedness. [Arrow 1967, p. 737]

NOTES

1. For defense and criticism of neoclassical economics, see the papers in this volume and the references therein.

2. "Being the son of Schumpeter, I am the grandson of Böhm-Bawerk and Menger. Being the son of Leontief, I am the grandson of Bortkiewicz and am the great-grandson of Walras" (Samuelson 1972, p. 684).

3. Keynes's perception of the economic world was essentially Marshallian (as opposed to Walrasian). "Marshall's analysis was half in historical time and half in equilibrium doctrine" (Robinson 1977, p. 132).

4. Samuelson's (1977, p. 889) down-to-earth advice to students when choosing a graduate school is: "If you have any reason to think you are good, beg, borrow, or steal the money to come to the top place. If you go to Rome, it is your classmates who will be the next cardinals and who will be picking popes."

5. Samuelson equivocates about the popular and controversial *simpliste* explanation that anti-Semitism was the reason behind his not being appointed to a "tenure-track" position at Harvard. On the one hand, he admits the incredible pre–World War II anti-Semitism in the seats of higher learning; on the other, he acknowledges many other contributing and not negligible factors (1977, p. 896). His proverbial *enfant terrible* behavior was probably

one of the factors that did not quite endear him to some of his teachers. A well-known story about his doctoral examination has Schumpeter asking Leontief: "Wassily, did we pass?"

6. What is and is not a dynamic theory is a bone of contention: "We damn another man's theory by terming it static, and advertise our own by calling it dynamic" (Samuelson 1947, p. 311). (For Samuelson's definition of dynamics, statics, and comparative statics, see 1966, p. 592; 1947, pp. 257–60, 284ff., and 311ff.) Some of the pioneers of modern dynamic theory were Frisch, Kalecki, and Tinbergen. On the development of dynamic theory, see Samuelson 1966, pp. 590–91; Baumol 1970; Feiwel 1975.

7. For the relation between Hicksian stability (which was essentially static and not derived from explicitly dynamic considerations) and the "true dynamic stability," see Samuelson 1966, p. 563. Samuelson did not take full cognizance of the implications of the assumptions underlying the perfectly competitive model. (See Arrow and Hurwicz 1958, Negishi 1962, p. 643). Arrow and Hurwicz questioned Samuelson's critique of Hicksian stability on two grounds: (1) Can a competitive economy have a dynamically unstable equilibrium? and (2) can Samuelson's mathematical example be wedded to a competitive economy? Both questions were answered in Samuelson's favor, (1) by Gale and Scarf and (2) by Sonnenschein and Debreu. (See Arrow and Hahn 1971.)

8. These two distinct approaches stemmed from two separate streams of thought. In particular, the postwar developments have their roots in prewar German language literature (e.g., such mathematicians as Abraham Wald). See Arrow 1974, pp. 260–63, where an illuminating survey of modern developments can be found. The evolution of the existence of competitive equilibrium theory is admirably pursued in Debreu 1981.

9. "The student of modern Sraffian analysis, even if he has no concern for international trade, will want to interest himself in the generalization to many primary factors of the nonsubstitution theorems, the factor-price frontiers, and other concepts of neo-neoclassical and neoclassical economics" (Samuelson 1977, p. 613).

10. When challenged by the eminent mathematician Stanislaw Ulam to name one proposition in the social sciences that is "both true and non-trivial," Samuelson admitted to having been stymied. Then, "some thirty years later, on the staircase so to speak, an appropriate answer occurs to me: The Ricardian theory of comparative advantage" (1972, p. 683). For Samuelson's awareness of and interesting discussion of the relevant political, social, and economic implications of following a policy of comparative advantage, see Samuelson 1977, pp. 571–93.

11. Samuelson noted that though he was aware of the catenary property of a Ramsey system when writing *Foundations,* it was not until 1949 (when visiting Rand) that he formulated the initial version of the theorem, which lacked adequate proof until Radner's 1961 paper (1972, p. 691; 1977, p. 122).

12. Samuelson (1966, p. 1739) facetiously noted his advantage over his British critics: "They read only their own writings, whereas we can get the benefit from reading their papers and our own too!" And, in the same vein, but in another context (ibid., p. 1593): "Cambridge economists, God bless them, also deserve justice; and since they cannot always be counted on to pour it on each other in buckets, it is up to us barbarians to join in the rituals." In this spirit he went on to extoll his most faithful and severe critic (in a passage that Joan Robinson told me she considers patronizing)

If an ignoramous in economics says that the current economic system cannot be interpreted as a rational scheme, that is nothing. But if one of the greatest analytical economists of our era says this, she is worth listening to. Joan Robinson . . . won fame young as one of the inventors of the theory of imperfect competition. She consolidated her worldwide reputation by becoming one of the leading contributors to the Keynesian macroeconomic literature. . . . [I]n recent decades Mrs. Robinson has been an important pioneer and critic of growth models. For any of these accomplishments she might well be awarded the Nobel Prize in Economics. [Samuelson 1970, p. 397]

13. The voluminous literature on the capital controversy, including the growing industry of commentators, defies brief synopsis. As so much misunderstanding enshrouds the controversy, and since it might be illusory that the participants are actually communicating with each other, the reader's attention is called to the statements of the chief contestants to convey an impression of their own perceptions of their positions and those of their opponents. Samuelson's position was clearly stated in a 1962 paper (1966, pp. 325–38). Referring to his 1966 summary of the debate, where he delineates his position from that of his opponents (Samuelson 1972, pp. 230–45) and the shots fired for another decade, Samuelson reports that his ''1966 discussion seems to stand up very well, and it would be hypocritical of me to give it other than a clean bill of health as a representation of my 1975 views'' (Samuelson 1977, pp. 134–35). For Joan Robinson's most recent statement of her position, see her contribution, Chapter 5, this volume. The two Cambridges' different perceptions of the Keynesian revolution are discussed in Part III, particularly by Feiwel, Chapter 14, this volume.

14. ''Properly formulated, the correct version of the Invisible Hand doctrine does not allege that dollar votes are distributed by the competitive regime of laissez faire so as to have equal ethical value. Its correct versions say, and it is important to know this, that once the initial distribution of wealth and economic voting power has been ethically rectified by non-laissez-faire forces, the algorithm of perfect market competition, if you could attain it, could *efficiently* achieve production and allocation of economic goods and services'' (Samuelson 1977, p. 864; see Samuelson 1966, p. 1410; 1947, pp. 203ff). As Arrow pointed out (1974, p. 269): ''General competitive equilibrium above all teaches the extent to which a social allocation of resources can be achieved by independent private decisions coordinated through the market. We are assured indeed that . . . the result will be Pareto efficient. But . . . there is nothing in the process which guarantees that distribution be just. . . . If we want to . . . achieve a more just distribution, the theory suggests the strategy of changing the initial distribution rather than interfering with the allocation process at some later stage.''

15. Samuelson (1973, p. 22) whimsically likened advisers to a mixed economy to dermatologists — the most fortunate practitioners of medicine — ''who never cure their patients but also . . . never kill them.''

REFERENCES

Arrow, K. J. 1963. *Social Choice and Individual Values*. New York: Wiley.
———. 1967. ''Samuelson Collected.'' *Journal of Political Economy* 75:730–37.
———. 1974. ''General Economic Equilibrium: Purpose, Analytic Techniques, Collective Choice.'' *American Economic Review* 64 (3):253–72.
———. 1975. ''Thorstein Veblen as an Economic Theorist.'' Technical Report No. 16, Harvard University.

————, and F. H. Hahn. 1971. *General Competitive Analysis*. San Francisco: Holden-Day.

————, and L. Hurwicz. 1958. "On the Stability of the Competitive Equilibrium." *Econometrica* 26:522–52.

Baumol, W. J. 1970. *Economic Dynamics*. New York: Macmillan.

Bhagwati, J. 1965. "The Pure Theory of International Trade." In *Surveys of Economic Theory*, Vol. 2. London: Macmillan.

Burkhead, J., and J. Miner. 1971. *Public Expenditure*. Chicago: Aldine.

Cass, D., and M. E. Yaari. 1976. "A Re-examination of the Pure Consumption Loans Model." *Journal of Political Economy* 74:353–67.

Debreu, G. 1981. "Existence of Competitive Equilibrium." In K. J. Arrow and M. D. Intriligator, eds. *Handbook of Mathematical Economics*, Vol. 2. Amsterdam: North-Holland.

Feiwel, G. R. 1975. *The Intellectual Capital of Michal Kalecki*. Knoxville: University of Tennessee Press.

Fisher, F. M. 1976. "The Stability of General Equilibrium." In M. J. Artis and A. R. Nobay, eds. *Essays in Economic Analysis*. Cambridge, England: Cambridge University Press.

Friedman, M. 1970. "Paul Samuelson." *Newsweek*, November 9, p. 80.

Hahn, F. H. 1973. *On the Notion of Equilibrium in Economics*. Cambridge, England: Cambridge University Press.

Harcourt, G. C. 1972. *Some Cambridge Controversies in the Theory of Capital*. Cambridge, England: Cambridge University Press.

Houthakker, H. S. 1961. "The Present State of Consumption Theory." *Econometrica* 29 (4):704–40.

Hurwicz, L. 1970. "Economics: Nobel Prize for 1970 Awarded to Samuelson of M.I.T." *Science* 170:720–21.

Kareken, J. H., and N. Wallace, eds. 1980. *Models of Monetary Economics*. Minneapolis, Minn.: Federal Reserve Bank.

Kemp, M. C. 1969. *Pure Theory of International Trade and Investment*. Englewood Cliffs, N.J.: Prentice-Hall.

Keynes, J. M. 1951. *Essays in Biography*. Ed. by Geoffrey Keynes. London: Horizon Press.

Negishi, T. 1962. "The Stability of Competitive Economy." *Econometrica* 30:635–69.

Robinson, J. 1977. "What Are the Questions?" *Journal of Economic Literature* 15:1318–39.

————. 1978. *Contributions to Modern Economics*. New York: Academic Press.

————. 1979a. "Foreword." In A. S. Eichner, ed. *A Guide to Post-Keynesian Economics*. White Plains, N.Y.: Sharpe.

————. 1979b. "Misunderstandings in the Theory of Production." *Greek Economic Review* 1:1–7.

Samuelson, P. A. 1947. *Foundations of Economic Analysis*. Cambridge, Mass.: Harvard University Press.

——. 1966. *The Collected Scientific Papers of Paul A. Samuelson.* 2 vols. Ed. by J. E. Stiglitz. Cambridge, Mass.: MIT Press.

——. 1970. *Readings in Economics.* New York: McGraw-Hill.

——. 1972. *The Collected Scientific Papers of Paul A. Samuelson,* Vol. 3. Ed. by R. C. Merton. Cambridge, Mass.: MIT Press.

——. 1973. *The Samuelson Sampler.* Glen Ridge, N.J.: Horton.

——. 1977. *The Collected Scientific Papers of Paul A. Samuelson,* Vol. 4. Ed. by H. Nagatani and K. Crowley. Cambridge, Mass.: MIT Press.

——. 1978a. "Economic Scares." *Newsweek,* September 11, p. 82.

——. 1978b. "Realistic Hopes." *Newsweek,* October 23, p. 85.

——. 1978c. "Time to Sell?" *Newsweek,* December 11, p. 90.

——. 1980a. "Arthur Okun, 1928–1980." *Newsweek,* April 7, p. 67.

——. 1980b. "The World Economy at Century's End." MIT, mimeographed.

——. 1981a. "The World Economy at Century's End." Typescript of speech given at the American Academy, January 14.

——. 1981b. "Bergsonian Welfare Economics." Typescript to appear in S. Rosefielde, ed. *Economic Welfare and the Economics of Soviet Socialism: Essays in Honor of Abram Bergson.* Cambridge, England: Cambridge University Press.

Solow, R. M. 1975. "Cambridge and the Real World." *Times Literary Supplement,* March 14, pp. 277–78.

Stiglitz, J. E. 1974. "The Cambridge-Cambridge Controversy in the Theory of Capital: A View from New Haven: A Review Article." *Journal of Political Economy* 82 (4):893–903.

I *FOUNDATIONS OF ECONOMIC ANALYSIS* AND EVOLUTION IN CONSUMPTION, PRODUCTION, AND DYNAMIC ANALYSIS

2 SAMUELSON AND CONSUMPTION THEORY

John S. Chipman

The task of reviewing a body of work as prodigious as Paul Samuelson's is so awesome that I confine myself in this essay and its sequel (Chapter 11) to only a small portion of his work: consumption theory and welfare economics. In the present paper I take up two branches of consumption theory that stem from quite different traditions: (1) revealed preference and the integrability problem and (2) the measurement of individual welfare. I try to show how Samuelson's contributions have led to a complete transformation of thought in both branches and have laid the basis for a synthesis of the two, allowing for the construction of utility functions and welfare measures that are firmly based on market observations of individual demand behavior.

In the first section I trace the development of revealed-preference and integrability theory from Samuelson's initial formulation and develop-

Research for this paper was supported by National Science Foundation grant SES–7924816 and a fellowship from the John Simon Guggenheim Memorial Foundation. I am grateful to Leonid Hurwicz and Marcel K. Richter for their comments on an earlier draft; however, they must not be held responsible for any defects that remain. Any opinions, findings, and conclusions or recommendations in this paper are those of the author and do not necessarily reflect the views of the National Science Foundation.

ment of the Weak Axiom of Revealed Preference (1938a) up to the most recent results of the last few years. To gain an impression of the extent of the professional turnabout in the last forty years, one need only read the literature of the 1930s to sense the strong tide of anti-utilitarianism and almost mid-Victorian abhorrence of any concept, such as utility, that smacked in the slightest degree of hedonism. That a strengthening and a definitive reintroduction of the utility concept would have been the ultimate result of the early efforts to "purge" it from consumption theory would not have been believed at the time.

I record that in 1938 Samuelson rejected the utility concept because he could not find a convincing economic interpretation of the symmetry of the Slutsky matrix. He showed that the Weak Axiom implied its negative semidefiniteness, but no economic meaning could be attached to its symmetry until Houthakker (1950) showed (indirectly) that it followed from his Strong Axiom. This inspired Samuelson's work on the integrability problem (1950a), in which, building also on the important early work of Allen (1932) and Georgescu-Roegen (1936), he explained the bizarre, spirallike consequences of failure of the symmetry condition and also developed the dual relation between direct and indirect demand functions and between the corresponding Slutsky and Antonelli integrability conditions. Uzawa's (1960, 1971) important development of Houthakker's work led to the fundamental partial differential equations (2.18) that form the link between the "finitistic" revealed-preference approach and the "infinitesimal" integrability approach and provide the basis for the important Hurwicz-Uzawa (1971) results establishing the sufficiency of the Slutsky symmetry and negative-semidefiniteness conditions for the existence of a utility function. Finally, one of the most recent results, due to Hurwicz and Richter (1979), shows that the axiom introduced by Ville (1946) provides exactly what is needed over and above the Weak Axiom in order to yield the Strong Axiom, and thus provides the long-sought economic interpretation of the Slutsky symmetry condition.

In the second section I take up the question of cardinal measurement of utility in the context of cost-benefit analysis, which seeks a cardinal measure of (individual) welfare, and I discuss the contrasting views on welfare measurement of Samuelson, Hotelling, and Hicks. Here I trace the evolution of Samuelson's thinking from the early period, when he was a staunch ordinalist and yet unwittingly provided some logical foundations for cardinal measurement, to the middle period when, faced with the findings of von Neumann and Marschak, he became a reluctant cardinalist, to the most recent period, in which cardinal measurement is accepted as having a valid role in certain well-defined uses. In his pathbreaking work (1942) characterizing the assumption of "constant marginal utility of income" that lies behind consumer's surplus analysis, he saw that this assumption was not invariant with respect to monotone transformations of the utility function and showed — building on Bergson's (1936) seminal work — that it had definite empirical implications concerning the nature of preferences. This connection between cardinal measurement and certain well-defined constraints on preferences was also brought out in many of his other contributions.

Taken together, these developments make possible a synthesis of the "pure" theory analyzed in the first section and the applied welfare analysis discussed in the second section. The theoretical work on revealed preference has laid the basis for practical construction of utility functions from demand functions, and a heightened understanding of the nature of cardinal measurement has made it possible to shift the issue from whether welfare should be measured to how to measure it correctly.

REVEALED PREFERENCE AND THE INTEGRABILITY PROBLEM

One of Samuelson's earliest contributions — and his first to consumption theory (1938a) — literally revolutionized the theory of consumer behavior. While the term "revealed preference" did not appear until a decade later (Samuelson 1948), it is in this paper that Samuelson introduced what subsequently (Samuelson 1950a) came to be known as the "Weak Axiom" of Revealed Preference.[1] If a bundle x^0 was purchased at prices p^0 when a different bundle x^1 could have been afforded (i.e., if $p^0 \cdot x^0 \geq p^0 \cdot x^1$ and $x^1 \neq x^0$), so that x^0 is "revealed preferred" to x^1, then if p^1 is a price vector at which x^1 is purchased, x^1 must not also be revealed preferred to x^0; hence we must have $p^1 \cdot x^1 < p^1 \cdot x^0$. The Weak Axiom thus reads:

$$[p^0 \cdot x^0 \geq p^0 \cdot x^1 \quad \& \quad x^1 \neq x^0] \Rightarrow p^1 \cdot x^1 < p^1 \cdot x^0. \qquad (2.1)$$

The importance of the axiom derives from the consequences Samuelson was able to deduce from it. Rewriting (2.1) in the form

$$[p \cdot x \geq p \cdot (x + \Delta x) \quad \& \quad \Delta x \neq 0] \Rightarrow (p + \Delta p) \cdot (x + \Delta x) < (p + \Delta p) \cdot x,$$

or equivalently,

$$[p \cdot \Delta x \leq 0 \quad \& \quad \Delta x \neq 0] \Rightarrow (p + \Delta p) \cdot \Delta x < 0,$$

it implies in particular that

$$[p \cdot \Delta x = 0 \quad \& \quad \Delta x \neq 0] \Rightarrow \Delta p \cdot \Delta x < 0. \tag{2.2}$$

Now, the preceding analysis implicitly assumes the existence of a demand function $x = h(p, I)$, where I is income, and since the budget set $p \cdot x \leq I$ is invariant with respect to multiplication of p and I by the same constant $\lambda > 0$, h is homogeneous of degree zero. Assuming it to be differentiable, the differential of its ith component, h^i, is equal to

$$dh^i = \sum_{j=1}^{n} h^i_j dp_j + h^i_I dI \qquad (h^i_j \equiv \partial h^i/\partial p_j, \; h^i_I \equiv \partial h^i/\partial I), \tag{2.3}$$

and the differential of the budget constraint $p \cdot h(p, I) = I$ is

$$dI = \sum_{j=1}^{n} h^j dp_j + \sum_{j=1}^{n} p_j dh^j.$$

If $p \cdot dh = 0$ this becomes $dI = h \cdot dp$, which, when substituted in (2.3), gives

$$dh^i = \sum_{j=1}^{n} (h^i_j + h^i_I h^j) dp_j.$$

Applying (2.2) and taking limits we then obtain,

$$dp \cdot dh = \sum_{i=1}^{n} \sum_{j=1}^{n} (h^i_j + h^i_I h^j) dp_i dp_j \leq 0 \quad \text{for } p \cdot dh = 0. \tag{2.4}$$

The expression $h^i_j + h^i_I h^j$ is the Slutsky term, as we now know it.[2] Accordingly, Samuelson concluded that the Weak Axiom implies the negative semidefiniteness of the Slutsky matrix.[3] He observed that "in the integrable case" the Slutsky matrix would also be symmetric, but did not pursue the matter further.

Samuelson's position on the integrability issue in 1938 was, in retrospect, quite curious, possibly reflecting the influence of some passages in Hicks and Allen (1934). In his words:

Concerning the question of integrability I have little to say. I cannot see that it is really an important problem, particularly if we are willing to dispense with the utility concept and its vestigial remnants. . . . The only possible interest that integrability can have . . . would be in providing us with additional knowledge concerning a certain reciprocal relation [in effect, the Slutsky symmetry conditions]. But it is this very implication which makes it doubtful and subject to refutation under ideal observational conditions, although I have little faith in any attempts to verify this statistically. I should strongly deny, however, that for a rational and consistent individual integrability is implied, except possibly as a matter of circular definition. [Samuelson 1938a, p. 68]

This position appears closer to the position Samuelson was later (1950a) to attribute to Allen than to the one he attributed to Hicks — namely, that the possibility of nonintegrability was too unimportant to exclude from consideration, as opposed to being too unimportant to take into consideration![4]

The matter was not allowed to rest there, however, and Samuelson was not one to stick rigidly to a previous position after new analyses came to light. The stimulus for change came from Little (1949), who presented an argument to the effect that by repeated application of the Weak Axiom and transitivity of revealed preference, one could build up what he called a "behavior line" in place of an indifference curve, by approximation from above and below. This idea was quickly taken up by Samuelson (1948) in an article that appeared before Little's was in print. In this paper Samuelson provided a sketch of a proof of Little's conjecture by means of the Cauchy-Lipschitz method of approximation. However, few mathematical details were provided, and only the case of two commodities, in which it is known that there is no integrability problem, was considered.

Houthakker's contribution, which soon followed (1950), was a major landmark. It made explicit the needed formal axiom that lay behind the informal reasoning of Little (1949) and Samuelson (1948), as well as a precise construction leading to a limiting differential equation that lay at the basis of the subsequent work of Uzawa (1960, 1971) and Hurwicz and Uzawa (1971). It also led to the fundamental work, along a different tack, of Richter (1966, 1971). Samuelson's (1950a) own follow-up contribution was likewise of crucial importance to this development. Before discussing it I shall briefly survey the development from Houthakker to Uzawa to Hurwicz and Uzawa.

The Strong Axiom of Revealed Preference introduced by Houthakker (1950) states that, for any positive integer s, if $x^t = h(p^t, p^t \cdot x^t)$ for $t = 1, 2, \ldots, s$, then

$$[p^t \cdot x^t \geqq p^t \cdot x^{t+1} \quad \& \quad x^t \neq x^{t+1}, \qquad t = 0, 1, \ldots, s - 1]$$

$$\Rightarrow p^s \cdot x^s < p^s \cdot x^0; \tag{2.5}$$

that is, the relation of (direct) revealed preference is not only asymmetric [as stated by (2.1)], but also acyclic. The bracketed statement in (2.5) defines the relation "x^0 is (indirectly) revealed preferred to x^s," which may be denoted "$x^0 P x^s$." The relation P, which by its definition is transitive, is thus postulated to be also asymmetric. The problem then is to show that the relation "not-P" is transitive and thus a total order.

Houthakker went about establishing this by constructing some "superior income sequences" and "inferior income sequences," as follows [the notation that ensues more closely follows Uzawa's (1971)]. Let a bundle x^0 be bought at prices p^0 and income I^0, and let p^1 be another price vector at which x^0 is not bought (say, $p^1 \neq p^0$, $p_n^1 = p_n^0 = 1$), and define intermediate price vectors by

$$p^t = p^0 + t(p^1 - p^0) \qquad (0 \leq t \leq 1). \tag{2.6}$$

Define $\bar{x}^{0s} = x^0 = h(p^0, I^0)$ and $\bar{I}^{0s} = I^0$, and recursively

$$\bar{I}^{k+1,s} = p^{(k+1)/s} \cdot \bar{x}^{ks}, \quad \bar{x}^{ks} = h(p^{k/s}, \bar{I}^{ks}) \quad (k = 0, 1, \ldots, s - 1). \tag{2.7}$$

This defines the superior income sequences $\bar{I}^{0s}, \bar{I}^{1s}, \ldots, \bar{I}^{ss}$ ($s = 1, 2, \ldots$). Since by the (explicit) assumption that all income is spent, we have $p^{(k+1)/s} \cdot \bar{x}^{k+1,s} = \bar{I}^{k+1,s} = p^{(k+1)/s} \cdot \bar{x}^{ks}$, so that $\bar{x}^{k+1,s}$ was chosen (at prices $p^{(k+1)/s}$) when $\bar{x}^{ks}$ was available, $\bar{x}^{k+1,s}$ is equal or revealed preferred to $\bar{x}^{ks}$; thus, $\bar{x}^{ss} P x^0$.

The inferior income sequences $\underline{I}^{0s}, \underline{I}^{1s}, \ldots, \underline{I}^{ss}$ are defined by setting $\underline{I}^{0s} = I^0$ and recursively solving the equations

$$\underline{I}^{ks} = p^{k/s} \cdot \underline{x}^{k+1,s}, \quad \underline{x}^{k+1,s} = h(p^{(k+1)/s}, \underline{I}^{k+1,s})$$

$$(k = 0, 1, \ldots, s - 1) \tag{2.8}$$

for $\underline{I}^{k+1,s}$ (given $\underline{I}^{ks}$), which is always possible (although, because of the possibility of inferior goods, the solution need not be unique; see Figure 2.1) since the function $p^{k/s} \cdot h(p^{(k+1)/s}, \cdot)$ ranges from 0 to ∞ and is continuous in income by virtue of an assumed Lipschitz condition on h with respect to I. Since $p^{k/s} \cdot \underline{x}^{k+1,s} = \underline{I}^{ks} = p^{k/s} \cdot \underline{x}^{ks}$, so that $\underline{x}^{ks}$ was chosen (at prices $p^{k/s}$) when $\underline{x}^{k+1,s}$ was available, $\underline{x}^{ks}$ is equal or revealed preferred to $\underline{x}^{k+1,s}$; thus $x^0 P \underline{x}^{ss}$.

We have $\bar{x}^{ss} P x^0$ and $x^0 P \underline{x}^{ss}$; hence $\bar{x}^{ss} P \underline{x}^{ss}$ [i.e., $\bar{x}^{ss} = h(p^1, \bar{I}^{ss})$ is (indirectly) revealed preferred to $\underline{x}^{ss} = h(p^1, \underline{I}^{ss})$]; and, since both are purchased at the same prices, it follows by the Strong Axiom that $\bar{I}^{ss} \geq \underline{I}^{ss}$. It was shown by Uzawa (1971, Lemma 1) that in the limit, as $s \rightarrow \infty$, these two incomes coincide.

Implicit in Houthakker's treatment, and subsequently rendered explicit in a related context by McKenzie (1957), was the important idea of an *income-compensation function*. This was formulated by Uzawa (1960, 1971) as follows. Given a bundle $x^0 = h(p^0, I^0)$, the supremum at prices p^1 of all incomes I such that x^0 is indirectly revealed preferred to $h(p^1, I)$ may be denoted (slightly modifying Uzawa's notation)

$$\rho(p^1; p^0, I^0) = \sup \{I: h(p^0, I^0) P h(p^1, I)\}. \tag{2.9}$$

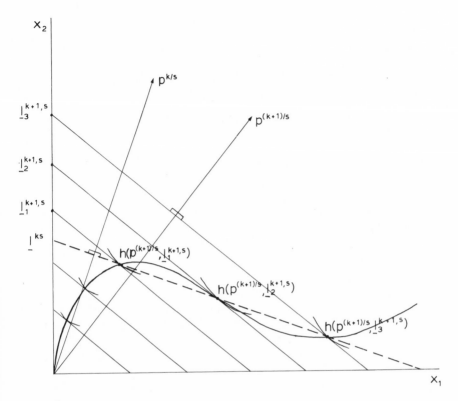

Figure 2.1

Likewise, the infimum at prices p^1 of all incomes I such that $h(p^1, I)$ is indirectly preferred or indifferent to x^0 may be denoted

$$\rho'(p^1; p^0, I^0) = \inf \{I: h(p^1, I)Ph(p^0, I^0)\}. \tag{2.10}$$

Since as shown above, $\bar{x}^{ss} = h(p^1, \bar{I}^{ss})Ph(p^0, I^0) = x^0$, clearly $\bar{I}^{ss} \geqq \rho'(p^1; p^0, I^0)$; likewise, since $x^0 = h(p^0, I^0)Ph(p^1, \underline{I}^{ss}) = \underline{x}^{ss}$, we have $\underline{I}^{ss} \leqq \rho(p^1; p^0, I^0)$. But since $\bar{I}^{ss}$ and $\underline{I}^{ss}$ approach a common limit as $s \to \infty$, it follows that the functions (2.9) and (2.10) coincide.

Since the indirect-revealed-preference relation P satisfies the monotonicity property $x \geq y \Rightarrow xPy$, it follows from (2.9) that

$$I < \rho(p^1; p^0, I^0) \Rightarrow h(p^0, I^0)Ph(p^1, I) \tag{2.9'}$$

and from (2.10) that

$$I > \rho'(p^1; p^0, I^0) \Rightarrow h(p^1, I)Ph(p^0, I^0). \tag{2.10'}$$

Consequently, if $x^0 = h(p^0, I^0)$ and $x^1 = h(p^1, I^1)$ are such that neither one is indirectly revealed preferred to the other, from the contrapositives of (2.9′) and (2.10′) we have $I^1 \geqq \rho(p^1; p^0, I^0)$ and $I^1 \leqq \rho'(p^1; p^0, I^0)$. Since $\rho = \rho'$ this means that

$$[\text{not-}x^0Px^1 \quad \& \quad \text{not-}x^1Px^0] \Rightarrow I^1 = \rho(p^1; p^0, I^0). \tag{2.11}$$

From here on, two different paths, both of which are indicated in Houthakker's classic article, can be taken to reach the desired result. One is to obtain a direct proof that the relation "not-P" is transitive, and the other is to arrive at an appropriate differential equation, which must then be integrated. First I shall describe Uzawa's very ingenious direct approach.

Uzawa showed that if a relation P is, as is the indirect-revealed-preference relation under the Strong Axiom, transitive and asymmetric as well as monotonic, then, in order that not-P be transitive (hence a total order), it is sufficient that P be convex and that not-P be upper semicontinuous. Uzawa showed that both of the latter properties were fulfilled by the indirect-revealed-preference relation P. I shall describe just the convexity result, since it uses the Strong Axiom in an essential way, and the continuity result is of a more technical nature. P is said to be convex if $x^0 \neq x^1$ and not-x^0Px^1 imply x^tPx^0 for $x^t = x^0 + t(x^1 - x^0)$, $0 < t < 1$. If $x^0 \neq x^1$ and not-x^0Px^1, and if $x^t = h(p^t, I^t)$ for $0 \leqq t \leqq 1$, then either (i) $p^t \cdot x^t - p^t \cdot x^0 = tp^t \cdot (x^1 - x^0) \geqq 0$ or (ii) $p^t \cdot x^t - p^t \cdot x^1 = (1-t)p^t \cdot (x^0 - x^1) > 0$. In Case (i), x^tPx^0 (the desired result). In Case (ii),

$$x^tPh(p^1, I^1 + \epsilon) \quad \text{for sufficiently small } \epsilon > 0 \tag{2.12}$$

(since h is continuous with respect to I). Now if x^1Px^0, then by monotonicity, $h(p^1, I)Ph(p^1, I^1)Ph(p^0, I^0)$ for $I > I^1$; that is,

$$h(p^1, I^1 + \epsilon)Px^0 \quad \text{for all } \epsilon > 0. \tag{2.13}$$

Alternatively, suppose not-x^1Px^0; then since also not-x^0Px^1, we have by (2.11) and the contrapositive of (2.10′) (and recalling that $\rho' = \rho$)

$$h(p^1, I)Ph(p^0, I^0) \quad \text{for all } I > I^1,$$

which is the same as (2.13). Combining (2.12) and (2.13) we have x^tPx^0 by the transitivity of P, which is the sought result.

I turn now to the alternative approach, which is of interest mainly because it provides the link between the "finite" revealed-preference approach of Samuelson (1938a) and Houthakker (1950) and the "infinitesimal'' differential-equations approach discussed by Samuelson (1950a) and by Hurwicz and Uzawa (1971).

Houthakker observed that the superior income sequences satisfy

$$\Delta \bar{I}^{ks} \equiv \bar{I}^{k+1,s} - \bar{I}^{ks} \equiv p^{(k+1)/s} \cdot \bar{x}^{k+1,s} - p^{k/s} \cdot \bar{x}^{ks}$$
$$= p^{(k+1)/s} \cdot \bar{x}^{ks} - p^{k/s} \cdot \bar{x}^{ks}$$
$$\equiv \Delta p^{k/s} \cdot \bar{x}^{ks} \tag{2.14}$$

and that the inferior income sequences satisfy

$$\Delta \underline{I}^{ks} \equiv \underline{I}^{k+1,s} - \underline{I}^{ks} \equiv p^{(k+1)/s} \cdot \underline{x}^{k+2,s} - p^{k/s} \cdot \underline{x}^{k+1,s}$$
$$= p^{(k+1)/s} \cdot \underline{x}^{k+1,s} - p^{k/s} \cdot \underline{x}^{k+1,s}$$
$$\equiv \Delta p^{k/s} \cdot \underline{x}^{k+1,s}$$
$$\equiv \Delta p^{k/s} \cdot (\underline{x}^{ks} + \Delta \underline{x}^{ks})$$
$$= \Delta p^{k/s} \cdot \underline{x}^{ks} + \Delta p^{k/s} \cdot \Delta \underline{x}^{ks}, \tag{2.15}$$

and thus that in the limit, as $s \to \infty$, both satisfy the same differential equation

$$dI = dp \cdot x = dp \cdot h(p, I). \tag{2.16}$$

If we make use of result (2.11), and define the relation R by xRy if and only if not-yPx, and finally define a new income-compensation function (as in Hurwicz and Uzawa 1971) by

$$\mu(p; p^0, I^0) = \inf \{I: h(p, I)Rh(p^0, I^0)\}, \tag{2.17}$$

then it is clear that the function μ coincides with ρ ($= \rho'$). It is thus possible to arrive at the system of partial differential equations

$$\frac{\partial \mu}{\partial p_i} = h^i(p, \mu) \quad (i = 1, 2, \ldots, n), \tag{2.18}$$

with the corresponding total differential equation

$$d\mu = \sum_{j=1}^{n} h^j(p, \mu)dp_j \tag{2.19}$$

as in (2.16).

The system of partial differential equations (2.18) is of fundamental importance. It is the basic system from which one may integrate the observable demand functions to obtain (as will become clear shortly) the consumer's *indirect* utility function. It also provides the link alluded to above between the "finite" revealed-preference approach and the "infinitesimal" differential-equations approach.

The differential equations (2.18) were used by Uzawa (1960, 1971) to derive the Slutsky symmetry conditions directly [an approach pioneered by McKenzie (1957) using a function close to (2.17)]. From the assumed Lipschitz condition, the Strong Axiom was shown by Uzawa (1971, p. 19) to imply that the demand function is continuous (jointly) in (p, I). If it is also continuously differentiable, differentiation of (2.18) yields

$$\frac{\partial^2 \mu}{\partial p_i \partial p_j} = \frac{\partial h^i}{\partial p_j} + \frac{\partial h^i}{\partial I} \frac{\partial \mu}{\partial p_j} = \frac{\partial h^i}{\partial p_j} + \frac{\partial h^i}{\partial I} h^j \equiv s_{ij}, \qquad (2.20)$$

hence $s_{ij} = s_{ji}$, where s_{ij} as defined in (2.20) is the Slutsky term. These Slutsky symmetry conditions are known to be necessary and sufficient for the "complete integrability" of the system (2.18) whenever the h^i are continuously differentiable — that is, for the existence of a function μ satisfying (2.18) and the initial condition $\mu(p^0; p^0, I^0) = I^0$ (cf. Hurwicz and Uzawa 1971, p. 124).

I now turn to Samuelson's (1950a) important paper on the integrability problem, which followed on the heels of Houthakker's contribution and which laid the basis for the contribution by Hurwicz and Uzawa (1971). Samuelson immediately saw that the Strong Axiom provided the long-sought economic explanation for the Slutsky symmetry conditions; he posed the problem in terms of the *inverse* demand functions defined by

$$p_i/p_n = B^i(x_1, x_2, \ldots, x_n) \qquad (i = 1, 2, \ldots, n - 1)$$

$$I/p_n = B^n(x_1, x_2, \ldots, x_n) \equiv \sum_{i=1}^{n-1} B^i(x)x_1 + x_n, \qquad (2.21)$$

where B^i is the marginal rate of substitution between commodity i and commodity n. This formulation assumes, of course, that a positive amount of each commodity is consumed, ruling out corner solutions; it also rules out indifference curves with kinks (but permits flat segments except that flats have also to be ruled out if the *direct* demand functions are to be single-valued).

If we momentarily assume (as we must, if we are looking for *necessary* conditions for integrability of the inverse demand functions) that the equations (2.21) result from maximization of a utility function $U(x_1, x_2, \ldots, x_n)$ subject to a budget constraint $p \cdot x = I$, the inverse demand functions are defined by

$$B^i(x) = \frac{\partial U/\partial x_i}{\partial U/\partial x_n} \qquad (i = 1, 2, \ldots, n - 1), \qquad (2.22)$$

giving rise to the system of homogeneous partial differential equations

$$\frac{\partial U}{\partial x_i} - B^i(x) \frac{\partial U}{\partial x_n} = 0 \qquad (i = 1, 2, \ldots, n-1) \qquad (2.23)$$

and the associated total differential equation

$$dU = \iota(x) \left[\sum_{i=1}^{n-1} B^i(x) dx_i + dx_n \right], \qquad (2.24)$$

where ι is an integrating factor (namely $\iota = \partial U/\partial x_n$). Now let us for convenience define as in Hurwicz (1971)

$$m = n - 1; z_i = x_i \, (i = 1, 2, \ldots, m); y = x_n. \qquad (2.25)$$

The equation of an indifference surface passing through the point $x^0 = (z^0, y^0)$ is defined implicitly by

$$U(z, \eta(z; z^0, y^0)) = U(z^0, y^0), \qquad (2.26)$$

where

$$y = \eta(z; z^0, y^0) \qquad (2.27)$$

expresses the amount of the nth commodity as a function of the amounts of commodities $1, 2, \ldots, n-1$, determined by the indifference surface through $x^0 = (z^0, y^0)$. We may refer to η as the *numéraire-compensation function*, since it defines the amount y of the numéraire required, as a function of the amounts z of the remaining $n-1$ commodities, to keep the consumer indifferent as between (z, y) and (z^0, y^0).

Differentiating (2.26) with respect to z_i, we obtain

$$\frac{\partial U}{\partial z_i} + \frac{\partial U}{\partial y} \frac{\partial \eta}{\partial z_i} = 0, \quad \text{or} \quad \frac{\partial \eta}{\partial z_i} = -\frac{\partial U/\partial z_i}{\partial U/\partial y} = -\frac{\partial U/\partial x_i}{\partial U/\partial x_n} \qquad (2.28)$$

so that, setting marginal utilities proportional to prices and setting $p_n = 1$, we have from (2.21) and (2.25) the system of nonhomogeneous partial differential equations

$$\frac{\partial \eta}{\partial z_i} = -B^i(z, \eta) \qquad (i = 1, 2, \ldots, m) \qquad (2.29)$$

with the associated total differential equation[5]

$$d\eta = -\sum_{i=1}^{m} B^i(z, \eta) dz_i. \qquad (2.30)$$

The system (2.29) is the basic system analyzed by Samuelson (1950a, p. 379). It is completely analogous to the system (2.18) in terms of direct demand functions (where we may also set $p_n = 1$).

If $\eta(\cdot; z^0, y^0)$ is twice continuously differentiable, upon differentiating (2.29) with respect to z_j, we obtain the "Antonelli coefficients"

$$-\frac{\partial^2 \eta}{\partial z_i \partial z_j} = \frac{\partial B^i}{\partial z_j} + \frac{\partial B^i}{\partial y}\frac{\partial \eta}{\partial z_j} = \frac{\partial B^i}{\partial z_j} - \frac{\partial B^i}{\partial y}B^j \equiv a_{ij} \qquad (2.31)$$

and thus the Antonelli-Allen integrability conditions $a_{ij} = a_{ji}$ (see Antonelli 1886; 1971, p. 347; Allen 1932, pp. 222–23n; Wold 1943, pp. 114–15; Samuelson 1950a, p. 378).[6] If the B^i are continuously differentiable, these conditions are known to be necessary and sufficient for the "complete integrability" of the system of partial differential equations (2.29) — that is, for the existence of a continuously differentiable function η satisfying (2.29) and $\eta(z^0; z^0, y^0) = y^0$ (see Hurwicz 1971, p. 191).

In order to complete the analogy between the system (2.29) and its dual (2.18), we may note that the function η of (2.26) and (2.27) satisfies, and therefore may be defined alternatively in the form,

$$\eta(z; z^0, y^0) = \sup \{y: (z^0, y^0)R(z, y)\}, \qquad (2.32)$$

where R is the (direct) preference relation (x^1Rx^2 means "x^1 is preferred or indifferent to x^2"). This is a convex function of z, just as the function μ of (2.17) is a concave function of p. Likewise, we may define the *indirect preference relation* R^* by the condition

$$(p^1, I^1)R^*(p^2, I^2) \Leftrightarrow h(p^1, I^1)Rh(p^2, I^2), \qquad (2.33)$$

and call a function $V(p, I)$ that represents R^* — i.e., is such that $V(p^1, I^1) \geqq V(p^2, I^2)$ if and only if $(p^1, I^1)R^*(p^2, I^2)$ — an *indirect utility function*, following Houthakker (1953). In case the direct preference relation R is representable by a utility function $U(x)$, so that $U(x^1) \geqq U(x^2)$ if and only if x^1Rx^2, then we have $V(p, I) = U[h(p, I)]$ and, conversely, $U(x) = V[B^1(x), B^2(x), \ldots , B^{n-1}(x), 1, B^n(x)]$.

In terms of the indirect utility function V, the analogue of the system (2.23) is the system of homogeneous partial differential equations

$$\frac{\partial V}{\partial P_i} + h^i(p, I)\frac{\partial V}{\partial I} = 0 \qquad (i = 1, 2, \ldots , n) \qquad (2.34)$$

first obtained by Antonelli (1886; 1971, p. 340) and subsequently rediscovered by Allen (1933, p. 190) and Roy (1942, p. 21).[7] The analogue of (2.24) is the total differential equation

$$dV = \lambda(p, I)\left[-\sum_{i=1}^{n} h^i(p, I)dp_i + dI\right], \qquad (2.35)$$

where $\lambda = \partial V / \partial I$ is the appropriate integrating factor. Since the function μ of (2.17) satisfies the property that $h(p, \mu(p; p^0, I^0))$ is indifferent to $h(p^0, I^0)$, it satisfies the identity [compare (2.26)]

$$V(p, \mu(p; p^0, I^0)) = V(p^0, I^0). \qquad (2.36)$$

Differentiating (2.36) with respect to p_i, we obtain by analogy with (2.28),

$$\frac{\partial V}{\partial p_i} + \frac{\partial V}{\partial I} \frac{\partial \mu}{\partial p_i} = 0, \quad \text{or} \quad \frac{\partial \mu}{\partial p_i} = - \frac{\partial V / \partial p_i}{\partial V / \partial I}. \qquad (2.37)$$

Just as (2.23) and (2.28) led to (2.29), (2.34) and (2.37) lead us back to our system of nonhomogeneous partial differential equations (2.18).

Since the function μ can be defined implicitly by (2.36), just as the equation (2.27) defined the (direct) indifference surface in commodity space passing through the point $x^0 = (z^0, y^0)$, likewise the equation

$$I = \mu(p; p^0, I^0) \qquad (2.38)$$

defines the *indirect indifference surface* in price-income space passing through the point (p^0, I^0).

Let us now set $p_n = p_n^0 = 1$, and denote

$$q_i = p_i \quad (i = 1, 2, \ldots, n - 1 = m), \quad D(q, I) = h(q, 1, I). \quad (2.39)$$

We may continue to use the notation R^* to denote the indirect preference relation between bundles of the form (q, I). It is not hard to see that

$$\begin{aligned} \mu(p; p^0, I^0) &= \inf \{p \cdot x : xRh(p^0, I^0)\} \\ &= \inf \{(q, 1) \cdot (z, y) : (z, y)RD(q^0, I^0) = (z^0, y^0)\} \quad (2.40) \end{aligned}$$

(see Figure 2.2) and that

$$\eta(z; z^0, y^0) = \sup \{(-z, 1) \cdot (q, I) : (q^0, I^0) = B(z^0, y^0)R^*(q, I)\} \qquad (2.41)$$

(see Figure 2.3). For convenience we define

$$\nu(q; q^0, I^0) = \mu(q, 1; q^0, 1, I^0). \qquad (2.42)$$

Samuelson's (1950a) procedure was to go from the direct demand function D of (2.39) to the inverse demand function B of (2.21) and to integrate the latter to obtain the indifference surface (2.27) through any given point $x^0 = (z^0, y^0)$. By the definitions of these functions, we have $D(B(z, y)) = (z, y)$ for $(z, y) > 0$, and conversely $B(D(q, I)) = (q, I)$ for $(q, I) > 0$ such that $D(q, I) > 0$ (i.e., $B = D^{-1}$ on these domains). The same is true of the corresponding *compensated* direct and inverse demand

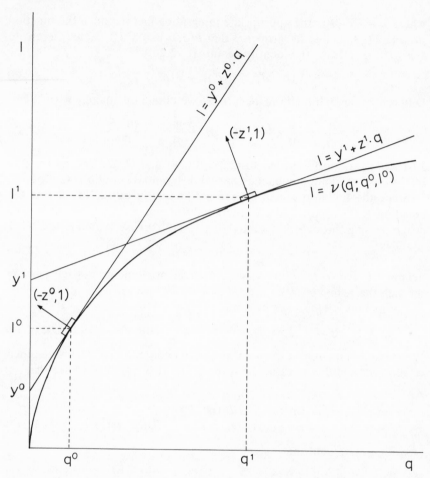

Figure 2.2

functions, although this is not immediately obvious. Samuelson's procedure was to find a factorization of the Jacobian matrix of the transformation $B(z, y) = (q, I)$ into the product of three matrices and to show
that the nth-order principal submatrix of the middle factor was the Antonelli matrix and its inverse the corresponding Slutsky matrix. The
following simpler and more direct approach was suggested to me by my
colleague Marcel Richter. So as not to prejudge the question of integrability, let us define the function η not by (2.32) or (2.26), but rather as

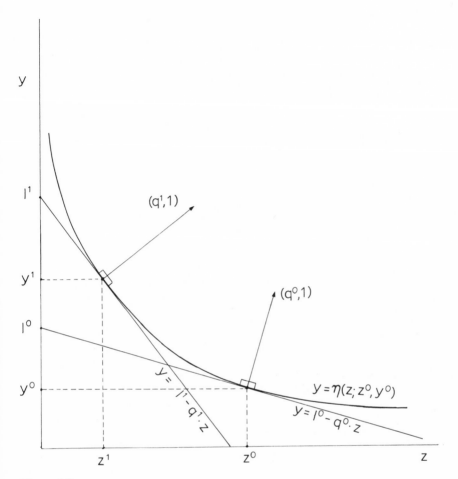

Figure 2.3

the solution of the system of partial differential equations (2.29); a necessary condition for the existence of such a solution is the symmetry of the Antonelli matrix $A = [a_{ij}]$ of (2.31). In place of the compensation function μ of (2.17), let us define the alternative income-compensation function (for $p_n = 1$)

$$M(q; z^0, y^0) = q \cdot z^0 + y^0 = p \cdot x^0. \qquad (2.43)$$

This corresponds to Slutsky's concept of compensation (1915, p. 14), according to which the consumer is compensated after a price change not so as to leave him as well off as before (see Hicks 1939, p. 31), but so as to allow him to afford the same bundle $x^0 = (z^0, y^0)$ that he was consuming in the initial situation. It is well known (see Mosak 1942) that in the limit, as $x \to x^0$, this coincides with the Hicksian concept of compensation — that is,

$$\frac{\partial}{\partial q_j} D^i[q, M(q; z^0, y^0)] = \frac{\partial D^i}{\partial q_j} + \frac{\partial D^i}{\partial I} z_j^0 = s_{ij}$$
$$\text{for } (z, y) = (z^0, y^0). \tag{2.44}$$

Now, from the identity $B(D(q, I)) = (q, I)$ we have

$$B^i[D(q, M(q; z^0, y^0)] = q_i \qquad (i = 1, 2, \ldots, m = n - 1). \tag{2.45}$$

Differentiating (2.45) with respect to q_j and making use of (2.44), we obtain, at $(z, y) = (z^0, y^0)$,

$$\sum_{k=1}^{n} \frac{\partial B^i}{\partial z_k} s_{kj} = \sum_{k=1}^{n-1} \left[\frac{\partial B^i}{\partial z_k} - q_k \frac{\partial B^i}{\partial y} \right] s_{kj} = \delta_{ij} \tag{2.46}$$

(where δ_{ij} is the Kronecker delta), where the first equality results from the condition

$$\sum_{k=1}^{n-1} q_k s_{kj} + s_{nj} = 0, \tag{2.47}$$

which is a consequence of the homogeneity of degree zero of the demand function h. Evaluating $B(z, y)$ at $(z, y) = (z^0, y^0)$, we may write (2.46) as

$$\sum_{k=1}^{n-1} a_{ik} s_{kj} = \delta_{ij}, \quad \text{or} \quad AS = I, \tag{2.48}$$

where $A = [a_{ij}]$ and $S = [s_{ij}]$ are the $m \times m$ Antonelli and Slutsky matrices respectively, $i, j = 1, 2, \ldots, m = n - 1$, and I in (2.48) denotes the identity matrix of order $m - 1$. Since a necessary condition for the integrability of (2.29) is that A be symmetric, an equivalent necessary condition (given the invertibility of B) is that $S = A^{-1}$ be symmetric.

This almost completes the survey of the subject, but there are still a few loose ends to be tied up. First of all, it should be noted that integration of the nonhomogeneous partial differential equations (2.29) leads, not to a utility function $U(x)$, but only to the equation (2.27) of an indifference surface through a point $x^0 = (z^0, y^0)$; to obtain a utility function one would need to integrate the system (2.23). Likewise, integration of the nonhomogeneous partial differential equations (2.18) leads not to an indirect utility function $V(p, I)$, but only to the equation (2.38) of an indirect indifference surface through a point (p^0, I^0); to obtain an indirect utility function, one would need to integrate the system (2.34). In the case of (2.18), however, it was shown, in effect, by Hurwicz and Uzawa (1971, Lemma 8) that the function

$$V_{\bar{p}}(p, I) = \mu(\bar{p}; p, I) \qquad (2.49)$$

is an indirect utility function representing R^*. This measures utility by the amount of income, $\bar{I}$, required to make $(\bar{p}, \bar{I})$ (indirectly) indifferent to (p, I); in Figure 2.2 it is measured by the height of an indirect indifference curve above a particular point, $\bar{q}$. It is therefore enough to know the entire function μ to obtain an integral of the Antonelli equations (2.34). It is tempting to conjecture that one may likewise represent R by the utility function

$$U_{\bar{z}}(z, y) = \eta(\bar{z}; z, y), \qquad (2.50)$$

measuring utility by the amount $\bar{y}$ of commodity n required to make the consumer indifferent between $(\bar{z}, \bar{y})$ and (z, y); in Figure 2.3 it would be measured by the height of an indifference curve above a particular point, $\bar{z}$. Unfortunately, however, here the duality breaks down; the domain of $\eta(\cdot; z, y)$ need not include all positive values of the bundle $\bar{z}$ (as is the case with C.E.S. utility functions with elasticity of substitution < 1), hence $\eta(\bar{z}; \cdot)$ need not be defined for some (z, y). For this reason one is led to what Samuelson (1974) called the "money metric," defined by

$$U_{\bar{q}}(x) = \nu(\bar{q}; B(x)) \qquad (2.51)$$

(see McKenzie 1957; Hurwicz and Uzawa 1971, p. 125).

Second, one may ask: What does the Strong Axiom add over and above the Weak Axiom? Indeed, does it add anything? We have seen that the Weak Axiom implies negative semidefiniteness of the Slutsky matrix (condition (2.4)), and that the Strong Axiom (which of course implies the Weak Axiom) implies its symmetry. It was remarked by Arrow (1959), however, that it was not known (at that time) that the Weak Axiom does not imply the Strong Axiom. This question was settled by Gale (1960), who provided an example (for $n = 3$) of a demand function that satisfies the Weak but not the Strong Axiom; his example carried out a suggestion made to him by Samuelson that one perturb slightly a demand function that satisfies the Slutsky symmetry and negative definiteness condition (see note 3). It was shown by Rose (1958), following Hicks (1956) and Afriat (1965), that the Weak Axiom implies the Strong when $n = 2$. More recently it was shown by Kihlstrom, Mas-Colell, and Sonnenschein (1976) that the negative semidefiniteness condition (2.4) implies (as well as is implied by) a slightly weakened version of the Weak Axiom.[8] There remains the question: What does the Strong Axiom add, or: Is there a condition that when added to the Weak Axiom, yields the Strong Axiom, which is known to be equivalent to the negative semidefiniteness and symmetry of the Slutsky matrix?

This question was posed by Uzawa (1960, 1971) who showed that a certain "regularity condition," when added to the Weak Axiom, would imply the Strong Axiom. This regularity condition states that the function ρ of (2.9) is strictly increasing in I^0, or equivalently that it is defined (finite) for all p^0, p^1 and that at the same time the function ρ' of (2.10) is continuous in I^0. It was remarked by Kihlstrom, Mas-Colell, and Sonnenschein (1976, p. 972), however, that Uzawa's condition "is marred by the fact that it looks very much like the *strong axiom* itself." There thus remains the question: Is there a condition *that does not itself imply the Strong Axiom* yet that, when added to the Weak Axiom, yields the Strong Axiom?

An answer to this question has been provided by Hurwicz and Richter (1979) on the basis of Ville's (1946) work. They have shown that Ville's axiom, while similar in spirit to Houthakker's but "infinitesimal" rather than "finitistic" in form, is equivalent to symmetry of the Antonelli matrix. Given a continuously differentiable demand function, it is thus equivalent to symmetry of the Slutsky matrix (see Richter 1979, pp. 178–79).

With this final step provided by Hurwicz and Richter (1979), all the fundamental problems in the theory of revealed preference may be said to be essentially solved. In particular, the long-sought problem of finding an economic interpretation of the Slutsky symmetry conditions, which eluded Samuelson in 1938, has finally been resolved after more than forty years of work by the best minds in the profession. It must be a very satisfying outcome for the originator of such a fruitful idea; it has in fact been one of the most glorious chapters in the history of economic thought. The contrast with Samuelson's predecessors is striking. By and large it may be said without too much injustice that Walras, Pareto, Edgeworth, and Fisher cast their pearls before swine; it was only in subsequent generations that a few sporadic and isolated, yet outstanding, contributions were made to the integrability problem, such as those of Johnson (1913), Slutsky (1915), Allen (1932), and Georgescu-Roegen (1936). Samuelson, on the other hand, cast his pearls before a grateful generation of economists eager to work out the theory to its conclusion, and he himself added crucial contributions along the way.

This does not mean that the subject is now dead. On the contrary, there are still numerous questions yet to be resolved, and it is in the nature of intellectual progress that one cannot foretell the development of a fruitful idea.[9] In fact, now that the logical foundations of the subject have been firmly laid, increasing attention has been paid to practical applications and the construction of utility functions from empirical data (see Afriat 1967). It is perhaps only when this practical aspect of the subject becomes fully worked out that one will finally be able to put to rest the long-standing controversies over welfare measurement that I take up in the next section.

CONSUMER'S SURPLUS AND THE MEASUREMENT OF UTILITY AND WELFARE

The principal motivation for the development of the theory of revealed preference and integrability outlined in the previous section arose from a desire to base demand theory on observable behavior and to free it from any unnecessary utility concepts. As we have seen, however, the outcome of the development was quite different — namely, it reestablished the utility concept precisely on the basis of postulates concerning observable behavior. Nevertheless, nothing in this development disconfirmed the Paretian view (Pareto 1898), so persuasively argued by Hicks and Allen (1934), that market behavior is invariant with respect to monotone transformations of a particular utility function generating the observed demand function. Subsequent developments have shown, however, that there is more to the "measurability" question than the proposition just cited. There were already hints of this in Samuelson's early papers dealing with the measurability issue (1937, 1938b), even on the occasions when he took a strongly "ordinalist" stance — in fact, especially on such occasions. This will be explained later. First I shall take up his seminal paper on the constancy of the marginal utility of income (1942).

Constancy of the Marginal Utility of Income

The question at issue arose from the practice of Marshall (1920, p. 842), following Dupuit (1844), of assessing the improvement in a consumer's welfare from an initial situation in which prices and income were given by (p^0, I^0) to a new one in which they were given by (p^1, I^1), in terms of a line integral[10]

$$- \sum_{i=1}^{n} \int_0^1 h^i[p(t), I(t)]dp_i(t) + I^1 - I^0 \qquad (2.52)$$

along a path $(p(t), I(t))$, $0 \leqq t \leqq 1$, from $(p(0),I(0)) = (p^0, I^0)$ to $(p(1), I(1)) = (p^1, I^1)$; or alternatively, in terms of a line integral in the commodity space, from $x^0 = h(p^0, I^0)$ to $x^1 = h(p^1, I^1)$ along a path $x(t) = h[p(t),I(t)]$ from $x(0) = x^0$ to $x(1) = x^1$, given by

$$\sum_{i=1}^{n-1} \int_0^1 B^i[x(t)]dx_i(t) + x_n^1 - x_n^0. \tag{2.53}$$

As is clear from (2.35) and (2.24), such a procedure is not legitimate, since the above expressions (2.52) and (2.53) are not exact differentials; to render them so, one must multiply them by the appropriate integrating factors — namely, the marginal utility of income $\lambda = \partial V/\partial I$ in the case of expression (2.52) and the marginal utility of the numéraire $\iota = \partial U/\partial x_n$ in the case of expression (2.53). This was admitted by Marshall, who specifically stipulated: "We assume that the marginal utility of money to the individual purchaser is the same throughout" (1920, p. 842). He argued — erroneously, as can easily be shown[11] — that variations in what he called the "marginal utility of money" could be neglected if the commodity under consideration (whose price is changing) "is only a small part of his whole expenditure." He nevertheless added, referring to the case of a change in the price of a single commodity, tea [say, commodity 1 in (2.52)]:

> If, for any reason, it be desirable to take account of the influence which his expenditure on tea exerts on the value of money to him, it is only necessary to multiply $f(x)$ within the integral given above [corresponding to $h^1[p(t), I(t)]$ in (2.52)] by that function of $xf(x)$ [corresponding to $p_1 h^1(p, I)$ above] (i.e. of the amount he has already spent on tea) which represents the marginal utility to him of money when his stock of it has been diminished by that amount. [Marshall 1920, p. 842]

Undeterred by the latter piece of advice, or confident that Marshall's previous argument made it unnecessary to heed, subsequent practitioners have adopted expressions such as (2.52) and (2.53), the so-called consumer's surplus, to measure the change in a consumer's welfare under the given conditions.

As Pareto (1892) had done before him (but largely unknown to Samuelson), Samuelson (1942) posed the question: What are the empirical implications of the assumed constancy of the marginal utility of income on the demand behavior of the individual consumer? Pareto had analyzed the question only in relation to the case in which the consumer's preferences could be represented by an additively separable utility function and had found that for the marginal utility of income to be independent of prices, the utility function would have to be log-linear (see Chipman 1976b, pp. 67–70).

Samuelson (1942) was apparently not aware of the concept introduced by Allen (1933) of an indirect utility function, but it was implicit in his discussion.[12] He showed that $\partial V/\partial I$ could not be constant for all values of (p, I) because, since V is homogeneous of degree 0, $\partial V/\partial I$ must be homogeneous of degree -1 and, since it is positive (owing to the budget equality), this would lead to a contradiction. He then considered the case treated by Marshall in which only prices change (not income) — so that the last two terms of (2.52) cancel out — and found that $\partial V/\partial I$ is independent of prices if and only if the demand function $h(p, I)$ is homogeneous of degree one in income — the case of "expenditure proportionality." He went further and showed (following Bergson 1936) that in this case, preferences could be represented by a utility function $\Phi(x)$ that is homogeneous of degree one, and that the required cardinal utility function would be of the form $U(x) = a \log \Phi(x) + b \ (a > 0)$.[13] From here one can reproduce his final result by defining $V(p, I) = U[h(p, I)]$ and noting that since

$$\log \{\Phi[Ih(p, 1)]\} = \log \{I\Phi[h(p,1)]\} = \log I + \log \Phi[h(p, 1)], \quad (2.54)$$

we have $\partial V/\partial I = a/I$.

Of particular interest is the fact that, should one seriously entertain the hypothesis of expenditure proportionality (homothetic preferences) as a realistic empirical hypothesis (and Samuelson, on the contrary, took the position that one could not reasonably do so, even locally), then the above result provides a basis for a scientifically legitimate theory of measurable utility. The class of utility functions representing such preferences, and having the property that the marginal utility of income is independent of prices, is unique up to increasing linear transformations of the above utility function U. It also has the nice classical property of diminishing marginal utility of income. More important is the general point that there exist restrictive hypotheses concerning consumer behavior (and possibly some that are more plausible than expenditure proportionality) that could serve as a basis for measuring utility in much the same way that physicists find it convenient to measure temperature. From this point of view, the objection that utility need not, and therefore must not, be measured because the consumer's market demand behavior is invariant with respect to monotone transformations of his utility function is not so much wrong as irrelevant. In a sense, it is even partly wrong. The proposition that a consumer's (indirect) preferences can be represented by an (indirect) utility function that has the property that the marginal (indirect) utility of income is independent of prices — a property that is obviously not invariant with respect to monotone transformations of the indirect utility function — is a proposition that carries strong empirical implications concerning the consumer's preferences, which can be verified or refuted by observations on his market demand behavior.

Samuelson (1942) also took up an alternative interpretation of "constancy" of the marginal utility of income — namely, the hypothesis that it is independent of income and of all prices save one, that of a numéraire (which we can take to be commodity n). This would be an appropriate way to pose the question if one restricted the use of (2.52) to comparisons between situations in which the price of the numéraire was unchanged or, alternatively, if one normalized income and other prices by this price. Samuelson showed that independence of $\partial V / \partial I$ of all variables other than p_n implied that the demand functions for all commodities but the nth were independent of income (for sufficiently high income, of course) and that they were generated by a utility function of the form $U(z, y) = \Phi(z) + ay + b$ [in the notation of (2.25) above]. Preferences yielding such demand behavior may be described as "parallel" with respect to commodity n (Samuelson 1964; Chipman and Moore 1976). Such preferences had previously been analyzed by Edgeworth (1891a, 1891b), who had shown that they were implicitly required in the types of consumer's surplus arguments employed by Auspitz and Lieben (1889). As before, whether or not one takes the hypothesis of parallel preferences seriously as an empirical postulate, it leads naturally to a cardinal measure of utility; in fact, this is one case in which the function (2.50) would be a natural and appropriate cardinal representation [but only for bundles at least as good as $(\bar{z}, 0)$], since it is a linear transformation of the above U.

The importance of Samuelson's contribution consisted in showing that the apparently innocent assumption of "constancy" of the marginal utility of income has very strong empirical implications concerning demand behavior; he pointed out further that other methods were available for assessing the desirability of prospective changes that did not prejudge the nature of consumers' tastes. One might have thought that the response of practitioners of cost-benefit analysis would have been either to pursue these alternative methods or to defend the empirical realism of homotheticity or parallelism of preferences. Instead, however — in stark contrast to the stimulating and profound effect on economic theory of his work on revealed preference and integrability — Samuelson's closely related work on the foundations of cost-benefit analysis has had virtually no impact on the methods of applied welfare economists. How can this be explained?

The Lack of Impact on Cost-Benefit Analysis

Three possible reasons suggest themselves. One is that there appears to be a strong preference among applied researchers for numerical results and measurements over qualitative comparisons. Measurement, particularly when it can be done in a standard manner among different research workers, provides the appearance of objectivity and scientific precision and thus enjoys much greater prestige than any qualitative method, no matter how soundly based. Moreover, it may simply be inconvenient to tabulate a ranking of a large number of alternative projects as opposed to furnishing each one with a numerical index of worth from which any binary comparison can be immediately read off. Thus, even such a staunch ordinalist as Hicks (1941, pp. 112–14) insisted that the role of consumer's surplus was to provide a cardinal measure of "the size of deviation" from an optimum, so as to be able to make comparisons of the form: a further reduction of output is more damaging than an initial reduction in output. This contrasts with Samuelson's position (1942, p. 87) that "one cannot fruitfully compare the gain derived from a movement between two given price situations with the gain between two other price situations." Samuelson added in a footnote the interesting point: "One can, however, compare the gains derived from a change in the basic price situation with an alternative price change from the *same* basic situation, since this resolves itself into an *ordinal* comparison of the alternative new situations" (ibid.). That is, if one has a cardinal indicator $W[(p^0, I^0)$, $(p^t, I^t)]$ of the improvement in going from a basic situation (p^0, I^0) to a new situation (p^t, I^t), then from the numerical comparison $W[(p^0, I^0)$, $(p^1, I^1)] \geqq W[(p^0, I^0), (p^2, I^2)]$ one can infer $(p^1, I^1)R^*(p^2, I^2)$ — that is, that (p^1, I^1) is (indirectly) preferred or indifferent to (p^2, I^2). In Hicks's illustration, if the welfare loss (by reference to an initial optimum) of a further reduction in output exceeds that of the initial reduction in output, one can infer that the situation after the further reduction in output is worse than the situation after the initial reduction in output.[14]

This brings me to a second possible reason why Samuelson's findings may have had so little impact on the practitioners of cost-benefit analysis. In the very same year, Hicks (1942) introduced an alternative indicator of welfare change, the compensating variation (already introduced as a concept in Hicks 1939, but not specifically as a welfare measure), that is widely regarded to be superior to the Marshallian consumer's surplus and immune from its deficiencies. In terms of the income-compensation function (2.17), the compensating variation in going from (p^0, I^0) to (p^t, I^t) is defined by

$$W^C[(p^0, I^0), (p^t, I^t)] = I^t - \mu(p^t; p^0, I^0). \tag{2.55}$$

Since $\mu(p^t; \cdot)$ is a proper indirect utility function, and $\mu(p^t; p^t, I^t) = I^t$, (2.55) furnishes an unobjectionable ordinal criterion of welfare change in the sense that $(p^t, I^t)R^*(p^0, I^0)$ if and only if $W^C[(p^0, I^0), (p^t, I^t)] \geqq 0$. However, if it is used in the manner proposed by Hicks (1941) in the case of the consumer's surplus measure (2.52), which (2.55) replaces — namely, to rank two alternatives (p^1, I^1) and (p^2, I^2) in terms of the relative magnitudes of (2.55) for $t = 1$ and $t = 2$ — then it implicitly assumes that the indirect preference relation R^* can be represented by the function

$$C_{(p^0, I^0)}(p, I) = I - \mu(p; p^0, I^0). \tag{2.56}$$

It can be shown, moreover (see Chipman and Moore 1980), that (2.56) can be expressed equivalently as a consumer's surplus integral in terms of the *compensated* demand function $g^i(p; p^0, I^0) \equiv h^i(p, \mu(p; p^0, I^0)) = \partial\mu(p; p^0, I^0)/\partial p_i$ [see (2.18)], as

$$C_{(p^0, I^0)}(p^1, I^1) = -\sum_{i=1}^{n} \int_0^1 g^i[p(t); p^0, I^0]dp_i(t) + I^1 - I^0, \tag{2.57}$$

along a path $(p(t), I(t))$ from (p^0, I^0) to (p^1, I^1), $0 \leqq t \leqq 1$. One may then pose the same question concerning the use of the Hicksian criterion (2.57) in making comparisons between two alternatives (p^1, I^1) and (p^2, I^2) as Samuelson posed with respect to the Marshallian criterion (2.52).

This question has in fact been posed by Chipman and Moore (1979, 1980), and it turns out that the answer is identical with Samuelson's answer to the analogous question — namely, that: (1) for unrestricted comparisons between pairs (p^1, I^1) and (p^2, I^2), (2.56) is never a valid indicator of preferences; and (2) if comparisons are restricted to pairs with (a) the same income, $I^1 = I^2$ or (b) the same price of commodity n, $p_n^1 = p_n^2$, then (2.55) furnishes a valid indicator of welfare change from (p^1, I^1) to (p^2, I^2) if and only if preferences are, respectively, homothetic in Case (a) or parallel with respect to commodity n in Case (b).[15] If one can take either of these hypotheses concerning consumer preferences seriously, it is of some interest to note that in Case (a) we have (see Chipman and Moore 1980)

$$\frac{\mu(p^0; p, I)}{I^0} = \frac{I}{\mu(p; p^0, I^0)}, \tag{2.58}$$

and that in Case (b) we have

$$\frac{\mu(p^0; p, I) - I^0}{p_n^0} = \frac{I - \mu(p; p^0, I^0)}{p_n}, \tag{2.59}$$

where in view of (2.49), in both cases the expression on the left is an indirect utility function representing the respective homothetic and parallel indirect preference relation R^*. In (2.59) differentiation with respect to I shows that in Case (b) the marginal utility of income is $1/p_n$ and is thus independent of nonnuméraire prices and income, while in Case (a) one must represent R^* by the *logarithm* of the expression in (2.58) in order that the marginal utility of income, which is then $1/I$, should be independent of prices. We thus obtain the same cardinal scales with the Hicksian as with the Marshallian measure in the case of parallel preferences, but different ones in the case of homothetic preferences; only the Marshallian measure yields diminishing marginal utility of income in Case (a).

I come now to a third and final possible explanation for the lack of impact of Samuelson's 1942 contribution on cost-benefit analysis — the authority and influence of Hotelling (1932, 1935, 1938). Hotelling's 1932 formulation departed from the classical Paretian formulation in that he assumed that the demand function was generated not by preference maximization subject to a budget constraint, but rather in a manner akin to that of a firm consuming amounts $x_1, x_2, \ldots, x_n$ as inputs into a production function $U(x)$ and maximizing "profits" $U(x) - \Sigma_{i=1}^n p_i x_i$ (Hotelling 1932, pp. 590–91). This leads to first-order conditions $\partial U(x)/\partial x_i = p_i$, as opposed to the customary first-order conditions $\partial U(x)/\partial x_i = \lambda p_i$ arising out of maximization of $U(x)$ subject to a budget constraint $\Sigma_{i=1}^n p_i x_i = I$. Writing inverse demand functions as $p_i = P^i(x)$, Hotelling was thus led to the "integrability conditions" $\partial P^i/\partial x_j = \partial P^j/\partial x_i$ for the recovery of U from the inverse demand functions via the partial differential equations

$$\frac{\partial U}{\partial x_i} = P^i(x_1, x_2, \ldots, x_n) \qquad (i = 1, 2, \ldots, n). \qquad (2.60)$$

Hotelling was perfectly well aware that this formulation was at variance with the Paretian one, and in fact wrote down the correct integrability conditions for the Paretian formulation (1932, p. 592). However, he defended his own formulation on the ground that he was "restricting attention to those cases in which money is spent, as the saying is, to make money." He continued:

This category of expenditures is very large, including not only all the articles commonly classed as producers' goods but such items as the haircuts and trousers-pressing paid for by the salesman in order to increase his sales. It includes even a good deal of food, clothing, and entertainment which are consumed, at least in part, with a view to making more money. [Hotelling 1932, p. 592]

If one accepts this hypothesis of consumer behavior underlying market demand functions, one has to accept the corresponding "integrability conditions." However, Hotelling's followers (e.g., Harberger 1964) have accepted his "integrability conditions" without, as far as I am aware, endorsing the theory of consumer behavior described in the above quotation.[16] The question naturally arises: If the Pareto-Samuelson theory of consumer behavior is accepted, what are the implications for consumer preferences of Hotelling's "integrability conditions" $\partial B^i/\partial z_j = \partial B^j/\partial z_i$ [in the notation of (2.31)]? By the invertibility of the demand functions, this is equivalent to replacing the Slutsky symmetry conditions of (2.20) by $\partial h^i/\partial p_j = \partial h^j/\partial p_i$, and it was remarked by Samuelson (1942, p. 81n) that these imply "expenditure proportionality" (i.e., homothetic preferences). (For proofs, see Chipman and Moore 1976).

Thus, within the context of the neoclassical theory of consumer behavior, Hotelling's "integrability conditions" are equivalent to the assumption that preferences are homothetic. It is to his credit that Hotelling (1935) recognized the need to verify his symmetry conditions statistically; he took comfort in the fact that they were not rejected by Schultz's (1933) statistical studies.[17] Subsequently, in his classic 1938 article, while still strongly defending consumer's surplus, he furnished an alternative proof of the Dupuit taxation theorem to the effect that a departure from marginal-cost pricing entailed a welfare loss. He emphasized Dupuit's (1844) "remarkable conclusion" that "the net loss is proportional to the *square* of the tax rate" and went on to meet the objection that pleasure is nonmeasurable "by establishing a generalized form of Dupuit's conclusion on the basis of a ranking only, without measurement, of satisfactions" (Hotelling 1938, p. 246). It is worth noting that Samuelson used those very same grounds to come to the opposite conclusion — namely, that "all valid theorems relating to the burden of taxation can be stated independently of any numerical measure of utility change" (Samuelson 1942, p. 87). Hotelling's procedure, which was remarkably similar to Samuelson's (1938a) in its approach and foreshadowed Arrow's (1951) pathbreaking methods for proving the Pareto optimality of competitive equilibrium, amounted essentially to using the compensating variation to evaluate the welfare loss, defined as "the total net loss of state revenue resulting from abandonment of the system of charging only marginal costs, and uncompensated by any gain to any individual" (p. 254). Dropping subscripts from C in (2.56) for convenience, we have from (2.18) the total differential equation

$$dC = dI - \sum_{i=1}^{n} h^i[p, \mu(p; p^0, I^0)]dp_i \qquad (2.61)$$

which coincides with the bracketed term of (2.35) at $(p, I) = (p^0, I^0)$. Since $\lambda > 0$, the sign of (2.61) is the same as that of (2.35). Leaving aside Hotelling's argument to the effect that (2.61) can be approximated by the famous "Dupuit triangle," we can conclude that examination of the sign of (2.61) is sufficient to warrant the conclusion, if this sign is negative, that the change involves a deterioration or brings about "deadweight loss." However, Hotelling went further in saying (p. 254) that "we have been able to arrive at [his approximation to (2.61)] as a valid approximation measuring in money a total loss of satisfactions to many persons." Such a conclusion is unwarranted, as Hotelling (1939a, 1939b) subsequently conceded in response to Frisch's (1939a, 1939b) criticisms; it would legitimize use of the compensating variation in making comparisons among alternative suboptimal situations, while Hotelling admitted that his method allowed one to show only that these were inferior to what we now call a Pareto-optimal situation.[18] The distinction between these two types of comparisons was brought out by Hicks:

> The first task of welfare economics is the formal study of the conditions of optimum organization in [the Pareto] sense. . . . The second task of welfare economics is the study of deviations from this optimum, and it is here that consumers' surplus has its part to play. The idea of consumers' surplus enables us to study in detail the effects of deviations from the optimum in a particular market. It is not merely a convenient way of showing when there will be a deviation (consumers' surplus is not necessary for that purpose, since the basic optimum conditions . . . show us at once when there will be a deviation); it also offers us a way of measuring the size of the deviation. This, if we are right in our general viewpoint, is a most important service. [Hicks 1941, p. 112]

The statement concerning the role of consumer's surplus agrees with the position held by Hotelling before 1939, and the statement as a whole appears to agree well with the general point of view of applied welfare economists today (e.g., Harberger 1964, 1971). But of course it is completely at variance with the fundamental results obtained by Samuelson in 1942.

The Quest for a "True" Cost-of-Living Index

I now skip thirty-two years and discuss Samuelson's second major investigation into the problem of welfare measurement, in Samuelson and Swamy (1974). Remarkably, this paper does not refer to Samuelson's 1942 contribution, but I shall try to show how closely they are in fact related. Samuelson and Swamy pose the old question concerning the possibility of constructing a "true" cost-of-living index. This may be posed by asking what such an index is supposed to do. In its use in calculating cost-of-living adjustments in union contracts, it is used to deflate nominal incomes on the supposition that, if $L(p)$ is the index expressed as a function of current prices, the individual will be just as well off in period 1 with prices and income (p^1, I^1) as in period 0 with prices and income (p^0, I^0) if and only if

$$\frac{I^1}{L(p^1)} = \frac{I^0}{L(p^0)},$$

where we may normalize the function L so that $L(p^0) = I^0$. We thus require the individual's indirect preferences to be representable by an indirect utility function of the form

$$V(p, I) = \frac{I}{L(p)} \tag{2.62}$$

for some function L. Since V must be homogeneous of degree zero, L must be homogeneous of degree one. Defining a new indirect utility function by $\log V$, we see immediately that $\partial \log V/\partial I = 1/I$; hence, in terms of $\log V$, the marginal utility of income must be independent of prices. The solution to the problem, obtained among many others in Samuelson and Swamy (1974) via a different route, is thus immediate from Samuelson's 1942 results: Preferences must be homothetic.[19] Representing them by a homogeneous-of-first-degree function $\Phi(x)$, we can set $L(p) = 1/\Phi[h(p, 1)]$ [from (2.54)]; alternatively, it is clear from (2.58) that we may choose $L(p) = \mu(p; p^0, I^0)$ and thus define Φ uniquely by $\Phi(x) = \mu(\xi^{-1}(x); p^0, I^0)$ where $\xi(p) = h(p, 1)$. This corresponds to Allen's (1933, p. 200) definition of the cost of living as the solution (2.38) to the equation (2.36) above.

It seems, however, only a matter of arbitrary convention, not to say sheer prejudice, to require a cost-of-living adjustment to be computed by "deflating" (dividing) income by a price index, as opposed, say, to *subtracting* the income-compensation function from current income (both expressed in terms of a numéraire), as in (2.59). This would be the appropriate procedure in the case in which preferences are parallel with respect to the numéraire. Depending on the nature of the preferences, different procedures would be appropriate.

The important general point that is brought out in these investigations is that the search for some standard measure of welfare or of the cost of living that is invariant with respect to consumer preferences is really a search for a philosopher's stone. On the other hand, if one is willing to make fairly stringent and definite assumptions about the nature of preferences, some natural measurement structures do emerge and are available.

Samuelson and Measurable Utility

This brings me finally to Samuelson's contributions specifically directed towards the question of measurability of utility. One of his earliest contributions (Samuelson 1937) was on this subject. He considered the intertemporal problem of maximizing $\int_0^b V(x, t)dt$ (x = income, t = time) and described a hypothetical experiment in which, supposing V to be of the separable form $V(x, t) = U(x)e^{-\pi t}$, one could retrieve information concerning the utility function and, in particular, obtain a measurable utility from knowledge of the rate of expenditure over time. He pointed out that if one specified a more general type of utility functional over time, this would not be possible.

In a second paper (1938b) he took issue with Lange (1934) with respect to Pareto's (1909, p. 264) proposition that one could measure utility on the basis of postulates permitting quaternary comparisons; he said that all one could show was that one such utility index was a linear transformation of the other. Of course, today it is agreed by all (including Samuelson) that this is exactly what is meant by measurability. But Samuelson went on to reject measurability on other grounds, in an argument that hinted at later developments (e.g., Debreu 1960; Georgescu-Roegen 1952) establishing a connection between separability and shapes of indifference curves.[20] In the *Foundations* (1947, pp. 174–81) he showed that the assumption that preferences could be represented by an additively separable utility function, permitting one to select one cardinal utility index $U(x)$ with $\partial^2 U/\partial x_i \partial x_j = 0$ for $i \neq j$, had extremely strong empirical implications and concluded:

> . . . if we are given as empirical observational data the two expenditure paths corresponding to the changes in quantities with income in each of two respective price situations, then from these observations, and these alone, the whole field of indifference curves can be determined by suitable extrapolation. [Samuelson 1947, p. 177]

This was presented as an argument against independent utilities and measurable utility. However, one could instead argue that this is just what one would like a good theory to be able to do; that unless and until economists can find empirical regularities sufficiently great to permit the making of such extrapolations, economics will not achieve the status of the physical sciences. Thus, Samuelson's argument can be turned on its head, and these very findings, combined with Samuelson's concern from the beginning with insisting on judging postulates in terms of their empirical implications, have had an important influence in shaping the way economists think about these questions and in clarifying the issues surrounding the question of measurability of utility.

By the time the economics profession had recovered from the shock of Hicks and Allen's (1934) demonstration that consumer demand behavior in competitive markets is invariant with respect to monotone transformations of any utility function yielding the demand function, it was presented with another, reverse shock in the form of the demonstration by von Neumann and Morgenstern (1947) that individual behavior in risk-taking situations, provided it conforms to their axioms that justify the Bernoulli rule of maximizing expected utility, is invariant only with respect to linear transformations of the utility function — and that utility is therefore, after all, measurable. Samuelson's (1950b) initial reaction to the von Neumann-Morgenstern result was strongly negative, partly on the basis of the argument from the *Foundations* quoted above. It did not help that the axioms put forward by von Neumann and Morgenstern (1947, pp. 617–32) were far from transparent. However, subsequent treatments, notably Marschak's (1950), brought out more clearly the logic behind the axioms; in particular, Marschak introduced the "independence axiom," to the effect that if a prospect f is indifferent to a prospect g, then for all prospects h, a probability mixture fph of f and h (f with probability, p, $0 < p < 1$, h with probability $1 - p$) is indifferent to the same probability mixture gph of g and h. It was not long before Samuelson (1953) became not only a convert to the cause, but one of its best exponents; he isolated the crucial axiom, called by him the "fundamental independence axiom," which states that if $0 < p \leq 1$, f is preferred or indifferent to g if and only if, for all prospects h, fph is preferred or indifferent to gph. His acceptance of the Bernoulli rule was still somewhat grudging, as when he stated (1953, p. 149) that "anyone rational enough to be consistent in this respect would probably be clever enough to sense the importance of binary-probability comparisons that define [the cardinal utility function], and he would probably find it convenient to do his 'taste calculations' in terms of this simplest form. In no other sense is the linear-additive utility indicator privileged." He might have added: In no other sense is the measurement of length, weight, or temperature privileged in physics. It should further be added that the theory does not require that the rational individual should himself perform calculations according to the Bernoulli rule; it is enough that his behavior should conform to the von Neumann-Morgenstern axioms, permitting the economist who is observing his actions to describe them in terms of this convenient rule.

In his comprehensive survey of the development of the concept of complementarity, Samuelson (1974) came back to the question of measurable utility. Edgeworth (1897) and Pareto (1909) had both adopted the definition of Auspitz and Lieben (1889), according to which two commodities i and j are said to be complements if $U_{ij}(x) \equiv \partial^2 U(x)/\partial x_i \partial x_j > 0$ and substitutes if $U_{ij}(x) < 0$, where U is a (concave) differentiable utility function. Allen (1934) had objected to this definition on the grounds that the sign of U_{ij} is not invariant with respect to monotone increasing transformations of the utility function U; he proposed instead an alternative definition (also used in Hicks and Allen 1934 and in the text of Hicks 1939), which Samuelson (1974, p. 1269) has shown to be equivalent to the so-called SHAS definition introduced by Slutsky (1915), Hicks (1939, Appendix), and Schultz (1938). According to this definition commodities i and j are complements (or substitutes) if the Slutsky terms s_{ij} of (2.20) are positive (or negative). Subsequently, Georgescu-Roegen (1952) furnished an ingenious diagrammatic analysis of complementarity, showing the formal equivalence of the SHAS definition to the Auspitz-Lieben-Edgeworth-Pareto (ALEP) definition. He showed in particular that ALEP complementarity has definite implications with regard to the possible shapes of indifference curves and questioned the scientific validity of the principle of Occam's razor invoked by Hicks (1939), asking rhetorically (1952, p. 2n): "Could we refuse to take account of animals with more than two feet, on the ground that only two feet are needed for walking?"

Samuelson (1974), strongly persuaded by this argument, agreed that despite its desirable properties of symmetry and invariance with respect to choice of utility index, the SHAS definition lacked intuitive appeal. He therefore proposed two alternative definitions, the second derived from the first. His first definition, which he called "money-metric complementarity," was precisely the ALEP definition but with a specific choice of utility indicator — namely, the utility function

$$U_p^0(x) = \mu(p^0; p, I), \tag{2.63}$$

where μ is the income-compensation function (2.17) and (p, I) is any price-income pair at which x is bought [i.e., $x = h(p, I)$] (cf. Hurwicz and Uzawa 1971, p. 125). [This is equivalent to the function $p_n^0 U_q^0(x)$

defined by (2.51), where $q_i^0 = p_i^0/p_n^0$ for $i = 1, 2, \ldots, n - 1$.] Samuelson provided a local definition of complementarity between i and j at the point $x^0 = h(p^0, I^0)$, as $\partial^2 U_p^0(x)/\partial x_i \partial x_j > 0$ evaluated at $x = x^0$.

Samuelson observed, however (1974, p. 1264), that in terms of this utility function, the marginal utility of income is constant for $p = p^0$. This is because μ has the property [evident from its definition (2.17)] that

$$\mu(p^0; p^0, I) = I, \tag{2.64}$$

hence $\partial \mu(p^0; p^0, I)/\partial I = 1$. As Samuelson expressed it:

> . . . the money-metric marginal utility *of income* is constant at unity. For how could it be otherwise? If you are measuring utility by money, it must remain constant with respect to money: a yardstick cannot change in terms of itself. [Samuelson, 1974, p. 1204]

This conflicts, however, with the classical law of diminishing marginal utility of income, which lies behind the hypothesis of risk aversion.

This led Samuelson to his second, improved definition of complementarity, which amounts to finding an appropriate von Neumann-Morgenstern utility function $f_p^0(I) = f_p^0(\mu(p^0; p^0, I)) \equiv V(p^0, I)$ by means of gambling experiments carried out at fixed prices p^0 and varying prospective incomes. Presumably this definition could be extended (at least in principle) to all price vectors p.

Support for the above kind of procedure may be found in the fact that the question of invariance with respect to the utility index is more subtle than Hicks and Allen's (1934) exposition makes it appear. To be sure, the inequality $U_{ij}(x) > 0$ is not invariant at a point $x = x^0$ with respect to monotone increasing transformations f yielding $W(x) = f(U(x))$. Nor is concavity of U, nor the strong-concavity property that the principal minors of the matrix $U = [U_{ij}]$ oscillate in sign, invariant with respect to such transformations. On the other hand, the question of whether or not there *exists* a strongly concave utility function U for which $U_{ij}(x^0) > 0$ for $i \neq j$ is (trivially) invariant with respect to any initial choice of utility index; furthermore, the affirmative answer to the question has empirical implications — namely, that demand for any commodity is a decreasing function of its own price (cf. Chipman 1977). These facts taken together provide a reason why it may be very convenient for the theorist to choose a particular, canonical utility function that is unique up to increasing linear transformations. Samuelson's proposed procedure accomplishes this.

Other unique ways of choosing a utility index are available. While it is not always possible to represent convex preferences by a concave (as opposed to merely quasiconcave) utility function (see Kannai 1977), in those cases in which it is possible (in which case preferences are said to be "concavifiable"), a unique representation is possible in terms of a "least concave utility function" (see Debreu 1976). Accordingly, one might wish to employ this particular representation when applying the ALEP definition of complementarity (see Kannai 1980). On the other hand, such a choice has the same kinds of disadvantages as Samuelson's money-metric utility function, since it admits of representations yielding constant marginal utility of income for fixed prices. For example, if preferences are convex and homothetic, a least-concave utility function $U(x)$ will be (up to increasing linear transformations) homogeneous of degree one, and thus the corresponding indirect utility function $U^*(p, I)$ $= U[h(p, I)]$ will be homogeneous of degree one in income; hence $\partial U^*(p, I)/\partial I = U^*(p, 1)$. This would conflict with risk aversion in risk-taking situations. However, as Debreu (1976, p. 122) has shown, if a risk-averse individual has a concave von Neumann-Morgenstern utility function $W(x)$, and $U(x)$ is his least-concave utility function, one can find an increasing concave function f such that $W(x) = f[U(x)]$. In the case in which U is homogeneous of degree one, f will necessarily be strictly concave. Defining $W^*(p, I) = f[U^*p, I)]$, since the individual is risk averse, this will satisfy $\partial^2 W^*/\partial I^2 < 0$ (diminishing marginal utility of income).

Consumption theory has come a long way since 1934. Samuelson's contributions have, at first unwittingly but subsequently quite purposively, played a major part in the development of a more sophisticated understanding of the proper scientific basis for measurement of utility and welfare.

NOTES

1. Initially called the "Weak Axiom of Consumer Behavior" (Samuelson 1950a, p. 370; Uzawa 1960).

2. Samuelson in (1938a) made no reference to Slutsky (1915), but did so in his follow-up paper (1938c). Slutsky's work was simultaneously and independently discovered by Schultz (1935) and by Allen (1936) and Hicks (1937).

3. See also Samuelson (1947, p. 116). It should be noted that the property of negative semidefiniteness of the Slutsky matrix $S = [s_{ij}] = [h_j^i + h_I^i h_j]$ is stronger than the statement (2.4), since not only does it not require the side condition $p \cdot dh = 0$, but it consists in the statement

$$\sum_{i=1}^{n} \sum_{j=1}^{n} [h_j^i(p, I) + h_I^i(p, I)h^j(p, I)]\xi_i\xi_j \leq 0 \qquad (2.4')$$

and does not require the inequality to hold only for $\xi_i = dp_i$, $\xi_j = dp_j$. Recently, a rigorous treatment has been provided by Kihlstrom, Mas-Colell, and Sonnenschein (1976), who distinguish between the conditions of negative semidefiniteness (NSD) and of negative definiteness (ND), which they define as $\xi'S(p, I)\xi \leqq 0$ and < 0, respectively, where in both cases ξ is required to satisfy $p \cdot \xi = 0$. [Since homogeneity of degree 0 of $h^i(p, I)$ implies along with the budget identity $\sum_{j=1}^n h^j(p, I)p_j = I$ that $S(p, I)p = 0$ (by Euler's theorem), (2.4′) follows for all ξ.] They also distinguish between the Weak Axiom (WA) and the "weak weak axiom" (WWA), the latter differing from (2.1) by the replacement of the weak inequality by a strict inequality $p^0 \cdot x^0 > p^0 \cdot x^1$. They show that WWA implies NSD (a strengthening of Samuelson's proposition WA $\Rightarrow$ NSD) and vice versa, that ND implies WA, and that WWA does not imply WA. Thus, WA implies but is not implied by NSD.

4. That is, in 1938 Samuelson was unable to attach a meaningful economic interpretation to symmetry of the Slutsky matrix and therefore saw no reason for imposing it. Hicks, on the other hand, apparently regarded it as a minor technical requirement (akin to differentiability), and therefore saw no reason for not imposing it. Already in 1947, however, Samuelson (1947, p. 116) conjectured that symmetry and negative semidefiniteness of the Slutsky matrix were sufficient to yield "an integrable preference field displaying the properties necessary for a maximum," and in a difficult footnote furnished what he described as "only the sketch of the proof."

5. This was the basic differential equation set up by Pareto (1911, p. 594), which formed the basis for the subsequent analyses by Allen (1932) and Georgescu-Roegen (1936). Pareto had previously (1893, pp. 296–300; 1902, p. 1104) worked with the homogeneous equations corresponding to (2.24), but his treatment of the integrability problem was faulty (see Volterra 1960; Pareto 1906; Wold 1943, pp. 114–17; Samuelson 1950a; and Chipman 1976b, pp. 80–86).

6. These integrability conditions had also been specified with reference to this particular economic application by Evans (1930, p. 120) and Hotelling (1932, p. 592), and were mentioned again by Hicks and Allen (1934, p. 211n). For further historical discussion, see Chipman 1976b, p. 82.

7. They are still commonly referred to by members of the Berkeley school as "Roy's identity," evidently after René Roy rather than Sir Roy Allen.

8. This is the "weak weak axiom" (WWA) referred to in note 3 above. See also Richter 1979, p. 173.

9. I mention briefly only a few of the many additional developments that have taken place. Richter (1966, 1971) introduced powerful set-theoretic methods in order to proceed from a general version of the Strong Axiom (the Congruence Axiom) to the existence of a preference ordering, without the need to introduce differentiability properties and differential equations. This led to the general treatment of Hurwicz and Richter (1971); it has also led to extension of the idea to other fields, including "revealed probability" (see Richter and Shapiro 1978). Debreu (1972) has pursued the integrability problem from a global point of view, in contrast with the local framework underlying all the differential-equations methods discussed in this section. The implications for demand theory of absence of symmetry or nonnegative definiteness of the Slutsky matrix — a question going back to Georgescu-Roegen (1936) — has been explored by Wold (1943), Samuelson (1950a), and Katzner (1970); these studies are valuable because they help us understand exactly what types of phenomena are being ruled out when the conditions are imposed. The meaning of the Lipschitz condition has been clarified by Mas-Colell (1977, 1978). The case in which the demand correspondence need not be a single-valued function, which in particular arises in connection with aggregate demand correspondences, has been analyzed in Chipman and Moore (1977).

10. Marshall omitted the income change $I^1 - I^0$ from his formula, showing that he assumed (at least implicitly) that nominal income was constant when using this measure. Likewise, he included only one of the price terms, so that we may infer that he assumed the other prices also to remain constant. In this case, (2.52) is always (provided the budget equality always holds) a correct measure of welfare improvement, with no restrictions on preferences (cf. Chipman and Moore 1980, p. 974n). A simpler measure still, with only p_1 varying, would be $1/p_1$.

11. See Chipman and Moore 1976, pp. 90–91.

12. Allen's concept was a rediscovery, the concept of an indirect utility function having been introduced by Antonelli (1886). The concept was rediscovered once again by Houthakker (1953), who also gave it its name.

13. See also Chipman and Moore 1976, pp. 86–87. The result was obtained by Pareto (1892, pp. 493–94) in the special case of additively separable preferences (independent utilities) (cf. Chipman 1976b, pp. 68–69).

14. This appears to agree well with the Harberger approach, summed up as follows (1971, p. 795): "Most applied welfare economics answers questions like . . . 'Which of two or three alternative actions helps most or hurts least, and by approximately how much?'"

15. For formal definitions of homothetic and parallel direct and indirect preferences, see Chipman and Moore 1980.

16. The theory has respectable antecedents, however, to be found in Marshall 1920, p. 335.

17. He might have felt less comfortable had he scrutinized Schultz's method more closely. For a cogent criticism of Schultz's method, see Samuelson 1974, p. 1284.

18. For a recent criticism similar to Frisch's (but not referring to Frisch), see Silberberg 1980.

19. This result can be traced back at least to Bergson (1936). The problem itself is an old one and can be traced back at least to 1898–1900, when the French actuary Hermann Laurent wrote a series of letters to Walras (see Jaffé 1956; Chipman 1976a) inquiring as to whether it would be possible to construct a "standard measure of value" by integrating the differential form $\Sigma_{i=1}^n p_i dx_i$ after expressing it as an exact differential; Walras's response was that in general this is not possible since the marginal utility of income would have to be constant. If the p_i are interpreted as inverse demand functions, expressing price-income ratios as functions of the quantities consumed as in (2.60), this becomes equivalent to Hotelling's problem.

20. Debreu (1960) showed that for three or more commodities, an independence axiom yields the property that preferences can be represented by an additively separable utility function, which is unique up to linear transformations. This result has been developed as well as applied to preferences over time by Gorman (1968) and Koopmans (1972a, 1972b).

REFERENCES

Afriat, S. N. 1965. "The Equivalence in Two Dimensions of the Strong and Weak Axioms of Revealed Preference." *Metroeconomica* 17:24–28.

———. 1967. "The Construction of Utility Functions from Expenditure Data." *International Economic Review* 8:67–77.

Allen, R. G. D. 1932. "The Foundations of a Mathematical Theory of Exchange." *Economica* 12:197–226.

————. 1933. "On the Marginal Utility of Money and Its Application." *Economica* 13:186–209.

————. 1934. "A Comparison between Different Definitions of Complementary and Competitive Goods." *Econometrica* 2:168–75.

————. 1935. "Professor Slutsky's Theory of Consumer's Choice." *Review of Economic Studies* 3:120–29.

Antonelli, G. B. 1886. *Sulla teoria matematica della economia politica* [On the mathematical theory of political economy]. Pisa: nella Tipografia del Folchetto. English trans. in J. S. Chipman, L. Hurwicz, M. K. Richter, and H. F. Sonnenschein, eds. *Preferences, Utility and Demand.* New York: Harcourt Brace Jovanovich, 1971.

Arrow, K. J. 1951. "An Extension of the Basic Theorems of Classical Welfare Economics." In *Proceedings of the Second Berkeley Symposium on Mathematical Statistics and Probability.* Berkeley: University of California Press, pp. 507–32.

————. 1959. "Rational Choice Functions and Orderings." *Economica* NS 26:121–27.

Auspitz, R., and R. Lieben. 1889. *Untersuchungen über die Theorie des Preises.* Leipzig: Duncker und Humblot.

Bergson (Burk), A. 1936. "Real Income, Expenditure Proportionality, and Frisch's 'New Methods of Measuring Marginal Utility'." *Review of Economic Studies* 4(1):33–52.

Chipman, J. S. 1976a. "An Episode in the Early Development of Ordinal Utility Theory: Pareto's Letters to Hermann Laurent." *Cahiers Vilfredo Pareto, Revue européenne des sciences sociales* 14(37):39–64.

————. 1976b. "The Paretian Heritage." *Cahiers Vilfredo Pareto, Revue européenne des sciences sociales* 14(37):65–171.

————. 1977. "An Empirical Implication of Auspitz-Lieben-Edgeworth-Pareto Complementarity." *Journal of Economic Theory* 14(1):229–31.

————. 1982. "Samuelson and Welfare Economics." In G. R. Feiwel, ed. *Samuelson and Neoclassical Economics.* Boston: Kluwer·Nijhoff.

————, L. Hurwicz, M. K. Richter, and H. F. Sonnenschein, eds. 1971. *Preferences, Utility and Demand.* New York: Harcourt Brace Jovanovich.

————, and J. C. Moore. 1976. "The Scope of Consumer's Surplus Arguments." In A. M. Tang, F. M. Westfield, and J. S. Worley, eds. *Evolution, Welfare and Time in Economics: Essays in Honor of Nicholas Georgescu-Roegen.* Lexington, Mass.: Heath.

————, and J. C. Moore. 1977. "Continuity and Uniqueness in Revealed Preference." *Journal of Mathematical Economics* 4(2): 139–62.

————, and J. C. Moore. 1979. "Compensating Variation as a Measure of Welfare Change." Typescript.

————, and J. C. Moore. 1980. "Compensating Variation, Consumer's Surplus, and Welfare." *American Economic Review* 70(5):933–49.

Debreu, G. 1960. "Topological Methods in Cardinal Utility Theory." In K. J. Arrow, S. Karlin, and P. Suppes, eds. *Mathematical Methods in the Social Sciences, 1959.* Stanford, Calif.: Stanford University Press, pp. 16–26.

————. 1972. "Smooth Preferences." *Econometrica* 40(4): 603–15.

————. 1976. "Least Concave Utility Functions." *Journal of Mathematical Economics* 3:121–29.

Dupuit, J. 1944. "De la mesure de l'utilité des travaux publics" [On the measurement of the utility of public works]. *Annales des Ponts et Chaussées, Mémoires et documents relatifs à l'art des constructions et au service de l'ingénieur* 8(2):332–75. English trans. in K. J. Arrow and T. Scitovsky, eds. *Readings in Welfare Economics.* Homewood, Ill.: Irwin, 1969.

Edgeworth, F. Y. 1891a. "Osservazioni sulla teoria matematica dell' economia politica con riguardo speciale ai principi di economia di Alfredo Marshall." *Giornale degli Economisti* [2] 2:233–45.

————. 1891b. "Ancora a proposito della teoria del baratto." *Giornale degli Economisti* [2] 3:316–18.

————. 1897. "La teoria pura del monopolio" [The pure theory of monopoly]. *Giornale degli Economisti* [2] 15:13–31, 307–20, 405–14. English trans. in *Papers Relating to Political Economy I.* London: Macmillan, 1925.

Evans, G. C. 1930. *Mathematical Introduction to Economics.* New York: McGraw-Hill.

Frisch, R. 1939a. "The Dupuit Taxation Theorem." *Econometrica* 7:145–50.

————. 1939b. "A Further Note on the Dupuit Taxation Theorem." *Econometrica* 7:156–57.

Gale, D. 1960. "A Note on Revealed Preference." *Economica* NS 27:348–54.

Georgescu-Roegen, N. 1936. "The Pure Theory of Consumer's Behavior." *Quarterly Journal of Economics* 50:545–93.

————. 1952. "A Diagrammatic Analysis of Complementarity." *Southern Economic Journal* 19:1–20.

Gorman, W. M. 1968. "The Structure of Utility Functions." *Review of Economic Studies* 35:369–90.

Harberger, A. C. 1964. "The Measurement of Waste." *American Economic Review Papers and Proceedings* 54:58–76.

————. 1971. "Three Basic Postulates for Applied Welfare Economics: An Interpretive Essay." *Journal of Economic Literature* 9:785–97.

Hicks, J. R., 1937. *Théorie mathématique de la valeur en régime de libre concurrence.* Paris: Hermann.

————. 1939. *Value and Capital.* Oxford: Clarendon Press.

————. 1941. "The Rehabilitation of Consumers' Surplus." *Review of Economic Studies* 8:108–16.

————. 1942. "Consumer's Surplus and Index-Numbers." *Review of Economic Studies* 9:126–37.

————. 1956. *A Revision of Demand Theory.* Oxford: Clarendon Press.

————, and R. G. D. Allen. 1934. "A Reconsideration of the Theory of Value." *Economica* NS 1:52–76, 196–219.

Hotelling, H. 1932. "Edgeworth's Taxation Paradox and the Nature of Demand and Supply Functions." *Journal of Political Economy* 40:577–616.

————. 1935. "Demand Functions with Limited Budgets." *Econometrica* 3:66–78.

————. 1938. "The General Welfare in Relation to Problems of Taxation and of Railway and Utility Rates." *Econometrica* 6:242–69.

————. 1939a. "The Relation of Prices to Marginal Costs in an Optimum System." *Econometrica* 7:151–55.

————. 1939b. "A Final Note." *Econometrica* 7:158–60.

Houthakker, H. S. 1950. "Revealed Preference and the Utility Function." *Economica* NS 17:159–74.

————. 1953. "Compensated Changes in Quantities and Qualities Consumed." *Review of Economic Studies* 19:155–64.

Hurwicz, L. 1971. "On the Problem of Integrability of Demand Functions." In J. S. Chipman, L. Hurwicz, M. K. Richter, and H. F. Sonnenschein, eds. *Preferences, Utility and Demand.* New York: Harcourt Brace Jovanovich.

————, and M. K. Richter. 1971. "Revealed Preference without Demand Continuity Assumptions." In J. S. Chipman, L. Hurwicz, M. K. Richter, and H. F. Sonnenschein, eds. *Preferences, Utility and Demand.* New York: Harcourt Brace Jovanovich.

————, and M. K. Richter. 1979. "Ville Axioms and Consumer Theory." *Econometrica* 47 (3):603–19.

————, and H. Uzawa. 1971. "On the Integrability of Demand Functions." In J. S. Chipman, L. Hurwicz, M. K. Richter, and H. F. Sonnenschein, eds. *Preferences, Utility and Demand.* New York: Harcourt Brace Jovanovich.

Jaffé, W. 1965. *Correspondence of Léon Walras and Related Papers.* 3 vols. Amsterdam: North-Holland.

Johnson, W. E. 1913. "The Pure Theory of Utility Curves." *Economic Journal* 23:483–513.

Kannai, Y. 1977. "Concavifiability and Constructions of Concave Utility Functions." *Journal of Mathematical Economics* 4:1–56.

————. 1980. "The ALEP Definition of Complementarity and Least Concave Utility Functions." *Journal of Economic Theory* 22(1):115–17.

Katzner, D. W. 1970. *Static Demand Theory.* New York: Macmillan.

Kihlstrom, R., A. Mas-Colell, and H. Sonnenschein. 1976. "The Demand Theory of the Weak Axiom of Revealed Preference." *Econometrica* 44(5):971–78.

Koopmans, T. C. 1972a. "Representation of Preference Orderings with Independent Components of Consumption." In C. B. McGuire and R. Radner, eds. *Decision and Organization.* Amsterdam: North-Holland.

————. 1972b. "Representation of Preference Orderings over Time." In C. B. McGuire and R. Radner, eds. *Decision and Organization.* Amsterdam: North-Holland.

Lange, O. 1934. "The Determinateness of the Utility Function." *Review of Economic Studies* 1:218–24.

Little, I. M. D. 1949. "A Reformulation of the Theory of Consumer's Behaviour." *Oxford Economic Papers* NS 1:90–99.

McKenzie, L. W. 1957. "Demand Theory without a Utility Index." *Review of Economic Studies* 24:185–89.

Marschak, J. 1950. "Rational Behavior, Uncertain Prospects, and Measurable Utility." *Econometrica* 18:111–41. "Errata." *Econometrica* 18 (July):312.

Marshall, A. 1920. *Principles of Economics*, 8th ed. London: Macmillan.

Mas-Colell, A. 1977. "The Recoverability of Consumers' Preferences from Market Demand Behavior." *Econometrica* 45:1409–30.

————. 1978. "On Revealed Preference Analysis." *Review of Economic Studies* 45(1):121–31.

Mosak, J. L. 1942. "On the Interpretation of the Fundamental Equation of Value Theory." In O. Lange, F. McIntyre, and T. O. Yntema, eds. *Studies in Mathematical Economics and Econometrics, in Memory of Henry Schultz*. Chicago: University of Chicago Press.

Neumann, J. von, and O. Morgenstern. 1947. *Theory of Games and Economic Behavior*, 2nd ed. Princeton, N.J.: Princeton University Press.

Pareto, V. 1892–93. "Considerazioni sui principi fondamentali dell'economia politica pura." *Giornale degli Economisti* [21] 4 (May 1892):389–420; 4 (June 1892):485–512; 5 (August 1892):119–57; 6 (January 1893):1–37; 7 (October 1893):279–321.

————. 1898. "Comment se pose le problème de l'économie pure." Mémoire présenté en décembre 1898, à la Societé Stella. Lausanne, 1898 (privately published), 12 pp. Reprinted in Vilfredo Pareto, *Oeuvres Completes*, Vol. 4: *Marxisme et économie pure*. Geneva: Librairie Droz, 1966.

————. 1902. "Anwendungen der Matematik auf Nationalökonomie." *Encyklopädie der Mathematischen Wissenschaften mit einschluss ihrer Andwendungen* 1:1094–1120.

————. 1906. "L'ofelimità nei cicli non chiusi" [Ophelimity in non-closed cycles]. *Giornale degli Economisti* [2] 33:15–30. English trans. in J. S. Chipman, L. Hurwicz, M. K. Richter, and H. F. Sonnenschein, eds. *Preferences, Utility and Demand*. New York: Harcourt Brace Jovanovich, 1971.

————. 1909. *Manuel d'Économie politique*. Paris: V. Giard et E. Brière.

————. 1911. "L'économie mathématique" [Mathematical economics]. *Encyclopédié des Sciences Mathématiques* Tome I, vol. 4. English trans. in W. J. Baumol and S. M. Goldfeld, eds. *Precursors in Mathematical Economics: An Anthology*. London: London School of Economics and Political Science, 1968.

Richter, M. K. 1966. "Revealed Preference Theory." *Econometrica* 34(3):635–45.

————. 1971. "Rational Choice." In J. S. Chipman, L. Hurwicz, M. K. Richter, and H. F. Sonnenschein, eds. *Preferences, Utility and Demand*. New York: Harcourt Brace Jovanovich.

————. 1979. "Duality and Rationality." *Journal of Economic Theory* 20(2):131–81.

————, and L. Shapiro. 1978. "Revelations of a Gambler." *Journal of Mathematical Economics* 5:229–44.

Rose, H. 1958. "Consistency of Preference: The Two-Commodity Case." *Review of Economic Studies* 25:124–25.

Roy, R. 1942. *De l'utilité. Contribution à la théorie des choix*. Paris: Hermann.

Samuelson, P. A. 1937. "A Note on Measurement of Utility." *Review of Economic Studies* 4:155–61.

————. 1938a. "A Note on the Pure Theory of Consumer's Behaviour." *Econ-*

omica NS 5:61–71. "A Note on the Pure Theory of Consumer's Behaviour: An Addendum." *Economica* NS 5:353–54.

———. 1938b. "The Numerical Representation of Ordered Classifications and the Concept of Utility." *Review of Economic Studies* 6:65–70.

———. 1938c. "The Empirical Implications of Utility Analysis." *Econometrica* 6(4):344–56.

———. 1942. "Constancy of the Marginal Utility of Income." In O. Lange, F. McIntyre, and T. O. Yntema, eds. In *Studies in Mathematical Economics and Econometrics, in Memory of Henry Schultz*. Chicago: University of Chicago Press.

———. 1947. *Foundations of Economic Analysis*. Cambridge, Mass.: Harvard University Press.

———. 1948. "Consumption Theory in Terms of Revealed Preference." *Economica* NS 15:243–53.

———. 1950a. "The Problem of Integrability in Utility Theory." *Economica* NS 17:355–85.

———. 1950b. "Probability and the Attempts to Measure Utility." *Economic Review* [Keizai Kenkyu] 1:167–73.

———. 1953. "Utilité, Préférence et Probabilité" [Utility, preference, and probability]. In *Econométrie*. Paris: Colloques Internationaux du Centre National de la Recherche Scientifique 40, pp. 141–50. English original in P. A. Samuelson, *The Collected Scientific Papers of Paul A. Samuelson*. 2 vols. Ed. by J. E. Stiglitz. Cambridge, Mass.: MIT Press, 1966.

———. 1964. "Principles of Efficiency — Discussion." *American Economic Review Papers and Proceedings* 54(3):93–96.

———. 1965. "Using Full Duality to Show that Simultaneously Additive Direct and Indirect Utilities Implies Unitary Price Elasticity of Demand." *Econometrica* 33(4):781–96.

———. 1966. *The Collected Scientific Papers of Paul A. Samuelson*. 2 vols. Ed. by J. E. Stiglitz. Cambridge, Mass.: MIT Press.

———. 1972a. "Unification Theorem for the Two Basic Dualities of Homothetic Demand Theory." *Proceedings of the National Academy of Sciences, U.S.A.* 69(9):2673–74.

———. 1972b. *The Collected Scientific Papers of Paul A. Samuelson*, Vol. 3. Ed. by R. C. Merton. Cambridge, Mass.: MIT Press.

———. 1974. "Complementarity: An Essay on the 40th Anniversary of the Hicks-Allen Revolution in Demand Theory." *Journal of Economic Literature* 12(4):1255–89.

———. 1977. *The Collected Scientific Papers of Paul A. Samuelson*, Vol. 4. Ed. by H. Nagatani and K. Crowley. Cambridge, Mass.: MIT Press.

———, and Swamy, S. 1973. "Invariant Economic Index Numbers and Canonical Duality: Survey and Synthesis." *American Economic Review* 64(4):655–93.

Schultz, H. 1933. "Interrelations of Demand." *Journal of Political Economy* 41:468–512.

————. 1935. "Interrelations of Demand, Price, and Income." *Journal of Political Economy* 43:433–81.

————. 1938. *The Theory and Measurement of Demand*. Chicago: University of Chicago Press.

Silberberg, E. 1980. "Harold Hotelling and Marginal Cost Pricing." *American Economic Review* 70:1054–57.

Slutsky, E. 1915. "Sulla teoria del bilancio del consumatore" [On the theory of the budget of the consumer]. *Giornale degli Economisti e Rivista di Statistica* [3] 51:1–26. English trans. in G. J. Stigler and K. E. Boulding, eds. *Readings in Price Theory*. Homewood, Ill.: Irwin, 1952.

Stigum, B. P. 1973. "Revealed Preference — A Proof of Houthakker's Theorem." *Econometrica* 41(3):411–23.

Uzawa, H. 1960. "Preference and Rational Choice in the Theory of Consumption." In K. J. Arrow, S. Karlin, and P. Suppes, eds. *Mathematical Methods in the Social Sciences, 1959*. Stanford, Calif.: Stanford University Press.

————. 1971. "Preference and Rational Choice in the Theory of Consumption." In J. S. Chipman, L. Hurwicz, M. K. Richter, and H. F. Sonnenschein, eds. *Preferences, Utility and Demand*. New York: Harcourt Brace Jovanovich.

Ville, J. 1946. "Sur les conditions d'existence d'une ophélimité totale et d'un indice du niveau des prix" [The existence conditions of a total utility function]. *Annales de l'Université de Lyon*, Sec. A(3), 1946, pp. 32–39. English trans. by P. K. Newman in *Review of Economic Studies* 19(2):123–28.

Volterra, V. 1906. "L'economia matematica ed il nuovo manuale del prof. Pareto" [Mathematical economics and Professor Pareto's new manual]. *Giornale degli Economisti* [2]32:296–310. English trans. in J. S. Chipman, L. Hurwicz, M. K. Richter, and H. F. Sonnenschein, eds. *Preferences, Utility and Demand*. New York: Harcourt Brace Jovanovich, 1971.

Wold, H. O. A. 1943. "A Synthesis of Pure Demand Analysis. I, II, III." *Skandinavisk Aktuarietidskrift* 26:85–118, 220–63; 27(1944):69–120.

3 REVEALED PREFERENCE AFTER SAMUELSON

Andreu Mas-Colell

The first and fundamental paper of P. A. Samuelson on revealed preference theory (1937) is now almost forty-five years old. He must have been barely twenty when it was written. One feels, nevertheless, that revealed preference has not just been a youthful interest, but has remained very close to his heart. He has written on it repeatedly (e.g., 1948, 1950), it features prominently in his Nobel Laureate lecture, and it was chosen by him as the subject of his 1973 Gibbs lecture at the American Mathematical Society meetings. Revealed preference is as foundational and purely theoretical a subject as one can find, and one cannot help thinking that this is part of its fascination. Indeed, of how many topics can it be said that, to paraphrase what Samuelson wrote in the Georgescu-Roegen *Festschrift,* people will be discussing them a hundred years from now? Certainly, the pure theory of rational choice is one, and I hope that it will be an appropriate appreciation of Samuelson's contributions if I devote these few pages to giving a nonscholarly and nonexhaustive account of some of the developments that his seminal revealed preference work inspired — to show, in a word, that if one starts the clock in 1937, his prediction has already become almost half fulfilled.

Revealed preference was born of the Pareto-Hicks program of purging consumer and demand theory of subjectivist components. Pareto and, very forcefully, Hicks in *Value and Capital,* discovered that for the purposes of the consumer theory of the day, it was sufficient if tastes were thought of as families of ordered indifference curves. Samuelson's insight was to push the idea one step further and enunciate the general methodological postulate that the basic axioms of a theory must be operational — that is, they must be refutable by observable data generated from feasible experiments.

Let's be more specific. In the language of binary relations, which became popular after the war, the Pareto-Hicks theory can be formulated as follows. There is a set X of commodity bundles. In X a typical consumer has defined a relation xRy to be read as "commodity bundle x is at least as good as commodity bundle y," which satisfies the rationality principles:

1. xRx (reflexivity);
2. Either xRy or yRx (completeness);
3. If xRy and yRz, then xRz (transitivity).

If xRy and yRx, we put xIy (x indifferent to y). If xRy but not yRx, we put xPy (x preferred to y). It must be noted at the outset that Pareto-Hicks theory passes in principle the operationality test. There is a trivial way to transform the indifference-preference framework into a choice-based theory: Just let the domain of choice experiments include every pair of commodity bundles. If we now interpret xRy to mean "when the decision agent is constrained to choose between x and y and is asked to eliminate a bundle if he does definitely not want it, he does not eliminate x," the three axioms have the obvious experimental meaning (and in fact only the third has any teeth). What Samuelson perceived is that these choice experiments may not be feasible in the sense of being observable in a given market environment. What he suggested was to stick to the given rather than hypothetical observables and to impose the rationality axioms on them. In the concrete case of competitive market behavior, he took the position that only the demand function would be observable and that this is therefore the entity to be axiomatized. He proceeded to propose a very basic axiom, the so-called Weak Axiom (WA) of Revealed Preference. Let us say that the commodity bundle x is revealed preferred to the commodity bundle y (written xSy) if for some competitive budget (i.e., for some given prices and income) x is chosen when y is affordable. The WA says then that whenever xSy, we cannot have ySx. This is a most intuitive and natural requirement, and Samuelson showed that, as we will describe later, it yields many of the implications of the Pareto-Hicks consumer theory. Many, but not all. Samuelson was aware that for some purposes the Weak Axiom needed extension. It was provided by Houthakker (1950) in the form of the Strong Axiom (SA) of Revealed Preference: If we have a finite domain of direct preference revelations $x_1 S x_2, \ldots, S x_n$, then we say that x_1 is indirectly revealed preferred to x_n (written $x_1 H x_n$), and we rule out the possibility that $x_n S x_1$. Again, from the standpoint of the rationality of choice, this is a most appealing and natural extension.

For years now the old cardinal versus ordinal utility dispute has been obsolete, and cardinal utilities are being widely used. It may therefore be worth emphasizing before proceeding any further that the Pareto-Hicks-Samuelson drive to liberate consumer theory from mysticism was theoretically sound. It has also been successful and fundamental for further progress. If cardinal utility has been restored, it is only because the theory of choice under uncertainty of von Neumann and Morgenstern (1944) has succeeded in putting it on a solid operational basis, well within the Pareto-Hicks-Samuelson tradition, since, in principle, it is possible to derive the cardinal utilities from observable choice experiments involving lotteries.

It was clear from the beginning that the consumer theory based on the revealed preference axiom had to be closely related to the theory based on the preference hypothesis (i.e., on the ordered indifference classes of Pareto and Hicks). Indeed, if demand derives from preferences, then obviously the Strong Axiom should be satisfied. Research has concentrated on the reverse direction: To what extent is it possible to work backwards (this is Samuelson's expression) and go from "rational demand" to "rational preferences"? As it turns out, it can be done, and by now this is well understood. In the next section we review some of the results that establish the compatibility of demand functions satisfying the Strong Axiom with underlying preferences (this is an *existence* issue). Then we discuss the uniqueness question (i.e., can preferences be unambiguously recovered from demand?). In the following section we comment on the relationships of revealed preference theory with integrability theory, an alternative and older (Antonelli 1886) approach to an axiomatic treatment of "rational" demand. Finally, we dwell on the demand theory one gets from the Weak, rather than the Strong, Axiom of Revealed Preference. After all, this was the original Samuelson postulate.

The "working backwards" from demand to preferences is not merely a matter of purely logical interest or of aesthetic perfection (although it is that too). What explains its centrality in the research effort over the years is that it is in a sense vital to an economic theory based on feasible choice experiments. The sense is this: Economic science is to a large extent a normative and predictive theory. From what is observed (say, in our case, competitive budget choices), one wants to evaluate and predict what would happen with a given change in the environment (say, the imposition of a tax). The task of evaluation is to ask for preferences and utility (welfare economics without them would be severely limited). The task of prediction does not quite ask for it, but, given the power of the preference hypothesis, it is most expedient to postulate the existence of preferences underlying the observable choices. If preferences can be recovered via revealed preference analysis, then they can be used for predictive purposes. Note that the overall result is a strictly operational (i.e., refutable) theory.

It should be stressed that the revealed preference approach and, more concretely, the revealed preference axioms, are quite general. They apply as well to the recovery of preferences from undistorted, competitive demand functions (to be used, perhaps, to predict in a distorted, non-competitive situation) as to their recovery from a collection of observations generated by a distorted, imperfectly competitive economic world (and to be used, say, to predict the ideal competitive outcome). The essence of revealed preference theory is the realization that the observable choice data will be far from inclusive of all conceivable choice experiments (if they did, then the Strong Axiom would amount to nothing but a rephrasing of the transitivity axiom on preferences), and that therefore the task of recovering preferences will typically be far from trivial. We will say more on all this in the next two sections.

As we have already said, it will be a conclusion of revealed preference analysis that one can go from "rational" demand functions (i.e., satisfying the Strong Axiom) to Pareto-Hicks preferences. Given the broader scope of those (they are not tied to a particular institutional specification), this is to be welcomed; indeed, the preference hypothesis is today at the basis of economic theory. Revealed preference has only reinforced it. The reader may ask: To end up where we started, was the trip worth it? I do not hesitate to answer in the affirmative: The house is now on a firmer foundation, and, lest anyone think that the whole enterprise was without difficulties, it could be pointed out that the conceptually close relative of the preference theory we have been discussing — namely, the von Neumann-Morgenstern theory of choice under uncertainty — is still at the Pareto-Hicks stage. It is operational because binary preferences on lotteries can be identified from choices over all conceivable pairs of lotteries. But those are not typically the budget choices that will be observable in a market situation. To my knowledge no one has yet provided an analog of the revealed preference axioms and theorems for choice functions over some restricted and economically natural class of lottery budgets.

THE EXISTENCE OF UNDERLYING PREFERENCES

The Weak Axiom of Revealed Preference alone does not imply the existence of preferences underlying a given demand function. For a two-commodity world the Weak Axiom implies the Strong, and so, for a while, there was some uncertainty whether this may not be the general situation. But an example of Gale's (1960), inspired by an informal argument of Samuelson's, settled the matter: There are demand functions that satisfy the Weak but not the Strong Axiom. Hence they cannot be generated from preferences.

The question is, then, if the Strong Axiom is equivalent to the preference hypothesis. The answer is yes, and we shall call this the revealed preference theorem. It has been established under a variety of conditions on demand by a central tradition that begins with Little (1949) and Samuelson (1948), continues with Houthakker's fundamental paper, (1950), and culminates in Uzawa (1959) and Stigum (1973). The mathematical treatment that this tradition gave to the problem, however, was quite cumbersome. Their techniques (i.e., the so-called price-income sequences) would lead one to believe that the revealed preference theorem belongs to the area of differential equations, which is definitely not the case since the revealed preference tests allow from the beginning for noninfinitesimals comparisons.

It was M. Richter (1966, 1971), who recognized the revealed preference theorem for what it is — a theorem in set theory. He abstracted the logical problem of existence of underlying preferences from the nonessential features of the competitive budget sets specification and with this laid bare the basic structure. What one has is a set of alternatives, X; a given family of budgets, B (each budget B is a subset of X); and a choice function, $C(B)$, which assigns a choice from B to B. Note that the family of budgets is totally unrestricted. Nevertheless, the Strong Axiom still makes sense in this context. It tells us that if we define x to be preferred to y (written xPy) whenever x is directly or indirectly revealed preferred to y, then P is transitive (i.e., we cannot get cycles). Of course, only some pairs x,y will stand in the relation, P, which, for this reason, constitutes what is called a partial order. The preference hypothesis amounts to the existence of a complete and transitive R underlying C. In particular, any complete and transitive extension of P will generate C and will, therefore, solve our problem. But a basic principle (Zorn's lemma) of the usual set theory asserts that every partial order has a complete, transitive extension. And we are done! There is nothing more to it. No other hypothesis but the Strong Axiom is made. Richter's revealed preference work is one of the best examples in economics of the power that an abstract treatment may have (but, of course, doesn't need to have; there is no automatism here).

While Richter's result is very general, it may be felt that it gives little clue to the nature of underlying preferences. This is true. In particular, the preferences one gets directly from the precedent construction are somewhat peculiar. No two alternatives are indifferent, for example. All this can be fixed up, and we refer to Richter's papers to see how. We would, nevertheless, like to report on an alternative approach to the revealed preference theorem that is much more specific about the obtained preferences. We refer to the important and seminal contribution of Afriat (1967), which, while as direct as Richter's, proceeds not by abstracting the economic aspects but by emphasizing them.

Afriat's analysis is placed on the perfectly competitive demand function's economic environment in which revealed preference theory was born. He begins by recognizing that in any practical situation only a finite number of competitive budget sets will be observable as data. He then writes down a linear program such that if the data do not satisfy the Strong Axiom, then it has no solution, and if it does have a solution, then this takes the form of a preference relation that is compatible with the given observations. Further, the solution is given by a piecewise linear, concave function. The point of the whole thing is that the solution is very nice and, via the simplex method, easily computable. In fact, once in the track opened by Afriat, it is not hard to convince oneself that even a linear program is not necessary. The solution can be computed recursively. Also, if one's standard for "being nice" is differentiability rather than piecewise linear, this can be obtained too.

Summing up: The Strong Axiom implies the preference hypothesis and, in quite different spirits, Richter and Afriat have provided very elegant, direct, and comparatively clean ways to proceed from demand to preferences.

THE UNIQUENESS OF UNDERLYING PREFERENCES

We saw in the previous section that the Strong Axiom guarantees the existence of underlying preferences. For applications, however, it may be important that those preferences be, in some appropriate sense, unique. Only then can we speak of "recovering" the preferences. Further, uniqueness in itself would be useless without an actual technique to accomplish the recovery in practice.

A first observation is the obvious need to narrow down the meaning of uniqueness. Indeed, even with the nicest sort of demand function, if there is an underlying preference relation, then there are infinitely many. Just take an indifference class and order its commodity bundles in some arbitrary way, leaving unaltered the preference ordering with the bundles in other indifference classes. The demand function will remain unaffected. The problem is, of course, that the family of competitive budgets is not large enough for a complete identification of the preference relation. The remedy, however, is also clear. We should look for uniqueness inside a natural class, one that will be large enough for any purpose for which the preferences have to be used. One such class is the class of preferences that satisfies the regularity property of continuity (or, more conveniently for revealed preference analysis, upper semicontinuity).

Restricting the sense of uniqueness to the one described in the previous paragraph, it is well established by now that underlying a given demand function there is a unique continuous preference relation if, besides the Strong Axiom, the demand satisfies (uniformly) a certain weak regularity condition (i.e., the so-called income lipschitzian property). Locally, this is somewhat stronger than continuity, but much weaker than differentiability. Therefore, if the reader believes that a hypothesis of differentiability imposes no empirical restriction, we need not worry about the income Lipschitzian property (which, it may be worthwhile to point out, is not implied by the continuity of preferences alone). The property was first explicitly identified by Houthakker (1950) and has been used by him, Samuelson (1948), Uzawa (1959), Stigum (1973), and many others for a simultaneous attack on the existence and uniqueness questions via the already alluded to price-income sequences, a constructive technique patterned on the approximation algorithms for the solution of differential equations. Another, less constructive, method is to establish on general grounds that under the technical hypotheses there can be at most one underlying preference relation, the existence of one coming from the results reported in the previous section.

In the setup proposed by Afriat (1967), where only a finite number of budget choices are available, nonuniqueness is inherent. But it can be shown that, under an appropriate version of the income lipschitzian property, as the number of choice observations increases in a regular manner, the set of possible underlying preferences narrows down in a well-defined way. Since, besides, Afriat's method is entirely constructive, it provides what is perhaps the most practical approach to revealed preference in the narrow (i.e., competitive demand choices) sense. The uniqueness problem is treated in Mas-Colell (1978), from which the observations of this section are taken.

REVEALED PREFERENCE AND THE INTEGRABILITY PROBLEM

When Samuelson invented revealed preference analysis, the search for demand restrictions that would imply (and be implied by) the preference hypothesis already had a long history (see Samuelson 1950 for an account). The older tradition is the so-called integrability approach, which was begun by Antonelli (1886). Its distinctive feature is that it focuses on infinitesimal conditions on demand — that is, conditions on derivatives.

There are two (dual) versions of integrability. The oldest begins with Antonelli. It imposes restrictions on indirect demand functions (dependent variables are prices and income; independent variables are commodity bundles) and recovers direct preferences (the usual type). For a modern treatment, see Debreu (1972). A more recent version imposes the integrability conditions on demand functions and obtains indirect preferences (i.e., preferences are defined on budgets rather than commodity bundles). A definitive treatment has been provided by Hurwicz and Uzawa (1971).

An advantage of the more recent version is that the integrability conditions are quite familiar. They are simply the symmetry and negative definiteness of the Slutsky matrix (i.e., the matrix of price derivatives of compensated demand). The negative definiteness condition has a clear economic interpretation; it is simply the law of demand for compensated demand function — that is, the (compensated) demand of any commodity, simple or composite, must increase when the price declines. Whether this should be looked at as a rationality or a stability condition is a question we shall not get into. The point is that it has an obvious economic meaning. The same cannot be said of the symmetry condition. While to get it as a theorem is very interesting (since it is just beyond what one can deduce about the logic of maximizing behavior without the help of mathematics), to impose it as a primitive axiom of the theory is economically quite opaque. In fact, in the 1930s a number of researchers hesitated to do so and entertained a notion of nonintegrable preferences that, once all is said, led to a dead end.

Regularity conditions aside, integrability and revealed preference theory are equivalent since both the Strong Axiom and the two integrability
conditions characterize the preference hypothesis by restrictions involving only the demand function. Integrability work has been important in
the development of the box of tools of consumer theory. But as a theory
that characterizes rational demand, one can only agree with Samuelson
that revealed preference is superior. While in the physical sciences it is
often the case that the primitives of a theory are laws of motion given in
terms of differential equations, there is no reason why this should be so
in consumer theory, where the postulate of a global optimizer does not
seem objectionable. Integrability theory, much influenced from the beginning by the mathematical methods of the physical sciences, considers
only infinitesimal comparisons and must depend, therefore, on an un-
intuitive condition, such as symmetry of the Slutsky matrix. Revealed
preference theory makes global comparisons (something, we repeat, not
unnatural in economics) and is able to accomplish the task with a very
intuitive hypothesis, the Strong Axiom. At the level of mathematical
techniques, revealed preference analysis was at the beginning still much
influenced by the differential equations methods proper to the integrability approach. Not until the contributions of Richter and Afriat did it
develop tools attuned to the new, global, finitistic point of view.

THE DEMAND THEORY OF THE WEAK AXIOM

With two commodities the Weak Axiom (the original Samuelson postulate) implies the Strong and, therefore, the preference hypothesis. This
does not generalize to more than two commodities. The reason was
perceived by Samuelson. He noted that with two commodities the Slutsky
symmetry condition is automatically satisfied, but with more than two it
is a substantive restriction. Take a demand function for three commodities that satisfies the integrability conditions (and therefore the Strong
Axiom) and perturb it slightly. Then we will destroy the symmetry of the
Slutsky matrix (and by implication the Strong Axiom), but we may still
hope that the Weak Axiom holds. This reasoning is correct. An implementation yielding an example was given by Gale (1968), and a general
argument can be found in Kihlstrom, Mas-Colell, and Sonnenschein
(1976), from which the remarks of this section are taken.

What turns out to be the case is that with differentiable demand the
Weak Axiom is essentially equivalent to the negative definiteness of the

Slutsky matrix (i.e., to the law of demand), but has no implications whatsoever for symmetry. This is something, incidentally, that Samuelson knew well. It would appear that if, in some sense, the Weak Axiom is satisfied but the Strong fails, this is akin to a failure of transitivity of underlying preferences. The sense, however, has not been made precise.

REFERENCES

Afriat, S. 1967. "The Construction of Utility Functions from Expenditure Data." *International Economic Review* 8:67–77.

Antonelli, G. B. 1886. *Sulla Teoria Matematica della Economia Politica*. Pisa: Nella Tipografia del Folchetto. English translation in J. Chipman et al., eds. *Preferences, Utility and Demand*. New York: Harcourt Brace Jovanovich, 1971.

Chipman, J., L. Hurwicz, M. Richter, and H. Sonnenschein, eds. 1971. *Preferences, Utility and Demand*. New York: Harcourt Brace Jovanovich.

Debreu, G. 1972. "Smooth Preferences." *Econometrica* 40:603–17.

Gale, D. 1960. "A Note on Revealed Preference." *Econometrica* 27:348–54.

Houthakker, H. 1950. "Revealed Preferences and the Utility Function." *Economica* 17:159–74.

Hurwicz, L., and H. Uzawa. 1971. "On the Integrability of Demand Functions." In J. Chipman et al., eds. *Preferences, Utility and Demand*. New York: Harcourt Brace Jovanovich.

Kihlstrom, R., A. Mas-Colell, and H. Sonnenschein. 1976. "The Demand Theory of the Weak Axiom of Revealed Preference." *Econometrica* 44:971–78.

Little, I. 1949. "A Reformulation of the Theory of Consumer Behaviour." *Oxford Economic Papers* NS 1:90–99.

Mas-Colell, A. 1978. "On Revealed Preference Analysis." *Review of Economic Studies* 45:121–31.

Neumann, J. von, and O. Morgenstern. 1944. *Theory of Games and Economic Behavior*. Princeton, N.J.: Princeton University Press.

Richter, M. 1966. "Revealed Preference Theory." *Econometrica* 34:635–45.

———. 1971. "Rational Choice." In J. Chipman et al., eds. *Preferences, Utility and Demand*. New York: Harcourt Brace Jovanovich.

Samuelson, P. 1938. "A Note on the Pure Theory of Consumer Behavior." *Economica* 5(17):61–71.

———. 1948. "Consumption Theory in Terms of Revealed Preference." *Economica* 15:243–53.

———. 1950. "The Problem of Integrability in Utility Theory." *Economica* 17(68):355–85.

Stigum, B. 1973. "Revealed Preference — A Proof of Houthakker's Theorem." *Econometrica* 41:411–23.

Uzawa, H. 1959. "Preference and Rational Choice in the Theory of Consumption." In K. Arrow, S. Karlin, and P. Suppes, eds. *Mathematical Methods in the Social Sciences, 1959*. Stanford, Calif.: Stanford University Press. (Revised version in J. Chipman et al., eds. *Preference, Utility and Demand*. New York: Harcourt Brace Jovanovich, 1971.)

4 SAMUELSON AND THE THEORY OF PRODUCTION

Lawrence J. Lau

Professor Samuelson's influence on the modern development of the theory of production can be found everywhere. To write about it in a way that does full justice to his important contributions in the field would have required a whole book. The editor, however, has imposed a binding constraint on the number of pages. I shall therefore limit my discussion to a few aspects of Samuelson's work, selected almost entirely on the basis of my personal preference (and, some may say, bias).

THE IMPORTANCE OF THE ASSUMPTION OF MAXIMIZATION

Samuelson was the first economist to recognize and emphasize the critical role of the assumption of maximization (or equivalently minimization) in the derivation of theorems in comparative statics. For example, the theorem that, for a profit-maximizing and price-taking firm, the supply curves for outputs are always upward sloping and the demand curves for inputs are always downward sloping may be derived from the maximization assumption alone.

83

Suppose at an initial vector of output prices p_0 and vector of input prices q_0, the profit-maximizing vectors of quantities of outputs and inputs are Y_0 and X_0, respectively. Suppose further that the vectors of prices change to p_1 and q_1, respectively, and the corresponding profit-maximizing vectors of outputs and inputs to Y_1 and X_1, respectively. By the assumption of profit maximization,

$$p_0 Y_0 - q_0 X_0 \geqq p_0 Y_1 - q_0 X_1 .$$

$$p_1 Y_1 - q_1 X_1 \geqq p_1 Y_0 - q_1 X_0 . \qquad (4.1)$$

Adding the two inequalities together and rearranging the terms, one obtains

$$(p_1 - p_0)(Y_1 - Y_0) - (q_1 - q_0)(X_1 - X_0) \geqq 0 \qquad (4.2)$$

or

$$\Delta p \, \Delta Y - \Delta q \, \Delta X \geqq 0 ,$$

which implies upward-sloping supply curves and downward-sloping demand curves. Note that this comparative statics result is obtained with hardly any assumption on the production function at all. Its validity is independent of whether the production function is differentiable or even concave. In particular, it is independent of whether the first-order conditions for a maximum hold. All the work is done by the assumption of profit maximization! Even in the case of a twice continuously differentiable production function, the second-order conditions for a maximum, rather than the first, give rise to the comparative statics result. This insight has had an important impact on the subsequent development of the theory of production, and in particular has provided the basis for the by now widely used duality approach.

THE REVEALED PREFERENCE APPROACH

The method of analysis of finite changes used in the previous section was pioneered and popularized by Samuelson. It is remarkable in its elegance and simplicity. This method can be used to test whether a given body of empirical data on prices and quantities could have been generated from, say, profit maximization, in a way that is analogous to a test of the axioms of the theory of revealed preference. For example, suppose there are three observations of prices of outputs (p_i) and inputs (q_i), and quantities of outputs (Y_i) and inputs (X_i), $i = 0,1,2$. Then the hypothesis of profit maximization requires that the following inequalities hold:

$$p_i Y_i - q_i X_i \geqq p_i Y_j - q_i X_j, \quad \text{all } i, j, \quad i \neq j \; ; i, j = 0, 1, 2 . \quad (4.3)$$

The hypothesis can well be refuted for arbitrarily given prices and quantities. If the hypothesis is not refuted, then it is possible to construct from the data a production function relating the outputs and inputs and satisfying the usual neoclassical assumptions (except for differentiability) that would have generated the observed quantities of outputs and inputs at the corresponding prices as profit maximizers. Such a production function is sometimes described as nonparametric, in order to distinguish it from the more common econometrically estimated variety. This line of research, which was obviously rooted in the theory of revealed preference, was initiated by Afriat (1967) and has been extended by others. It has the advantage that no restrictive assumption needs to be made on the functional form.

THE COST FUNCTION

Today almost every economics graduate student knows what a cost function is. The cost function and its properties are routinely invoked. This, however, has not always been the case. In his *Foundations* Samuelson provided the first derivation and *complete* characterization of the properties of the cost function as the minimum total cost of inputs required to achieve a given level of output at given prices of inputs, where the level of output is related to the levels of inputs through a production function (Samuelson 1947, pp. 57–89). Under the assumption of twice differentiability of the production function, Samuelson showed that a (variable) cost function must be nonnegative, homogeneous of degree one, monotonically increasing, and concave in the prices of inputs, and monotonically increasing in the level of output. He also showed that a system of cost-minimizing input demand functions must be nonnegative and homogeneous of degree zero in the prices of inputs and that its Jacobian matrix with respect to the prices of inputs must be symmetric and negative semidefinite for any given level of output. These conditions on a system of input demand functions also provide a test for the integrability of an arbitrarily given system of input demand functions. He also gave the formula that is now commonly referred to as Shephard's Lemma:

$$X = \frac{\partial C}{\partial q}(q, Y) . \quad (4.4)$$

That is, the cost-minimizing vector of quantities of inputs X for given level of output Y and prices of inputs q is equal to the gradient of the cost function with respect to q [Shephard 1953, p. 68, equation (55)].[1] Shephard's Lemma, or some variant thereof, is used nowadays by practically every economist in estimating empirical cost or input demand functions to derive an appropriate and convenient functional form.

Although Samuelson assumed differentiability in his derivation, it appears that he could have easily carried out the same program without it. For example, using his method of finite changes, it is straightforward to show that the cost function is concave in the prices of inputs. Let q_0 and q_1 be any two arbitrary input price vectors, and $q_\lambda \equiv (1 - \lambda)q_0 + \lambda q_1$, $1 \geqq \lambda \geqq 0$, be an arbitrary convex combination of q_0 and q_1. Let X_λ be the vector of cost-minimizing input demands at input price vector q_λ and level of output Y. Then, by definition:

$$q_0 X_\lambda \geqq C(q_0, Y) \tag{4.5}$$

and

$$q_1 X_\lambda \geqq C(q_1, Y) .$$

Multiplying the first inequality by $(1 - \lambda)$ and the second inequality by λ and adding them together, one obtains:

$$q_\lambda X_\lambda = C(q_\lambda, Y)$$

$$\geqq (1 - \lambda)C(q_0, Y) + \lambda C(q_1, Y) . \tag{4.6}$$

That is, $C(q, Y)$ is a concave function of q. It also appears from his 1949 Rand Corporation memoranda (Samuelson 1966, pp. 425–92) that he was aware of the concept of a supergradient (sometimes also called a subgradient) of a not necessarily differentiable concave function, which, like the gradient for the differentiable case, can be identified with the set of cost-minimizing vectors of input demands.

DUALITY

It is not clear why Samuelson did not proceed in his *Foundations* to establish the full duality between production and cost functions, since the Legendre transformation was certainly well known to him at the time. In 1953 and 1954 Samuelson enunciated the basic duality between constant-returns-to-scale production functions and factor-price frontiers (which may be interpreted as unit cost functions) (Samuelson 1966, pp. 888–908).[2]

The potential applicability of duality in both the theory and empirical analysis of production was not fully realized until more than a decade later.[3] In the 1970s, however, concepts such as cost, revenue, and profit functions have largely supplanted the concept of the production function, at least as far as empirical analysis is concerned.

LE CHATELIER PRINCIPLE

The Le Chatelier principle was a vaguely worded, little understood, and almost metaphysical principle occasionally invoked in chemistry and physics — until Samuelson came along. He gave the principle substance, precision, and rigor (Samuelson 1947, pp. 36–39). As an application of this principle in the theory of production, he deduced such elegant theorems as: "The demand for a factor like labor is less elastic in the short run when land cannot be varied than in the long run when land can be bought at a fixed rental — and this *independently* of whether labor and land are *complementary* or *rival* factors." Now who would have thought of that a priori? The degree of generality of this result is truly remarkable. It also has wide applicability, especially in the comparison between short- and long-run production behavior. Samuelson extended this principle to linear programming technologies and to Leontief input-output systems.

FACTOR-PRICE FRONTIER AND THE AGGREGATE PRODUCTION FUNCTION

In the 1950s Samuelson developed the concept of a factor-price frontier for both the one-period and the multiple-period cases (Samuelson 1966, pp. 341–69; 888–908). The factor-price frontier, as the locus of all wage and interest rates that are consistent with economic equilibrium, can, for certain quantities such as the distribution of factor shares, be regarded as a "sufficient statistic" of the economy.

An aggregate production function expressing a measure of aggregate output as a function of measures of aggregate capital and labor (or what Samuelson called a surrogate production function) is not really a production function in the technological sense. Yet economists have always manipulated aggregate production functions in the same way as technology-based production functions. For example, economists would equate the marginal rate of substitution between aggregate capital and labor to the rental-wage ratio. Although Samuelson did not seem to approve of the practice, he nevertheless derived conditions under which the use of such an aggregate production function can be justified (Samuelson 1966, pp. 325–38).

CHARACTERIZATION OF MULTIPLE-OUTPUT, MULTIPLE-INPUT PRODUCTION FUNCTIONS

In a model of a productive economy in which multiple outputs and multiple inputs are distinguished, one can always represent the economywide set of production possibilities by a production function expressing the level of output of one commodity as a function of the levels of the remaining outputs and inputs. Under the assumption that each output is produced individually with primary inputs — that is, there is no joint production — Samuelson derived the fundamental singularity theorem for the economywide production function described above. Its Hessian matrix must have the property that if the ith row and the jth column are deleted, where both the ith and jth commodities are outputs, the resulting submatrix is always a singular matrix (Samuelson 1972, pp. 179–86).

It is possible to view a nonsubstitution theorem as a theorem on the economywide production function. Consider a multisectoral interindustry model of production with a single primary input, say, labor. Then, under the assumption of nonjoint production and constant returns to scale in every sector, the transformation surface relating the outputs can be described by a linear function of the quantities of output for any given level of labor. In other words, the relative prices of the outputs are independent of the final demand conditions. This implies also that the input proportions in each industry are also independent of final demand conditions. For any given level of labor, the economy *behaves* as if the individual production functions of each sector all have fixed coefficients of production, even though technologically they may exhibit varying degrees of substitutability.

This remarkable theorem was first proved by Samuelson in 1951 (1966, pp. 515–19).[4] In the case of two primary inputs, one of which can be produced using the other — for example, capital (indirect labor) and labor — the nonsubstitution theorem is true in long-run equilibrium for any given levels of interest rate and labor. Thus, the long-run, economywide transformation surface can again be described by a linear function (ibid., pp. 520–36).[5] The nonsubstitution theorems are of more than theoretical interest. They are frequently exploited in the numerical computation of general equilibrium.

CONCLUDING REMARKS

Space limitations do not permit discussion of Samuelson's other contributions to the theory of production. These include in particular his work on linear programming, either by himself or with his collaborators; on capital theory, which may properly be regarded as the study of efficient intertemporal production; on induced innovation; and on elasticities of substitution. Finally, although Samuelson never did much empirical work himself, his constant insistence on "operational meaningfulness" of theorems focused attention on their empirical refutability and provided a major impetus for the econometric analysis of production.

NOTES

1. Earlier, Hotelling (1932) had derived a similar result for a profit function.

2. A complete proof, using the concept of a distance function, was first given by Shephard (1953).

3. Among the contributors were Diewert, McFadden, Jorgenson, and Lau, to name only a few.

4. Independently and simultaneously Georgescu-Roegen also proved a similar theorem (see Georgescu-Roegen 1966).

5. This second nonsubstitution theorem was anticipated by Morishima (1964).

REFERENCES

Afriat, S. N. 1972. "Efficiency Estimation of Production Function." *International Economic Review* 13(3): 568–98.

Arrow, K. J. 1967. "Samuelson Collected." *Journal of Political Economy* 75(5): 730–37.

Dorfman, R., P. A. Samuelson, and R. M. Solow. 1958. *Linear Programming and Economic Analysis*. New York: McGraw-Hill.

Georgescu-Roegen, N. 1966. *Analytical Economics: Issues and Problems*. Cambridge, Mass.: Harvard University Press.

Hotelling, H. 1932. "Edgeworth's Taxation Paradox and the Nature of Demand and Supply Functions." *Journal of Political Economy* 40(5): 577–616.

Morishima, M. 1964. *Equilibrium, Stability, and Growth*. Oxford: Clarendon Press.

Samuelson, P. A. 1947. *Foundations of Economic Analysis*. Cambridge, Mass.: Harvard University Press.

———. 1966. *The Collected Scientific Papers of Paul A. Samuelson*. 2 vols. Ed. by J. E. Stiglitz. Cambridge, Mass.: MIT Press.

———. 1972. *The Collected Scientific Papers of Paul A. Samuelson*, Vol. 3. Ed. by R. C. Merton. Cambridge, Mass.: MIT Press.

Shephard, R. W. 1953. *Cost and Production Functions*. Princeton, N.J.: Princeton University Press.

5 MISUNDERSTANDINGS IN THE THEORY OF PRODUCTION

Joan Robinson

Any contribution to economic theory that is not merely repeating slogans must pass through a stage of what Janos Kornai (1971) has called intellectual experiment. Concepts are defined and logical relations between them worked out under the shelter of "other things equal" and "other things remaining the same." When inconsistencies have been eliminated and implausible assumptions discarded, the next stage is to propose the most promising-looking hypotheses to be confronted with evidence from reality.

Unfortunately, the textbooks are littered with broken-down thought experiments. Kornai himself shows that the entire structure of general equilibrium is in that state. Piero Sraffa's critique has done irreparable damage to the "marginal productivity of capital."

Sraffa cannot go on from intellectual experiment to the second stage; the *Production of Commodities by Means of Commodities* (1960) is set up in terms of long-period relationships in the sense that inputs are

This paper has been reprinted with permission from *Greek Economic Review* 1, no. 1 (1979):1–7.

correctly adjusted to outputs and a stock of means of production is being operated by a given labor force at its designed level of utilization. A long-period model cannot be directly confronted with evidence because any actual situation is affected by short-period influences, such as the state of effective demand and the distribution of money income, which occupy the forefront of the picture. (Looking back now, I see that in the tumultuous years when Keynes's *General Theory* was being written, Piero never really quite knew what it was that we were going on about.)

THE PSEUDO-PRODUCTION FUNCTION

For me, the Sraffa revolution dates from 1951, the *Introduction* to Ricardo's *Principles* (Sraffa 1951), not from 1960. The thought experiment is simple and robust — the corn model. I set about to dismantle the neoclassical production function by introducing what I called a book of blueprints showing the concrete stock of means of production required for each level of output with a given labor force. From this developed what Professor Solow called a pseudo-production function. (Bob! I thank thee for that word.) I do not think I ever misused it as Professor Samuelson does nowadays,[1] but it certainly took me a long time to understand its meaning and its limitations.

A pseudo-production function represents a list of mutually nonsuperior techniques with a flow of homogeneous final output and given employment of labor, each in a self-reproducing state with its appropriate stock of means of production. Each technique is eligible at at least one rate of profits (with the corresponding share of wages in the value of net output). Between each pair is a switch point at which both yield the same rate of profits.

In the "Unimportance of Reswitching" (Robinson 1975), I emphasized the fact that this construction permits only of comparisons of imaginary equilibrium positions already in existence, not a process of accumulation going on through time. Samuelson's (1975) "Reply" is instructive. (I checked with him recently; he stands by it today.)

First, in respect to accumulation, it seems that he is still a completely unreconstructed pre-Keynesian neoclassic. He expects to find the rate of interest (which is what he calls what Sraffa calls the rate of profits) lowered by successful saving-investment abstaining from consumption. But let that pass.

Substantive Vindication?

Where then does the possibility of misinterpretation arise? It arises from the ambiguity of English speech and grammar. Thus, in my first paragraph, I speak of "switching back at a low interest rate. . ." and of ". . .as the interest rate falls in consequence of abstention from present consumption. . . ." Suppose that here, and in a score of other innocent passages, I had rewritten these as ". . .a switch back had *permanently* occurred at a *permanent* low interest rate to the techniques *permanently* viable at a *permanent* high interest rate *subsequent* to successful saving-investment abstaining in the past from then-current consumption [as envisaged by the neoclassical writers being quoted]." If I had done this, even a hostile critic could not have managed to fall into a misunderstanding; and a critic of neoclassical views, sensitized to past propensities of some writers to err on related matters, would have had no reason to quarrel with my revised text.

So, to narrow down misunderstanding, I authorize any reader to make such purely verbal alterations at a score of places. This done, how much of my substantive argument evaporates, or is vitiated, or needs amendment and elucidation? None that I can see. No diagram needs redrawing. No substantive contention need be withdrawn or qualified. [Samuelson 1975, pp. 43–44]

Evidently, we are in an era when a slow secular fall in the rate of profits is going on. Each time it passes a switch point (toward a technique that requires either a higher or a lower value of capital than the last), there must be a certain period of investment and disinvestment installing the stock required for the latest technique and clearing away the debris of the former one. We are not told anything about what goes on in these interludes, which seem to pass as though in a dream.

The whole process may take centuries, but all the while there is no technical progress or learning by doing. The specifications of all the techniques were available in the original book of blueprints.

In the reply to Harcourt (Samuelson 1975, footnote 7) also there are strange episodes. In a case of double switching, the rate of interest may drop from more than 100 percent to below 50 percent "without any physical movement at all." Would not a violent change in the ratio of profits to wages require readjustment in the flows of output?

After a backward switch, a transition is made to a technique with lower net output, but since the value of capital is going to be less than before, there is at the same time a transient period of "negative abstinence" or excess consumption. Professor Samuelson raises the question whether such transitions could be made *efficiently* in market or planned economies in the real world.

The reply to Harcourt ends with a declaration of faith by Samuelson in himself:

> I am not aware that my own part in this discussion contains *invalid* "habits of thought so ingrained as for [me] to be unconscious of their presence," but I shall be happy to recant if such logical errors can be found.

Then, patronizingly, to me:

> I do not think that the real stumbling block has been the failure of a literary writer to understand that when a mathematician says, "*y* rises as *x* falls," he is implying nothing about temporal sequences or anything different from "when *x* is low, *y* is high." [Samuelson 1975, p. 45].

My dear sir! That is *my* point. I really cannot allow you to get away with that.

In 1974 I finally took the pseudo-production function to pieces again. Obviously, stocks of equipment appropriate to different techniques cannot coexist both in time and space. It should never have been drawn in a plane diagram in the first place. Different techniques are not isolated from each other on "islands." They succeed each other through time as new discoveries and inventions become operational. Normally, a new technique is *superior* to the one in use and does not have to wait for a change in the rate of profit to be installed.

PSEUDO-PRODUCTION FUNCTIONS MARK II

There was a second, independent, appearance of pseudo-production functions after 1960. The model in *Production of Commodities* is a one-technique system in a self-reproducing state, but it does permit of some variations (Sraffa, 1960). One of the ingredients among the inputs exists in two versions or brands. The difference between them is in the time pattern of reproduction, not any physical characteristic. Sraffa did not intend this for a pseudo-production function. His purpose was to refute marginalism by showing that the least conceivable difference alters the whole system. As one or the other brand is eligible, according to the level of the rate of profits, everything is transformed. There is a different pattern of prices, distribution, and value of capital. Even the numéraires are different, for each brand appears in its own standard commodity. The brand eligible at the higher rate of profit may require the higher value of capital, as in the case of a backward switch point on a pseudo-production function.

Samuelson is correct in saying that grammar is awkward. It is hard to describe a map without using the language of moving about on it. Sraffa habitually uses the language of change but, properly speaking, there are no events in his world except the cycle of self-reproduction and the flow of net output to wages and net profits. The second brand was not *introduced* at some date. It had always existed in the specification of the model, but it was mentioned only when a certain point in the argument was reached.

There is no movement from one position to another, merely a comparison of positions corresponding to different levels of the rate of profits at which different brands are eligible. This comparison was an important element in his prelude to the critique of economic theory, clearing the ground for further analysis that, however, Sraffa himself did not supply. Certainly, thought experiments are justified by preparing the ground for an analysis of change, but to identify a comparison of static positions with an event, as Samuelson does, is not a practicable short cut.

Samuelson's (1962) first reaction to Sraffa was to produce a form of pseudo-production function in which, beyond each switch point, a higher rate of interest is associated with a lower ratio of value of capital to output so that backward switching cannot occur. This was countered by the construction of a spate of pseudo-production functions exhibiting switches of all kinds.[2] They are now so elaborate, elegant, and beautiful and their designers have become so fond of them that it seems cruel to point out that they are unable to say anything without falling into Samuelson's fallacy.

HISTORICAL TIME AND UNCERTAINTY

Keynes, at the opposite extreme to Sraffa, discusses only events. In businesses, households, public agencies, and so forth, each within its own sphere, decisions are taken under the influence of convention, imperfect information, and uncertain expectations. Their interaction as they are implemented brings about the movements of the whole economy.

Objection is sometimes raised to the emphasis on expectations as introducing an unduly subjective element into analysis. But if we cannot mention expectations, we cannot say anything at all. Any economic action — say, buying a bus ticket — is made with a view to its future consequences and is influenced by beliefs about what the outcome will be. Expectations are revealed in intentions, and intentions are revealed in actions. However, a businessman is not a black box. You can ask him about his intentions. You will not necessarily believe what he says, but you are bound to learn a lot from how he answers.

It is sometimes supposed that the aim of a business is to maximize its rate of profit. This is a gross confusion. Investment plans must be guided by views of the possible *rates of return* on alternative schemes of investment, but these are highly problematical. The aims of a business, this year, are concerned with the *flow* of profits this year. The accountants can work out, according to the accepted conventions, what the *rate of profit on capital* has been after the year is over. Only in Sraffa's intellectual experiment does the rate of profits have an exact meaning, for it is a *postulate* of the system that prices are such as to make the rate of profits uniform over the whole value of capital reckoned at these prices.

A short-period thought experiment can be clear and precise. What is to "remain the same" can be specified. Within a general frame of institutions, knowledge, and habits, the stock of means of production in existence, the capability and training of the labor force, the distribution of wealth, habitual patterns of consumption, business and financial organization are all taken as given; what can change from week to week is the amount and content of expenditure, causing changes in employment and the utilization of resources. New bargains can be made for pay and prices adjusted to them. The quantity of money changes mainly to accommodate these, but it may also exercise an influence of its own through the relation of the supply of credit to requirements.

In real life the dichotomy between short- and long-period aspects of a situation is not so sharp; every week long-period changes, resulting from past decisions, are coming into being — stocks are changing slowly through time while flows may run rapidly to and fro. The underlying historical movements ensure that the economy is not as madly unstable as Keynes was sometimes tempted to suppose. There may even be times when the short- and long-period influences are sufficiently in harmony with each other to allow a run of near-steady growth to be enjoyed for a time. But if we are going to bring history into the analysis, we must consider the effects of technical change.

This is the question that we have neglected to discuss for twenty-five years.

NOTES

1. Samuelson was piqued at my saying, "The professors at MIT took over my book of blueprints" (see Samuelson 1975, footnote 10). He says that he used my nickname, as a

compliment, for a very well-known concept. But if it was all well known, how account for the famous error (Samuelson 1966) that he had to admit in 1966?

2. This began in *Quarterly Journal of Economics,* November 1966, and has been going on ever since.

REFERENCES

Kornai, J. 1971. *Anti-equilibrium.* Amsterdam: North Holland.

Robinson, J. 1975. "The Unimportance of Reswitching." *Quarterly Journal of Economics* 89:32–39. See also *Collected Economic Papers,* vol 5. Oxford: Basil Blackwell, 1979.

Samuelson, P. 1962. "Parable and Realism in Capital Theory: The Surrogate Production Function." *Review of Economic Studies* 29:193–206.

———. 1966. "A Summing Up." *Quarterly Journal of Economics* 80:568–83.

———. 1975. "Steady-State and Transient Relations: A Reply on Reswitching." *Quarterly Journal of Economics* 89:40–47.

Sraffa, P., ed. 1951. *Works and Correspondence of David Ricardo,* vol. 1. Cambridge, England: Cambridge University Press.

———. 1960. *Production of Commodities by Means of Commodities.* Cambridge, England: Cambridge University Press.

6 THE DYNAMIC INTERDEPENDENCE BETWEEN INFORMATION, VALUATION, AND PRODUCTION IN A SOCIETY

Wilhelm Krelle

Economic theory would not be on the level it is now without the numerous and outstanding contributions of Paul A. Samuelson. He is one of the very few scholars who are specialists as well as generalists in many fields. He has pushed the frontier of economic knowledge into previously unknown regions, and he has maintained a general view of economics in its entirety as well as of the interrelations between the economic, social, and political aspects of society. Thus, even where he opened up a new field, as in the case of consumer demand theory in general and especially in revealed preference theory (see Samuelson 1938, 1947, p. 109 ff.), he knew the limitations of that approach. The theory, as he developed it and as it stands now, assumes a given state of preferences (or valuations) for each person and treats them as independent from other persons' preferences and from the production activities of the economy. This can be considered only as a first approximation in the very short run.

Samuelson stated that explicitly:

> . . . in recent years many economists . . . have insisted upon the degree to which individual tastes and wants are socially conditioned by advertising and custom so that they can hardly be said to belong to him in any ultimate sense. All this is recognized in the witticism of the soap box speaker who said to the

97

recalcitrant listener: "When the revolution comes, you will eat strawberries and cream, and like it!" [Samuelson 1947, pp. 223-24]

In this spirit we suggest a coherent approach to utility and demand theory that explains the long-term development of the intellectual, ethical, and productive sides of a society simultaneously. There have been some attempts in this direction (e.g., by Peston 1967; Gorman 1967; von Weizsäcker 1971; Frey and Schneider 1975; and Krelle 1973, 1980). Thus this paper may be viewed as an attempt to extend Samuelson's work in the direction that he himself suggested.

THE THESIS AND SOME DEFINITIONS

We start with some definitions. A person, $\mu = 1, \ldots, m$, is characterized:

1. By his *amount of information*, b_μ^ρ, on the object ρ. All objects $\rho = 1, \ldots, r$ that may conceivably become known to any person will be enumerated. There are r of them. The amount of information b_μ^ρ on the object ρ is measured in bits; thus $b_\mu^\rho \geq 0$.

2. By the *credibility*, c_μ^ρ, that person μ assigns to the information b_μ^ρ — that is, by the degree of faith the person has that the information b_μ^ρ is true, $0 \leq c_\mu^\rho \leq 1$. "Zero" indicates a subjective certainty that the information is false, and "one" indicates the subjective certainty that it is true.

3. By the *valuation*, v_μ^ρ, of the information b_μ^ρ by person μ. These value figures v_μ^ρ are normalized to lie between -1 (for objects that are disliked to the highest degree) and $+1$ (for objects that are liked as much as possible). $v_\mu^\rho = 0$ indicates indifference; thus $-1 \leq v_\mu^\rho \leq 1$.

4. By his productive skill or *ability*, a, in the field ρ. By this we mean the actual performance of a person in changing the state of the world in a specific field. It may be measured by the number of well-defined operations that the person is able to perform in a certain time; thus $a_\mu^\rho \geq 0$.

If $a_\mu = (a_\mu^1, \ldots, a_\mu^r)$ and b_μ, c_μ, v_μ accordingly, a *person* μ is defined by $p_\mu := (a_\mu, b_\mu, c_\mu, v_\mu)'$ and a *society* by $p := (p_1, \ldots, p_m)'$.

A part of the information and the valuations of a person $p_{\mu,t-\tau}$ in former periods $t - \tau, \tau = 1, \ldots, T$, may be preserved in "stores of knowledge and valuations" such as books, tapes, instruments, objects of art, and so on. Let $b_\mu := (b_\mu^1, \ldots, b_\mu^r)'$ be the information vector of person μ, $b := (b_1, \ldots, b_m)'$, the vector information in the society

and $\bar{B} = \begin{pmatrix} \bar{B}_{11} & \cdots & \bar{B}_{m1} \\ \vdots & & \\ \bar{B}_{1m} & \cdots & \bar{B}_{mm} \end{pmatrix}$, where $\bar{B}_{ij} = \begin{pmatrix} \bar{b}_{ij}^1 & & \\ & \ddots & \\ & & \bar{b}_{ij}^r \end{pmatrix}$ is a diagonal matrix

of *transfer coefficients* $\bar{b}_{ij}^q \geq 0$. They indicate the proportion of information of person i concerning the object g that is stored in such a way that it may become information of person i. Usually, $\bar{b}_{i1}^q = \bar{b}_{im}^q$. Then

$$\bar{b}_t := \bar{B}_t \cdot b_t \tag{6.1}$$

gives the amount of information available at period t out of information storages. Similarly, $\bar{c}_t$ and $\bar{v}_t$ give the stored credibilities of the information and the stored valuations, respectively. Thus total information b_t^* available in a society in period t becomes

$$b_t^* = (b_t, \bar{b}_{t-1}, \ldots, \bar{b}_{t-T}) , \tag{6.2}$$

where b_t is "active" information of persons in period t and $\bar{b}_{t-T}$ is "stored" information of persons T periods before. c_t^*, v_t^* are similarly defined.

We now assume transfer coefficients that determine the relative amounts of information, credibility, valuation, and productive ability in a field that are transferred from one person or from one store of information to another person (or from one person in one period to the same person in the next period). Similarly, we assume transfer coefficients that determine the part of newly created knowledge and newly established valuations that are going to become internalized by a person. We shall show that if the transfer coefficients are constant, the information and ability system converges to a final state, whereas the credibility system and the valuation system may not converge.

THE ORIGIN AND TRANSFER OF INFORMATION

Let $\hat{B}_{t-\tau}$ be the transfer matrix that indicates the transfer of knowledge from person to person (including within a person) or from an information storage to a person. The transfer takes one period. Let $\hat{e} := (e_1, \ldots, e_m)'$, $e_\mu := (e_\mu^1, \ldots, e_\mu^r)'$ be a vector of observations by all persons on all subjects; let E be a transfer matrix that transforms observations into information of a person, and $\tilde{b}$ the vector of new ideas ("inventions"), also measured in bits. $\tilde{b}$ may be considered as a chance vector. Thus

$$b_t = \hat{B}_{t-1} \cdot b_{t-1} + \sum_{\tau=2}^{T} \hat{B}_{t-\tau} \cdot \bar{b}_{t-\tau} + E_{t-1}\hat{e}_{t-1} + \tilde{b}_t ,$$

which may be written as

$$b_t = \sum_{\tau=1}^{T} B_{t-\tau} \cdot b_{t-\tau} + E_{t-1}\hat{e}_{t-1} + \tilde{b}_t , \tag{6.3}$$

where

$$\bar{B}_{t-1} := \hat{B}_{t-1} \text{ and } B_{t-\tau} := \hat{B}_{t-\tau}B_{t-\tau} , \qquad \tau = 2 , \dots , T ,$$

or, in case the transfer matrices are constant:

$$x_t = G\, x_{t-1} + F\, e_{t-1} + \tilde{x}_t , \tag{6.4}$$

where

$$x_t = \begin{pmatrix} b_t \\ b_{t-1} \\ \vdots \\ b_{t-T+1} \end{pmatrix}, \ \tilde{x}_t = \begin{pmatrix} \tilde{b}_t \\ \hline 0 \\ \vdots \\ 0 \end{pmatrix}, \ e_t = \begin{pmatrix} \hat{e}_t \\ \hline 0 \\ \vdots \\ 0 \end{pmatrix},$$

$$G = \begin{pmatrix} B_{-1} & \cdots & B_{-T+1} & B_{-T} \\ \hline I & 0 & & 0 \\ 0 & \ddots & & \\ & & & \\ 0 & \cdots & I & 0 \end{pmatrix}, \ F = \begin{pmatrix} E_{-1} & 0 \\ \hline & \\ 0 & 0 \\ & \end{pmatrix}.$$

All components are nonnegative; the row sums of all components of $G + F$ are smaller than or equal to one (since the human brain is able to store only a finite number of bits). Thus the Brauer-Solow conditions apply, and $(I - G)^{-1}q \geq 0$ for all $q \geq 0$. For the same reason the sum of the off-diagonal elements in the first $r \times m$ rows of the matrix G are smaller than $1 - g_{ii}$, which is the rate of forgetting; if no knowledge comes from outside (i.e., if $\hat{e} = \tilde{b} = 0$), mankind will eventually lose information by the information transfer. Thus the matrix $I - G$ has a dominant main diagonal; for constant e and $\tilde{x}$ the system (6.4) converges to

$$x = (I - G)^{-1}(F \cdot e + \tilde{x}). \tag{6.5}$$

The total amount of information in the society reaches a final limit (measured in bits), but the content of information always changes. We may define the *degree of modernity*, $\bar{m}_\mu^\rho(T)$, of the information of person μ on the object ρ as the part of this information that is not older than T years. From (6.4) we get for $Fe_{t-1} + \tilde{x}_t =: q_t$:

$$x_1 = G\,x_0 + q_1$$
$$x_2 = G\,x_1 + q_2 = G^2\,q_0 + G\,q_1 + q_2$$
$$\vdots$$
$$x_t = G^t\,q_0 + G^{t-1}\,q_1 + \ldots + G\,q_{t-1} + q_t$$

and therefore for period t:

$$\overline{m}_\mu^\rho(T) = \left[\sum_{\tau=0}^{T} G^\tau q_{t-\tau} \right]_{\mu\rho} \bigg/ [q]_{\mu\rho} , \qquad (6.6)$$

where the index $(\mu\rho)$ means the component $(\mu\rho)$ of the vector in question, for $[q]_{\mu\rho} \neq 0$.

THE ORIGIN AND TRANSFER OF PRODUCTIVE ABILITIES

Productive skills, a_t, are transferred from person to person (and, for the same person, from one period to the next) in much the same way as information. But abilities may be improved by actual information, b_t, in this specific or in a related field. They will also improve by actual observations (or experiments), $\hat{e}_t$, and by actual production, $\hat{q}_t$. There may be new inventions, $\tilde{a}_t$, in skill; $\tilde{a}_t$ may be a chance variable. Thus we get similarly as in (6.4):

$$a_t = \sum_{\tau=1}^{T} A_{t-\tau} a_{t-\tau} + D_{t-1} b_{t-1} + \hat{L}_1 \hat{e}_{t-1} + \hat{L}_2 \hat{q}_{t-1} + \tilde{a}_{t-1} , \qquad (6.7)$$

which in the case of constant transfer matrices A and D may be written as

$$y_t = H\,y_{t-1} + K\,x_{t-1} + L_1\,e_{t-1} + L_2 q_{t-1} + \tilde{y}_t , \qquad (6.8)$$

where

$$y_t = \begin{pmatrix} a_t \\ a_{t-1} \\ \vdots \\ a_{t-T+1} \end{pmatrix}, \tilde{y}_t = \begin{pmatrix} \tilde{a}_t \\ 0 \\ \vdots \\ 0 \end{pmatrix}, e_t = \begin{pmatrix} \hat{e}_t \\ 0 \\ \vdots \\ 0 \end{pmatrix}, q_t = \begin{pmatrix} \hat{q}_t \\ 0 \\ \vdots \\ 0 \end{pmatrix},$$

$$H = \begin{pmatrix} A_{-1} & \cdots & A_{-T+1} & A_{-T} \\ I & 0 & \cdots & 0 \\ 0 & \cdots & \cdots & 0 \\ 0 & \cdots & I & 0 \end{pmatrix}, L_i = \begin{pmatrix} \hat{L}_i & 0 \\ 0 & 0 \end{pmatrix}, i = 1,2.$$

The components of all vectors and matrices are nonnegative; the rows of $H + K + L_1 + L_2$ sum up to a figure smaller or equal to one; and the matrix $I - H$ has a dominant main diagonal. Thus, for constant and nonnegative x, e, q, and $\bar{y}$, the system (6.8) converges to

$$y = (I - H)^{-1}[Kx + L_1 e + L_2 q + \bar{y}] . \qquad (6.9)$$

Skills reach a final amount in this case, in the same way as information. A degree of modernity of skill may be defined for the productive skill as well.

THE CREDIBILITY OF INFORMATION

Each information, b_μ^ρ, carries a degree of credibility, c_μ^ρ, where $0 \le c_\mu^\rho \le 1$. The latter is transferred simultaneously with the former, but perhaps with other transfer coefficients. Let $w(\hat{e}_t)$ be the credibility weights assigned to an observation (or experiment), $\hat{e}_t$, where $0 \le w(\hat{e}_t) \le 1$. Let $\bar{c}_t$ be a spontaneous, unexplained influence on credibility due to a change of mind of a person, $0 \le \bar{c}_t \le 1$, and let C_t , . . . , C_{t-T}, M_t, N_t be nonnegative transfer matrices such that the row sums of $\Sigma_{\tau=1}^T C_{t-1} + M_{t-1} + N_{t-1}$ are smaller or equal to one. Now the creation and the transfer of credibilities of information may be reflected by

$$c_t = \sum_{\tau=1}^T C_{t-\tau} c_{t-\tau} + M_{t-1} w(\hat{e}_{t-1}) + N_{t-1} \bar{c}_{t-1} , \qquad (6.10)$$

which, in the case of constant transfer matrices, may be written as

$$z_t = P z_{t-1} + Q \cdot w(e_{t-1}) + R \bar{z}_{t-1} . \qquad (6.11)$$

The vectors z, $w(e)$, $\bar{z}$ and the matrices P, Q, R are similarly defined as the vectors x, e, $\bar{x}$ and the matrices G and F in (6.4).

For constant $w(e)$ and $\bar{z}$ the system converges to

$$z = (I - P)^{-1}[Q \cdot w(e) + R\bar{z}], \qquad (6.12)$$

if it converges at all. But this is not sure since the main diagonal of $(I - P)$ might not be dominant.

THE VALUATION OF INFORMATION

Each information, b_μ^ρ, also carries an evaluation, v_μ^ρ, where $-1 \le v_\mu^\rho \le 1$. Valuations stem from valuations of other people (alive or dead, if their opinions are preserved in "stores") and from their own valuations of the period before. Moreover, they are influenced by the "state of nature" with respect to the person in question (e.g., if the person feels hungry, food will be highly valued). There are natural laws that influence the valuation of commodities according to the needs of the person. Since for human beings the state of nature (as far as needs are concerned) depends very much on man's own production, we make this valuation a function, $v(\hat{q}_t)$, of production, where $-1 \leq v(\hat{q}_t) \leq 1$. Let $\bar{v}_t$ be an autonomous change of valuations, $-1 \leq \bar{v}_t \leq 1$. Let the matrices $V_t, \ldots, V_{t-T}, S_t, T_t$ be nonnegative transfer matrices, where the row sums of $\Sigma_{\tau=1}^{T} V_{t-\tau} + S_{t-1} + T_{t-1} =: \Gamma$ are equal to one. Thus we have

$$v_t = \sum_{\tau=1}^{T} V_{t-\tau} v_{t-\tau} + S_{t-1} \cdot v(\hat{q}_{t-1}) + T_{t-1} \cdot \bar{v}_t . \tag{6.13}$$

For constant transfer matrices this may be written

$$\xi_t = U\xi_{t-1} + W \cdot v(q_{t-1}) + Z \cdot \tilde{\xi}_{t-1}, \tag{6.14}$$

where the vectors ξ, $v(q)$, $\tilde{\xi}$ and the matrices U, W, Z are similarly defined as the vectors x, e, $\tilde{x}$ and the matrices G and F in (6.4).

For constant $v(q)$ and ξ the system (6.14) would converge to

$$\xi = (I - U)^{-1}[W \cdot v(q) + Z \tilde{\xi}] \tag{6.15}$$

if at least one row sum of Γ is smaller than one. But we cannot assume this. Thus, U does not have a dominant main diagonal, ξ_t will not converge, and society will always change its evaluation. The process of history does not end.

THE TOTAL SYSTEM

Now the system (6.4), (6.8), (6.11), (6.14) becomes

$$\eta_t = A_1\eta_{t-1} + A_2\omega_{t-1} + A_3\tilde{\eta}_t, \tag{6.16}$$

where

$$\eta = \begin{pmatrix} x \\ y \\ z \\ \xi \end{pmatrix}, \quad \omega = \begin{pmatrix} e \\ w(e) \\ q \\ v(q) \end{pmatrix}, \quad \tilde{\eta} = \begin{pmatrix} \tilde{x} \\ \tilde{y} \\ \tilde{z} \\ \tilde{\xi} \end{pmatrix}, \quad A_1 = \begin{pmatrix} G & 0 & 0 & 0 \\ \hline K & H & 0 & 0 \\ \hline 0 & 0 & P & 0 \\ \hline 0 & 0 & 0 & U \end{pmatrix},$$

$$A_2 = \begin{pmatrix} F & 0 & 0 & 0 \\ \hline L_1 & 0 & L_2 & 0 \\ \hline 0 & Q & 0 & 0 \\ \hline 0 & 0 & 0 & W \end{pmatrix}, A_3 = \begin{pmatrix} I & 0 & 0 & 0 \\ \hline 0 & I & 0 & 0 \\ \hline 0 & 0 & R & 0 \\ \hline 0 & 0 & 0 & Z \end{pmatrix}$$

The transfer matrices A_1, A_2, A_3 may not be constant. If the political system changes, the information structure changes, and therefore the components of the A-matrices change as well. Since we cannot offer a theory for it, we disregard this case. But since observations (or research), e_t, and production, q_t, are vector functions f_e and f_q of the economic situation, s_t, and the state of knowledge and valuations, η_t, in society:

$$e_t = f_e(s_t, \eta_t), \qquad q_t = f_q(s_t, \eta_t) \tag{6.17}$$

and since the economic situation, s_t, might be considered as a function, f_s, of the economic situation, s_{t-1}, of production, q_{t-1}, and of research, e_{t-1}, in the preceding period, we get the stochastic feedback system:

$$s_t = f_s(s_{t-1}, f_e(s_{t-1}, \eta_{t-1}), f_q(s_{t-1}, \eta_{t-1})) =: F_1(s_{t-1}, \eta_{t-1})$$

$$\eta_t = A_1 \eta_{t-1} + A_2 \cdot \begin{pmatrix} f_e(s_{t-1}, \eta_{t-1}) \\ w_e(f_e(\cdot)) \\ f_q(s_{t-1}, \eta_{t-1}) \\ v(f_q(\cdot)) \end{pmatrix} + A_3 \tilde{\eta}_t =: F_2(\eta_{t-1}, s_{t-1}) + \tilde{\tilde{\eta}}_t. \tag{6.18}$$

It describes the interrelationship between the intellectual and ethical sides and the productive side of a society, unfortunately only on the theoretical level. To implement the system and to make it operational would be a huge task. We now relate the system developed above to the usual production and consumption theory.

PRODUCTION AND CONSUMPTION FROM THE VIEWPOINT OF THIS THEORY

Production theory starts from the assumption of a production possibility set or, more simply, from a production function, $q = F(x_1, \ldots, x_n)$, where $x_1, \ldots, x_n$ are the factors of production. From the point of view of this theory, persons $p_\mu := (a_\mu, b_\mu, c_\mu, v_\mu)$, $\mu = 1, \ldots, m$, should appear in the production function.

Let $p_\mu^l := (p_\mu, l_\mu)$ be the vector determining the working hours, l_μ, of person μ in production and let Ω be the productive organization that assigns each person a role in the production process and defines the rules of the performance of each person. The production function, Φ:

$$q = \Phi(p_1^l, \ldots, p_m^l, \Omega, K_1, \ldots, K_n) \qquad (6.19)$$

relates the output, q, to the performance of person $1, \ldots, m$ in the organization, Ω, and to the available physical primary and secondary means of production, $K_1, \ldots, K_n$. Φ is now a technical relation. Of course, by keeping the organization and the characteristics (a,b,c,v) of a person constant, one arrives at the usual production function.

For consumption theory, one has to relate the theory to a preference ordering or (more specifically) to a utility function. For this purpose the "objects" to which values are assigned have to be defined in more detail.

Let $x = (x_1, \ldots, x_n)$ be a commodity bundle that might be bought by a household. This bundle constitutes an "object" in the sense of our theory. Thus in a certain period the household values r commodity bundles, $x^1, \ldots, x^r$, by figures $v^1 = v(x^1), \ldots, v^r = v(x^r)$, respectively, where $-1 \leq v^\rho \leq 1, \rho = 1, \ldots, r$.

If the household has an amount, y, of money to spend and the prices of the commodities are $\pi_1, \ldots, \pi_n$, the household buys the bundle, x^*, where

$$x^* \leftarrow \max \{v(x^1), \ldots, v(x^r) | \sum_{i=1}^{n} x_i^* \pi_i \leq Y, x^* \epsilon \{x^1, \ldots, x^r\}\} . \qquad (6.20)$$

If one fits a utility function that is identical to $v(x^1), \ldots, v(x^r)$ at the points $x^1, \ldots, x^r$ and smooth everywhere else in the relevant region, one may use as an approximation the common approach of maximizing a utility function under the budget constraint. Since there is an upper bound for the values of all possible bundles, the law of diminishing marginal utility follows for large enough x.

CONCLUSION

The paper suggests an approach to economic theory that makes it possible to consider the interdependence of preferences within a society and the interrelation of information and valuation. This approach might give some insight into the forces behind the historical process and might be used to formulate dynamic preferences for planning. After all, the long-term decisions to be taken would have to be optimal in the light of the future rather than the present generation because the future generation is affected by them.

REFERENCES

Frey, B. S., and F. Schneider. 1975. "On the Modeling of Politico-Economic Interdependence." *European Journal of Political Research* 3:339–60.

Gorman, W. M. 1967. "Tastes, Habits and Choices." *International Economic Review* 8:218–22.

Kramer, G. H. 1971. "Short-Term Fluctuations in U.S. Voting Behavior, 1896–1964." *American Political Science Review* 65: S 131–43.

Krelle, W. 1973. "Dynamics of the Utility Function." In J. R. Hicks and W. Weber, eds. *Carl Menger and the Austrian School of Economics.* London: Oxford University Press.

———. 1980. "Ein System der allgemeinen Interdependenz der geistigen und wirtschaftlichen Entwicklung." In E. Küng, ed. *Wandlungen in Wirtschaft und Gesellschaft, Festschrift für W. A. Jöhr.* Tübingen: Mohr.

Peston, M. H. 1967. "Changing Utility Functions." In M. Shubik, ed. *Essays in Mathematical Economics in Honor of Oskar Morgenstern.* Princeton, N.J.: Princeton University Press.

Samuelson, P. A. 1938. "A Note on the Pure Theory of Consumer's Behaviour." *Economica* NS 5:61–71.

———. 1947. *Foundations of Economic Analysis.* Cambridge, Mass.: Harvard University Press.

Weizsäcker, C. C. von. 1972. "Notes on Endogenous Change of Tastes." *Journal of Economic Theory* 3:345–72.

7 DEVIATIONS BETWEEN EARNINGS AND MARGINAL PRODUCTIVITY: Two Studies Compared

Jan Tinbergen

PRODUCTION FUNCTIONS: SOME ALTERNATIVE DEFINITIONS AND THEIR ROLE

In line with alternative interpretations of a number of variables used in economic science, a number of alternative interpretations of functions used in economics may be distinguished. In this essay we concentrate on production functions (see Samuelson 1947, Chap. 4). The alternatives that will enter our argument are *actual* or *ex post* versus *expected* or *intended* (or *planned*) — all of them are entitled to the characterization *ex ante*. As a rule an expected production function reflects a more passive observation, while an intended or planned production function reflects a more active involvement. Active involvement occurs when a production process is set up deliberately, just as in the theory of markets we speak of price setters for a variable such as price.

Our main problem will be the incomes, and more particularly earnings, of a category of actors (used in the sense given this word by Tinbergen 1956) whom we will call the "bearers of competition." By this phrase we try to identify occupations relevant to the phenomenon of competition — that is, they are more particularly involved in competition with other firms. In the language of the Census of Population of the United States, this category is to be sought among the main occupational groups of "managers, administrators, etc." and of "sales workers." More precisely, the problem we intend to tackle is how the incomes of the bearers of competition are determined and, in addition, whether other ways of determining them are "better," according to a criterion to be proposed after the analysis of the determination has been attempted.

The empirical material I propose to use is taken from two recent studies, one by Gottschalk (1978) and one by Kol and Tinbergen (1980). This empirical material gave rise to the title chosen for this essay. Both Gottschalk and the two of us — unaware at the time of writing of Gottschalk's interesting study — tried to answer the question whether there are deviations between median earnings of some categories of occupations and their estimated marginal products. Both studies used American data; the second study also used Japanese material. The methods used are different in several important respects. Gottschalk developed a highly imaginative method of estimating marginal productivities; ours was more traditional. In contradistinction, I venture to submit that our attempts to interpret our — somewhat strange — results was more daring and led me to formulate the main problem of this essay. Even though the results of the two studies are in some respects quite different, in other respects they seem to support each other remarkably well. All this will be taken up *in concreto* later. In the next section a central part of the interpretation is discussed, detached from empirical research, followed by some supporting, down-to-earth empirical material. In the two final sections, I attempt to give an answer to what we called our main problem.

THE PHENOMENON OF COUNTERPRODUCTION

In a Dutch article (Tinbergen 1980) I proposed to introduce into economic science the concept of counterproduction. It has some similarity to the concept of antimatter in physics. Counterproduction is an activity intending to annihilate, wholly or partially, the production of another individual or group of individuals. A direct concrete example is the demolition of something produced by somebody else. In an era of increasing vandalism, we may have to pay increasing attention to this form of counterproduction. A number of other examples are less visibly concrete, but of fundamental importance to our social order. One is the activity of those we have called the bearers of competition, or at least part of their activity. This example will be our central case. It is the effort made to induce a buyer of some product not to buy it from firm A but from firm B, where A and B both supply that product. The situation prevailing in a competitive market is that sales managers and sales workers spend a considerable part of their working effort to ''neutralize'' each other, to keep the market shares of A and B what they turn out to be (ex post) and not to let them be either what A or B intended them to be.

As stated, this will be our central case. In order, however, to clarify further the concept of counterproduction, some other examples will be added. Counterproductive elements may be present in the process of supervision of one person's work by another. The ideal type of supervision contains this element in a negative way; true supervision corrects an error made by or expected from the person under supervision. It does annihilate a piece of negative production. But not all supervision is of this ideal type. A second type of supervision implies that the supervised labor did not make an error, and the supervision in that case does not add anything to production. A third type of supervision may imply irritation by the supervised person and, as a consequence, a negative contribution to production. This is what Bahro (1977) has in mind when he points out that the present system of production in the German Democratic Republic is suffering from a plethora of supervisory labor.

Related examples can be drawn from what happens in large hierarchies. One example is that there may be too many levels of supervision. Officer A of lowest rank writes a draft text. Officer B of the next higher rank changes the draft and passes it on to the next higher officer, C, who deletes part of the change. So part of B's work is counterproductive. Whoever has worked in a hierarchy has observed such processes. A second example observed in a hierarchy: Librarian X finds that he has not yet exhausted his budget for buying books. Since an unexhausted budget for year t may induce the authority under whom X works to reduce the budget for year $t + 1$, X buys some additional books. Counterproduction! A third example in a hierarchy consists of competence quarrels. Two parts of an agency claim the ''right'' to deal with some problem regarding the agency. This may be conducive to either unnecessary discussions or duplication of work. The relationship with Parkinson's Law is clear, too.

Some Empirical Material on Counterproduction

Some simple figures may be given in order to show that the extent of counterproduction is not negligible. In the United States about 3 to 4 percent of national income ($64 billion in 1976) is spent on advertising

(Janus and Roncagliolo 1974). While an element of (productive) information is included, another part of advertising is typically counterproductive.

Part of counterproduction is the production of unhealthy commodities or the too-large production of others. Examples of the former are tobacco products and alcoholic beverages. In the Netherlands 1.53 percent of national income was spent on tobacco products in 1976 (*Statistical Pocketbook,* 1977). Fortunately, this figure has declined since 1965. This does not apply to the consumption of alcoholic beverages. In 1965, 1.89 liters per head were consumed (expressed in pure alcohol); in 1975, 3.39 liters. The 1976 figure was lower (2.49 liters), but still twice as high as in 1929. Beer consumption grew from 37.2 liters in 1965 to 93.9 liters in 1976, as compared with 28.0 in 1929.

Although not generally considered unhealthy, meat and sugar are being consumed in larger quantities than the Dutch National Health Council deems optimal. Annual per capita consumption of meat amounted to 57.4 kg in 1976, while the optimum is 36.5 kg. The value of overconsumption (actual minus optimal consumption) in 1976 constituted about 2 percent of national income. Sugar is used in such quantities that dentists spend 25 percent of their working time to neutralize the damage done by candy consumption to the teeth of youngsters.

INCOMES AND ESTIMATED MARGINAL PRODUCTIVITIES OF "BEARERS OF COMPETITION": A COMPARISON OF TWO STUDIES

As previously mentioned, Gottschalk (1978) made an attempt to estimate marginal productivities of six types of labor in the United States in 1959. Independently Kol and Tinbergen (1980) made another attempt for five types of labor in the United States in 1959 and Japan in 1975. In both cases cross-section data for states (prefectures in Japan) were used. Kol and Tinbergen estimated a Cobb-Douglas production function expressing per capita income as a function of the quantities of five labor types (expressed as a proportion of the total labor force in each state or prefecture) and a proxy for capital per employee. A proxy was used since no figures on capital by state are available (see Sattinger 1980, p. 165). The way in which this proxy was calculated is very similar to the method used by Gottschalk.

Gottschalk launched a very inventive method to avoid multicollinearity in his estimates of marginal productivities. He assumed that each production process consists of two separate phases, one of production and one of administration. His method required that these two processes have one common factor of production, for which he chose the total of clerical and service workers and laborers. In addition, production-specific factors were assumed to be capital, operatives, and craftsmen, and administration-specific factors, professionals, and so forth, managers, and so forth, and sales workers. Formulas for the derivation of marginal productivity were obtained from two production functions, for the two phases, constrained by the necessity to produce and administer the same quantity of product; the common factor has to be distributed over the two processes in an optimal way. The two production functions were "normalized" by considering the natural logarithm of value added divided by the natural logarithm of the quantity of one specific factor (capital for the production process and sales workers for the administration process). Linear relationships in these (relative) logarithms were then tested for 267 observations, each concerning one manufacturing industry in one state. Corrected multiple correlation coefficients as well as the t-values for most of the regression coefficients were quite satisfactory; these coefficients are used to estimate marginal productivities. The Cobb-Douglas exponents found added up to one and hence indicated no economies or diseconomies of scale. Median earnings of each of the six types of labor were then divided by marginal product found. A further difference is that Gottschalk considered manufacturing only, while Kol and Tinbergen covered all activities. Table 7.1 compares the results.

Table 7.1. Median Earnings to Marginal Product Ratios, United States, 1959

Occupational Groups	Gottschalk	Kol/Tinbergen
Managers, etc.	2.03	2.55
Sales workers	2.64	0.64[c]
Professional workers	1.12	0.98
Craftsmen	0.35	−4.67[d]
Operatives	0.44	−4.67
Clerical workers	0.63[a]	0.64[c]
Laborers	0.54[a]	−4.67[d]
Service workers	0.49[a]	−4.67[d]
Farm managers and workers	NA[b]	−1.46

[a] Combined as "supporting workers."

[b] Not available.

[c] Combined as "white-collar workers."

[d] Combined as "blue-collar workers."

Gottschalk did not give an interpretation of his findings and said so explicitly in footnote 30. A possible and interesting interpretation would seem to be that there is no free competition in the labor markets between the organizers of production. Free competition is a precondition for the equality of earnings and marginal productivity. Expressed otherwise, the organizers of production are not pricetakers but are to some extent pricesetters. Contrary to what Gottschalk seems to hold (see his footnote 25), we accepted negative marginal productivities as a possibility. For small entrepreneurs (farmers and retail traders, for instance) this may be a consequence of (1) erroneous calculation of their costs, omitting or underestimating the price of their own labor and capital, and of (2) the psychic income derived from being independent. For blue-collar workers negative marginal productivity may be a consequence of their being "hoarded" by their employers if they expect larger production to be desirable at a later time.

The main point Kol and Tinbergen made in their interpretation was the phenomenon of counterproduction. Interestingly enough, Gottschalk makes a very similar point, hidden in footnote 29. Interestingly too, our findings concerning overpayment of managers, etc., and the earnings-to-productivity ratio of about one for professional workers, etc., are almost the same. The large difference between Gottschalk's ratio for sales workers and ours may be due to our having combined sales and clerical workers; the latter are much more numerous than the former. Gottschalk's and our ratios for clerical workers are identical. In fact, Gottschalk's high figure for sales workers suits our counterproduction theory quite well!

A last comment on the subject of empirical verification should be that our two inquiries are clearly only in their initial stages and are beset with question marks. Gottschalk, in his footnotes, illustrates this by a number of additional bits of information. In footnote 25 he informs us that TSLS yielded a negative marginal productivity to capital. The alternative shown in footnote 32 (aggregating his supporting workers in a somewhat different way) shows a few large deviations from his Table 1 "central" case. His "within-occupation" analysis at the end adds to his own doubts. Similarly, in our work the omission of the District of Columbia makes for a considerable shift in our results. So all of us agree that much remains to be done, and, on our side, quite a few additional estimates have already been made (using the 1970 Census in addition) or are in the process of being elaborated. A considerable advantage of the 1970 Census is the availability of economic state areas, which raises the number of observations about eightfold. Combination of 1959 and 1969 data with a simple assumption on technological development has also been planned.

DETERMINATION OF EARNINGS OF BEARERS OF COMPETITION

Returning now to our main problem — the manner of determining the earnings of the bearers of competition — it seems natural that the earnings are connected with an ex ante production function of the firm that employs the bearers of competition. If the firm were a pricetaker, earnings would be equal to the marginal products as intended or planned by that firm. One way of planning may be based on the maintenance of the firm's market share; another, more aggressive way of planning, on the expansion of that share by some percentage; still another on the acceptance of a shrinkage by no more than some percentage ("satisficing").

The statistics used in both empirical studies do not, of course, disclose such an ex ante production function of the firm. They provide us with ex post figures, after the fight between the different firms in the industry has taken place. In line with Gottschalk's footnote 29 and our counterproduction theory, the sales workers and the sales managers of different firms have partly or wholly annihilated each other's efforts. If, therefore, we assume that their income should be determined by their ex post marginal productivity, these incomes would be much smaller than the actual incomes, derived from some of the ex ante production functions. This is what both Gottschalk's and our figures bring out quite clearly for managers and Gottschalk's figures for sales workers, whose ex post marginal productivity is 1/2.64, or 38 percent, of their median income.

It would be wrong to conclude, however, that their actual incomes should be reduced so drastically — namely, to 40 or 50 percent for managers and to less than 40 percent for sales workers. As the bearers of competition they render an important service to society, and their incomes should reflect the value of that service to society.[1] This requires quite another type of analysis. We propose to outline in the present and the next section the sort of analysis that seems to us to be relevant to the question raised.

To begin with we need to make a comparison between an economy showing competition in all its markets and one characterized by the absence of competition, especially among producers of finished products. We will illustrate this comparison by a simple theoretical model,[2] where all production is vertically integrated (i.e., all groups of finished products considered are produced by one firm, which produces not only the finished products but also the intermediary products and the raw materials needed). The groups of finished products considered are only very weakly competing with the other groups; if it were different, no (quasi-)monopolization would be possible. In the next section we will add an additional detail by showing a model for one group in which the vertical stages are subdivided into consecutive processes, each handled by a monopolist.

Let there be J (groups of) finished products, the quantities produced being x_i ($i = 1, \ldots, J$) or x_j and the prices, p_i or p_j. Let demand be given by the implicit demand function

$$x_i p_i = x_i^0 + \sum_j \delta_{ij} x_j \tag{7.1}$$

with the restrictions that

$$\sum_i x_i^0 = Y \tag{7.2}$$

$$\sum_i \delta_{ij} = 0 \tag{7.3}$$

where Y is national income, supposed to be given, for instance by a Friedmanian monetary policy. The two restrictions are imposed in order that

$$\sum_i x_i p_i = Y. \tag{7.4}$$

Production costs $C_i(x_i)$ are supposed to be given by

$$C_i(x_i) = c_{0i} + c_i x_i + \tfrac{1}{2} x_i^2 , \tag{7.5}$$

where the coefficient 1/2 constitutes no loss of generality since the units of x_i can be chosen accordingly. Marginal costs of x_i will be:

$$C_i'(x_i) = c_i + x_i . \tag{7.6}$$

Indicating the state of a competitive economy by an upper index of C and a monopolist situation by an upper index M, we will find x_i^M by the maximum condition for profits $Z_i = x_i p_i - c_{0i} - c_i x_i - \tfrac{1}{2} x_i^2$; hence:

$$x_i^M = \delta_{ii} - c_i \qquad (i = 1, \ldots, J). \tag{7.7}$$

From it we derive:

$$p_i^M = \left\{ x_i^0 + \sum_j \delta_{ij}(\delta_{jj} - c_j) \right\} \Big/ (\delta_{ii} - c_i) \qquad (i = 1, \ldots, J). \tag{7.8}$$

The state of a competitive economy will be characterized by:

$$p_i^C = c_i + x_i^C \qquad (i = 1, \ldots, J) \tag{7.9}$$

and

$$(x_i^C)^2 + c_i x_i^C - x_i^0 - \sum_j \delta_{ij} x_j^C = 0 \qquad (i = 1, \ldots, J). \tag{7.10}$$

The system of quadratic equations (7.10) does not permit an explicit solution, but numerical solution for given values of all parameters is, of course, possible. Approximate solutions are possible also because of the weak substitution possibilities we must assume to exist as a precondition of the J monopolization attempts. This implies that all $\delta_{ij} \ll 1$; as a consequence also the $c_i \ll 1$; otherwise no positive x_i^M would result [cf. Equations (7.7)]. Under these conditions we may neglect the last sum in Equations (7.10) and solve for approximate values of x_i^C:

$$x_i^C \simeq -\tfrac{1}{2}c_i + \sqrt{\tfrac{1}{4}c_i^2 + x_i^0} \simeq \sqrt{}\ x_i^0 . \tag{7.11}$$

Comparing (7.7) and (7.11) it is clear that

$$x_i^C > x_i^M \qquad (i = 1 , \ldots , J) \tag{7.12}$$

and the system (7.12) yields an approximate measure of the welfare gain as a consequence of competition — namely, $\sqrt{}\ x_i^0$ for the bearers of competition in industry i.

The Effects of Cumulative Monopolization

As announced we will now illustrate the effect of a succession of monopolizations in each vertical chain of the production of one group of finished products, contained in x_i. Not unrealistically, such a system of "cumulative monopolies" assumes that raw material producers are much fewer than semifinished goods producers and these again much fewer than finished product makers.[3] Thus, in each of the consecutive markets, buyers are competing and sellers are able to monopolize. This implies that input prices are considered given but output prices manipulated in order to maximize profit in that stage. Instead of x_i we will leave out the index i, since we will deal with one column only, and introduce z for the quantity of finished product, y for the quantity of semifinished product, and x for the quantity of raw material used. Units will be chosen so as to make $x = y = z$. Prices will be written as r, q, and p, respectively. Parameters of the transformation process producing and selling z will carry two primes, those of the previous process one, and those of the initial process none.

Let demand for z be:

$$z = a'' - b''r \tag{7.13}$$

and costs of production $c_0'' + (q + c'')z$, where c_0'' are fixed costs; q, unit costs of raw materials, and c'', transformation costs per unit. Profit will be

$$Z'' = r(a'' - b''r) - c_0'' - (q + c'')(a'' - b''r) \tag{7.14}$$

and q will be considered given. The monopoly price r^M will then obey

$$\frac{\partial Z''}{\partial r} = a'' - 2b''r^M - (q + c'')b'' = 0, \tag{7.15}$$

or

$$r^M = a''/2b'' + (q^M + c'')/2, \tag{7.16}$$

since q is assumed to be the outcome of a monopoly of semifinished-product suppliers.

In exactly the same way the two preceding operations will yield:

$$q^M = a'/2b' + (p^M + c')/2 \tag{7.17}$$

and

$$p^M = a/2b + c/2 . \tag{7.18}$$

Substitution of (7.18) into (7.17) and of (7.17) into (7.16) yields:

$$r^M = \frac{a''}{2b''} + \frac{a'}{2b'} + \frac{a}{2b} + \frac{1}{2}c'' + \frac{1}{4}c' + \frac{1}{8}c . \tag{7.19}$$

Considering that $z = y = x$, we may eliminate a', b', a, and b by using demand equation (7.13) and the corresponding expressions for y and x:

$$a'' - b''r = a' - b'q = a - bp \tag{7.20}$$

and equations (7.16) through (7.18). The results are

$$a'/2b' = (a'' - b''c'')/2b'' \tag{7.21}$$

and

$$a/2b = (a'' - b''c'' - b''c')/2b''. \tag{7.22}$$

With the aid of (7.21) and (7.22) we obtain

$$r^M = 7a''/8b'' + (c'' + c' + c)/8 \tag{7.23}$$

from which we can calculate

$$z^M = a''/8 - b''(c'' + c' + c)/8 . \tag{7.24}$$

For a production column with competitive price formation, prices will equal marginal costs:[4]

$$r^C = c'' + c' + c \tag{7.25}$$

leading to:

$$z^c = a'' - b''(c'' + c' + c), \tag{7.26}$$

which implies:

$$z^M = \tfrac{1}{8}z^C . \tag{7.27}$$

It will be easily understood that the chain of three consecutive processes can be generalized into one of n processes, and that in that case

$$z^M = \frac{1}{2^n} z^C . \tag{7.28}$$

Our example illustrates that cumulative monopolies are extremely restrictive. Breaking up one large, vertically integrated firm into smaller and possibly chain monopolists means, from the social point of view, making things worse. Breaking up a "horizontal" monopoly into a set of competing firms is socially useful.

NOTES

1. At this point we assume that optimal earnings are equal to the marginal productivity of the group considered. These earnings are not the ones called "equitable" in Tinbergen (1975). Equity as defined there is not necessarily attainable at once.

2. This simple model may be considered as an algebraic counterpart to Joan Robinson's treatment of the same problem (Robinson 1933, pp. 307 ff.).

3. In most branches the number of semifinished goods is larger than the number of raw materials, and the number of finished products larger than the number of semifinished products.

4. In the model given competitive prices make for permanent losses, unless all goods are sold to consumers and charge them for part of the overheads (two-part price system, as usual for power). It would require more complicated models, such as that given in the preceding section, to deal adequately with this aspect, but we have preferred the extreme simplicity of the present model, meant as an illustration only.

REFERENCES

Bahro, R. 1977. *Die Alternative, Zur Kritik des real existierenden Sozialismus.* Köln/Frankfurt am Main: Europäische Verlagsanstalt.

Gottschalk, P. T. 1978. "A Comparison of Marginal Productivity and Earnings by Occupation." *Industrial and Labor Relations Review* 31:368–78.

Janus, N., and R. Roncagliolo. 1979. "Advertising, Mass Media and Dependency." *Development Dialogue* 1:81–97. Uppsala: Dag Hammarskjöld Foundation.

Kol, J., and J. Tinbergen. 1980. "Market-Determined and Residual Incomes — Some Dilemmas." *Economie appliquée* 33: 285–301.

Robinson, J. 1933. *The Economics of Imperfect Competition.* London: Macmillan.

Samuelson, P. A. 1947. *Foundations of Economic Analysis.* Cambridge, Mass.: Harvard University Press.

Sattinger, M. 1980. *Capital and the Distribution of Labor Earnings, Contributions to Economic Analysis.* Amsterdam: North-Holland.

Tinbergen, J. 1956. *Economic Policy: Principles and Design.* Amsterdam: North-Holland.

――――. 1975. *Income Distribution: Analysis and Policies.* Amsterdam: North-Holland.

――――. 1980. "Contraproduktie" [Counterproduction]. In P. J. Eijgelshoven and L. J. van Gemerden, eds. *Inkomensverdeling en openbare financiën, Opstellen voor Jan Pen* [Income distribution and public finance, essays for Jan Pen]. Utrecht/Antwerpen: Het Spectrum, Aula Paperback.

8 FROM SAMUELSON'S STABILITY ANALYSIS TO NON-WALRASIAN ECONOMICS

Takashi Negishi

Samuelson's work on stability (collected in Samuelson 1947, pp. 257–349) contains the first rigorous attempt to analyze the dynamic stability of Walrasian tâtonnement. It is interesting, however, to see that a recent trend in microeconomics called non-Walrasian economics has developed, via the stability analysis of the so-called non-tâtonnement process, from this study of the most typically Walrasian problem.

THE SINGLE-MARKET CASE

Let us start with the case of a single market or, to be more exact, the case of two-good economy with the one good being numéraire. Samuelson considered the process of price change according to excess demand,

$$dp/dt = H[D(p) - S(p)], \qquad (8.1)$$

where $H(0) = 0$, $H' > 0$, and t, p, D, S signify respectively the time, price, demand, and supply of the nonnuméraire good. The equilibrium price, p^0, such that $D(p^0) = S(p^0)$, is locally stable — that is, for the solution of (8.1) with $p(0)$ close to p^0

$$\lim_{t \to \infty} p(t) = p^0, \qquad (8.2)$$

if $dD/dp - dS/dp < 0$ at p^0 — that is, the so-called Walrasian stability condition is satisfied.

The dynamic process (8.1) is, however, a special case of a more general process,

$$dp/dt = H[D(p) - S].\tag{8.3}$$

$$dS/dt = G[p - C(S)],\tag{8.4}$$

where $G(0) = 0$, $G' > 0$, $C(S)$ is an inverse supply function indicating marginal cost (supply price) of competitive suppliers as a function of output, and the consumers' adjustment to price change is assumed to be instantaneously made. If the speed of adjustment for supply is infinite, we have instead of (8.4)

$$p = C(S),\tag{8.5}$$

which can be solved for $S = S(p)$. By substituting it into (8.3), we obtain (8.1). The Walrasian stability condition is relevant, therefore, when the adjustment of supply to price is very quick.

On the other hand, if the speed of adjustment for the price is infinite, we have instead of (8.3)

$$D(p) = S,\tag{8.6}$$

which can be solved for $p = p(S)$ — that is, demand price. By substituting it into (8.4), we have the process of supply being changed according to the difference between demand and supply prices,

$$dS/dt = G[p(S) - C(S)],\tag{8.7}$$

the stability condition that Samuelson called the Marshallian stability condition. The Marshallian stability condition presupposes the Marshallian temporary equilibrium so that the market is always cleared by the quick adjustment of price for the given supply, while the adjustment of supply to price is rather slow. Although Samuelson seems to be considering the case of Marshall's long-run theory of normal price, it is also the case in Marshallian short-run theory, in which supply is slowly adjusted, under the given capital stock, to the price established in the temporary equilibrium.

In view of (8.5) and (8.6), the Marshallian stability condition is $1/(dD/dp) - 1/(dS/dp) < 0$ at p^0. Since Walrasian and Marshallian conditions are relevant for different specifications of speed of adjustment, however, there is no need to worry about the contradiction of the conditions when, in addition to the demand curve, the supply curve is downwardly sloping.[1]

Incidentally, an aim of the study of the stability condition is its use in comparative statics. Since the equilibria to be compared must be stable ones, the stability condition can be assumed to be satisfied and used to derive results in comparative statics, which is the correspondence principle suggested by Hicks (1946) and named by Samuelson. One must be careful, however, since the Walrasian and Marshallian stability conditions mentioned above are obtained by considering the linearly approximated equations of (8.1) and (8.7). The stability of the linearly approximated equation is sufficient, but not necessary, for the local stability of the original nonlinear equation, since the latter may have higher-order stability — a possibility that was also considered by Samuelson.[2]

THE CASE OF MULTIPLE MARKETS

Samuelson considered the stability of multiple markets, or the stability of an $n + 1$ good economy with the last good being numéraire, by

$$dp_i/dt = H_i[E_i(p_1, \ldots, p_n)], \quad i = 1, \ldots, n, \quad (8.8)$$

where p_i and E_i denote respectively the price and excess demand of the ith good. The condition for the stability of the linear differential equations approximated to (8.8) at the general equilibrium prices, $p^0 = (p_1^0, \ldots, p_n^0)$ such that $E_i(p^0) = 0, i = 1, \ldots, n$, is that the real parts of all the eigenvalues of an $n \times n$ Jacobian matrix $[H_i' \partial E_i / \partial p_j]$ evaluated at p^0 are negative. Samuelson further showed the necessary and sufficient condition for this stability condition, which is originally due to Routh and Hurwitz.[3]

Samuelson insisted that the so-called Hicksian stability condition, which is obtained by Hicks (1946) with a kind of generalization of the Walrasian stability condition for a single market into the case of multiple markets, is in general neither necessary nor sufficient for this so-called Samuelsonian dynamic stability condition. It can be shown, however, that the Hicksian condition for the imperfect stability of the ith market is the Samuelsonian dynamic stability condition for a special case of (8.8), where the adjustment speeds of other markets are assumed to be infinite; that is,

$$dp_i/dt = H_i[E_i(p_1, \ldots, p_n)] \quad (8.9)$$

$$0 = E_j(p_1, \ldots, p_n), \quad j \neq i.[4]$$

To derive the stability condition, Samuelson did not explicitly utilize such economically meaningful conditions as Walras's law and homogeneity, which must be satisfied by the excess demand functions E_i in (8.8). Following Metzler, therefore, he simply stated that the stability condition is identical to the Hicksian condition for perfect stability if all goods are gross substitutes — that is, $\partial E_i/\partial p_j > 0$, for all $i \neq j$. It was left for Arrow, Hurwicz, Hahn, and Negishi to show that (8.8) is locally stable if all goods are gross substitutes by using Walras's law or homogeneity:

$$\sum_{i=1}^{i=n} p_i E_i = 0, \tag{8.10}$$

or

$$\sum_{j=1}^{j=n} (\partial E_i/\partial p_j)p_j = 0.[5] \tag{8.11}$$

Morishima (1950) emphatically argued that the dynamic process described by (8.8) is the process of price change within a Hicksian week and not that of over weeks, and that exchange transactions among individuals are assumed not to be carried out or recontract is always possible until the general equilibrium is reached. Even for the adjustment process in a Hicksian week, this assumption of Walrasian tâtonnement is certainly too stringent. Although it does exist sometimes, such a way of auctioneering is very exceptional even in a well-organized exchange, let alone in less-organized competitive markets. If exchange transaction is permitted, however, at disequilibria, excess demand functions are shifted owing to the income effects, as was recognized by Hicks (1946), and the dynamic path of prices cannot be described by (8.8).[6]

DISEQUILIBRIUM TRANSACTIONS

A natural extension of Samuelson's stability analysis of Walrasian tâtonnement is, therefore, an attempt to introduce disequilibrium transactions and their effects on excess demands explicitly into the model, which is called the study of the non-tâtonnement process.

If we consider the most simple case — that is, that of pure exchange without production[7] — the tâtonnement process (8.8) is extended into the non-tâtonnement process

$$dp_i/dt = H_i[E_i(p,\overline{X})], \qquad i = 1, \ldots, n, \tag{8.12}$$

$$d\overline{X}_{ij}/dt = F_{ij}(p,\overline{X}), \qquad i = 1, \ldots, m, \qquad j = 1, \ldots, n, \tag{8.13}$$

where p is an n vector of p_i and $\overline{X}$ is an $m \times n$ matrix of $\overline{X}_{ij}$, the stock of the mth good held by the ith individual. Equation (8.13) describes how the stock of goods held by individuals is changed by the transactions among individuals, which are assumed very generally to be a function of prices and distribution of goods among individuals.

To make it more specific, Hahn and Negishi (1962) proposed a rule that transactions at disequilibria are carried out so that the condition

$$\text{sign } E_{ij} = \text{sign } E_i, \qquad \text{if } E_{ij} \neq 0, \qquad (8.14)$$

where E_{ij} signifies the excess demand of the jth good for the ith individual — that is, $\Sigma_i E_{ij} = E_j$. In words, if there is an aggregate surplus of a good, any individual who seeks to increase his stock can easily and quickly achieve his plan. If there exists, on the other hand, a shortage of a good, any individual who wants to dispose of his stock can easily and quickly do so. A trouble with (8.14) is that it may conflict with another plausible rule of transaction, that is, the rule of voluntary exchange or no overfulfillment,

$$F_{ij} \gtreqqless 0 \qquad \text{if } E_{ij} \gtreqqless 0. \qquad (8.15)$$

Arrow and Hahn (1971, pp. 337–46) solved this problem by introducing money explicitly into the model and by imposing (8.15) only on nonmonetary goods. After the sale and before purchase, at least temporarily, people often have more money than they want to keep ultimately.

As for equation (8.12), Clower (1965) insisted that in disequilibria notional income and realized income are different and the price change must be influenced not by the notional excess demand based on notional income but by the effective excess demand based on realized income.

By introducing money as the sole medium of exchange, Arrow and Hahn (1971) also took care of this problem, so that we are now almost at the gate of recent studies of non-Walrasian economics. If we suppose that the adjustment speed of price in (8.12) is very slow so that we can regard p as constant in (8.13), we have a standard model of recent non-Walrasian economics (i.e., the fixprice model of Barro and Grossman, Benassy, Dreze, Malinvaud, Younes, and so on). The condition (8.14) of non-tâtonnement stability analysis is nothing but the short-side principle that plays a central role in such a model of non-Walrasian disequilibrium analysis.[8]

It may not be out of place to give some comments on the fixprice model. The assumption of fixed price has to be questioned if one considers investment and saving in order to argue the microeconomic foundations of Keynesian economics. In the case of current markets with unexpected excess supply, price rigidity might be explained by the slow adjustment of prices relative to adjustment of output. If future excess supply is expected well in advance so that there is sufficient time to adjust capital stock, however, it is inconceivable that there is not enough time to adjust prices. This strongly suggests that fixed price should not be merely assumed, but should be explained endogenously. Unlike the case of homogeneous Walrasian markets where information is perfect, even a competitive supplier, who cannot raise the price by supplying less, has to perceive an inelastic demand curve for the amount of sale larger than the currently realized one in heterogeneous, non-Walrasian (i.e., Marshallian and Keynesian) markets where information is imperfect and the reduction of price made by a supplier might not be fully perceived by demanders who are currently buying from other suppliers. If the demand curve perceived is sufficiently inelastic, suppliers would not reduce price in the face of insufficient effective demand, even though they wish to sell more at the current price. This may explain, at least partly, the downward rigidity of price in the Keynesian situation.[9]

NOTES

1. See Samuelson 1947, pp. 263–64; Newman 1965, pp. 106–08; Negishi 1972, pp. 192–95. For the contradiction between Walrasian and Marshallian stability conditions, see Henderson and Quandt 1958, pp. 110–12.

2. See Samuelson 1947, pp. 258–60; Kemp 1964, pp. 59–62, for the comparative statics and stability. As for the higher-order stability, see Samuelson 1947, pp. 294–96.

3. See Samuelson 1947, pp. 269–71 and p. 434. Yasui (1948), on the other hand, discussed the stability condition of the difference equation version of (8.8) due to Schur and Cohn.

4. See Samuelson 1947, pp. 271–74. As far as I know, it was Furuya (1949) who first discussed the Hicksian condition by using (8.9).

5. See Samuelson 1947, pp. 273, 438 and Negishi 1972, pp. 195–97.

6. See Hicks 1946, p. 122 for the definition of the Hicksian week and pp. 127–29 for the effect of trade at disequilibria on demand function.

7. For the non-tâtonnement process with production, see Fisher 1976.

8. For the recent fixprice model, see Malinvaud 1980 and Negishi 1979, pp. 53–72.

9. See Negishi 1979, pp. 27–37, 87–98.

REFERENCES

Arrow, K. J., and F. H. Hahn. 1971. *General Competitive Analysis*. San Francisco: Holden-Day.

Clower, R. W. 1965. "The Keynesian Counter-Revolution: A Theoretical Appraisal." In F. H. Hahn and F. P. R. Brechling, eds. *The Theory of Interest*. New York: Macmillan.

Fisher, F. M. 1976. "The Stability of General Equilibrium: Results and Problems." In H. J. Artis and A. R. Nobay, eds. *Essays in Economic Analysis*. Cambridge, England: Cambridge University Press.

Furuya, H. 1949. "Keizaikinko no Anteibunseki" [Stability analysis of economic equilibrium]. Department of Economics, University of Tokyo. *Rironkeizaigaku no Shomondai* [Problems in economic theory]. Tokyo: Yuhikaku.

Hahn, F. H., and T. Negishi. 1962. "A Theorem on Non-Tâtonnement Stability." *Econometrica* 30:463–69.

Henderson, J. M., and R. E. Quandt. 1958. *Microeconomic Theory*. New York: McGraw-Hill.

Hicks, J. R. 1946. *Value and Capital,* 2nd ed. London: Oxford University Press.

Kemp, M. C. 1964. *The Pure Theory of International Trade*. Englewood Cliffs, N.J.: Prentice-Hall.

Malinvaud, E. 1980. *Profitability and Unemployment*. Cambridge, England: Cambridge University Press.

Morishima, M. 1950. *Dogakuteki Keizairiron* [Dynamic economic theory]. Kyoto: Kobundo.

Negishi, T. 1972. *General Equilibrium Theory and International Trade*. Amsterdam: North-Holland.

————. 1979. *Microeconomic Foundations of Keynesian Macroeconomics*. Amsterdam: North-Holland.

Newman, P. 1965. *The Theory of Exchange*. Englewood Cliffs, N.J.: Prentice-Hall.

Samuelson, P. A. 1947. *Foundations of Economic Analysis*. Cambridge, Mass.: Harvard University Press.

Yasui, T. 1948. "Keizaitekikinko no Dogakuteki Anteijoken" [Dynamic stability condition of economic equilibrium]. *Keizai-Shicho* 9:1–30.

9 SAMUELSONIAN THEORY AND THE PROCESS OF CHANGE

Earl F. Beach

When Friedman reviewed the Jaffé translation of Walras's great work, he concluded with a significant statement:

> This conception — or rather misconception — of economic theory has helped to produce an economics that is far better equipped in respect to form than of substance. In consequence, the major work that needs to be done is Marshallian rather than Walrasian in character. [Friedman 1955, p. 909]

Samuelson's work is very much in this Walrasian tradition. In the introductory chapter to his *Foundations,* he made it quite clear that the form of the analysis is to be considered to be the "foundations" of analysis.

In contrast, Marshall's use of the word in the Preface to the eighth edition of the *Principles* is quite different:

> The main concern of economics is thus with human beings who are impelled, for good or evil, to change and progress. Fragmentary statical hypotheses are used as temporary auxiliaries to dynamical — or rather biological — conceptions: but the central idea of economics, even when its Foundations alone are under discussion, must be that of living force and movement. [Marshall 1920, p. xv]

Marshall was very careful in his use of words, and it is notable that this key word begins with a capital letter. Thus, when Samuelson announced that "Marshall's dictum . . . should be exactly reversed," he signaled a very different approach.[1]

NEOCLASSICAL THEORIZING

Late in the nineteenth century, the newer tools of analysis that were fashioned shifted interest toward the theory of value and made it the keystone of economic analysis as a whole. The work of Cannan in criticizing the classics helped to emphasize logical consistency. Frank Knight's work was also in this tradition; he found Marshall's theory seriously deficient (1921, p. 15): "almost anti-theoretical."

Logical consistency is a valuable aid to analysis, but it can be frustrating to innovative thought. It has been so during the twentieth century. Emphasis on value theory, supported by an array of analytical tools that are suitable to it, has inhibited the development of a theory of evolutionary change that was begun by Smith and Marshall. Instead of real change, there is but pseudochange, or alternative positions of equilibrium.

Samuelson's approach is part of this trend. He has played a leading role in building up an impressive array of analytical tools and has applied them to a wide range of problems. It is the technique, however, that is to him the interesting and important aspect of his analysis. His discussion of and, indeed, his approach to a problem are dictated by the technique that he chooses to use. This is in contrast to the suggestion of Phelps Brown (1972, p. 8) that a clinical approach should be tried; the problem is studied first, and then the various techniques are assessed for their suitability.

The development of technique is not unimportant, and Samuelson has performed a valuable service for the profession in keeping in touch with developments in other scientific fields. This emphasis on technique has, however, been so great that it has resulted in distortion of the results. This may be seen in a comment by Hahn and Matthews in their noted review of growth theory:

> Considering the prominent part played by *increasing returns* in past discussions of growth since Adam Smith, the mainstream of the recent neoclassical theory has neglected it to a surprising extent. . . . The reason for the neglect is no doubt the difficulty of fitting increasing returns into the prevailing framework of perfect competition and marginal productivity pricing. [Hahn and Matthews 1964, p. 833]

The word "neglect" is too gentle a word to be used in this situation. The concepts of perfect competition and marginal productivity pricing are key elements of mainstream technique, and increasing returns (the italics are used by the authors!) has surely been one of the most characteristic aspects of economic development of the last two or three centuries. The theoretical apparatus has played too strong a role in determining what problems are to be selected for study.[2]

The dominating influence of technique may be seen to determine the analytical approach. The elementary text by Lipsey and Steiner (1972) treats the analysis of industry in a way that appears strange to those who are not attuned to current methods of economic analysis. In the short run, capital is fixed. In the long run, capital may be varied. Technological change is varied only in the very long run and exogenously. Students show some skepticism of an approach that is so much at variance with their own observation that technology is changing frequently, almost continuously, and much of it in response to economic variables.

The power of "The Noxious Influence of Authority" (Jevons 1931, p. 275) was felt personally when a manuscript was rejected by an editor of a professional journal on the ground that I employed the concept of an average period of unemployment in the analysis of technological unemployment. Presumably such a concept has no place in a comparison of two equilibrium positions, when "jobs" are lost permanently. Thus, the concept is ruled out in such analysis, even though government statisticians regularly make estimates of the average.

Allyn Young expressed fears of such a situation fifty years ago:

> I suspect, indeed, that the apparatus which economists have built up for dealing effectively with the range of questions to which I have just referred may stand in the way of a clear view of the more general or elementary aspects of the phenomena of increasing returns. [Young 1928, p. 527]

Young was then attempting to stem the tide toward formal analytical technique, which was undermining the credibility of Marshall. Sraffa and Robbins, in criticizing Marshallian theory, used the assumption of the conditions of equilibrium, inferring that Marshall did also. He did not do so, and hence their criticisms were inappropriate (see Beach 1979).

One more example. Recently Samuelson produced "The Canonical Classical Model of Political Economy," in which Smith is bunched with the rest. The model turns out to be:

> . . . self-propelled into development by capital accumulation and parallel population growth . . . to their long-run equilibrium rates when they barely earn their costs of reproduction. . . . The classicists earned for our subject Carlyle's title of the dismal science precisely because their expositions erred in overplaying the law of diminishing returns and underplaying the counter-

forces of technical change. They lived during the industrial revolution, but scarcely looked out from their libraries to notice the remaking of the world. [Samuelson 1978, pp. 1426, 1428]

It could be argued that the classical political economists were more familiar with the real world than are most modern neoclassical theorists. Smith was noted for his habit of observation, and his work shows it. Ricardo made himself wealthy while still young. J. S. Mill had a lifetime job with the East India Company.

There are, however, much more important items in the quotation to be criticized, such as the inclusion of Smith with such a model. It was not by inadvertance. The article begins with his name, and in the literary appendix the question is considered whether the model "minimized the basic differences between . . . Ricardo . . . [and] Smith." Samuelson replies to his own question as follows:

The considered answer I would give is this: "Yes, Ricardo differed with Smith, and thought these differences important. But upon detailed examination, we find that their differences do not mainly involve differences in their behavior equations, short-run or long-run, but rather involve their semantic preferences about what names could be given to the same agreed-upon effects. To moderns, it is a quarrel about nothing substantive, being carried out by Ricardo, often with somewhat unaesthetic logic. [Samuelson 1978, p. 1430]

It is a travesty to state that Smith "underplayed" technological change. The opening pages of *The Wealth of Nations* show that the division of labor is at the heart of economic change and development. The first three chapters are devoted to the subject. Throughout the book there is little that would support the idea that the earnings of workers are to be squeezed toward subsistence. It was not Smith who earned Carlyle's description.[3]

Consider, in contrast, two authors who were not blinded by the neoclassical apparatus. Young carried on with the development of the Marshallian analysis of industry. He concentrated on

. . . Adam Smith's famous theorem that the division of labour depends upon the extent of the market. That theorem, I have always thought, is one of the most illuminating and fruitful generalizations which can be found anywhere in the whole literature of economics. In fact, as I am bound to confess, I am taking it as the text of this paper. [Young 1928, p. 529]

Better known for his work in history, Fay gave this judgment of Smith:

His prodigious feat was to take over a theory of dynamic growth from the panoply of force and apply it to wellbeing. Before him power was dynamic, driven home by sword and shot. He taught the nations to find it in the peaceful act of getting a living, in the making of pins and watches, in butchering, brewing and the like. Viewed historically, this change was "a revolution of the greatest importance to the public happiness." [Fay 1930, pp. 27–28]

The internal quote is from *The Wealth of Nations*.[4]

ECONOMIC MODELING

The construction of theoretical models has become a way of life for economic theorists. In this way the interrelations of a number of variables can be appraised and tested, a distinct advance over purely literary attempts to explain such relations.[5]

The exogenous variables, which represent the outside causative forces, are separated from the endogenous variables, which have their equilibrium values determined by the restraints of the model. It is important to observe that these latter are assumed to be equilibrating toward a stable equilibrium, with equilibrating forces that are strong enough to make the operation meaningful. Each of these points deserves examination.

If the equilibrium is not stable, but unstable, then the endogenous variables move away from the equilibrium point, and the model is of little help. If the equilibrating forces are continually offset by countervailing forces, we may never get close enough to the equilibrium point for the equilibrium to be realistic.

This latter point is important. Schumpeter describes at length such countering forces in the early pages of his *Business Cycles* (1939). Theorists seem to feel that it is enough to determine that the equilibrium exists and that it is stable, both "in the small" and "in the large." Little is known about how close we may be to an equilibrium at any time, and there is not much discussion of how such a "distance" might be measured.[6]

There is, indeed, some ambivalence. Theorists wish the system to be close enough to equilibrium that their equilibrium equalities may be imposed, and yet it is the movement toward equilibrium,[7] not the position itself that is of interest. Chipman states:

> . . . equilibrium is a state of affairs in which things are at rest. It is obvious, however, that things which never change would not warrant much study. The real content of the equilibrium concept is to be found not so much in the state itself as in the laws of change which it implies: that is, in the tendencies to move towards it, away from it, or around it. [Chipman 1965a, p. 36]

Samuelson has given a classification of static and dynamic systems (1947, Chap. 11), but the only form of endogenous movement is that of an equilibrating variable toward its equilibrium. The equilibrium positions themselves are changed only as the result of exogenous change. There is no form of endogenous movement that changes the equilibrium (except when a longer-run equilibrium shifts a shorter-run equilibrium) or results in a movement that is not equilibrating.

This is not just a quibbling over esoteric matters. There are two pesky variables that any respectable economic model should internalize as endogenous variables but that seem to have no easily designated equilibrium levels. They are productivity and capital. The rate of investment may be conceived of as an equilibrium flow, but it has long been supposed that an economy will adjust to any level of capital that exists. Similarly, the level of productivity is seen to move in response to economic pressures, and yet it is not easy to conceive of an equilibrium level of productivity in an economy at any time.

Clearly, the type of mathematical model that is so generally used in economic theorizing is incapable of fitting the complexity of life itself, as Schrodinger has noted.[8] Why should we have such faith in them, or indeed in the "fundamental"[9] nature of equilibrium itself? It will be suggested below that there is an alternative that is better suited to a theory of change, as against a theory of condition, relevant to a theory of value.[10]

DIFFICULTIES WITH THE EQUILIBRIUM OF A FIRM

A consumer is assumed to make the best use of the spending money available by making the proper choice of goods to buy. The job is likely to be done well if the consumer is familiar with the situation, so that knowledge is adequate, and prices do not change very much. Even when the circumstances are not ideal, the consequences of a shortfall from an optimum are unlikely to be serious (cf. Georgescu-Roegen 1966, p. 119).

In contrast, a firm that seeks to make the best use of its resources in competition with other firms may face serious consequences if it does not achieve its optimum. In a perfect competition situation, that firm will be eliminated. When competition is not "perfect" but vigorous, strenuous efforts may have to be made in order to avoid catastrophe. The number of bankruptcies attests to the difficulties.

There is another important way in which these two equilibrium situations differ. A consumer who does not attain a maximum may have another chance on next week's trip to the supermarket, and sometimes it is possible to return unwanted articles that were selected too quickly. On the other hand, a firm that is not in equilibrium will find that changes are not so easy. If equipment has been rented it may be changed when the lease expires; firms that own their own capital goods will require longer periods to adjust. Labor contracts and government restrictions impose additional burdens. Clearly there is a longer and more painful adjustment entailed. Time[11] and additional resources are usually required, but that is not all.

Compare a firm that makes its own equipment with a firm that hires it or buys it from another. The second firm will make some assessment of its situation and plan changes accordingly. The first firm is not finished when it has made a cost-benefit study and has decided on changes to be made. It must also plan the financing and manning of the making of the new equipment to be installed.

It is generally assumed that the effects of a particular firm can be aggregated to those of an industry, or even a whole economy.[12] This is to assume that all firms make their own equipment, like the first firm above, and to miss some important interfirm effects — that is, when one firm decides to alter its production equipment, other firms feel the effects in their demands. Discussions of technological unemployment have long suffered from this kind of myopia.[13]

Consider Samuelson's analysis of induced innovation (1965). A neoclassical production function, in both a micro and a macro sense, is assumed, with all of the proper derivatives, and his "short-run equilibrium" displays the appropriate equivalences between derivatives and factor prices. On page 344 he notes that "a director of research and development, who makes a decision about innovational effort, would find it valuable to know about the feasible effects." As stated above, a cost-benefit study is usually helpful, but is not enough to tell us about the consequences of change. In moving from a micro to a macro model, he deems it sufficient to "drop the assumption that factor prices are constant" (p. 346). He should recognize that actual movement entails time and resources and interfirm effects.

Pigou (1929, Pt. IV, Chap. 4) tried to work with integrated industries,[14] which included their "subsidiary industries," and he mentioned the difference between "waiting" and "capital," even though he was not successful in taking them all into account. Samuelson ignores these problems of adjustment, which Salter emphasized.

The neoclassical production function treats factors as equivalent and interchangeable, but it has long been recognized that capital is not a factor like the others, since it requires labor in its production. This becomes important when considering changes such as those that Samuelson contemplates. Samuelson does recognize that some of his assumptions may be "monstrous" (1965, p. 345), but he does not hesitate to apply his results to the real world:

> Be it noted that the argument does not rest upon wages being in some sense "high." High compared to what? . . . Nor does the argument apply to a land-rich country like America. [Samuelson 1965, p. 349]

Later he examines the historical literature in the light of his findings. He states that "Wicksell corrected what appears to be one of Ricardo's rare outright errors . . ." by using "the first modern discussion of technical change and distribution." (ibid., pp. 353–54). This "modern technique" is, of course, the use of equilibrium theorizing, indeed, equilibrium conditions. Ricardo may have been "in error" (see Beach 1971), but Wicksell's equilibrium technique is not generally suitable for this kind of analysis.

Samuelson makes further presumptions that are based on his neoclassical theorizing. On p. 355: "We have the unfortunate tendency to use labor as the denominator in making productivity statements." Yes, and for very good reasons, in particular because we have a special interest in the welfare of that factor. Furthermore, Samuelson should be reminded that he has himself stated: "Such computed value totals, it need hardly be said, cannot be fed into production functions, kicked, or leaned against" (1966, p. 523).

The technical apparatus of the production function seems to have seduced its users into forgetting that the factors are not interchangeable entities, but have personalities of their own. In particular, an increase in capital, in real form, entails an increase in the use of labor, at least in a macro function. Yet, Samuelson states:

> For the most part, labor-saving innovation has a spurious attractiveness to economists because of a fortuitous verbal muddle. . . . That this is all fallacious becomes apparent when one examines a mathematical production function and tries to describe in advance whether a particular described invention changes the partial derivatives of marginal productivity imputation one way or another. [Samuelson 1965, p. 355]

Would such an abstract production function tell us as much as more mundane calculations? Here it is important to know what is meant by "capital," which he nowhere attempts to make clear. Yet, if it is in terms of physical capital, one factor for each type of machine, then it must be recognized that these machines include stored-up labor. If, on the other hand, he is dealing with abstract "waiting," he is then assuming a time frame that is long enough for the production and using up of such machines to be unimportant, and such a time frame is so absurdly long as to be quite unrealistic. It is quite clear that he leans too heavily on his theoretical apparatus.

FACTOR SUBSTITUTION

The analysis of the causes and effects of factor substitution is of special interest because of its practical importance and because it brings out sharply the weaknesses of the method of equilibrium theorizing. Samuelson has given it attention at various times. In his Stamp Memorial Lecture in 1961, he offered "A Bouquet of Problems," in which the third was:

> . . . the alleged effects of alleged automation on unemployment and real wages. Never did so many write so much that is nonsense and inconclusive as on this topic . . . a murky issue. [Samuelson 1966, p. 1673]

In the same year he produced, in the Akerman volume, "A New Theorem of Nonsubstitution" (ibid., pp. 520–36), which is an analysis of the effects of an increase in wages on the likelihood of mechanization. His answer is clear from the title. The increase in wages will, *in time,* become part of the cost of the machines. He feels free to neglect the "short-term" effect in applying his finding to real-life situations. He wonders briefly why such a wage increase might occur in the first place, a problem that is imposed by his theoretical apparatus.

The proof of the theorem is based on a comparison of two points of equilibrium, a once-for-all change. Short-run adjustments are recognized, but the equilibrium conditions are taken to be the important aspect to be analyzed, and he dismisses "simple-minded people" and "scientists who prattle about automation." He does appeal to "cold statistics" and finishes with a parable to answer:

> . . . the final question: Suppose society learns how to make robots that are very close substitutes for man himself? What will the effect of that be on real wages paid to man? [Samuelson 1966, p. 534]

The robots are then produced in a state of perfection, which reminds one of "the celebrated winch argument" of Sismondi (Gide and Rist 1913, p. 181), in which a king of England does all the work of the island by turning a winch. It is, of course, implicitly assumed that (1) there is no need to fuel or maintain the machines, (2) they need not be replaced, and (3) they are in such a state of perfection that no improvement is contemplated. Samuelson's robots have a given life span and are regularly replaced, but by other robots! It seems clear that the proof of Samuelson's theorem under static conditions — and other simplifying conditions, only some of which he removes — is considered by him to be adequate, and no consideration need be given to continuously changing conditions, some of which are endogenous, like saving or "waiting."

Kaldor (1932) had suggested that the optimistic conclusions of equilibrium theory follow straightforwardly from the assumptions, and detailed proof is often thought to be unnecessary. Simon (1965) used this form of theorizing to show that automation does not rob workers of jobs, but only increases real wages, under extremely simplifying assumptions, and yet twice in the course of the argument he suggested that bored readers may jump to the conclusions at the end.

Yet it is the detail of this form of argument that must be examined with care. Salter (1966) tells us that equilibrium theory does not fit the real world, especially when technological change and factor substitution are entailed. It is important to be precise as to why this is so.

COMPARATIVE STATICS VERSUS REAL CHANGE

The effects of a shift in demand are usually shown with a "Marshallian cross." In this way a shift in demand from a labor-intensive commodity to a capital-intensive commodity is presumed to result in a reduction in the demand for labor [Neisser 1942]. In contrast, a continuing shift, as in the shift from coal to electricity, or from horses to motor vehicles, continued over very long periods, with rather continuous pressure to increase the capacity to produce the favored commodity and its related commodities. Clearly such shifts did not result in a lessening in the demand for labor while they were taking place — which is to say, over some decades — and when they were complete, the economy was transformed, so that a comparison before and after would have little meaning.

Consider the process of mechanization that went on in the textile industry in England during the Industrial Revolution. Most studies confine their attention to the textile industry, but during this period of, say, a century, there was a shift in employment from the textile industry to the machine industry, which was storing up the labor in textile-making machinery. Similarly, employment was shifted from agriculture to the industries that made machinery and supplies for the farmers. Yet equilibrium theory consists of comparing two points on an isoproduct curve of a production function, ignoring the new investment that is required to get from one point to the other, even in this case of mechanization, in which, by definition, there is an increase in the use of capital. It has been shown, moreover, that the amount of employment created by the act of storing up is large relative to the loss in employment from the displacement (Beach 1971).

Some economists (Morawetz 1974) think that they have adequately recognized the effects of the investment when they have taken into account the replacement of the new machinery through depreciation allowances. The inadequacy of this approach is seen in the discussion of the "naive argument" (Beach 1979). The changing of the production technology by the original introduction of such machines is a very different thing from subsequently preserving that new technology by allowing for the continuation of the employment of such machines. The former changes the number of "workplaces"; the latter merely preserves them.

Perhaps the greatest fear of all has been that of "automation." Ever since (and perhaps before) Montesquieu complained about the employment effects of the building of windmills in the middle of the eighteenth century, such a fear has been expressed in some form. The intensity of the fear varies with the level of economic activity, and usually there is some new technological breakthrough that can be found to hold new fears; the more capital intensive and labor saving, the greater the fear. Equilibrium theorists have not been successful in convincing others. It is time that another way be tried, one that does not ignore the fact that the more capital-intensive the automation, the more stored up labor will be entailed (Beach 1980).

Marshall was interested in real change and repeatedly warned about the misuse of "statical theory," but such warnings have since been forgotten in the professional pressure to make the theory more "precise" and "consistent." It is appropriate to be reminded that:

> the statical theory of equilibrium is only an introduction to economic studies; and it is barely even an introduction to the study of the progress and development of industries which show a tendency to increasing return. Its limitations are so constantly overlooked, especially by those who approach it from an abstract point of view. [Marshall 1920, p. 461]

Sraffa's classic attempt to "tidy up" Marshallian theory fell into this trap. He assumed the firm to be in equilibrium, whereas Marshall's firms were not in equilibrium and did have "normal access to the economies, external and internal, which belong to that aggregate volume of production.'' Thus Sraffa's criticism of Marshallian theory was inappropriate. Furthermore, Marshall did not assume perfect competition. Sraffa continued to use Marshall's term *free competition* but in his hands it assumed more and more the implications of uniformity of price rather than the older and more robust assumption of freedom of entry.

On the same grounds, Robbins's criticism of the representative firm was not relevant.[15] Samuelson's chapter in the Kuenne volume (1967) is a particularly vituperative tirade about Marshall's refusal to use the *conditions* of equilibrium and bespeaks his misunderstanding of Marshall's model of industrial change (Beach 1979).[16]

Samuelson's desire to reverse Marshall's dictum requires a further comment. In his Ely Lecture, Georgescu-Roegen quoted at length a criticism of ''blind symbolism'' by ''a well-known British Engineer'':[17]

> Contrary to common belief it is sometimes easier to talk in mathematics than to talk in English; this is the reason why many scientific papers contain more mathematics than is either necessary or desirable. Contrary to common belief it is also less precise to do so. For mathematical symbols have a tendency to conceal the physical meaning that they are intended to represent; they sometimes serve as a substitute for the arduous task of deciding what is and what is not relevant. . . . It is true that mathematics cannot lie. But it can mislead.
>
> However, the dangers of over-indulgence in formula spinning are avoided if mathematics is treated, wherever possible, as a language into which *thoughts may only be translated after they have first been [clearly] expressed in the language of words*. The use of mathematics in this way is indeed disciplinary, helpful, and sometimes indispensable. [Georgescu-Roegen 1970, p. 1]

SOME CONSEQUENCES

Some of the neoclassical theorists have recognized that some of their assumptions are extreme, but they have always consoled themselves that there is no alternative body of theory. I have suggested that there is such an alternative, and in some ways, at least, it is better. It fits reality better. It predicts the employment consequences of change better. It implies that the economy is indeed, as Marshall emphasized, a biological entity, which should be treated as such, maintained in good health, and expected to respond by growing and adjusting. In the past two centuries, such a ''pragmatic'' economy has produced better results in terms of output, equality of distribution, and indeed of such noneconomic characteristics as tolerance, than have the more idealistic societies based on presumably fairer theories, such as communism, or theology.

In contrast, the Samuelson approach implies a constantly sick or incompetent economy that needs the continuing attention and bolstering of a government.[18] One may well ask whether the Industrial Revolution would have developed better — or indeed at all — if the government had had as much control of the economy as it does today. The earlier indications were that technological change should be severely limited. The consequences of this point of view in dealing with the current debates over the role of government are obvious.

NOTES

1. This interest in technique is again emphasized in his 1970 Nobel Lecture (1972). Samuelson has, of course, been much interested in the real world and has taken an active part in policy formulation and in politicking. Hence his lack of interest in the fitting of his models is disturbing. It might be argued that Samuelson is considering the foundations of *analysis* while Marshall was considering the foundations of economics, but that would be quibbling. There can be little doubt that Marshall was interested in analyzing economic forces just as much as is Samuelson, who states in the last paragraph of his introductory chapter of the *Foundations*: "My own interest in mathematics has been secondary and subsequent to my interest in economics" (1947, p. 6).

2. Ferguson's popular text dismisses the subject: "The phenomenon of decreasing cost is not examined inasmuch as it is not consistent with all the requirements of perfect competition" (1972, p. 276).

3. Baumol (1959) finds his "magnificent dynamics" in the work of Ricardo and Malthus. Smith is not even listed in his index. When he comes to Marshall, the only item of importance is his market equilibration system, contrasted, as usual with one named after Walras (see Beach 1979). Hicks (1965) is one of the few who pays much attention to Smith and Marshall in a discussion of growth theory.

4. The *JEL* of March 1980 carried a discussion of the progress of the pin industry since Smith's time. The history of the pin industry before *The Wealth of Nations* is of a great deal more interest. In the fourteenth and fifteenth centuries, pins were an expensive and scarce item. Parliamentary laws gave them special attention, and limited their sale to certain days of the year. Money was saved in preparation for such times, and the term *pin money* has become an interesting item in the language, even though its meaning has changed with the value of the objects themselves. A revolution in the production of pins had brought down the price of pins by the eighteenth century, and Smith's choice of the pin as an example of the division of labor was made with a lesson in mind that seems to have been lost on most of his readers. Despite Schumpeter's derisive remark, Smith did indeed understand what was going on around him.

5. One may wonder whether Marshall might soften his insistence on the translation of mathematics into words if he were faced with the models employed by modern theorists, but it should be kept in mind that Marshall himself worked out the elements of a mathematical model of growth in his early years and apparently discarded it (see Whitaker 1974).

6. I once amused myself by setting up a computer program that would measure the relative change from one period to the next in a set of national accounts, or in the items of an international balance of payments of a country. The relative change in each item was

squared and weighted, and the total of such squares gave the total amount of change from one period to another. A plotting of such a total over a period would show when such change was minimal and hence provide a base for greater change. In this way, countries and times can be compared in respect to intensity of change; a lack of equilibrium is implied, the distance from equilibrium being directly related to the amount of change activity.

7. On the same page as the quote, Chipman makes a curious statement: "Equilibrium . . . is a concept as fundamental in economics as it is in physics. The reason it is so fundamental is that the concept is much more complex than might at first be supposed."

8. See Georgescu-Roegen 1966, p. 415.

9. See note 7 above.

10. The fitting of production functions has been an active sport of econometricians. Kotowitz estimated the elasticity of demand for labor for Canadian manufacturing industries and concluded:

> For the industries which appear to fit these conditions, it is clear that a change in wages has a small influence relative to technological and demand conditions. This analysis suggests that wage reductions are not an effective tool in regaining employment lost due to changes in demand for output or labour saving technical change. [Kotowitz 1969, p. 112]

As a test, I fitted regressions to similar Canadian data on wages, output, and investment, first to contemporary data, and then to data arranged to remove the contemporaneous investment effects — that is, the wage and output data were lagged by one, two, three, and four years, while investment was cumulated. I found a dramatic change in sign in the wage coefficient, showing a great difference between a relation among contemporaneous figures and figures that were adjusted to allow for the disappearance of the investment effect.

11. See Salter:

> . . . it is obviously impossible to employ the long-period schema for the analysis of technical change and productivity; for, by definition, the long-period approach assumes away the adjustment process which leads to this gap. Moreover, once we admit the existence of continuous disturbance and slow adjustment, the long-period framework is unsuitable for analysis of the cost and price movements accompanying technical change. [Salter 1966, p. 7]

12. Green (1964) and Gupta (1969) have pointed out the requirements for simple aggregation, which are very severe. Yet it is common practice to imply macro effects from simple aggregation of micro effects (see Beach 1975). Nelson and Winter (1974) have experimented with a simulation model of evolutionary growth, but have not allowed for interfirm and interindustry effects adequately.

13. See Beach 1971.

14. Hicks (1932) notes Pigou's contribution in this area, but Pigou is not mentioned by Hahn and Matthews (1964, p. 825). It is interesting to note that Pigou's treatment bears some similarity to that of Johnson (1906), although there is no mention by Pigou of the earlier article.

15. See Stigler 1976, p. 215, and Chipman 1965b on Allyn Young.

16. Samuelson has had a penchant for digs at Marshall (see 1966, p. 53).

17. Georgescu-Roegen (1970) quotes these words from Kapp, *Towards a Unified Cosmology*, (New York, 1960), p. 111. The italics are those of Georgescu-Roegen, who makes

no reference here to Marshall or to Samuelson. See also Krehm 1975, Appendix B, where physicists are seen to have done just as Kapp suggests.

18. This may be seen in the 1966 edition of the Samuelson introductory text (Samuelson and Scott 1966, pp. 363–65).

REFERENCES

Baumol, W. J. 1959. *Economic Dynamics*. New York: Macmillan.

Beach, E. F. 1971. "Hicks on Ricardo on Machinery." *Economic Journal* 81 (324):916–22.

———. 1975a. "Marxian Analysis." *Industrial Relations* 30 (4):772–75.

———. 1975b. "Marshall and Samuelson in Perspective." *Eastern Economic Journal* 2 (3), Supp., pp. 164–74. Proceedings of the 1974 Convention, July.

———. 1978. "Modèles statiques et modèles dynamiques en développement économique." *L'Actualité Economique* (October-December), pp. 539–49.

———. 1979. "Towards a Realistic Dynamics." *Journal of Economics* 5:39–41.

———. 1980. "A Search for a Theory of Change." *Journal of Economics* 6:161–64.

Chipman, J. S. 1965a. "The Nature and Meaning of Equilibrium Theory." In D. Martindale, ed. *Functionalism in the Social Sciences*. Philadelphia: American Academy of Political and Social Science.

———. 1965b. "A Survey of the Theory of International Trade: Part 2: The Neo-classical Theory." *Econometrica* 33:736–49.

———. 1970. "External Economies of Scale and Competitive Equilibrium." *Quarterly Journal of Economics* 84 (3):347–85.

Fay, C. R. 1930. "Adam Smith and the Dynamic State." *Economic Journal* 40 (157):25–34.

Ferguson, C. E. 1972. *Microeconomic Theory*. Homewood, Ill.: Irwin.

Friedman, Milton. 1955. "Walras and His Economic System," *American Economic Review* 45 (5):900–09.

Georgescu-Roegen, N. 1966. *Analytical Economics*. Cambridge, Mass.: Harvard University Press.

———. 1970. "The Economics of Production." *American Economic Review* 60 (2):1–9.

Gide, C., and C. Rist. 1913. *A History of Economic Doctrines*. Trans. from the French edition of 1913. Boston: Heath (no date).

Gordon, R. A. 1976. "Rigor and Relevance in a Changing Institutional Setting." *American Economic Review* 66 (1):1–14.

Green, H. A. J. 1969. *Aggregation in Economic Analysis: An Introductory Survey*. Princeton, N. J.: Princeton University Press.

Gupta, K. L. 1969. *Aggregation in Economics: A Theoretical and Empirical Study*. Rotterdam: Rotterdam University Press.

Hahn, F. H., and R. O. C. Matthews. 1964. "The Theory of Economic Growth: A Survey." *Economic Journal* 74 (296):779–902.

Harrod, R. F. 1949. *Towards a Dynamic Economics*. London: Macmillan.
Hickman, B. G. 1965. *Investment Demand and U.S. Economic Growth*. Washington, D.C.: Brookings.
Hicks, J. R. 1932. *Theory of Wages*. London: Macmillan.
———. 1965. Capital and Growth. London: Oxford University Press, 1965.
Jevons, W. S. 1931. *The Theory of Political Economy*. London: Macmillan.
Johnson, A. 1906. "The Effect of Labor-Saving Devices upon Wages." *Quarterly Journal of Economics* 20:86–109.
Kaldor, N. 1932. "A Case against Technical Progress?" *Economica* 12:180–96.
Knight, F. H. 1921. *Risk, Uncertainty and Profit*. Boston: Houghton Mifflin.
Kotowitz, Y. 1969. "Technical Progress, Factor Substitution and Income Distribution in Canadian Manufacturing 1926–39 and 1946–61." *Canadian Journal of Economics* 2 (91):106–14.
Krehm, W. 1975. *Price in a Mixed Economy: Our Record of Disaster*. Toronto: Thornwood.
Lipsey, R. G., and P. O. Steiner. 1972. *Economics*. New York: Harper & Row.
Machlup, F. 1958. "Equilibrium and Disequilibrium: Misplaced Concreteness and Disguised Politics." *Economic Journal* 68 (269):1–24.
Marshall, A. 1920. *Principles of Economics*. London: Macmillan.
Morawetz, D. 1974. "Employment Implications of Industrialisation in Developing Countries." *Economic Journal* 84 (335):491–542.
Morgenstern, O. 1972. "Thirteen Points in Contemporary Economic Theory: An Interpretation." *Journal of Economic Literature* 10 (4):1163–89.
Neisser, H. 1942. "'Permanent' Technological Unemployment." *American Economic Review* 32 (1):50–71.
Nelson, R. R., and S. G. Winter. 1974. "Neoclassical vs. Evolutionary Theories of Economic Growth: Critique and Prospectus." *Economic Journal* 84 (336):886–905.
Phelps Brown, E. H. 1972. "The Underdevelopment of Economics." *Economic Journal* 82 (325):1–10.
Pigou, A. C. 1929. *The Economics of Welfare*. London: Macmillan.
Robbins, L. 1928. "The Representative Firm." *Economic Journal* 38 (151):387–404.
Salter, W. E. G. 1966. *Productivity and Technical Change*. Cambridge, England: Cambridge University Press.
Samuelson, P. A. 1947. *Foundations of Economic Analysis*. Cambridge, Mass.: Harvard University Press.
———. 1965. "A Theory of Induced Innovation along Kennedy-Weisäker Lines." *Review of Economics and Statistics* 47 (4):343–56.
———. 1966. *The Collected Scientific Papers of Paul A. Samuelson*. 2 vols. Ed. by J. E. Stiglitz. Cambridge, Mass.: MIT Press.
———. 1967. "The Monopolistic Competition Revolution." In R. E. Kuenne, ed. *Monopolistic Competition Theory: Studies in Impact*. New York: Wiley.
———. 1972. "Maximum Principles in Analytical Economics." *American Economic Review* 62 (3):249–62.

———. 1978. "The Canonical Classical Model of Political Economy." *Journal of Economic Literature* 16 (4):1415–35.

———, and A. Scott. 1966. *Economics*. Toronto: McGraw-Hill.

Schumpeter, J. A. 1939. *Business Cycles*. New York: McGraw-Hill.

Shubik, M. 1970. "A Curmudgeon's Guide to Microeconomics." *Journal of Economic Literature* 8 (2):405–34.

Simon, H. A. 1965. *The Shape of Automation for Men and Management*. New York: Harper & Row.

Solow, R. M. 1965. *Capital Theory and the Rate of Return*. Chicago: Rand McNally.

Sraffa, P. 1926. "The Laws of Returns under Competitive Conditions." *Economic Journal* 36 (144):535–50.

Stigler, G. J. 1976. "The Xistence of X-Efficiency." *American Economic Review* 66 (1):213–16.

Whitaker, J. K. 1974. "The Marshallian System in 1881: Distribution and Growth." *Economic Journal* 84 (333):1–17.

Young, A. 1928. "Increasing Returns and Economic Progress." *Economic Journal* 38 (152):527–42.

II TRADE THEORY AND WELFARE ECONOMICS

10 SAMUELSON AND TRADE THEORY:

From the Methodological Perspective

Henry Y. Wan, Jr.

It is both an honor and a considerable intellectual challenge to evaluate in this essay the impact of Samuelson's contributions. The relationship between Samuelson and trade theory is unique. When Samuelson started his work, trade was already an established field, imprinted with the footsteps of Ricardo, Mill, Edgeworth, and Marshall, to cite a few. With his wide-ranging interests Samuelson could never devote his effort exclusively to trade. Between 1938 and 1954 he published his first dozen trade-related articles. Interspersed in between are his two books and another sixty essays, all on other subjects. Yet, by 1954 he had totally transformed the landscape of trade theory, a feat unsurpassed by any other economist, past or living.

One must now dispel a misconception. Samuelson did not achieve all this because he was *the first* economist bombarding the field with *the most* mathematics. Functional equations and fixed point theorem had been hurled at economics and related areas in late 1920s, a decade ahead of Samuelson.

To attain so much during his crowded research life, Samuelson, the researcher, had to be selective to the extreme. He drew strength from his deep grasp of the nature and needs of economics and his commitment to meet such needs. Of course, his analytical prowess, his expository skill, and his indefatigable vitality all played important roles. But his unique strength lay in his perception. His perception enabled him to identify issues that are both researchable and enduringly significant, to formulate models that are both tractable and pragmatically relevant, and to limit his research scope to landmark propositions, leaving the extensions and generalizations to other economists.

Today, many results and methods pioneered by Samuelson have become the standard content of the undergraduate curriculum on trade. His professional impact is fully attested in authoritative textbooks and survey articles, in manners more eloquent than I can ever possibly emulate. Yet within his seminal papers there lies a most precious lesson, which students rarely learn — the research strategy underlying the spectacular fruitfulness of his contributions. It should be important to all economists, present or yet unborn, just as Cannae is important to generations of cadets at St. Cyr and Sandhurst twenty-two centuries after the passing of war elephants. In the present essay, research strategy is our theme.

Samuelson himself is, of course, a methodologist of the first order, yet it is never his style to illuminate his discourses with his own citations. I think that it is apropos today to conjecture and to discuss those factors instrumental to Samuelson's success; the master has the full opportunity to favor us by correcting our misconceptions. In today's world most young economists are beleaguered by surrogate payoffs of tenure promotions, awards, and honors. To them, the personal example of Samuelson should be most inspiring. He is an example of the rare scholar, fully committed to the true mission of his profession and, in return, honored by his profession for such commitment.

TANQUAM EX LEONUM—
SPECIAL FEATURES OF SAMUELSON'S WORK

Throughout Samuelson's papers on international trade, several features are ever present. The subject is usually rooted in policy discussions. The model is invariably formulated as a general equilibrium. Special assumptions are introduced to obtain sharp conclusions. There often exist situations in which the approximate validity of those assumptions is self-evident.

Economics is a social science, receiving social attention for its relevance to policy. In each of Samuelson's major findings, the subject is traceable to earlier literature with real-life significance. The trading gain problem dates back to classical advocacies for free trade. The factor price equalization problem evolves from the views of Heckscher and Ohlin. The Stolper-Samuelson theorem is related to the unions' traditional concern about competition from cheap foreign labor. The transfer issue harks back to the German indemnity discussions. Samuelson is never attracted to a theorem only because of its elegance.

Trade theory explains commodity exchanges among agents. To recognize fully "mutual interdependence" and "simultaneous determination," Samuelson adheres exclusively to models of general equilibrium.

For certain problems (e.g., compensated trading gain), the general equilibrium framework yields sharp results under most robust conditions. For other problems equally significant in trade (e.g., factor price equalization), the more general formulations do not provide relevant implications. Instead of confining himself to isolated, annecdotal examples or to concluding that anything might happen, Samuelson typically searches for meaningful sufficient conditions to prove the desired theorems. For applied fields, such specialized general equilibrium models are most fruitful in his hands. In addition to trade theory, he also employed such models for public goods as well as consumption loans.

One might observe that the simpler the special conditions, the more insights one may obtain. Ideally, the satisfaction of those conditions may be self-evident under some circumstances (e.g., petrochemical production is *unambiguously more capital intensive* than garment making). Much of Samuelson's work involves conditions that require little quantitative information to verify. As he noted in his *Foundations,* it is precisely in such cases that qualitative theoretic analysis has its strongest justification for existence — eliminating the necessity to run elaborate simulations. We now turn to the major areas of Samuelson's work for illustration.

GAINS FROM TRADE

Ever since the days of Ricardo and Mill, economists have grappled with the problem of trading gain under various assumptions. From his work on welfare economics, Samuelson recognized that, in general, the opening of trade may benefit some persons and harm others. Avoiding interpersonal welfare comparisons, Samuelson asked whether the opening of trade could be made harmless to all citizens under some compensations. In a series of three papers written in 1938, 1939, and 1962 (Samuelson 1966, pp. 775–801), Samuelson showed that the answer is yes if the country has no influence on the world prices, and the answer is still yes if the country has influence, but some external tariff is imposed.

Typically, Samuelson's papers have been trailblazers that have inspired future research. Take his gains from trade papers, for example. The method of his proof was a harbinger of the axiomatic economics that flourished much later. The theorems he has proved also represent a class of subsequent results including (1) the potential harmlessness of the opening of free trade for all countries, without cross-country compensation (Grandmont and McFadden 1972); (2) the potential harmlessness of the opening of free trade, for one country, given other countries' demands, without cross-country compensation (Kemp and Wan 1972); and (3) the potential harmlessness of the formation of customs unions, without compensations across the union boundary. All these results hold under great generality (Grinols 1980). In retrospect, Samuelson's decisive choice of studying the compensated trading gain (rather than the uncompensated gains) is responsible for his having achieved definite and objective results.

FACTOR PRICE EQUALIZATION

The notion that countries with different factor endowments may face identical factor prices is not new, according to Chipman's masterful survey (1966). This was discovered and rediscovered by half a dozen economists independently over the thirty years between 1919 and 1948. Samuelson's papers in 1948–1949 (1966, pp. 847–85) galvanized much of the profession overnight. The original two-factor, two-product case was extended to the general case of any number of factors and products, extensive interpretations were made of such propositions, and alternative sufficient conditions were given. This advanced knowledge in mathematics as well as in economic theory. In all such works, Samuelson played a central role.

It is our task, however, to ask why the basic result gathered dust for thirty years but suddenly became fashionable in Samuelson's hand. A careful sifting of the evidence shows there is no mystery and it is no coincidence. To early discoverers of the result, the proposition is an isolated phenomenon, either not important enough to merit early publication or deserving only a passing reference of a few pages. To Samuelson (1966, p. 888), it is central to the cost-production duality in general equilibrium, and it is a natural extension of the mathematical theorems on implicit functions. He alone appreciated the full potential of the result and devoted time and effort to bring out its various ramifications and convince the profession of what the result is worth, despite its apparent inconsistency with daily experience. Like Ms. Doolittle in *My Fair Lady,* while dozens may identify her as the girl next door, it takes Professor Higgins to mastermind her meteoric transformation.

RECIPROCITY THEOREM, STOLPER-SAMUELSON THEOREM, AND THE SAMUELSON-RYBCZYNSKI THEOREM

Clearing up the literature on tariff and welfare, which started with Adam Smith, the Stolper-Samuelson theorem (1966, pp. 831–46) showed that labor is unambiguously hurt by a reduction of the tariff on labor-intensive imports. The feat was achieved both through the use of a general equilibrium analysis and through the postulation of various sufficient conditions. This celebrated result generated an entire literature that tested its generalizability in various directions. Samuelson (1966, pp. 888–901), meanwhile, related this result to the factor price equalization theorems he derived. He showed that the Stolper-Samuelson theorem has its dual: the Samuelson-Rybczynski theorem that a population increase will raise the output of the labor-intensity product. Both of these were then shown to be special cases of the reciprocity theorem: The output response to an input increment equals the factor price response to a product price increment. Both the reciprocity theorem and the factor price equalization theorem were then shown to be implications of a general equilibrium model under constant returns and without joint product.

Samuelson's work in this sphere illustrates several facts. First, his deep grasp of the general equilibrium structure enabled him to derive various theorems in trade. Second, his overall vision of microeconomic theory helped him to combine the isolated results into an integrated system. Third, his perseverance allowed him to pursue logical reasoning to its natural conclusions, despite the apparent lack of realism of some theorems (e.g., factor price equalization) and the obvious unpopularity of some other results (e.g., the Stolper-Samuelson theorem).

Samuelson's 1953 article essentially completed the Heckscher-Ohlin-Samuelson paradigm. It has since become *the* principal paradigm in trade, and it admits a wide range of possibilities for extension, generalization, and adaptation, not only in trade but also in allied fields like development. But unlike many other scholars, Samuelson is never a single-paradigm researcher. Leaving the extension and generalization of the H-O-S model largely to other economists, he experimented with alternative formulations [e.g., the admission of a stock-capital along with a flow-labor as inputs (Samuelson 1972, p. 356), the incorporation of a production lag in the Ricardian technology, or the postulation of a Ricardo-Viner model in which each product is produced with one sector-specific input together with an all-purpose labor input (Samuelson 1977, pp. 594 and 667)]. For Samuelson each model idealizes some aspects of reality. Insight is obtained by considering these tractable models, one at a time. This outlook is shared by physicists. Recognizing that atoms possess both corpuscular and wave properties, physicists make progress by considering models dealing with either aspect in isolation.

THE TRANSFER PROBLEM AND BALANCE OF PAYMENT ADJUSTMENT

Another topic Samuelson clarified definitively is the transfer problem of Keynes and Ohlin. Reasoning in the context of fully specified models of general equilibrium, he delineated where deduction ends and subjective estimation starts, an exemplary *policy analysis* that deserves emulation. After his fixed production models without or with trade impediments, Samuelson synthesized (1972, p. 356) the first general equilibrium model with Ricardian technology, Marshallian preferences, and alternative mechanisms for balance of payment adjustments, including the gold flow scheme of Hume. Such a model has much to offer to the studies of international finance literature today.

THE CONTINUUM OF GOODS MODEL

Space allows me only to mention Samuelson's latest contribution: the Dornbusch-Fischer-Samuelson (1977) model with a continuum of goods. This formulation is especially suitable for studying the determination and variation of the product mix that is produced and traded. Since each commodity has only a negligible share in resource and expenditure allocation, such a model sidesteps the complexity that some marginal good may be produced in more than one country.

Such models appear most relevant today. The erosion of competitiveness of traditional industries and the development of new products are events of paramount importance to both advanced and developing economies. The continuum of goods model is likely to be a key for analyzing such issues.

A SIMPLE THOUGHT

At this point it is conventional to sum up the *Leibenswerk* of the scholar. This is obviously out of the question in the present case, since Samuelson's productivity is at its prime. In fact, as one of his former students, I am always waiting avidly for the next installment — the next volume of Samuelson's collected scientific papers, the next, the next, and. . . .

It appears fitting, nonetheless, to quote what apparently came *first* to Samuelson's mind when he wrote the *first* paragraph of his *first* article on trade:

> Historically, the development of economic theory owes much to the theory of international trade. . . . the classical theory of international trade rose in the thoughts of "practical" men, interested as *citizens* in problems of public policy. [Samuelson 1966, p. 775]

This is a digression about the very beginning; it is perhaps also a suggestion about the ultimate end all theoretical research must serve. Characteristically, in most of Samuelson's papers on trade theory, allusions to their pragmatic implications are made with care.

REFERENCES

Chipman, J. S. 1966. "A Survey of the Theory of International Trade, Part 3." *Econometrica* 34 (1):18–76.

Dornbusch, R., S. Fischer, and P. A. Samuelson. 1977. "Comparative Advantage, Trade and Payments in a Ricardian Model with a Continuum of Goods." *American Economic Review* 67 (5):823–39.

Grandmont, J.-M., and D. McFadden. 1972. "A Technical Note on Classical Gains from Trade." *Journal of International Economics* 2 (2):109–25.

Grinols, E. 1981. "An Extension of the Kemp-Wan Theorem on the Formation of Customs Unions." *Journal of International Economics* 11, forthcoming.

Kemp, M. C., and H. Y. Wan, Jr. 1972. "The Gains from Free Trade." *International Economic Review* 13 (3):509–22.

Samuelson, P. A. 1966. *The Collected Scientific Papers of Paul A. Samuelson.* 2 vols. Ed. by J. Stiglitz. Cambridge, Mass.: MIT Press.

———. 1972. *The Collected Scientific Papers of Paul A. Samuelson,* Vol. 3. Ed. by R. C. Merton. Cambridge, Mass.: MIT Press.

———. 1977. *The Collected Scientific Papers of Paul A. Samuelson,* Vol. 4. Ed. by H. Nagatani and K. Crowley. Cambridge, Mass.: MIT Press.

11 SAMUELSON AND WELFARE ECONOMICS

John S. Chipman

In this essay I try to show how Samuelson, in four major works, has made a unique contribution that has set up welfare economics as a separate discipline: the study of the relationships between economic policies and value judgments. This contribution, which grew out of Bergson's seminal work, has consisted of setting up a formal framework for the description and classification of value judgments and the analysis of their relationships to economic systems and policies. By an exact example I make precise his point that an improvement in potential welfare can bring about a reduction in actual welfare in terms of some value judgments. I also go through the detailed argument to show how separability of the social ordering leads to the possibility of optimal decentralized decision making according to that ordering. I finally make a plea

This work was supported by National Science Foundation grant SES–7924186 and a fellowship from the John Simon Guggenheim Memorial Foundation. Any opinions, findings, and conclusions or recommendations in this paper are those of the author and do not necessarily reflect the views of the National Science Foundation. I have had the advantage of Samuelson's reactions to the original draft of this essay; it should be pointed out, however, that my interpretations can in no way be considered as constituting an "approved version" of his work and indeed may in places be considerably at variance with his views.

for a "revealed preference" approach to welfare economics and indicate ways in which the structure Samuelson has built can be used to determine configurations of empirical assumptions and implicit value judgments that are consistent with observed economic systems and policies.

When one examines the field of welfare economics today, one cannot help but be struck by the large extent to which it has been shaped by Samuelson's contributions. These have consisted in furnishing a general framework for the discussion of policy questions, comprising a few key concepts that have made it possible to achieve a better understanding than existed heretofore of the relationships between value judgments and policy recommendations.

THE UTILITY-POSSIBILITY FRONTIER AND THE CONCEPT OF POTENTIAL IMPROVEMENT

One of the key concepts was that of a utility-possibility frontier, introduced in Samuelson's fundamental contribution to the subject of the "evaluation of real national income" (1950).[1] Hicks (1940) had argued that a national-income comparison of the form $p^2 \cdot x^2 > p^2 \cdot x^1$, where x^t is the aggregate consumption bundle in period t, and p^t is the price vector in period t, would permit the inference that "real social income" was higher in period 2 than in period 1 because, as he argued, it would not be possible to redistribute bundle x^1 among the m individuals in such a way as to make them each as well off as they were in period 2 with aggregate consumption bundle x^2. He considered the logical possibility that one might also observe the opposite inequality $p^1 \cdot x^1 > p^1 \cdot x^2$, but dismissed it on the grounds that (1940, pp. 112–13) "something has gone wrong with the assumptions. The most likely explanation will usually be that we are dealing with a situation to which our original hypothesis of constant wants is inapplicable." Samuelson (1950, p. 2) interpreted Hicks in this passage to be assuming the Weak Axiom of revealed preference to hold for the community. He pointed out that one could easily find examples in which it is violated.[2]

He then introduced the concept of a utility-possibility frontier associated with a particular aggregate commodity bundle x, defined with reference to a set of cardinal utility functions[3] $U^i(x_i)$, where $x_i = (x_{i1}, x_{i2}, \ldots, x_{in})$ is the bundle consumed by individual i, $i = 1, 2, \ldots, m$; given these utility functions, Samuelson's concept is strictly analogous to the concept of a production-possibility frontier, with utility functions taking the place of production functions and consumption bundles taking the place of factor-input combinations. Thus, defining the *utility-possibility set* as

$$\mathbb{U}(\mathbf{x}) = \left\{ u = (u_1, u_2, \ldots, u_m): u_i = U^i(\mathbf{x}_i), \sum_{i=1}^{m} \mathbf{x}_i = \mathbf{x} \right\}, \quad (11.1)$$

the *utility-possibility frontier*[4] is defined as its outer boundary

$$\hat{\mathbb{U}}(\mathbf{x}) = \{u \in \mathbb{U}(\mathbf{x}): u' \geq u \text{ for no } u' \in \mathbb{U}(\mathbf{x})\}, \quad (11.2)$$

where $u' \geq u$ means that $u_i' \geq u_i$ for all i and $u_i' > u_i$ for at least one i, $i = 1, 2, \ldots, m$.

On this basis, Samuelson introduced the concept of potential welfare improvement. A bundle $\mathbf{x}^2$ is said to be *potentially better* than a bundle $\mathbf{x}^1$ if and only if for all $u' \in \hat{\mathbb{U}}(\mathbf{x}^1)$ (i.e., for all points u' on the utility-possibility frontier for $\mathbf{x}^1$) there exists a $u'' \in \hat{\mathbb{U}}(\mathbf{x}^2)$ (a point u'' on the utility-possibility frontier for $\mathbf{x}^2$) such that $u'' \geq u'$. This requires the utility-possibility frontier for $\mathbf{x}^2$ to lie uniformly outside (though possibly touching at some points) the utility-possibility frontier for $\mathbf{x}^1$. Samuelson pointed out that the 1940 Hicks criterion consisted in defining $\mathbf{x}^2$ to be superior to $\mathbf{x}^1$ provided only that the utility-possibility surface for $\mathbf{x}^1$ passed below the point u^2 on the utility-possibility surface for $\mathbf{x}^2$ corresponding to the actual allocation of $\mathbf{x}^2$ among individuals in the observed situation. In fact, he pointed out that to reach this conclusion, Hicks's 1940 reasoning had to be supplemented by a proof that if $\mathbf{p}^2 \cdot \mathbf{x}^2 > \mathbf{p}^1 \cdot \mathbf{x}^1$, then there exists a *Pareto-optimal* allocation of $\mathbf{x}^1$ that is Pareto inferior to the given allocation of $\mathbf{x}^2$; he provided an ingenious geometric proof of this for the two-commodity, two-individual case (1950, p. 8n.).[5] He went on to point out, however, that this did not prevent $\hat{\mathbb{U}}(\mathbf{x}^1)$ from lying above $\hat{\mathbb{U}}(\mathbf{x}^2)$ in a neighborhood of some other point $\bar{u}^2 \in \hat{\mathbb{U}}(\mathbf{x}^2)$ (see Figure 11.1).

THE SOCIAL WELFARE FUNCTION

The significance and proper interpretation of Samuelson's criterion for potential improvement cannot be adequately appreciated except in conjunction with his concept, borrowed from Bergson (1938), of a social welfare function (Samuelson 1947, pp. 219–28). Bergson had expressed social welfare as a function of the amounts of commodities allocated to individuals as well as the allocation of factor services, the latter defined with reference to the particular employments of labor services and the particular industries in which labor was employed. Introducing some

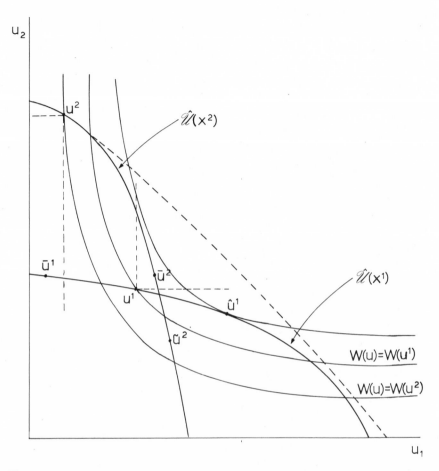

Figure 11.1

additional postulates, notably indifference as to alternative occupations (his Postulate 4), the requirement that "individuals' preferences are 'to count'" (Postulate 5), and absence of externalities in consumption (Postulate 6), Samuelson simplified the social welfare function to the separable form[6]

$$W[U^1(\mathbf{x}_1), U^2(\mathbf{x}_2), \ldots, U^m(\mathbf{x}_m)] \equiv F(\mathbf{x}_1, \mathbf{x}_2, \ldots, \mathbf{x}_m). \quad (11.3)$$

It should be stressed that in introducing these postulates, Samuelson's avowed aim was to provide a convenient framework for analyzing and classifying various commonly (and usually only implicitly) held ethical principles and beliefs and, in particular, for studying and isolating those combinations of empirical assumptions and ethical principles from which one could deduce the optimality of competitive equilibrium. In his words:

> It is a legitimate exercise of economic analysis to examine the consequences of various value judgments, whether or not they are shared by the theorist, just as the study of comparative ethics is itself a science like any other branch of anthropology. [Samuelson 1947, p. 220]

From this point of view, the seven postulates enumerated by Samuelson leading to a social welfare function of the form (11.3) should be judged not on their intrinsic merits or ethical appeal to the enlightened welfare economist, but rather on their empirical realism as an appropriate description of the general principles that are actually applied in the policy-making process, or at least can reasonably be inferred to provide an adequate explanation of observed policy behavior.

Let us consider now the manner in which Samuelson employed the concept of a social welfare function to justify his criterion of potential welfare improvement. If we are given two bundles x^1 and x^2, it is only when the utility-possibility frontier for x^2 lies entirely outside that of x^1 (i.e., when for each $u' \in \mathfrak{U}(x^1)$ one can find a $u'' \in \mathfrak{U}(x^2)$ such that $u'' > u'$) that one can be sure that for *any* social welfare function $W(u_1, u_2, \ldots, u_m)$ that is a strictly increasing function of its arguments [in the sense that $u'' \geq u'$ implies $W(u'') > W(u')$], the maximum of W over $\mathfrak{U}(x^2)$ will exceed the maximum of W over $\mathfrak{U}(x^1)$.

This justification contains two components. The first is acceptance of the Paretian value judgment involved in the partial ordering of allocations. If we denote by X^t the $m \times n$ matrix whose rows are the m allocations $x_i^t = (x_{i1}^t, x_{i2}^t, \ldots, x_{in}^t)$ of the aggregate commodity bundle $x^t = \Sigma_{i=1}^m x_i^t$ among the m individuals, and by

$$u^t = U(X^t) \equiv (U^1(x_1^t), U^2(x_2^t), \ldots, U^m(x_m^t)) \qquad (11.4)$$

the corresponding vector of utilities $u_i^t = U^i(x_i^t)$, allocation X^2 is defined as Pareto superior to allocation X^1 (which may be written $X^2 P X^1$) if $U(X^2) \geq U(X^1)$. Writing (11.3) in the form $W[U(X)] = F(X)$, in accepting the Paretian value judgment, we assume that $X^2 P X^1$ implies $F(X^2) > F(X^1)$, which requires W to be increasing in the sense defined above. An ethical judgment may be defined as "relatively *wertfrei* (value free)" if it holds for all increasing social welfare functions W. This much is fairly uncontroversial.

The second component is the crucial one. It is an essentially *empirical* hypothesis that "society" acts so as to maximize *some* increasing social welfare function $W(u)$ over $\mathfrak{U}(x)$, for each aggregate commodity bundle x; the observed situations being compared must be assumed to be optima in terms of the same increasing W function — no matter which. Unless this empirical assumption is made, the potential-welfare criterion cannot (within Samuelson's framework) be described as "relatively value-free."

Samuelson illustrated this point in many ways. One of his examples (1950, p. 12) is depicted geometrically in Figure 11.1. Two competitive equilibria are compared, and information is supplied concerning the price vector $\mathbf{p}^t$ and the aggregate consumption bundle $\mathbf{x}^t$ in each of two periods $t = 1,2$. It is given that $\mathbf{p}^2 \cdot \mathbf{x}^2 > \mathbf{p}^2 \cdot \mathbf{x}^1$, so that the Hicks criterion is satisfied — that is, there exists a Pareto-optimal allocation $\overline{\mathbf{X}}^1$ of $\mathbf{x}^1$ that is Pareto inferior to the actual allocation $\mathbf{X}^2$ of $\mathbf{x}^2$ in the second period, so that (see Figure 11.1)

$$u^2 \equiv U(\mathbf{X}^2) \geq U(\overline{\mathbf{X}}^1) \equiv \bar{u}^1. \tag{11.5}$$

It is also given that the famous "double criterion" of Scitovsky (1941) is satisfied — namely, that there exists in addition a (Pareto-optimal) (re)allocation $\overline{\mathbf{X}}^2$ of $\mathbf{x}^2$ that is Pareto superior to the actual allocation $\mathbf{X}^1$ of $\mathbf{x}^1$ in the first period — that is,

$$\bar{u}^2 \equiv U(\overline{\mathbf{X}}^2) \geq U(\mathbf{X}^1) \equiv u^1. \tag{11.6}$$

In these circumstances it cannot be the case that $\mathbf{p}^1 \cdot \mathbf{x}^1 > \mathbf{p}^1 \cdot \mathbf{x}^2$, since this would imply (by the previously cited result) that there existed a Pareto-optimal allocation $\overline{\mathbf{X}}^2$ of $\mathbf{x}^2$ that was Pareto inferior to $\mathbf{X}^1$, so that $U(\overline{\mathbf{X}}^2) \geq U(\mathbf{X}^1) \geq U(\overline{\mathbf{X}}^2)$, contradicting the assumed Pareto optimality of $\overline{\overline{\mathbf{X}}}^2$. Hence it follows that $\mathbf{p}^1 \cdot \mathbf{x}^2 \geq \mathbf{p}^1 \cdot \mathbf{x}^1$, and Kuznets's (1948) "base reversal test" is satisfied. Nevertheless, as Figure 11.1 makes clear, for the given social welfare function W we have $W(u^1) > W(u^2)$. Moreover, the optimum point is $\hat{u}^1 \in \hat{\Pi}(\mathbf{x}^1)$.[7]

This can be seen more explicitly as follows (see Figure 11.2). Let us suppose that $m = n = 2$, and that two competitive equilibria are observed with prices $\mathbf{p}^1 = (3,4)'$ and $\mathbf{p}^2 = (4,4)'$ and aggregate quantities $\mathbf{x}^1 = (6,6)$ and $\mathbf{x}^2 = (4,9)$ respectively, with the respective allocations

$$\mathbf{X}^1 = \begin{bmatrix} 39/8 & 39/128 \\ 9/8 & 729/128 \end{bmatrix}, \mathbf{X}^2 = \begin{bmatrix} 243/80 & 27/80 \\ 77/80 & 693/80 \end{bmatrix}, \tag{11.7}$$

where it is assumed that the two individuals' preferences can be represented by the respective utility functions

$$U^1(x_{11}, x_{12}) = (3x^{\frac{1}{2}}_{11} + x^{\frac{1}{2}}_{12})^2, \quad U^2(x_{21}, x_{22}) = (x^{\frac{1}{2}}_{21} + 3x^{\frac{1}{2}}_{22})^2. \tag{11.8}$$

Since $\mathbf{p}^2 \cdot \mathbf{x}^2 = 52 > 48 = \mathbf{p}^2 \cdot \mathbf{x}^1$, the Hicks criterion is satisfied, and thus there exists a Pareto-optimal allocation of $\mathbf{x}^1$ that is Pareto inferior to $\mathbf{X}^2$. (An example of such an allocation, as can be readily verified from (11.8),

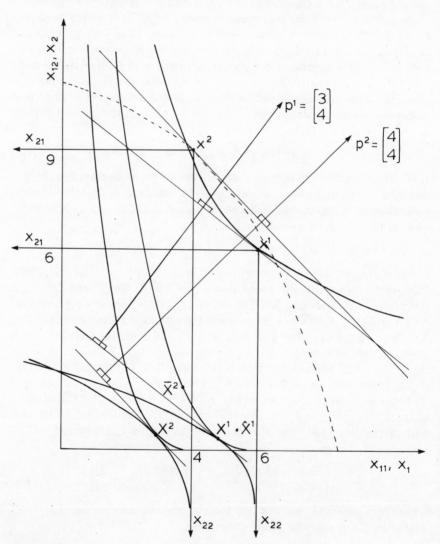

Figure 11.2

is that in which all of bundle x^1 is allocated to individual 2.) On the other hand, it can be seen that the Scitovsky criterion is also satisfied, since the allocation $\overline{X}^2$ of x^2 defined by

$$\overline{X}^2 = \begin{bmatrix} 3.75 & 1.86686 \\ .25 & 7.13314 \end{bmatrix} \tag{11.9}$$

leaves individual 1 just as well off as under the allocation X^1, but makes individual 2 better off (since $U^1(3.75, 1.86686) = 51.49 = U^1(39/8, 39/128)$ and $U^2(.25, 7.13314) = 72.46 > 67.57 = U^2(9/8, 729/138)$). This is seen in Figure 11.2 by the fact that the "Scitovsky indifference curve" (see Scitovsky 1942), showing the locus of all points at which both individuals would be at the same utility level as at X^1, passes beneath the point x^2. Because of this we must have $p^1 \cdot x^2 \geqq p^1 \cdot x^1$; and indeed we have $p^1 \cdot x^2 = 48 > 42 = p^1 \cdot x^1$.

Now to make Samuelson's point precise, we may choose a social welfare function W of the (symmetric) form

$$W(u_1, u_2) = (u_1^{-2} + u_2^{-2})^{-1/2}; \tag{11.10}$$

with this particular function we verify from (11.7) and (11.8) that

$$W[U(X^1)] = 40.96 > 31.85 = W[U(X^2)]. \tag{11.11}$$

We may also note that, by symmetry, the optimal allocation of $x^1 = (6,6)$ (in terms of W) is the competitive allocation at prices $p = (1,1)$, which is

$$\hat{X}^1 = \begin{bmatrix} 27/5 & 3/5 \\ 3/5 & 27/5 \end{bmatrix}, \tag{11.12}$$

and comparing this to (11.9) we have, by (11.8) and (11.10),

$$W[U(\hat{X}^1)] = 42.43 > 41.97 = W[U(\overline{X}^2)]. \tag{11.13}$$

It should be noted that the above conclusion that $W(u^1) > W(u^2)$ would remain unchanged if the utility-possibility curve for x^2 were altered so as to dominate that for x^1, as indicated by the dashed curve in Figure 11.1, showing that situation 1 could be judged ethically preferable to situation 2 (in terms of some increasing symmetric social welfare function) even though the latter is potentially superior in Samuelson's sense. This possibility is shown in Figure 11.2 by the dashed production-possibility frontier associated with the point x^2, which lies uniformly outside of that associated with x^1. This illustrates the objection raised by Samuelson (1950, pp. 11–12) against the framework introduced by Kaldor (1939) and Hicks (1939), according to which the welfare problem can be divided into two parts: an economic-efficiency problem, which is the concern of the

t, and a politico-distributive problem, which is the concern of
ßamuelson pinpointed the difficulty in the following passage:

> the new welfare economics cannot make the definite statement: "The
> ~ ı Laws should be repealed, and the owners should *not* be compensated."
> It can only assert in a negative way: "'Twere better that the Corn Laws be
> repealed, and compensation be paid, *if necessary*." It gives no real guide to
> action. [Samuelson 1947, p. 250]

In Chipman and Moore (1978, pp. 579–80), the issue was posed in the
following way: If it is given in advance that the economic policy adviser
is operating in a "collectivist environment," in which it is known that
income distribution will be manipulated so as to maximize a social welfare
function, then the potential-welfare criterion provides a positive guide to
action; whereas if the policy adviser is operating in a "laissez-faire environment," advice based on the potential-welfare criterion could be
irresponsible, in the sense that it could lead to an outcome that represents
a deterioration in social welfare in terms of *some* value judgments. Even
this way of posing the issue should be subjected to some qualification,
however. In the first place, such a formulation depends on the prior
acceptance of Samuelson's postulates, including in particular what might
be called "Postulate 0" to the effect that a set of ethical beliefs can be
represented as a total ordering of allocations. Many thoughtful writers
(e.g., Little 1949, 1950, and Mishan 1962, 1980) recoil from the idea that
such all-encompassing comparisons can always be made, or that it is
necessary in building a theory of welfare economics to assume that they
are always capable of being made. Even if one disagrees with such a
position, as long as one adheres to the objective empirical approach to
welfare economics originally set forth by Samuelson in the *Foundations*
(1947, p. 220) as quoted above, one has to accept an explicitly nontotal
ordering of allocations as representing a legitimate system of value judgments that a complete theory of welfare economics should be able to
accomodate.

Thus, some would argue that "society" has a strong social obligation
to prevent any of its members from sinking below a certain level of
poverty or distress, but that it has no obligation to perform wholesale
"social engineering" among those above the poverty line.[8] Such a point
of view has been described as "conservative" by Arrow (1951c) and
Meade (1959), on the grounds that it tends in practice to favor the status
quo; but this need not at all be the case. If, for example, one actively
adopts a potential-welfare criterion in the knowledge that no one's utility
will be allowed to fall short of a certain critical level, policies designed

to switch the economy to (uniformly) potentially superior situations (e.g., the introduction of labor-saving machinery or of free trade) may inflict definite hardships on some. The classic illustration is precisely that of the landlords after the repeal of the Corn Laws; another is Hotelling's illustration (1938, p. 267) of "the hand weavers who tried to wreck the power looms that threatened their employment." Whether one describes such a position as "liberal" (in the old-fashioned sense) or "conservative," it seems deserving of the status of a widely accepted system of value judgments. While Samuelson has convincingly shown that the "'twere better" (or "let-the-chips-fall-where-they-may") precept cannot find a place in *his* system, it remains possible that it could be fitted into an explicitly partially ordered ethical system — the principal difficulty being that of finding a rule in such a system for sharing the burden of necessary compensation.[9] Nevertheless — and this must not be forgotten — such a "rugged individualist" philosophy could not be passed off as "relatively *wertfrei*," as the early new welfare economists believed; it would represent a very definite system of value judgments.

A second qualification needs to be made to the position that adoption by the economic policy adviser of the potential-welfare criterion can be justified in an environment in which it is known that some other agency is taking measures to distribute income in such a way as to maximize some social welfare function. While it is true that the rule yields an optimal result (in terms of W) no matter what W is chosen, the justification is vacuous unless a particular W *is* chosen. And as Arrow (1951b) has shown, there is no reasonable way to build up democratically a consensus social ordering of allocations (and associated F function) from the individual orderings of allocations (corresponding to the individual $F(X) = W[U(X)]$ functions reflecting the ethical beliefs of the different members of society). In short, no particular W can be put into place except by intimidation. And needless to say, policies resulting from an *imposed* W function will invariably lead to a reduction in social welfare in terms of some *individual* W functions.

In his seminal paper on social utility, Samuelson (1956) suggested a different way of arriving at a W function: by a kind of consensus, analogous to that of a family. In an extreme form, such a consensus would not be incompatible with Arrow's results; one can imagine a Hobbesian social contract in which society (tacitly) submits to a firm but fair dictator in return for law and order and the protection of property and certain freedoms. The theoretical problem of formulating the process of social consensus has so far proved extremely elusive. Arrow's use of the ethically loaded term "dictator" has perhaps made the profession unduly reticent in acknowledging the ubiquity of compulsion in everyday life, even in the most liberal democracies. Dictatorship is resented and resisted when there is some chance of its being overcome, but accepted — even cheerfully — if there is no chance of dislodging it. If one substitutes the word "taxation" for "dictatorship," this fact may be more readily acknowledged.

Difficult as it may be to formulate the process whereby a family or nation arrives at a social compact, it is nevertheless quite legitimate and reasonable to assume as an empirical hypothesis that the family does so; and once this is granted, it is only a matter of degree of empirical realism, and no longer a matter of principle, to accept the hypothesis that the nation does so. Accordingly, how does such a society act, and how does it or can it achieve its aims in a decentralized fashion? That is the key question posed in Samuelson's classic 1956 paper.

THE SOCIAL UTILITY FUNCTION AND THE OPTIMAL DISTRIBUTION OF INCOME

Formally, the problem is simply that of maximizing $W(u)$ over the utility-possibility set (11.1) to determine the optimal allocations $\mathbf{x}_i = \xi_i(\mathbf{x})$ of each $\mathbf{x}$; this defines the "social utility function"

$$U_W(\mathbf{x}) = \max W[U(\mathbf{X})] = W[U(\Xi(\mathbf{x}))] \qquad (11.14)$$
$$\sum_{i=1}^{m} \mathbf{x}_i = \mathbf{x},$$

where $W[U(\mathbf{X})]$ is shorthand for (11.3) and $\mathbf{X} = \Xi(\mathbf{x})$ is the allocation matrix that maximizes $W[U(\mathbf{X})]$ for $\sum_{i=1}^{m} \mathbf{x}_i = \mathbf{x}$. If the individual utility functions U^i can be and are chosen to be increasing and concave, it can be shown (and is well known from the analogous problem in production theory) that the utility-possibility set (11.1) is convex. Further, if W is assumed to be continuous, concave, and weakly increasing [in the sense that $u \geqq u'$ implies $W(u) \geqq W(u')$ and $u > u'$ implies $W(u) > W(u')$], it can be shown that the function U_W of (11.14) is concave and strictly increasing (see Samuelson 1956; Gorman 1959b; Negishi 1963; Chipman and Moore 1972, p. 162). Under these conditions, U_W has all the desirable properties of individual utility functions, and one can pose the problem of deriving an aggregate demand function

$$\mathbf{x} = h_W(\mathbf{p}, I) \qquad (11.15)$$

by maximizing $U_W(\mathbf{x})$ subject to the budget constraint $\mathbf{p} \cdot \mathbf{x} \leqq I$, where I is aggregate national income. The interesting question now arises:

Suppose that from the formal solution $X = \Xi(x)$ of the problem (11.14) one defines the allocation rule

$$\delta_i = D^i_W(\mathbf{p},I) = \xi_i[h_W(\mathbf{p},I)]\mathbf{p}/I, \tag{11.16}$$

which gives to individual i an income $\mathbf{x}_i\mathbf{p} = \xi_i(\mathbf{x})\mathbf{p}$ equal to the cost at prices $\mathbf{p}$ of the optimal allocation $\mathbf{x}_i = \xi_i(\mathbf{x})$ of the aggregate bundle $\mathbf{x} = h_W(\mathbf{p},I)$, where $\xi_i(\mathbf{x})$ is the ith row of the matrix $\Xi(\mathbf{x})$. Formula (11.16) then expresses the optimal income-distribution rule in terms of the share of individual i's income in total income. The question is then: if each individual is free to maximize his own utility subject to the budget constraint $\mathbf{p} \cdot \mathbf{x}_i \leqq I_i \equiv \delta_i I = \xi_i[h_W(\mathbf{p},I)]\mathbf{p}$, will his demand be precisely

$$h^i(\mathbf{p},\xi_i[h_W(\mathbf{p},I)]\mathbf{p}) = \xi_i[h_W(\mathbf{p},I)]? \tag{11.17}$$

That is to say, is it enough to simply distribute *income* in an optimal manner in order to ensure that each individual will voluntarily choose the commodity bundle that is optimal according to the maximization problem (11.14)? The affirmative answer to this question is the main insight of Samuelson's 1956 paper.

Samuelson merely sketched a partial proof (1956, pp. 17–18), involving an ingenious application of Hicks's (1939a) composite-commodity theorem. This would seem to be an appropriate occasion to furnish the precise details.

The composite-commodity theorem may be stated in the following general form. Suppose the $n \times 1$ vector p of prices satisfies the linear restriction

$$p = C\bar{p} \tag{11.18}$$

where $\bar{p}$ is an $\bar{n} \times 1$ vector and C is an $n \times \bar{n}$ matrix of rank $\bar{n}$. In the special case in which C is a block-diagonal matrix with diagonal blocks consisting of $n_i \times 1$ vectors c^i, with $\Sigma^{\bar{n}}_{i=1} n_i = n$, (11.18) may be written

$$\begin{bmatrix} p^1 \\ p^2 \\ \vdots \\ p^{\bar{n}} \end{bmatrix} = \begin{bmatrix} c^1 & 0 & \ldots & 0 \\ 0 & c^2 & \ldots & 0 \\ \vdots & \vdots & \ddots & \vdots \\ 0 & 0 & \ldots & c^{\bar{n}} \end{bmatrix} \begin{bmatrix} \bar{p}_1 \\ \bar{p}_2 \\ \vdots \\ \bar{p}_{\bar{n}} \end{bmatrix} = \begin{bmatrix} c^1\bar{p}_1 \\ c^2\bar{p}_2 \\ \vdots \\ c^{\bar{n}}\bar{p}_{\bar{n}} \end{bmatrix}. \tag{11.19}$$

This partitions the set of n commodities into $\bar{n}$ groups such that for each $i = 1, 2, \ldots, \bar{n}$, within the ith group the n_i prices in that group remain proportionate to one another, as $p^i = c^i\bar{p}_i$, $\bar{p}_i$ being the factor of proportionality. Now, define the bundle $\bar{x}$ of amounts of $\bar{n}$ composite commodities as the $1 \times \bar{n}$ row vector

$$\bar{x} = xC, \tag{11.20}$$

where $x = (x_1, x_2, \ldots, x_n)$ is the vector of amounts of the original n commodities. In the special case given by (11.19), (11.20) becomes

$$(\bar{x}_1, \bar{x}_2, \ldots, \bar{x}_{\bar{n}}) = (x^1, x^2, \ldots, x^{\bar{n}}) \begin{bmatrix} c^1 & 0 & \ldots & 0 \\ 0 & c^2 & \ldots & 0 \\ \vdots & \vdots & \ddots & \vdots \\ 0 & 0 & \ldots & c^{\bar{n}} \end{bmatrix}$$

$$= (x^1 c^1, x^2 c^2, \ldots, x^{\bar{n}} c^{\bar{n}}), \tag{11.21}$$

where $x = (x^1, x^2, \ldots, x^{\bar{n}})$ is the original bundle partitioned into $\bar{n}$ groups, and $\bar{x}_i = x^i c^i$ is (by definition) the amount of the ith composite commodity.

The composite-commodity theorem states that if $x = h(p,I)$ is the demand function generated by maximization of a utility function $U(x)$ subject to the budget constraint $p \cdot x \leq I$, and if h is differentiable and satisfies $p \cdot x = I$, then, assuming p to be restricted by (11.18), it follows that there exists a demand function $\bar{x} = \bar{h}(\bar{p},I)$ satisfying

$$\bar{h}(\bar{p},I) = h(C\bar{p},I)C, \tag{11.22}$$

which is generated by maximization of a utility function $\bar{U}(\bar{x})$ subject to the budget constraint $\bar{p} \cdot \bar{x} \leq I$.

To prove the result, we may define $\bar{h}$ by (11.22) and compute the Slutsky terms

$$\bar{s}_{ij}(\bar{p},I) = \frac{\partial \bar{h}^i(\bar{p},I)}{\partial \bar{p}_j} + \frac{\partial \bar{h}^i(\bar{p},I)}{\partial I} \bar{h}^j. \tag{11.23}$$

Routine computations show that the $\bar{n} \times \bar{n}$ Slutsky matrix $\bar{S} = [\bar{s}_{ij}]$ is related to the $n \times n$ Slutsky matrix $S = [s_{ij}]$ by

$$\bar{S}(\bar{p},I) = C'S(C\bar{p},I)C. \tag{11.24}$$

Since S is symmetric and negative semidefinite, it follows immediately that $\bar{S}$ is. We verify also that

$$\bar{S}(\bar{p},I)\bar{p} = C'S(C\bar{p},I)C\bar{p} = C'S(p,I)p = 0. \tag{11.25}$$

By the results of Hurwicz and Uzawa (1971), it follows that $\bar{h}(\bar{p},I)$ is generated by maximization of a utility function $\bar{U}(\bar{x})$ subject to the budget constraint $\bar{p} \cdot \bar{x} \leq I$.

Now, applying this result to the problem at hand, we may imagine that each individual, i, faces a distinct price, p_{ij}, of commodity j, which happens, however, to be equal to the same market price, p_j, for each i. Denoting the $m \times n$ matrix of these prices by $\mathbf{P} = [p_{ij}]$ and its ith row by

$\mathbf{p}'_i = (p_{i1}, p_{i2}, \ldots, p_{in}) \equiv$ row $\mathbf{P}$, we have in place of (11.18) the restriction

$$(\text{row } \mathbf{P})' \equiv \begin{bmatrix} \mathbf{p}^1 \\ \mathbf{p}^2 \\ \vdots \\ \mathbf{p}_m \end{bmatrix} = C\mathbf{p} , \tag{11.26}$$

where $\mathbf{p}$ is the $n \times 1$ column vector of market prices p_j and C is an $mn \times n$ matrix consisting of m identity matrices of order n stacked on top of one another. Thus, (11.26) simply states that $\mathbf{p}_i = \mathbf{p}$ for $i = 1, 2, \ldots, m$. Likewise, equation (11.20) is replaced by

$$\mathbf{x} = (\mathbf{x}_1, \mathbf{x}_2, \ldots, \mathbf{x}_m)C \equiv (\text{row } \mathbf{X})C, \tag{11.27}$$

which simply states that $\mathbf{x} = \Sigma_{i=1}^m \mathbf{x}_i$. Applying the composite-commodity theorem, with n and $\bar{n}$ replaced by mn and n, p and $\bar{p}$ replaced by (row $\mathbf{P}$)′ and $\mathbf{p}$, and x and $\bar{x}$ replaced by row $\mathbf{X}$ and $\mathbf{x}$, respectively, we may replace the function $U(x)$ of the theorem by the function $F(\text{row } \mathbf{X})$ of (11.3); this is maximized subject to $\Sigma_{i=1}^m \mathbf{x}_i \mathbf{p}_i \leq I$, yielding in place of (11.22) the equation

$$\bar{\mathbf{h}}(\mathbf{p}, I) = \sum_{i=1}^m \mathbf{h}_i(\mathbf{p}, \mathbf{p}, \ldots, \mathbf{p}, I), \tag{11.28}$$

where $\mathbf{x}_i = \mathbf{h}_i(\mathbf{p}_1, \mathbf{p}_2, \ldots, \mathbf{p}_m, I)$ is the demand for the bundle $\mathbf{x}_i$ consumed by individual i as a function of the m price vectors faced by all m individuals and of the national income. In accordance with the composite-commodity theorem, the function $\bar{\mathbf{h}}$ defined by (11.28) is generated by a utility function $\bar{U}(\mathbf{x})$ where $\mathbf{x} = \Sigma_{i=1}^m \mathbf{x}_i$, $\mathbf{x}_i = (x_{i1}, x_{i2}, \ldots, x_{in})$; that is, $\bar{\mathbf{x}} = \bar{\mathbf{h}}(\mathbf{p}, I)$ maximizes $\bar{U}(\mathbf{x})$ subject to the budget constraint $\mathbf{x}\mathbf{p} \leq I$.

It is at this point that the proof was left by Samuelson (1956, p. 18). However, it does not quite establish the result that was presumably intended — namely, that

$$h_W(\mathbf{p}, I) = \sum_{i=1}^m h^i(\mathbf{p}, D^i_W(\mathbf{p}, I)I), \tag{11.29}$$

where $h^i(\mathbf{p}, I_i)$ is individual i's demand function, which maximizes $U^i(\mathbf{x}_i)$ subject to $\mathbf{x}_i \mathbf{p} \leq I_i$ and where the individual's income I_i is set equal to $D^i_W(\mathbf{p}, I)I$, D^i_W being the optimal income-distribution rule defined by (11.16). The proof is therefore incomplete. In the following paragraphs I shall suggest some possible steps one might take to complete it.

We may observe from the definition of the social demand function (11.15) and of the social utility function (11.14) from which it is generated that h_W maximizes, over the budget set $\{\mathbf{x} : \mathbf{x}\mathbf{p} \leq I\}$, the maximum of

$W[U(\mathbf{X})]$ over the set $\{\mathbf{X} : \Sigma_{i=1}^{m}\mathbf{x}_i = \mathbf{x}\}$; this is equivalent to its simultaneously maximizing $W[U(\mathbf{X})]$ over the set of allocations $\mathbf{X}$ for which $\iota\mathbf{X}\mathbf{p} = (\Sigma_{i=1}^{m}\mathbf{x}_i)\mathbf{p} = \mathbf{x}\mathbf{p} \leqq I$ [where $\iota = (1, 1, \ldots, 1)$]. Now, consider the function

$$\mathbf{X} = \mathbf{H}(\mathbf{p}_1, \mathbf{p}_2, \ldots, \mathbf{p}_m, I) = \begin{bmatrix} \mathbf{h}_1(\mathbf{p}_1, \mathbf{p}_2, \ldots, \mathbf{p}_m, I) \\ \mathbf{h}_2(\mathbf{p}_1, \mathbf{p}_2, \ldots, \mathbf{p}_m, I) \\ \vdots \\ \mathbf{h}_m(\mathbf{p}_1, \mathbf{p}_2, \ldots, \mathbf{p}_m, I) \end{bmatrix} \quad (11.30)$$

where $\mathbf{h}_i$ (row $\mathbf{P},I$) is individual i's consumption of all n commodities as a function of the mn prices of the n commodities faced by all m individuals, and I is the national income. By definition, $\mathbf{H}$ maximizes $W[U(\mathbf{X})]$ subject to (row $\mathbf{X}$) (row $\mathbf{P}$)$'$ = $\Sigma_{i=1}^{m}\mathbf{x}_i\mathbf{p}_i = \mathbf{x}\mathbf{p} \leqq I$, where $\Sigma_{i=1}^{m}\mathbf{x}_i = \mathbf{x}$; accordingly, the function $\iota\mathbf{H}(\mathbf{p}, \mathbf{p}, \ldots, \mathbf{p},I) = \bar{\mathbf{h}}(\mathbf{p},I)$ of (11.28) maximizes $W[U(\mathbf{X})]$ over the set of allocations $\mathbf{X}$ for which $\iota\mathbf{X} = \Sigma_{i=1}^{m}\mathbf{x}_i = \mathbf{x}$ and $\mathbf{x}\mathbf{p} \leqq I$. Thus, the functions $\bar{\mathbf{h}}$ and h_W of (11.28) and (11.29) are one and the same.

The proof will be completed if we can show that

$$\mathbf{h}_i(\mathbf{p}, \mathbf{p}, \ldots, \mathbf{p}, I) = h^i(\mathbf{p}, D_W^i(\mathbf{p},I)I) \quad \text{for } i = 1, 2, \ldots, m. \quad (11.31)$$

Since by the previous reasoning $\bar{\mathbf{h}} = h_W$, it follows that $\bar{\mathbf{h}}$ is generated by U_W; thus, $\mathbf{H}(\mathbf{p}, \mathbf{p}, \ldots, \mathbf{p}, I)$ determines the optimal allocation $\mathbf{X} = \Xi(\mathbf{x})$ of $\iota\mathbf{X} = \mathbf{x}$, or

$$\mathbf{h}_i(\mathbf{p}, \mathbf{p}, \ldots, \mathbf{p}, I) = \xi_i[\bar{\mathbf{h}}(\mathbf{p},I)] = \xi_i[h_W(\mathbf{p},I)]. \quad (11.32)$$

The optimal income-distribution rule of (11.16) may therefore be defined by

$$D_W^i(\mathbf{p},I) = \mathbf{h}_i(\mathbf{p}, \mathbf{p}, \ldots, \mathbf{p}, I)/I. \quad (11.33)$$

It remains to show that if income is distributed to individual i in accordance with (11.33), this individual will voluntarily demand the optimal allocation (11.32), in accordance with (11.31). I will now indicate a way in which the latter result can be proved, but it will be apparent that the method to be described enables one to establish the entire result much more simply, without any need to have recourse to the composite-commodity theorem.

The method of proof was first presented in Chipman and Moore (1972). It rests heavily on the techniques introduced by Arrow (1951a) and further developed by Koopmans (1957) and Debreu (1959, pp. 68–71). Since it can be described rather simply, I shall do so here.

Consider an arbitrary price-income pair $(\mathbf{p}^0,I^0)$. Let $\mathbf{x}^0 = h_W(\mathbf{p}^0,I^0)$, and let the optimal share of individual i in national income, defined by (11.16), be given by $\delta_i^0 = D_W^i(\mathbf{p}^0, I^0)$. Denoting the optimal allocation of $\mathbf{x}^0$ by $\mathbf{X}^0 = \Xi(\mathbf{x}^0)$, by definition we have $\delta_i^0 = \mathbf{x}_i^0 \mathbf{p}/I$. Now we may define two sets: the "Samuelson set," which may be denoted "$R_W \mathbf{x}^0$" (see Figure 11.3), which consists of all aggregate bundles $\mathbf{x}$ that are socially preferred or indifferent to $\mathbf{x}^0$ (denoted "$\mathbf{x} R_W \mathbf{x}^0$") [i.e., all $\mathbf{x}$ such that $U_W(\mathbf{x}) \geqq U_W(\mathbf{x}^0)$]; and the "Scitovsky set," which consists of all aggregate bundles $\mathbf{x}$ that

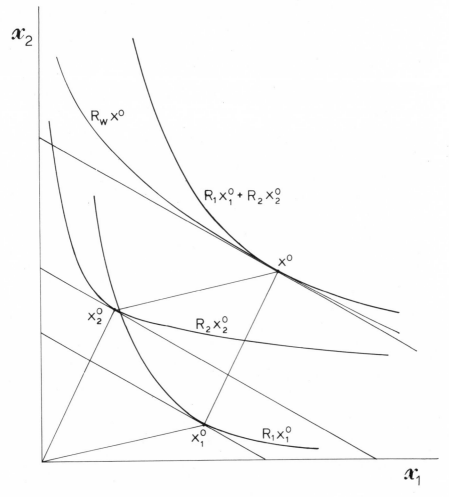

Figure 11.3

can be allocated to the m individuals in such a way that if $\mathbf{x}_i$ is the ith individual's allocation (where $\Sigma_{i=1}^m \mathbf{x}_i = \mathbf{x}$), $\mathbf{x}_i$ is preferred or indifferent to $\mathbf{x}_i^0$ by individual i (denoted "$\mathbf{x}_i R_i \mathbf{x}_i^0$") [i.e., $U^i(\mathbf{x}_i) \geqq U^i(\mathbf{x}_i^0)$, for $i = 1$, $2, \ldots, m$]. The Scitovsky set of $\mathbf{x}^0$ is then simply the algebraic sum $\Sigma_{i=1}^m R_i \mathbf{x}_i^0$, where $R_i \mathbf{x}_i^0$ denotes the set of all $\mathbf{x}_i$ that are preferred or indifferent to $\mathbf{x}_i^0$ by individual i (see Figure 11.3). The boundary of the Scitovsky set is, in the case $n = 2$, the well-known "Scitovsky indifference curve" introduced by Scitovsky (1942). The boundary of the Samuelson set is, of course, the corresponding "social indifference curve." Since the social welfare function W has been assumed to be increasing, the Scitovsky set is necessarily a subset of the Samuelson set (see Figure 11.3). That is to say, if a bundle $\mathbf{x}^1$ is such that one can find an allocation $\mathbf{X}^1$ of $\mathbf{x}^1$ (where $\iota\mathbf{X}^1 = \Sigma_{i=1}^m \mathbf{x}_i^1 = \mathbf{x}^1$) that is Pareto superior or indifferent to $\mathbf{x}^0$ [i.e., $U^i(\mathbf{x}_i^1) \geqq U^i(\mathbf{x}_i^0)$ for $i = 1, 2, \ldots, m$], then

$$U_W(\mathbf{x}^1) \geqq W[U(\mathbf{X}^1)] \geqq W[U(\mathbf{X}^0)] = U_W(\mathbf{x}^0). \tag{11.34}$$

Since U_W is a quasi-concave function, the Samuelson set is convex. Likewise, since each U^i is quasi-concave, for each i the set of $\mathbf{x}_i$ such that $U^i(\mathbf{x}_i) \geqq U^i(\mathbf{x}_i^0)$ is convex; and since the Scitovsky set is simply the algebraic sum of these sets (see Koopmans 1957, pp. 12–13), it is also convex. The point $\mathbf{x}^0$ is a common boundary point of both sets.

Now, from the duality between utility maximization and expenditure minimization (see Debreu 1959, pp. 68–71), since $\mathbf{x}^0$ maximizes $U_W(\mathbf{x})$ subject to $\mathbf{xp} \leqq I$, it also minimizes $\mathbf{xp}$ subject to $U_W(\mathbf{x}) \geqq U_W(\mathbf{x}^0)$ (and vice versa). Since $\mathbf{x}^0$ minimizes $\mathbf{xp}$ over the (convex) Samuelson set, and belongs to the convex and smaller Scitovsky set, it also minimizes $\mathbf{xp}$ over the Scitovsky set. At this point we bring in the very simple but powerful results isolated by Koopmans (1957, pp. 12–13): Since $\mathbf{x}^0 = \Sigma_{i=1}^m \mathbf{x}_i^0$ minimizes $\mathbf{xp}$ over the Scitovsky set $\Sigma_{i=1}^m R_i \mathbf{x}_i^0$, where $R_i \mathbf{x}_i^0$ denotes the set of all $\mathbf{x}_i$ such that $U^i(\mathbf{x}_i) \geqq U^i(\mathbf{x}_i^0)$, each $\mathbf{x}_i^0$ minimizes $\mathbf{x}_i \mathbf{p}$ over the corresponding set $R_i \mathbf{x}_i^0$. Now, using duality once again we can conclude that for each individual, i, $\mathbf{x}_i^0$ maximizes $U^i(\mathbf{x}_i)$ over the budget set $\mathbf{xp} \leqq \mathbf{x}_i^0 \mathbf{p} = \delta_i^0 I$ — that is, $\mathbf{x}_i^0 = h^i(\mathbf{p}, \delta_i^0 I)$ where $\delta_i^0 = D_W^i(\mathbf{p}^0, I^0)$, $i = 1, 2, \ldots, m$. This establishes the result (11.29) directly. Indirectly, therefore, it establishes (11.31).

The argument in the preceding two paragraphs assumed that the utility functions U^i and the social welfare function W were quasi-concave. In fact, the argument used by Gorman (1959b) and Negishi (1963) (and followed in Chipman and Moore 1972) to prove that the function U_W of (11.14) was quasi-concave assumed more — namely, that each U^i was actually concave. However, even if preferences are convex in the sense that the sets $R_i \mathbf{x}_i^0$ of bundles $\mathbf{x}_i$ preferred or indifferent to $\mathbf{x}_i^0$ (by individual i) are convex for all $\mathbf{x}_i^0$, it need not be the case that one can find a concave function U^i to represent these preferences — that is, a function U^i such that for $\mathbf{x}_i^t = (1 - t)\mathbf{x}_i^0 + t\mathbf{x}_i^1$, $U^i(\mathbf{x}_i^t) \geqq (1 - t)U^i(\mathbf{x}_i^0) + tU^i(\mathbf{x}_i^1)$ for $0 < t < 1$; in other words, preferences need not be *concavifiable*. This somewhat bewildering result, which goes back to de Finetti (1949) and Fenchel (1956), has recently been exhaustively analyzed by Kannai (1977). It will be recalled that concavity of each U^i (rather than merely its quasi-concavity) was needed to ensure the convexity of the utility-possibility set (11.1), which in turn was needed (in conjunction with quasi-concavity of W) to ensure that there would be a unique optimum point. Indeed, Kannai and Mantel (1978) have shown that if the individual preferences are not concavifiable, the utility-possibility set may be "non-convexifiable"; they have also provided a simple example.[10] Samuelson himself took care never to depict utility-possibility frontiers as convex to the origin, and remarked (1956, p. 17) that he did not regard convexity of preferences to be a realistic assumption, but assumed concavity of the function F of (11.3) above only "to save space."

It is nevertheless possible to extend the result (11.29) to the case in which the functions W and U^i are no longer assumed concave, or even quasi-concave, as long as they are continuous and W is increasing, and preferences are such as to ensure that all income is spent. This has been shown in Chipman and Moore (1979). Of course, under these conditions the individual and social demand functions, as well as the optimal income-distribution rule, need no longer be single valued, and the functions h^i, h_W, and D_W must therefore be interpreted as multivalued correspondences. With this interpretation it is shown in Chipman and Moore (1979) that, assuming certain mild regularity conditions to hold to be described below, if $\mathbf{d} = (d_1, d_2, \ldots, d_m)$ is an optimal income distribution for prices $\mathbf{p}$ and national income I [i.e., if $d_i I = \bar{\mathbf{x}}_i \mathbf{p}$ where $\bar{\mathbf{X}}$ is any optimal allocation of an aggregate bundle $\bar{\mathbf{x}} \in h_W(\mathbf{p}, I)$ — in which case we write $\mathbf{d} \in D_W(\mathbf{p}, I)$], then: (a) any allocation $\mathbf{X}^*$ resulting from individual demands $\mathbf{x}_i^* \in h^i(\mathbf{p}, d_i I)$ is also an optimal allocation of some bundle $\mathbf{x}^* \in h_W(\mathbf{p}, I)$; and (b) $\bar{\mathbf{X}}$ itself can be effectuated by individual demand behavior in the sense that its rows satisfy $\bar{\mathbf{x}}_i \in h^i(\mathbf{p}, d_i I)$, $i = 1, 2, \ldots, m$. Thus, (11.29) is generalized to

$$\mathbf{d} \in D_W(\mathbf{p}, I) \Rightarrow \sum_{i=1}^{m} h^i(\mathbf{p}, d_i I) = h_W(\mathbf{p}, I). \tag{11.35}$$

The proof is quite straightforward, following basically the same argument as before. It is illustrated in Figure 11.4 for the case $n = m = 2$. It will

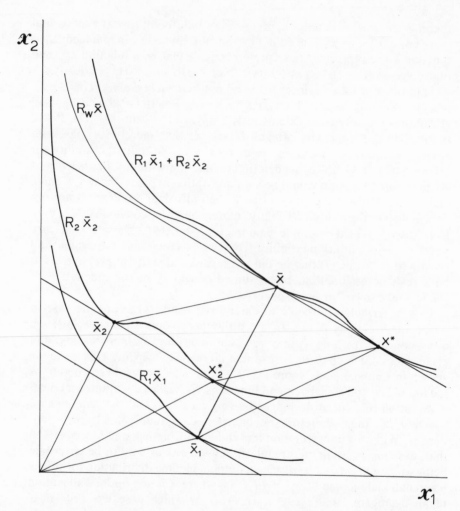

Figure 11.4

be assumed that all prices and national income are strictly positive. Since $\mathbf{x}_i^* \mathbf{p} = d_i I = \bar{\mathbf{x}}_i \mathbf{p}$, so that $\bar{\mathbf{x}}_i$ was affordable even though $\mathbf{x}_i^*$ was chosen, it follows that $U^i(\mathbf{x}_i^*) \geqq U^i(\bar{\mathbf{x}}_i)$, and thus (since W is increasing) $W[U(\mathbf{X}^*)] \geqq W[U(\bar{\mathbf{X}})]$; but by definition of $\bar{\mathbf{X}}$, $W[U(\bar{\mathbf{X}})]$ is equal to the maximum of $U_W(\mathbf{x})$ subject to the budget constraint $\mathbf{xp} \leqq I$; and since $\mathbf{x}^*$ also satisfies this constraint, it follows that $W[U(\mathbf{X}^*)] = W[U(\bar{\mathbf{X}})]$, and thus that $\mathbf{X}^*$ is also an optimal allocation of $h_W(\mathbf{p}, I)$. This establishes (a). To establish

(b) we proceed as follows. For any individual, k, if $d_k \equiv \bar{\mathbf{x}}_k \mathbf{p}/I = 0$, then certainly $\bar{\mathbf{x}}_k = 0 \in h^i(\mathbf{p}, d_k I)$. If $d_k > 0$, let $\mathbf{x}_k$ be any bundle such that $U^k(\mathbf{x}_k) \geqq U^k(\bar{\mathbf{x}}_k)$; define the allocation $\mathbf{X}^k$ by $\mathbf{x}_k^k = \mathbf{x}^k$ and $\mathbf{x}_i^k = \bar{\mathbf{x}}_i$ for $i \neq k$, and the aggregate bundle $\mathbf{x}^k$ by $\mathbf{x}^k = \Sigma_{i=1}^m \mathbf{x}_i^k = \mathbf{x}_k + \Sigma_{i \neq k} \bar{\mathbf{x}}_i$. Since $U^k(\mathbf{x}_k)$ $\geqq U^k(\bar{\mathbf{x}}_k)$, it follows by the definition (11.14) of U_W, the monotonicity of W, and the definition of $\bar{\mathbf{X}}$, that

$$U_W(\mathbf{x}^k) \geqq W[U(\mathbf{X}^k)] \geqq W[U(\bar{\mathbf{X}})] = U_W(\bar{\mathbf{x}}), \qquad (11.36)$$

hence $\mathbf{x}^k \mathbf{p} \geqq \bar{\mathbf{x}} \mathbf{p}$; but from the definition of $\mathbf{x}^k$ the latter inequality is equivalent to $\mathbf{x}_k \mathbf{p} \geqq \bar{\mathbf{x}}_k \mathbf{p}$. Since $\mathbf{x}_k$ was an arbitrary bundle preferred or indifferent by individual k to $\bar{\mathbf{x}}_k$, this shows that $\bar{\mathbf{x}}_k$ minimizes $\mathbf{x}_k \mathbf{p}$ subject to $U^k(\mathbf{x}_k) \geqq U^k(\bar{\mathbf{x}}_k)$. By duality, it follows that $\bar{\mathbf{x}}_k$ maximizes $U^k(\mathbf{x}_k)$ subject to $\mathbf{x}_k \mathbf{p} \leqq \bar{\mathbf{x}}_k \mathbf{p} = d_k I$ [i.e., $\bar{\mathbf{x}}_k \in h^k(\mathbf{p}, d_k I)$].[11] This holds for each individual, $k = 1, 2, \ldots, m$.

The above argument has all been cast in terms of specific numerical (cardinal) utility functions, U^i, and a specific numerical social welfare function, W. Although Samuelson has always taken pains in his writings to stress that no significance should be attached to the particular numerical indices chosen, the suspicion has always lurked among some of his readers that some hidden cardinality assumption was involved. This suspicion should finally be dispelled by his most recent comprehensive restatement of the theory (1981), in which he has started out as in Arrow (1951b) with a total ordering of allocations, $\mathbf{X}$. Following the notation of Chipman and Moore (1979), we can denote this relation by B, where $\mathbf{X}^1 B \mathbf{X}^2$ means that $\mathbf{X}^1$ is socially preferred or indifferent to $\mathbf{X}^2$. Denoting the Pareto (quasi-)ordering by R, where $\mathbf{X}^1 R \mathbf{X}^2$ means that $\mathbf{X}^1$ is Pareto superior or indifferent to $\mathbf{X}^2$ (i.e., $\mathbf{x}_i^1 R_i \mathbf{x}_i^2$ for $i = 1, 2, \ldots, m$), B has the property that $\mathbf{X}^1 R \mathbf{X}^2$ implies $\mathbf{X}^1 B \mathbf{X}^2$. A social welfare function $F(\mathbf{X})$ is any real-valued function representing B [i.e., any numerical function such that $F(\mathbf{X}^1) \geqq F(\mathbf{X}^2)$ if and only if $\mathbf{X}^1 B \mathbf{X}^2$].

Samuelson's concept of a social utility function is one that represents a relation between aggregate commodity bundles $\mathbf{x} = \iota \mathbf{X} = (1, 1, \ldots, 1)$ $\mathbf{X} = \Sigma_{i=1}^m \mathbf{x}_i$ derived from the social ordering B of allocations $\mathbf{X}$. Again using the notation of Chipman and Moore (1979), the relation in question, which may be denoted G_B, is defined by the condition that $\mathbf{x}^1 G_B \mathbf{x}^2$ if and only if, for all allocations $\mathbf{X}''$ of $\mathbf{x}^2$ ($\iota \mathbf{X}'' = \Sigma_{i=1}^m \mathbf{x}_i'' = \mathbf{x}^2$), there exists an allocation $\mathbf{X}'$ of $\mathbf{x}^1$ ($\iota \mathbf{X}' = \Sigma_{i=1}^m \mathbf{x}_i^1$) such that $\mathbf{X}^1 R \mathbf{X}^2$. According to this notation, G_R is simply the potential-welfare (quasi-)ordering, hence G_B has the property that $\mathbf{x}^1 G_R \mathbf{x}^2$ ($\mathbf{x}^1$ is potentially superior to $\mathbf{x}^2$) implies $\mathbf{x}^1 G_B \mathbf{x}^2$ ($\mathbf{x}^1$ is socially preferred to $\mathbf{x}^2$). As shown in Chipman and Moore

(1979), if B can be represented by a continuous real-valued function F, then the function

$$U(\mathbf{x}) = \max_{\iota\mathbf{X} = \mathbf{x}} F(\mathbf{X}) \tag{11.37}$$

is itself continuous and represents G_B, and is thus a social utility function in Samuelson's sense.

Without introducing additional structure, there is not much further that one can go. The key to the result described above — that the maximization of U with respect to an aggregate budget constraint can be effectuated by a decentralized process involving lump-sum distributions of income followed by individual preference maximization in the market — lies in the separability of F [i.e., in the possibility of representing it in the form (11.3) for *some* numerical functions W and U^1, U^2, . . . , U^m].[12]

In his recent paper (1981) Samuelson has indicated a method for building up a particular separable social welfare function $F = W \circ U$. Samuelson states the separability assumption in the following form: if $\mathbf{X}'$ and $\mathbf{X}''$ are such that each individual, i, is indifferent between $\mathbf{x}'_i$ and $\mathbf{x}''_i$, then society must be indifferent between $\mathbf{X}'$ and $\mathbf{X}''$.[13] He postulates that for each $\mathbf{x}_i$ one can find a z such that individual i is indifferent between $\mathbf{x}_i$ and $z_i\iota = (z, z, . . . , z)$; this defines a particular cardinal utility function $z_i = U^i(\mathbf{x}_i)$. Likewise, denoting by J the $m \times n$ matrix of mn ones, he postulates that for each $\mathbf{X}$ one can find a z such that society is indifferent as between $\mathbf{X}$ and zJ; this defines a particular cardinal representation $z = F(\mathbf{X})$. Then he observes that separability implies the existence of a function W satisfying (11.3). From the knowledge of the slopes in mn-dimensional space of the indifference surfaces $F(\mathbf{X}) = z$, he writes down the associated system of partial differential equations [corresponding to (2.29), Chap. 2, this volume] and the associated Antonelli-Allen integrability conditions stipulating the symmetry of the Antonelli coefficients. To get a definite (cardinal) welfare function, he stipulates the boundary condition $F(zJ) = z$. Finally, he imposes the above separability condition in order to obtain a system of partial differential equations from which one may retrieve W.

THE BEARING OF ARROW'S IMPOSSIBILITY THEOREM

Much confusion has been caused in the literature, as Samuelson observes (1981), by the fact that Arrow (1951b) used the same term "social welfare function" to denote something quite different from Samuelson's conception. Arrow's concept is indeed quite distinct. Let us suppose that each of the m individuals in society is also an "ethical observer" with a social ordering B_i over the set of allocations X. The ordering B_i may but need not coincide with the preference ordering R_i — that is, it may but need not be the case that $X^1 G_i X^2$ if and only if $x_i^1 R_i x_i^2$, where x_i^t is the ith row of X^t. [For example, someone may bargain hard in the market and engage in rigorous comparison shopping and yet donate the money saved to charity (see Arrow 1951b, pp. 17–19, and the discussion in Chipman and Moore 1979, p. 116).] Arrow's concept of a social welfare function is a function of the form

$$B = f(B_1, B_2, \ldots, B_m), \tag{11.38}$$

which determines a consensus social ordering from the individual social orderings. Such a function has been called by Samuelson (1967) a "constitution function," following Kemp and Asimakopulos (1952).

This may be related to Samuelson's approach in (at least) two different ways. In the first place, it may be observed that Samuelson's method described above for constructing a particular representation $F = W \circ U$ can be used to construct a particular f function, as follows. Let us assume that $X^1 B_i X^2$ if and only if $x^1 R_i x^2$. Given an initial set of preferences, one determines cardinal functions U^i and F satisfying $U^i(z_i t) = z_i$ and $F(z J) = z$, and thence the function W. Now let us fix this W and hypothetically vary individual preferences, obtaining with each different profile of individual preferences R_i a corresponding m-tuple of cardinal utility indicators U^i; in this way we obtain a new F function for each set of preferences and thus a new social ordering B. This determines the function f. I hasten to add that there is no reason to believe that Samuelson would approve of such a procedure, and it has specifically been disapproved of by Graaff (1957, p. 37).

In accordance with Arrow's Impossibility Theorem, such an f (indeed any f) will necessarily violate some of his postulates. Samuelson (1967) has responded to this outcome by suggesting that if one specifically limits oneself to the case of a fixed profile $(R_1, R_2, \ldots, R_m)$ of individual orderings, this difficulty will not arise. Without going into the details, I shall merely cite the contributions of Parks (1976) and Kemp and Ng (1976, 1977), in which an Impossibility Theorem has been established for this case (see the discussion by Pollak 1979). Samuelson (1977b, 1981), in an example, has specifically rejected the crucial "neutrality" or "independence" axioms adopted by these authors.

There is another way to compare the Bergson-Samuelson approach with Arrow's, which is simply to observe that a Bergson-Samuelson social welfare function is merely a representation F of a particular social ordering B, whereas Arrow's is a way of constructing B from the individual B_i's in accordance with (11.38) (see Chipman and Moore 1979, p. 116n.). It does not seem particularly helpful to describe Arrow's Impossibility Theorem, or those of Parks and of Kemp and Ng, as proving that a Bergson-Samuelson social welfare function F, or a Bergsonian welfare ordering B, "does not exist" (see Kemp and Ng 1976). On the other hand, if one is to build the entire structure of welfare economics upon the Bergson-Samuelson concept, one is naturally led to inquire as to how a particular B is or should be chosen. On this point Samuelson confesses:

> I have not shown much interest in the process by which particular social welfare functions arise and are deemed to be of interest or relevance. I have been satisfied to consider it not to be the task of economics as such to pass judgments on whether this social welfare function is in some sense more important than that social welfare function. [Samuelson 1981]

A superficial reading of this passage might lead a reader to ask: Is not such a stance perilously close to that of the compensationists (notably Kaldor 1939; see the discussion in Chipman and Moore 1978, p. 579), so effectively criticized by Samuelson himself (1950, pp. 11–12), to the effect that one can divide the problem of policy into two parts — that which is properly the domain of the economist (efficiency) and that which is best left to the political authorities (equity)?

Another way to express these gnawing doubts is to ask whether and to what extent the Bergson-Samuelson framework stands up to the same kinds of criticisms and tests to which Samuelson (1947, p. 250) subjected that of the compensationists. Does it provide a real guide to action?

If action is based on a particular B furnished by an "ethical observer," it goes without saying that such a criterion for action will not be "relatively *wertfrei*," any more than those defined by the compensation tests, since it will in general lead to reduction in welfare in terms of some B_i. Should B be interpreted as an actual revealed–social preference relation observed in a particular society, whether dictatorially imposed or not? This would be the interpretation of Pareto (1913), as I have indicated elsewhere (Chipman 1976, pp. 109–10). If so, it would simply reflect the relative political power of the various segments of society and hence would hardly have any claims to objective ethical status. (Indeed, some philosophers contend that there is no such thing.) The best one could say is that it provides an ethical rationalization for actual policies, should one be sought. Perhaps one should not expect welfare economics to be able to do much more than this.

The relevance of Arrow's Impossibility Theorem, it seems to me, is that it provides the main stumbling block preventing the Bergson-Samuelson (or indeed any other) approach from having any pretensions to providing a real "guide to action." [14] It warns us not to engage in a ceaseless quest for a philosopher's stone. Ironically, the huge literature it has spawned could be regarded as constituting precisely such a quest!

Welfare economics should perhaps have a more modest objective: that of promoting clear thinking on policy issues and sorting out the relationships between policies and value judgments. There can hardly be any doubt that in this respect Samuelson's contributions have excelled. One need only reread pre-Samuelsonian welfare economics to be convinced of this fact. And it is primarily this objective that was set forth as the appropriate one in Samuelson's original formulation (1947).

THE INTERPRETATION OF CONVENTIONAL MEASURES
OF WELFARE

This leads me to reconsider briefly some of the issues raised at the beginning of this paper, which did much to move the whole subject forward. What is the status of conventional welfare measures and criteria, such as, in particular, real national income?

There is one theme that was present in Chapter 2 that is still lacking here. The subject of the first section was the derivation of preference relations and utility functions from demand functions: consumption theory from the bottom up rather than from the top down. These results had a definite bearing on the subject of the second section, which was concerned with conditions under which certain particular kinds of individual welfare measures could be derived from knowledge of individual demand behavior. Samuelson showed that highly stringent conditions were required in order for consumer's surplus to provide a correct welfare measure, and the same was seen to be true of the compensating variation.

The same types of questions can be, and have been, asked with respect to the validity of conventional measures of group welfare. Under what conditions, and in what sense, is real national income a valid measure of the welfare of the community? This is part of the general question of inferring implicit value judgments from knowledge of actual policies or actual welfare criteria. I shall cite some results of this type obtained by James C. Moore and me, which I think can illustrate the way in which Samuelson's framework can be helpful as a guide to rational thinking about policy problems.

We can ask the question Q1: Is there a set of preference profiles $(R_1,$ $R_2, \ldots, R_m)$ for which it is true that, given any arbitrary competitive equilibria in two given periods that satisfy the national-income inequalities $\mathbf{p}^2 \cdot \mathbf{x}^2 \geqq \mathbf{p}^2 \cdot \mathbf{x}^1$ and $\mathbf{p}^1 \cdot \mathbf{x}^2 \geqq \mathbf{p}^1 \cdot \mathbf{x}^1$, we can always conclude that potential welfare has improved from period 1 to period 2? If so, how can this set of preference profiles be described? The answer to Q1 provided in Chipman and Moore (1973, 1976) is that there is such a set, which is precisely the set of identical and homothetic preferences $R_1 = R_2 = \ldots$ $= R_m$.[15] This means that if preferences are not identical and homothetic, it is always possible to find an example of an allocation $\mathbf{X}^1$ of $\mathbf{x}^1$ for which there does not exist a Pareto-superior allocation $\mathbf{X}^2$ of $\mathbf{x}^2$.

We can replace Q1 by a related question Q2, in which the individual preferences R_i are assumed in advance to be homothetic and the distribution of income among the m individuals is assumed to be constant as between the two periods.[16] The answer to Q2 is then (see Chipman and Moore 1980) that the individual preferences must be identical to one another. This answer remains unchanged if the criterion of potential improvement is replaced by that of actual Pareto improvement.

Now we replace Q2 by question Q3, in which the criterion of improvement is the Bergson-Samuelson one — that is, we ask whether there exists a Bergson-Samuelson individualistic social welfare ordering B of allocations such that situation 2 is an improvement over situation 1. Here we can make use of the result in Chipman (1974) that if preferences are homothetic and represented by utility functions U^i, which are homogeneous of degree one, and if W is chosen to be of the form

$$W(u) = u_1^{\delta_1} u_2^{\delta_2} \ldots u_m^{\delta_m} \ (\delta_i > 0, \sum_{i=1}^{m} \delta_i = 1), \qquad (11.39)$$

then the optimal income-distribution rule (11.16) is precisely $D_W^i (\mathbf{p},I) = \delta_i$. This is what Samuelson (1947, p. 225; 1956, p. 11) described as a "shibboleth."[17] We can conclude that if the δ_i's in (11.39) are chosen to be the common distributive shares observed in periods 1 and 2, welfare has improved according to this particular social welfare function.

This example also points to a trap. If preferences are homothetic and the distribution of income is constant, then aggregate demand is generated by an aggregate preference ordering, and Hicks's conjecture that aggregate demand will satisfy the Weak Axiom of Revealed Preference will be correct in this case (in fact, of course the Strong Axiom will be fulfilled). One can legitimately employ community indifference curves, for purposes of positive economics. But one has to be very careful in giving them a welfare interpretation. A higher indifference curve does not even enable us to infer an improvement in *potential* welfare, unless preferences are also identical; it allows us to infer an improvement in *social* welfare, but only if the existing distribution of income is considered to be the optimal one in both periods. The example thus gives us two possible configurations of empirical assumptions (about preferences and income distributions) and value judgments that enable us to attach a reasonable interpretation to the inference that a rise in real national income is "a good thing."

The researches of Sonnenschein (1973) have led to the result (see Mantel 1974; Debreu 1974; McFadden, Mas-Colell, Mantel, and Richter 1974) that, given any continuous mathematical form for a market excess-demand function satisfying Walras's law, it can be expressed as the sum of n individual excess-demand functions. In other words, as long as the number m of individuals exceeds or equals the number n of commodities, if individual preferences are sufficiently disparate, the aggregate excess-demand function can have any shape whatsoever. Since empirical verifications of demand theory necessarily deal with aggregates, the hypothesis of rational behavior has no empirical implications for observed demand behavior unless either the number of individuals falls short of the number of commodities (and the determination of this depends on the arbitrary manner in which "individuals" and "commodities" are grouped and counted) or definite restrictions are imposed enforcing special structures and a certain amount of similarity in people's tastes. One hesitates to accept as a scientific principle the proposition that individual preferences must be postulated to be similar and to have certain special forms just so that we can apply standard economic theory (for if it were otherwise, how could we justify all the work that has gone into building up modern demand and revealed-preference theory?); but we must hope (and pray!) that this is so as an empirical fact. If this is accepted, then one should surely use and incorporate this kind of information as an integral part of the theoretical structure of welfare economics.

Welfare economics can proceed along one of two roads. One is the road of casuistry: Detailed and ingenious tax-and-bounty schemes can be worked out that will maximize a symmetric (egalitarian) social welfare function. Perusal of our journals in public finance and public economics will confirm that this type of quantitative casuistry has become a widely accepted norm. Such work can be useful in helping us understand the full implications of certain (rather extreme) value judgments, but its usefulness is limited since, as a rule, no other hypothetical value judgments are considered, and by implication they are deemed unworthy. Persuasive and innocuous-sounding terms like "symmetry" and "neutrality" are often used (sometimes quite unwittingly) to advance a particular value judgment.[18] The *B* relation of the public-finance theorists has thus subtly but firmly ("dictatorially") imposed itself on a wide segment of the economics profession by essentially the same means as did the doctrines of its two predecessors — the New Welfare Economics and, before that, Utilitarianism — by "putting up a smokescreen of technical jargon to terrify an ignorant antagonist" as Robbins (1938, p. 638) so well expressed it.

The other road on which welfare economics can proceed is the one indicated by Samuelson in 1947 — the objective study of the relation between economic policies and value judgments. For this to be relevant to actual policy making, it would best proceed as in Samuelson's revealed preference theory, not from the top down but from the bottom up: from observed policies to revealed value judgments, making use of empirical information concerning the structure of individuals' preferences and the distribution of income. In such a program, the basic postulates leading to the separable social welfare function would have to be reexamined; after all, such observed phenomena as food stamp programs are in flagrant violation of Bergson's (1938) principle of consumer sovereignty. Samuelson himself has analyzed departures from these postulates — in his recent work (1981) and in his classic analysis of "public goods" (1954). The framework Samuelson has provided, which has been the subject of the present survey, may thus be regarded as just a first step, but the most important one, in the development of a comprehensive theory of policy analysis.

NOTES

1. Already contained in embryonic form in the *Foundations* (1947, p. 244). Samuelson himself has reminded me of Graaff's (1957, p. 59) observation that the concept of a utility-possibility frontier had already been introduced by Allais (1943, p. 640). The full significance of the concept was, however, not apparent until Samuelson showed how it could be put to use.

2. The first such example, but containing unnecessarily special features, was furnished by Kuznets (1948); cf. Chipman and Moore 1978, pp. 556–57. For examples without these features, see Chipman and Moore 1971, pp. 49–51; 1978, pp. 565–66.

3. There is no particular significance to the particular cardinal utility indices chosen, as Samuelson has repeatedly emphasized and finally definitively settled in his latest contribution to the subject (1981). All that is involved is the existence of *some* numerical functions U^i and W for which the social preference ordering among allocations can be expressed in the separable form (11.3).

4. The essential idea of a utility-possibility frontier is also contained in Lange 1942. For a formal development, see Chipman and Moore 1971.

5. The method of proof unfortunately does not go through in higher dimensions, but the proposition itself does (cf. Chipman and Moore 1978, footnotes 12 and 16).

6. See also Lange 1942, where the function W is introduced and described as a "social value function." A similar formulation was introduced earlier by Pareto (1913); (cf. Chipman 1976).

7. I do not discuss here the intransitivities in the various compensation tests put forward by Kaldor, Hicks, Scitovsky, and Kuznets, which were pointed out by Samuelson (1950) and Gorman (1955), since this subject has been covered in detail in Chipman and Moore 1978.

8. An analogy might be helpful. While societies, by their actions in helping victims of earthquakes, floods, and volcanic eruptions, reveal their abhorrence of these climatic disasters, they do not (at least so far!) feel compelled out of a sense of logical consistency or otherwise to compensate inhabitants of a region for slightly inclement weather. Another way to explain this would be in terms of the bureaucratic transaction costs of small transfers (as opposed to a partial ordering).

9. This is far from being the only difficulty. As Samuelson pointed out (1947, p. 248), such a policy would provide a strong disincentive to work for workers at the margin. The entire problem of the effect of redistributive schemes on incentives (or the possibility of "lump-sum transfers") is glossed over in the present discussion, but its importance can hardly be overemphasized. I have not focused on such difficulties in the present survey, but they must be regarded as empirically the most vulnerable parts of the edifice whose internal logical structure is being analyzed.

10. It has been shown by both Kannai (1974) and Mas-Colell (1974) that, in a certain precise sense, continuous convex preferences can be approximated by concavifiable preferences. However, it is doubtful whether this kind of result could be used to prove that the utility-possibility set can be well approximated by a convex set — well enough to yield a unique optimum.

11. Use of these duality results requires some mild restrictions on the "consumption sets" of individuals (called the "weak duality condition" in Chipman and Moore 1979, p. 122), which are always fulfilled if the consumption sets are chosen to be the nonnegative orthant (or any cone, or any closed convex set).

12. There is an interesting analogy between this problem and the one formulated by Strotz (1957), in which an individual "decentralizes" his own decision making by first. allocating his income among m different broad categories of commodities and then optimizing within each category. Unfortunately the analogy does not go through, since if we interpret x_i as the bundle of commodities in category i, we would have to assume that there is an equal number n of commodities in each category and that the prices $p_{1j}, p_{2j}, \ldots, p_{nj}$ across categories are equiproportional, for each $j = 1, 2, \ldots, n$ — which is manifestly artificial. Thus in Strotz's formulation separability is not enough, as Gorman (1959a) showed; a much stronger condition, such as additive separability, is needed.

13. This axiom was first introduced by Harsanyi (1955), who used it to show that if both individual and social preferences satisfied Marschak's axiom for behavior under risk, the resulting social ordering could be represented by an additively separable function $F(X) = \sum_{i=1}^{m} a_i U^i(x_i)$. Samuelson has described this result as "one of the few quantum-jump improvements on the classic A. Bergson clarification of welfare economics" (1974, p. 1267n.; see also Samuelson 1966, pp. 124–26).

14. The sin of the compensationists was perhaps not so much the one ascribed to them

by Samuelson (1947) of failing to provide a positive guide to action, but rather of providing a positive guide to action (e.g., *do* repeal the Corn Laws, *do* introduce the power looms) and supporting it by specious "'twere better" arguments, and in maintaining that these arguments were (relatively) free of value judgments.

15. If individuals' consumption is assumed to take place in the strictly positive orthant, then for sufficiently small disturbances this condition can be weakened to the condition first obtained by Antonelli (1886), and subsequently by Gorman (1953) and Nataf (1953) (see also Theil 1954), that demand functions should be linear (affine) in income, with coefficients depending on the prices and with the income coefficient being the same function of prices across individuals. See also Samuelson (1956, p. 5n.). Note that this Antonelli-Gorman-Nataf (AGN) condition was found by those authors to be necessary for the existence of an aggregate demand function (with aggregate income as an argument) invariant with respect to redistribution of income. This, of course, is logically quite distinct from the statement that the AGN condition is necessary for the affirmative answer to $Q1$. There is no direct relation between $Q1$ and the existence of an aggregate demand function; in fact, as the answer to $Q2$ makes clear, the existence of an aggregate demand function (with constant income shares) is not sufficient for the affirmative answer to $Q1$.

16. The assumption of constancy in income distribution as between the two periods under comparison was explicitly introduced by Pigou (1932, pp. 51–52).

17. Samuelson originally stated (1947, p. 225): ". . . it is easy to show that the rule of equality of income . . . applied to individuals of different tastes, but made to hold in all circumstances, is actually inconsistent with any determinate, definite W function." This statement is contradicted by the result just quoted. Samuelson's subsequent statement was more cautious (1956, p. 11): ". . . such a rule . . . is generally incompatible with the maximization of a social welfare function . . . that involves real goods." In a recent paper (1977c) Samuelson has corrected the original statement and provided an independent derivation of the 1974 Chipman result cited in the text.

18. I do not mean to imply that the building-up of a system of value judgments on the basis of a set of first principles is an illegitimate academic pursuit. On the contrary, it is a legitimate branch of ethics to which economists are eminently well suited to make a contribution, and to which Lerner (1944, Chap. 3) and Samuelson (1964, 1976) have in fact made important contributions.

REFERENCES

Allais, Maurice. 1943. *Traité d'économie pure*. 4 vols. Paris: Imprimerie nationale.

Antonelli, G. B. 1886. *Sulla teoria matematica della economia politica* [On the mathematical theory of political economy]. Pisa: nella Tipografia del Folchetto. English trans. in J. S. Chipman, L. Hurwicz, M. K. Richter, and H. F. Sonnenschein, eds. *Preferences, Utility and Demand*. New York: Harcourt Brace Jovanovich, 1971.

Arrow, K. J. 1951a. "An Extension of the Basic Theorems of Classical Welfare Economics." In *Proceedings of the Second Berkeley Symposium on Mathematical Statistics and Probability*. Berkeley: University of California Press.

———. 1951b. *Social Choice and Individual Values*. New York: Wiley.

———. 1951c. "Little's Critique of Welfare Economics." *American Economic Review* 41:923–34.

Bergson (Burk), A. 1938. "A Reformulation of Certain Aspects of Welfare Economics." *Quarterly Journal of Economics* 52:310–34.

Chipman, J. S. 1974. "Homothetic Preferences and Aggregation." *Journal of Economic Theory* 8(1):26–38.

———. 1976. "The Paretian Heritage." *Cahiers Vilfredo Pareto, Revue européenne des sciences sociales* 14(37):65–171.

———. 1982. "Samuelson and Consumption Theory." In G. R. Feiwel, ed. *Samuelson and Neoclassical Economics*. Boston: Kluwer•Nijhoff.

———, L. Hurwicz, M. K. Richter, and H. F. Sonnenschein, eds. 1971. *Preferences, Utility and Demand*. New York: Harcourt Brace Jovanovich.

———, and J. C. Moore. 1971. "The Compensation Principle in Welfare Economics." In Arvid M. Zarley, ed. *Papers in Quantitative Economics*, Vol. 2. Lawrence: University Press of Kansas.

———, and J. C. Moore. 1972. "Social Utility and the Gains from Trade." *Journal of International Economics* 2(2):157–72.

———, and J. C. Moore. 1973. "Aggregate Demand, Real National Income, and the Compensation Principle." *International Economic Review* 14(1):153–81.

———, and J. C. Moore. 1976. "Why an Increase in GNP Need Not Imply an Improvement in Potential Welfare." *Kyklos* 29(3):391–418.

———, and J. C. Moore. 1978. "The New Welfare Economics, 1939–1974." *International Economic Review* 19(3):547–84.

———, and J. C. Moore. 1979. "On Social Welfare Functions and the Aggregation of Preferences." *Journal of Economic Theory* 21(1):111–39.

———, and J. C. Moore. 1980. "Real National Income with Homothetic Preferences and a Fixed Distribution of Income." *Econometrica* 48(2):401–22.

Debreu, G. 1959. *Theory of Value*. New York: Wiley.

———. 1974. "Excess Demand Functions." *Journal of Mathematical Economics* 1:15–21.

Fenchel, W. 1956. "Über konvexe Funktionen mit vorgeschriebenen Niveaumannigfaltigkeiten." *Mathematische Zeitschrift* 63:496–506.

Finetti, B. de. 1949. "Sulle stratificazioni convesse." *Annali di Matematica Pura ed Applicata* 30:173–83.

Gorman, W. M. 1953. "Community Preference Fields." *Econometrica* 21:63–80.

———. 1955. "The Intransitivity of Certain Criteria Used in Welfare Economics." *Oxford Economic Papers* NS 7:25–35.

———. 1959a. "Separable Utility and Aggregation." *Econometrica* 27:469–81.

———. 1959b. "Are Social Indifference Curves Convex?" *Quarterly Journal of Economics* 73:485–96.

Graaff, J. de V. 1957. *Theoretical Welfare Economics*. Cambridge, England: Cambridge University Press.

Harsanyi, J. C. 1955. "Cardinal Welfare, Individualistic Ethics, and Interpersonal Comparisons of Utility." *Journal of Political Economy* 63:309–21.

Hicks, J. R. 1939a. *Value and Capital*. Oxford: Clarendon Press.

———. 1939b. "The Foundations of Welfare Economics." *Economic Journal* 49:696–712.

———. 1940. "The Valuation of the Social Income." *Economica* NS 7:105–24.

Hotelling, H. 1938. "The General Welfare in Relation to Problems of Taxation and of Railway and Utility Rates." *Econometrica* 6:242–69.

Hurwicz, L. and H. Uzawa. 1971. "On the Integrability of Demand Functions." In J. S. Chipman, L. Hurwicz, M. K. Richter, and H. F. Sonnenschein, eds. *Preferences, Utility and Demand*. New York: Harcourt Brace Jovanovich.

Kaldor, N. 1939. "Welfare Propositions in Economics and Interpersonal Comparisons of Utility." *Economic Journal* 49:549–52.

Kannai, Y. 1974. "Approximation of Convex Preferences." *Journal of Mathematical Economics* 1:101–06.

———. 1977. "Concavifiability and Constructions of Concave Utility Functions." *Journal of Mathematical Economics* 4:1–56.

———, and R. R. Mantel. 1978. "Non-Convexifiable Pareto Sets." *Econometrica* 46(3):571–75.

Kemp, M. C., and A. Asimakopulos. 1952. "A Note on 'Social Welfare Functions' and Cardinal Utility." *Canadian Journal of Economics and Political Science* 18:195–200.

———, and Y.-K. Ng. 1976. "On the Existence of Social Welfare Functions, Social Orderings and Social Decision Functions." *Economica* NS 43:59–66.

———, and Y.-K. Ng. 1977. "More on Social Welfare Functions: The Incompatibility of Individualism and Ordinalism." *Economica* NS 44:89–90.

Koopmans, T. C. 1957. *Three Essays on the State of Economic Science*. New York: McGraw-Hill.

Kuznets, S. 1948. "On the Valuation of Social Income — Reflections on Professor Hicks' Article." *Economica* NS 15:1–16, 116–31.

Lange, O. 1942. "The Foundations of Welfare Economics." *Econometrica* 10:215–28.

Little, I. M. D. 1949. "The Foundations of Welfare Economics." *Oxford Economic Papers* NS 1:227–46.

———. 1950. *A Critique of Welfare Economics*. Oxford: Clarendon Press.

McFadden, D., A. Mas-Colell, R. Mantel, and M. K. Richter. 1974. "A Characterization of Community Excess Demand Functions." *Journal of Economic Theory* 9(4):361–74.

Mantel, R. R. 1974. "On the Characterization of Aggregate Excess Demand." *Journal of Economic Theory* 7(3):348–53.

Mas-Colell, A. 1974. "Continuous and Smooth Consumers: Approximation Theorems." *Journal of Economic Theory* 8(3):305–36.

Meade, J. E. 1959. "Review of *A Critique of Welfare Economics*, 2nd ed., by I. M. D. Little." *Economic Journal* 49:124–29.

Mishan, E. J. 1962. "Welfare Criteria: An Exchange of Notes. V. A Comment." *Economic Journal* 72:234–44.

————. 1980. "The New Welfare Economics: An Alternative View." *International Economic Review* 21:691–705.

Nataf, A. 1953. "Sur des questions d'agrégation en économétrie." *Publications de l'Institut de Statistíque de l'Université de Paris* 2(4):5–61.

Negishi, T. 1963. "On Social Welfare Function." *Quarterly Journal of Economics* 77:156–58.

Pareto, V. 1894. "Il massimo di utilità data dalla libera concorrenza." *Giornale degli Economisti* [2] 9:48–66.

————. 1913. "Il massimo di utilità per una collettività in Sociologia." *Giornale degli Economisti e Rivista di Statistica* [3] 46:337–41.

Parks, R. P. 1976. "An Impossibility Theorem for Fixed Preferences: A Dictatorial Bergson-Samuelson Welfare Function." *Review of Economic Studies* 43:447–50.

Pigou, A. C. 1932. *The Economics of Welfare*, 4th ed. London: Macmillan.

Pollak, R. W. 1979. "Bergson-Samuelson Social Welfare Functions and the Theory of Social Choice." *Quarterly Journal of Economics* 93:73–90.

Robbins, L. 1938. "Interpersonal Comparisons of Utility: A Comment." *Economic Journal* 48:635–41.

Samuelson, P. A. 1947. *Foundations of Economic Analysis.* Cambridge, Mass.: Harvard University Press.

————. 1950. "Evaluation of Real National Income." *Oxford Economic Papers* NS 2:1–29.

————. 1954. "The Pure Theory of Public Expenditure," *Review of Economics and Statistics* 36(4):387–89.

————. 1956. "Social Indifference Curves," *Quarterly Journal of Economics* 70:1–22.

————. 1964. "A. P. Lerner at Sixty." *Review of Economic Studies* 31(3):169–78.

————. 1966. *The Collected Scientific Papers of Paul A. Samuelson.* 2 vols. Ed. by J. E. Stiglitz. Cambridge, Mass.: MIT Press.

————. 1967. "Arrow's Mathematical Politics." In S. Hook, ed. *Human Values and Economic Policy: A Symposium.* New York: New York University Press.

————. 1972. *The Collected Scientific Papers of Paul A. Samuelson,* Vol. 3. Ed. by Robert C. Merton. Cambridge, Mass: MIT Press.

————. 1974. "Complementarity: An Essay on the 40th Anniversary of the Hicks-Allen Revolution in Demand Theory." *Journal of Economic Literature* 12(4):1255–89.

————. 1976. "Optimal Compacts for Redistribution." In R. E. Grieson, ed. *Public and Urban Economics: Essays in Honor of William S. Vickrey.* Lexington, Mass.: Lexington Books.

————. 1977a. *The Collected Scientific Papers of Paul A. Samuelson,* Vol. 4. Ed. by H. Nagatani and K. Crowley. Cambridge, Mass.: MIT Press.

————. 1977b. "Reaffirming the Existence of 'Reasonable' Bergson-Samuelson Social Welfare Functions." *Economica* NS 44:81–88.

————. 1977c. "When It Is Ethically Optimal to Allocate Money Income in Stipulated Fractional Shares." In A. S. Blinder and P. Friedman, eds. *Natural Resources, Uncertainty, and General Equilibrium Systems*. New York: Academic Press.

————. 1981. "Bergsonian Welfare Economics." In S. Rosefielde, ed. *Economic Welfare and the Economics of Soviet Socialism: Essays in Honor of Abram Bergson*. Cambridge, England: Cambridge University Press.

Scitovsky, T. 1941. "A Note on Welfare Propositions in Economics." *Review of Economic Studies* 9:77–88.

————. 1942. "A Reconsideration of the Theory of Tariffs." *Review of Economic Studies* 9:89–110.

Sonnenschein, H. 1973. "Do Walras' Identity and Continuity Characterize the Class of Community Excess Demand Functions?" *Journal of Economic Theory* 6(4):345–54.

Strotz, R. H. 1957. "The Empirical Implications of a Utility Tree." *Econometrica* 25:269–80.

Theil, H. 1954. *Linear Aggregation of Economic Relations*. Amsterdam: North-Holland.

12 ON THE EVALUATION OF SOCIAL INCOME IN A DYNAMIC ECONOMY:

Variations on a Samuelsonian Theme

Murray C. Kemp and Ngo Van Long

Given the undisputed facts of capital accumulation and decumulation, of growing and decaying technical knowledge, and, therefore, of changing relative commodity prices, is it possible to define social income in such a way that it is both welfare relevant and ideally computable? Early writers like Marshall, Fisher, and Pigou were inclined to answer the question in the affirmative. In contrast, Paul Samuelson, in a classical exposition (1961, p. 57), has argued that in general "the only valid approximation to a measure of welfare comes from computing *wealth-like* magnitudes, not income magnitudes of the Haig, Fisher or any other type."

More recently, Martin Weitzman (1976, p. 156) has put forward the moderating view that ". . . it is not really a question of choosing between a conventional but inappropriate current income concept and an impractical but correct wealth-like magnitude, because in principle they are merely different sides of the same coin." More specifically, he has shown that, under very special assumptions, conventionally defined net national

We acknowledge with gratitude the helpful comments of Hans-Werner Sinn.

185

product can serve as "a proxy for the [wealthlike] present discounted value of future consumption." In particular, to avoid "the index number problem," Weitzman assumed that there is a single consumption good subject to choice (with the implication that primary factors like labor are inelastically supplied), that all utility functions are linear, and that both utility functions and the technology of the economy are stationary — that is, independent of time.

In the present note we show that, even without the first two of Weitzman's assumptions (a single consumption good, linear utility functions), our question can be answered in the affirmative. In particular, we show that net national product or net social income, redefined in terms of utility, can serve as a proxy for the wealthlike present discounted value of the stream of future utility.

The assumption of stationarity remains and might be thought to be so restrictive as to deprive our conclusions of all interest. However, as Weitzman (1976, p. 157) has noted, states of knowledge resulting from learning or research activities can be treated as capital goods and accommodated in a stationary technology. It is arguable, moreover, that all changes in knowledge can be traced to learning and research. However, we do not wish to take a firm stand on this question. Accordingly, in the end we face up to the difficulties created by exogenous changes in knowledge and show that they can be circumvented by a suitable extension of the notion of net national product.

ANALYSIS

There are n commodities, including leisure. The production and consumption vectors at time s are, respectively,

$$y(s) \equiv (y_1(s), \ldots, y_n(s))$$

and

$$c(s) \equiv (c_1(s), \ldots, c_n(s)).$$

The vector of capital stocks and the investment vector are, respectively,

$$k(s) \equiv (k_1(s), \ldots, k_n(s))$$

and

$$\dot{k}(s) \equiv (\dot{k}_1(s), \ldots, \dot{k}_n(s)),$$

where a dot indicates the time derivative. Each of $y(s)$, $c(s)$, and $k(s)$ may contain entries that are identically zero, indicating that some commodities cannot be produced or consumed or held as stocks, as the case may be. Similarly, $\dot{k}(s)$ may contain entries that can be only nonpositive, indicating that some commodities are exhaustible and nonreplenishable. These restrictions can be described by the vector of inequalities

$$g(y(s), c(s), k(s), \dot{k}(s)) \geqq 0. \tag{12.1}$$

We have also the accounting restriction

$$\dot{k}(s) \leqq y(s) - c(s). \tag{12.2}$$

Introducing the social utility functional

$$\int_t^\infty \exp(-\rho(s - t))u(c(s))dt \qquad (\rho \geqq 0, \text{ constant}) \tag{12.3}$$

and the set of production possibilities, defined by

$$\phi(y(s), k(s)) \geqq 0, \qquad y(s) \geqq 0, k(s) \geqq 0, \tag{12.4}$$

we can state the social problem at time t of maximizing the present value of the stream of future utility subject to the initial conditions

$$k(t) = k_t \tag{12.5}$$

and to the inescapable production and accounting constraints:

> maximize (12.3) with respect to $y(s)$ and $c(s)$,
> subject to (12.1), (12.2), (12.4), and (12.5). $\hfill\text{(P)}$

Notice that, at this stage, neither the utility function nor the production set is allowed to vary with time. Notice also that a more compact formulation could be achieved by subsuming (12.4) in (12.1). It is assumed that (P) has a solution.

Let $H(y, c, \psi) \equiv u(c) + \psi \cdot (y - c)$ be the Hamiltonian for (P), where $\psi(s) \equiv (\psi_1(s), \dots, \psi_n(s))$ and $\psi_i(s)$ is the shadow price, at time s and in terms of utility, of the ith capital stock; let $V(k(t))$ be the required maximum of (P); and let asterisks indicate optimal values. Then

$$z(s) \equiv u(c^*(s)) + \psi(s) \cdot \dot{k}^*(s) \tag{12.6}$$

can be interpreted as the optimal national income in terms of utility at time s.

LEMMA. *If the utility functions and technology are stationary, then, for all t, $z(t) = \rho V(k(t))$.*

PROOF. For any t_0 and t_1, with $t_0 \leqq t_1$,

$$V(k(t_0)) = \max_{\substack{\{c(s),\, y(s), \\ t_1,\, k(t_1)\}}} \left[\int_{t_0}^{t_1} \exp(-\rho(s - t_0))u(c(s))ds + \exp(-\rho t_1)V(k(t_1)) \right].$$

As transversality conditions we have

$$\exp(-\rho t_1)H(t_1) = -\frac{\partial}{\partial t_1}[\exp(-\rho t_1)V(k(t_1))] = \rho \exp(-\rho t_1)V(k(t_1))$$

$$\exp(-\rho t_1)\psi(t_1) = \frac{\partial}{\partial k(t_1)}[\exp(-\rho t_1)V(k(t_1))] = \exp(-\rho t_1)V'(k(t_1))$$

[see Hestenes (1966, theorem 11.1)]. Hence

$$\rho V(k(t_1)) = H(t_1) = u(c(t_1)) + V'(k(t_1)) \cdot (y(t_1) - c(t_1)). \qquad (12.7)$$

By virtue of the principle of optimality, this is true for all $t_1 \in [t_0, \infty)$ Q.E.D.

It is straightforward to show that if the production set is convex and if there are no externalities or public goods, then the solution to (P) can be reproduced by a competitive economy. Further, whether or not the production set is convex, if there are no externalities or public goods, then any competitive equilibrium that satisfies the transversality condition is a solution to (P). Thus we have the following:

PROPOSITION. *In an efficient competitive economy with stationary preferences and technology, social income in terms of utility can be viewed as interest on the wealthlike present value of the stream of future utility; it is the constant equivalent of that stream.*

Remark. The Lemma and Proposition are valid even for $\rho = 0$. Of course, $H(t)$ then is zero and no longer can serve as a proxy for $V(t)$. Consider, as an example, the problem of eating a cake of size $R(t)$ known at the planning point t, with a convex-concave utility function. If $\rho = 0$, it is optimal to consume at the rate

$$E(s) = \begin{cases} E^* & \text{if } s \in [t, t + T^*] \\ 0 & \text{if } s > t + T^* \end{cases}$$

where the positive constant E^* solves $u'(E) = u(E)/E$ and $T^* = R(t)/E^*$. The value of the program is

$$V(t) = [R(t)/E^*]u(E^*),$$

and the Hamiltonian

$$H(s) = u(E(s)) - u'(E(s)) \cdot E(s)$$

vanishes for all $s \geqq t$.

Finally, we go back on our tracks to allow for exogenous changes in knowledge. If u and ϕ depend on t, then so does V:

$$V = V(k(t), t).$$

The transversality condition (12.7) then becomes

$$\rho V(k(t_1), t_1) - \partial V(k(t_1), t_1)/\partial t_1 = H(t_1)$$
$$= u(c(t_1), t_1) + (\partial V(k(t_1), t_1)/\partial k(t_1)) \cdot (y(t_1) - c(t_1)),$$

where $\partial V/\partial t_1$ is the shadow price at time t_1 of the exogenous change in knowledge. Thus, if one takes seriously the possibility of exogenous changes in knowledge, then Samuelson's view that none of the familiar income measures (including net national product) has welfare significance is vindicated. Notice, however, that the Lemma and Proposition remain valid under nonstationary conditions if $z(s)$ is redefined as $u(c(s), s) + \psi(s) \cdot k(s) + \partial V/\partial s$.

COROLLARY. *Differentiating (12.7) with respect to t, we see that if u^* is constant for all $t \geqq t_0$, then $\psi^* \cdot \dot{k}^* = 0$ for all $t \geqq 0$. Thus we have, as a corollary of the Proposition, Hartwick's rule that, along an optimal path with utility constant, investment in new producible capital goods must be exactly equal to the rent yielded by the community's exhaustible resources* (see Hartwick 1977, and Dixit, Hammond, and Hoel 1980).

REFERENCES

Dixit, A., P. Hammond, and M. Hoel. 1980. "On Hartwick's Rule for Regular Maximin Paths of Capital Accumulation and Resource Depletion." *Review of Economic Studies* 47:551–56.

Hartwick, J. M. 1977. "Intertemporal Equity and the Investing of Rents from Exhaustible Resources." *American Economic Review* 66:972–74.

Hestenes, M. R. 1966. *Calculus of Variations and Optimal Control Theory.* New York: Wiley.

Samuelson, P. A. 1961. "The Evaluation of 'Social Income': Capital Formation and Wealth." In F. A. Lutz and D. C. Hague, eds. *The Theory of Capital.* New York: St. Martin's Press.

Weitzman, M. L. 1976. "On the Welfare Significance of National Product in a Dynamic Economy." *Quarterly Journal of Economics* 90:156–62.

III THE NEOCLASSICAL SYNTHESIS AND TRENDS IN CONTEMPORARY ECONOMICS

13 ECONOMIC ECLECTICISM:
The Neoclassical Component
Martin Bronfenbrenner

Professor Feiwel assures me convincingly that this volume will contain its full share of attacks on and denunciations of whatever the attackers and denouncers choose to call neoclassical economics. He also asks me (among others!) to defend the citadel of conventional wisdom as best I can. He does not require that defense involve denunciation of any or all rival positions, such as, for example, his own. This is fortunate in my case, for my defense is at best a limited affair that some will label half-hearted. It is limited to neoclassical economics as one important component of an eclectic, not to say syncretic, mixture of ideas and notions. I have never been able to fuse or otherwise combine these ideas and notions into a usable all-purpose compound. Now, at 65, I am reconciled to never being able to do so.

A PERSONAL ECLECTICISM

The upshot of all this has been an eclectic (or syncretic) outlook. (As Molière has said: "Je prends mon bien où je le trouve.") This outlook has five principal components, one of which is admittedly neoclassical economics. I list it below together with the other four:

1. Neoclassical economics. In my case this involves a special affinity for the Chicago School under which I received postgraduate training. (Actually I think there are two Chicago Schools. The older group — my teachers — tended to be price-level stabilizers in macroeconomic policy and trustbusters in microeconomic policy. The younger group — my approximate contemporaries and their own students — rely on monetary rules on the macro side and worry less about monopoly on the micro side. Being influenced by both groups, I should perhaps divide principle 1 into 1-a, and 1-b.)

2. The Keynesian tradition, which differs significantly from principle 1, at least for me, by casting doubt on both the macroeconomy's basic stability and its tendency to any full-employment equilibrium position. My interpretation of this tradition, I am afraid, owes less to what Professor Axel Leijonhufvud calls "the economics of Keynes [himself]," whom I never met, than to "Keynesian economics" filtered through Alvin Hansen, Paul Samuelson, and others.

3. The Marxian tradition, more in "the other social sciences" (or "social studies"), including economic history, than in economics proper. Again there has been filtering; I owe more to Rosa Luxemburg, Leon Trotsky, Paul Sweezy, and Oskar Lange than to the dominant dynasty of Lenin, Stalin, and perhaps Mao Tsetung.

4. A number of historical and institutional schools, all of which try to look at economic and social history and development (primarily, for me, as they affect America and Japan) from the viewpoint of "what actually happened, and why" rather than as hindsight illustrations of preconceived general and nonhistorical theories. (I have become painfully aware that complete emancipation from "preconceived general and nonhistorical theories," like complete objectivity, is impossible of attainment; on the other hand, "Not failure but low aim is crime.")

5. Behavioral schools, particularly my former Carnegie-Mellon colleagues, who doubt the realism and usefulness of assuming "maximizing" or "optimizing" or otherwise "rational" behavior in social or economic matters and rely on primarily empirical (meaning statistical) routines and regularities, especially in considering short-run problems.

This is a short list, and obviously incomplete. One of its omissions, however, is intentional enough to warrant explicit pointing out. This omission is "nonrational ways of knowing." That category includes not only reading the entrails of birds and communing with the stars or the dead but also Faith, in any of its standard religious senses and likewise in the mutual consistency of the positive and normative worlds. (I cannot, specifically, accept the comfortable proposition that good economics cannot be bad ethics, or its obverse, or its converse.)

Professor Feiwel has not shown me this book's particular wave of attacks on neoclassical economics, and so I write these lines in considerable ignorance of their contents. I have, however, read fairly widely in dissident literatures of various sects, secular and religious, and have even built up a teaching field in "Comparative Economic Systems" defined by me as comparative economic theories Left, Right, Utopian, and Dystopian. Faced with eclectic statements like the one above, these dissidents would react, I think, in different ways, and it will be difficult to reply to all of them simultaneously. I must, in the first instance, invoke "personal privilege" to rule out "dishonesty" objections that I don't mean what I say, and that I am really, basically, deep-down, 99.44 if not a full 100 percent neoclassical — a wolf in sheep's clothing, and therefore what I say you needn't mind. (I wish my McCarthyite and pre-McCarthyite tormentors of 1943–1955 might have accepted this criticism!) Turning to serious critics granting me the benefit of some doubt on personal honesty issues, I presume the more extreme among them would want neoclassical economics shifted from my category (1) all the way to the outer darkness of astrology, tea leaves, Jim Jones, and the Ayatollah Khomeini. (The Veblenian institutionalist Clarence Ayres took some such position in asserting that technology determines economic activity as meteorology determines the weather, with the price system reduced to the role of prayers and rain dances.) The more reasonable critics would, I hope, limit themselves to the defensible proposition that, where conflict exists between the implications of my five positions, neoclassical economics is more likely than most to be either wrong or incomplete, with the incompleteness so extreme as to be trivial. All the criticisms reduce themselves, or so it seems, to the book-burning theory of the conquerors of Alexandria. Where the volumes in the library of Alexandria agreed with the Bible or the Koran they were useless, where they disagreed they were dangerous, and so they were burnt in any case. (Subtle distinction: Mainstream economics should not perhaps be burnt, but merely left unread on the shelves or in storage!)

My mathematics is completely, as distinguished from "giftedly," amateurish. I do remember a little arithmetic, a little algebra, a little geometry, a little calculus, and a little mathematical statistics. Faced with a problem involving applied mathematics — computing income tax liability or present value, solving an economic model in terms of its parameters, testing an economic plan for feasibility — I think I proceed by deciding or guessing which of my snippets of numeracy is most apt to be relevant. Then I go ahead with my problem and ignore all the other snippets unless and until I run into serious trouble. My history and economics are better than my mathematics, but I think I proceed in much the same way here as well. That is to say, I let my problem determine my approach in a loose and haphazard fashion and ignore those aspects in which my nose has not been rubbed by the nature of the problem, or rather the nature of the problem *as stated to* or conceived initially by myself. This factual statement is in no sense boastful, since the procedure is shot full of logical holes and flaws. At the same time, I cannot see how Marxian analysis or Veblenian institutionalism can help one forecast next year's price level, or how neoclassical economics will help historians decide whether the Meiji Restoration was a bourgeois revolution of merchants against samurai or a palace revolution within the single samurai class.

INCONSISTENCIES OF ECLECTICISM

Now eclecticism and syncretism are all very well in music, art, literature, and cookery. Electronic sounds combined and sequenced in accordance with a computer program and the laws of chance may be heard on the same program with the music of Bach or Beethoven. Duke University's radio affiliate plays classics all day, then jazz all night. An art museum may separate a Rembrandt and a Picasso with an anonymous Northwest Indian totem pole. A literary scholar may enjoy Homer in the original Greek, Goethe in the original German, and *Finnegan's Wake* in the original Joyce. If the diner's stomach is big or the portions small, he can combine Japanese sashimi, Italian ravioli, and Mexican frijoles in one meal.

In other fields there are problems. The greatest of these is inconsistency. Early missionaries to the Orient report more difficulty in persuading the heathen to abandon pagan superstitions than to heed the Christian insights, but even today I cannot quite fathom the Japanese combination of Shinto weddings, Buddhist funerals, and Christian Christmases celebrated as New Year's Eve cum Santa Claus. In economics as in most other disciplines striving for scientific status, eclecticism and syncretism are taboo. In the typical mainstream economics department, Marxism is mentioned, if at all, as just another aberration in a doctrinal history course (while campus radicals learn their radical economics underground or in some other department). At the same time, on the other side of one or another curtain, Marxism is the secular faith, and neoclassical economics is written off as "vulgar economy" and ascribed to "learned handmaidens of Wall Street."

The greatest problem the eclectic faces, we have just said, is inconsistency — Emerson's "hobgoblin of little minds" — not only over time, but over problems at a point in time. How can I, or any other eclectic economist, rest assured that one's neoclassical treatment of Problem Alpha yields answers consistent with those of one's Keynesian or institutional treatment of Problem Beta? The unfortunate answer is that we cannot; inconsistencies are brought to my attention by students, colleagues, and others more frequently than I should like. This difficulty, however, is just one aspect of a larger one — the all-too-common reliance on a method or a methodology as insurance against one's own stupidity and carelessness. Stupidity insurance and carelessness insurance are intellectual equivalents of a free lunch; "there ain't any."

But now go on to suppose that, within the bounds of a single problem, two or more of my eclectic quintet give two or more mutually inconsistent answers; what should one do then? Here is what I plan to do myself in the future but have not always done in the past: Compare the two or more answers, together with their implications, and select whichever one seems to fit the facts or figures best, with minimal regard for labels and their "radical" or "reactionary" connotations. If this test is inconclusive, and if the multiple answers cannot be combined in any intellectually respectable manner, I pick the solution that is simplest and most natural or that accords best and with least friction to my previous views about similar problems.

It is much easier to state what I oppose than what I advocate or what I think I do. I oppose discarding or suppressing any answers or its implications because it is "neoclassical," "Keynesian," "Marxist," or anything else, and I oppose the intuitionism, emotionalism, and "thinking with one's blood" (as well as the logical fallacy of *argumentum ad hominem*) of the old Barry Goldwater slogan "In your heart you know he's right" and its equivalents.

SOME EXAMPLES

The preceding section has been abstract and general. Here are three illustrations, which I hope will lend more concreteness, from my own recent experience at Duke University and elsewhere.

1. The scene is Japan. The problem is the relation, if any, between the country's endemic inflation and its "economic miracle" of 1960–1973. I have argued along basically Keynesian lines that the inflation led to "forced saving" or "forced frugality," which in turn increased both investment and growth. To illustrate my case, I used a little model whose variables were:

Y: National Income (actual)
C: Consumption Spending (actual)
I: Private Investment (actual)
G: Public Spending (actual)
Y': Y, as planned or anticipated
C': C, as planned or anticipated
S':   Saving, as anticipated
T':   Taxes, as anticipated.

The *sources* of national income are expenditures. The (anticipated) uses of national income are consumption, saving, and taxes. We therefore have:

$$Y = C + I + G \quad \text{and} \quad Y' = C' + S' + T'.$$

If the anticipations are correct in the aggregate, so that $Y = Y'$ approximately:

$$(I + G) > (S' + T') \quad \text{implies} \quad (C < C').$$

If inflation is brought about by making additional funds available by bank loans and fiscal deficits for private investment and public spending, $(I + G)$ can be greater than $(S' + T')$, which the public had anticipated saving and paying in taxes. It follows that the public can spend for consumption, in real terms, less than it had anticipated spending. The difference constitutes "forced saving" or "forced frugality."

Thus my little model. It was objected in the United States that this is inconsistent with neoclassical economics, at least in its "rational expectations" variant. You can't fool consumers more than once or twice, runs the rational-expectations objection, or impose forced saving upon them. They will see you coming, so to speak, and buy on credit before prices rise. My rebuttal: Perhaps Japanese consumers *can* be fooled, or at least constrained by the height of down payments and the paucity of consumer credit under Japanese conditions. At any rate, the neoclassical and rational-expectations labels settle nothing in themselves, and the objection should have been supported by Japanese evidence of some sort.

2.   The last generation has seen a revulsion of academic economists — and of other economists not required to produce results after lunch or overnight — against "scientific fishing expeditions," "data mining," and "ad hockery." These three expressions all refer to reliance on empirical (statistical) relations not justified by any theoretical model and therefore often fragile when extended into periods before or after those for which the statistical relation was actually observed to hold.

So far, I agree, so good. But this "no-no" or prohibition has been extended in some quarters to the a priori rejection of all small-model results (like the one above), unless the perpetrator has also stated and fit the larger model into which the smaller one is embedded, and unless that larger model also appeals to the decisionmaker's methodological esthetic. I recently attempted to solve a so-called Friedman problem: Assuming a close relation between the nominal money supply and nominal income, and given a change in the money supply, what variables determine the division of the resulting increase in nominal income between real income and the price level? I worked out a little model, which fit quarterly data less well than I had hoped it might, and which gave reasonable but not earthshaking solutions for this Friedman problem. The objection was not that I had failed to shake the earth, but that I had not presented, let alone fitted, some complete model from which my own minimodel should have been derived. Methodological pedantry, I thought (and still think); in this case, skeptical suspicion run wild against the fourth and fifth members of my family of eclectic components.

3.   The most famous passage in John Maynard Keynes's *General Theory of Employment, Interest and Money* has turned out to be its final paragraph, which has nothing to do with employment, interest, or money; I reproduce a lengthy excerpt:

> The ideas of economists and political philosophers, both when they are right and when they are wrong, are more powerful than is commonly understood. Indeed the world is ruled by little else. Practical men, who believe themselves to be quite exempt from any intellectual influences, are usually the slaves of some defunct economist. Madmen in authority, who hear voices in the air, are distilling their frenzy from some academic scribbler of a few years back. I am sure that the power of vested interests is vastly exaggerated compared with the gradual encroachment of ideas. Not, indeed, immediately, but after a certain interval; for in the field of economic and political philosophy there are not many who are influenced by new theories after they are twenty-five or thirty years of age, so that the ideas which civil servants and politicians and even agitators apply to current events are not likely to be the newest. But, soon or late, it is ideas, not vested interests, which are dangerous for good or evil. [Pp. 383–84]

Neoclassical economists agree on these points with their Keynesian rivals, "these points" being the ultimate triumph of ideas over vested interests and of competition over monopoly in the so-called marketplace of ideas — at least in reasonably free societies. They also accept, I believe, a corollary implied but not stated by Lord Keynes in the passage quoted — namely, that errors in economic policy are traceable to policymakers' errors in economic theory. The conventional wisdom of that day or the particular heretical frenzy of the contemporary madmen in authority is wrong — or, at the very least, irrelevant to the contemporary situation.

Keynes's view, I have said, most neoclassical and Keynesian economists accept, and so do I. But when one leaves the antiseptic confines of the economics and business buildings and visits our colleagues in history, politics, and sociology, he is apt to find their left wings, both Marxist and non-Marxist, shot through with the precise position against which Keynes was campaigning. If an economic policy has been wrong — supposing that we agree that such is the case — the error should be sought, they tell us, less in the logical or empirical deficiencies of its underlying theory than in the power relations between those favored by the policy and the rest of society, particularly those positively injured by it. Who gained from the policy, in economic or political power, including social prestige? How did those (wicked) people conspire to foist that policy on the long-suffering public? How did they use that policy to grind the faces of the masses further into the mire? My colleagues' ultrasensitive noses for "gunpowder, treason, and plot" verge suspiciously on the paranoid, and I insist on implicit evidence in addition to the easy analogues and generalizations about the way "the Interests" or "the Establishment" usually act before I pay them as much attention as I sometimes wish I had. Even paranoids may occasionally be right, as witness Watergate and Nazi Germany. And perhaps we rationalists may be too quick to underestimate the public's natural immunity to nonsense and lunacy from the high susceptibility of our university classes, especially their lower halves.

IN CONCLUSION

Rereading the preceding paragraphs and sections, I find more space, and more reader time, devoted to my apology for eclecticism in general than to the rationale for including neoclassical economics as an important component of my personal eclectic stance. To avoid disappointment for

Professor Feiwel, let me devote this final section to redressing the balance. But first this message, as the television commercials say.

Common, garden-variety, or middle-level economics is practiced in "operating" agencies of governments or similar organizations, in private agencies not specializing in research, or in teaching at the undergraduate level "service" courses in programs aimed at law or business administration. As practiced in any of these connections, it requires full professional training at the doctoral level no more than house painting requires certification from an art school. I make bold to go further: A reasonably earnest and intelligent man or woman can eventually learn the technical aspects of any workaday economic job at home, with minimal aid, almost regardless of his prior field of concentration. (If he cannot, the usual difficulty is an inferiority complex of some kind.) A particularly outstanding example of learning by doing in economics is provided by a recent chairman of the President's Council of Economic Advisors, who was trained as a musician; his instrument was the clarinet.

Do not, however, overlook the word "eventually" in our last paragraph. One learns workaday economic jobs more quickly, more easily, with less and less conflict with one's economic philosophy — if my personal experience with revenue estimation in Washington and Tokyo is representative — with a background in economics and statistics than with a background in music and art — or in social philosophy. And in such cases, too, neoclassical economics as currently taught seems to me a better background than most of its more abstract or purely literary-historical alternatives.

This is not to claim that Marxists, fascists, or Islamic republicans cannot learn to estimate public revenues in local or national finance offices. I am sure that they can and that they do. My claim is rather that neoclassical economics is a better background for the requisite learning processes than are its alternatives. And perhaps, also, that some of the learning processes that the economic dissenter goes through are more apt to be purely mechanical in the robot or button-pushing sense than were my own, or even more apt to involve gaps in or inconsistencies with the main body of his economic thinking than were my own. For which reason among others, I continue to resist any urges to excise or purge "mainstream economics" from my eclectic mix of economic and social philosopies.

REFERENCE

Keynes, J. M. 1936. *The General Theory of Employment, Interest and Money.* London: Macmillan.

14 SAMUELSON AND THE AGE AFTER KEYNES

George R. Feiwel

TWO PERCEPTIONS OF THE ECONOMY

Much could be said about the major themes and philosophical perceptions that reappear periodically in the history of economic ideas and condition the vision and conceptions of the economic process and mechanism. For the purposes of this essay, I would like to single out in broad contours: (1) the tendency to focus on the beneficial effects of competitive laissez-faire and defects of government intervention and (2) the tendency to focus on market failures and on the need for "something more" than the market. Economists evincing either of these tendencies fall into two distinct groups, but even within a group they differ sharply on many aspects of the discipline.

Economists belonging to the first group generally emphasize that the competitive market economy excels in allocative and productive efficiency, that it is an inherently stable, self-equilibrating mechanism capable of eliminating excess supply or demand, and that it is a source of economic freedom and a means for achieving political freedom. Characteristically, they tend to minimize "market imperfections" and the dynamics and costs of "transitional" processes.

In the "age before Keynes," the "classical" macroeconomic theory that dominated economic thought (and is resurfacing at present in a sophisticated guise) viewed the economy as a more or less self-propelled and self-regulating mechanism, where a tendency to establish full employment prevails. The flexibility of wages, prices, and interest rates ensures the operation of the mechanism. In such a system lapses from full employment are transitory and disequilibria are eliminated rapidly and effectively. Full employment is that which is determined by the factors of supply and demand on the market — whatever it may be. Unemployment is thus considered to be merely an accidental and temporary displacement from such a state.

The modern disciples of Adam Smith do not regard government intervention in the economy as promoting welfare.[1] Rather, they view it as impairing the system's adaptive capacity and flexibility, allocative efficiency, and speed of return to equilibrium. Thus there is hardly room for an active policy. In Milton Friedman's words:

> The free market enables millions of men to cooperate with one another in complex tasks without compulsion and without centralized control. The invisible hand of the free market, whereby men who intend only to serve their own interests are led to serve the public interest, is a far more sensitive and effective source of both growth and freedom than the dead hand of the bureaucrat, however well intentioned he may be. [Friedman 1970a, p. 597]

As Samuelson (1973a, p. 159) has reminded us: "The truths of economics cannot be captured in even a hundred laws. But somewhere on the sacred tablets this truth is written: do not render unto the market that which is not the market's." Economists belonging to the second group generally stress that, however great the merits of the market, a laissez-faire economy tends to be seriously underachieving, suffering from many market failures. It is particularly vulnerable to waste due to massive underutilization of labor and capacity; to output, employment, and price instabilities; and to an inability to provide a "socially desired" rate of economic growth. Some of the other market deficiencies or failures of markets to exist (Pareto inefficiencies), which lead to misallocation of resources, include externalities and public goods, monopolistic elements, increasing returns, informational flaws, and transaction costs. The idealization of freedom through the market is illusory because the market does not provide a justifiable income distribution and because the market can exist in a repressive regime such as present-day Chile. Thus the need is recognized for a public policy at least to amend, supplement, stabilize, and steer market processes and to reduce or correct distributional injustices.

THE KEYNESIAN REVOLUTION

Whatever else needs to be said about the Keynesian revolution in macroeconomics and its various interpretations, it undermined the myth that full employment is the normal state of the economy (see Keynes 1936). It focused on the seriousness of the macroeconomic failures of the system, on effective demand as a central problem, on the mechanism generating fluctuations in activity, on prolonged periods of underemployment equilibrium or persisting disequilibrium, and on the fallacies of the classical saving-investment-interest rate mechanism and of the doctrine of full employment via flexible wages and prices.

The Keynesian revolution means different things to different people. In essence it refers to the impact of the theory of the determination of and fluctuations in the level of aggregate output and employment; underscores the dependence and impact of the level of effective demand on the degree of utilization of labor and capacity; provides the analytical innovation of the consumption function; focuses on expectations in an uncertain world; cogently distinguishes between the acts of saving and investment and the problems of offsets to saving; and emphasizes, inter alia, the fluctuations in total investment demand (and its dependence on shifts in expected profitability, which in turn depends on fairly unpredictable dynamic factors and subjective psychology and is beneficially influenced by a reduction of uncertainty about the future when the economy is steadily working in high gear) as a source of macroeconomic instability. The policy implicit in the theory assigns a crucial role to deliberate government policy for influencing (if not regulating) effective demand, and, in a broader sense, to use whatever policy instruments are most appropriate to influence and coordinate both demand and supply and to keep the system reasonably close to a desirable full employment growth path, while minimizing adverse side effects.

Ten years after the publication of the *General Theory,* Paul Samuelson vividly depicted how it originally affected economists of his generation:

> I have always considered it a priceless advantage to have been born as an economist prior to 1936 and to have received a thorough grounding in classical economics. It is quite impossible for modern students to realize the full effect of what has been advisably called "The Keynesian Revolution" upon those of us brought up in the orthodox tradition. What beginners today often regard as trite and obvious was to us puzzling, novel, and heretical. . . .
>
> The *General Theory* caught most economists under the age of thirty-five with the unexpected virulence of a disease first attacking and decimating an isolated tribe of south sea islanders. [Samuelson 1966, p. 1517]

He went on to elucidate:

> I myself believe the broad significance of the *General Theory* to be in the fact
> that it provides a relatively realistic, complete system for analyzing the level
> of effective demand and its fluctuations. More narrowly, I conceive the heart
> of its contribution to be in that subset of its equations which relate to the
> propensity to consume and to saving in relation to offsets-to-saving. In addi-
> tion to linking saving explicitly to income, there is an equally important denial
> of the implicit "classical" axiom that motivated investment is *indefinitely*
> *expansible or contractable,* so that whatever people *try* to save will always be
> fully invested. [Samuelson 1966, p. 1523]

The significance was that this was a new theory, for "it takes a theory
to kill a theory; facts can only dent the theorist's hide" (ibid., p. 1568).
How did Samuelson view the relationship of this revolution to what it
aimed at overthrowing?

> Of course, the Great Depression of the thirties was not the first to reveal the
> untenability of the classical synthesis. . . . But now for the first time, it was
> confronted by a competing system — a well-reasoned body of thought con-
> taining among other things as many equations as unknowns; in short, like
> itself, a synthesis; and one which could swallow the classical system as a
> special case. [Samuelson 1966, p. 1520]

Writing three decades later, Samuelson saw the *General Theory* as representing "a culmination of Smith's 1776 *Wealth of Nations,* not its *coup
de grace*" (1977a, p. 862).

Like many breakthroughs the *General Theory* gave rise to different
and often conflicting (but also in many respects overlapping) interpretations and spinoffs. Some of them derived strongly clashing implications
due to differences in underlying philosophies and descent from different
intellectual family trees (say, Walrasian or Marshallian). In fact one
group may even question whether the other is "Keynesian" at all.[2] Even
among similar versions there is an abundance of variants — and not only
for reasons of product differentiation. Some of the most representative
variants are:[3] Kalecki's independent version of the *General Theory*;
"Hicksian Walrasianism" (IS-LM), prior to his "reincarnation" as a
"born-again Keynesian"; American neoclassical Keynesians (including
Alvin Hansen, Samuelson, Lawrence Klein, Franco Modigliani, James
Tobin, and Robert Solow); "Cambridge-on-the-Cam Keynesians" (in-
cluding Richard Kahn, Joan Robinson, Nicholas Kaldor, and Geoffrey
Harcourt) and their "cousins" the American post Keynesians (including
Sidney Weintraub, Paul Davidson, Hyman Minsky, Alfred Eichner, and
Jan Kregel); and the general disequilibrium theorists (including Robert

Clower, Axel Leijonhufvud, the "old" Robert Barro, Herschel Gross-man, Jean-Pascal Benassy, and Edmond Malinvaud). Such a listing begs more questions than it answers. For obvious reasons, I shall concentrate on the American neoclassical Keynesian school, touching upon the others for discussion purposes only, even though the subject merits much more careful elaboration than the treatment allowed for by the confines of this essay.[4]

THE SAMUELSONIAN NEOCLASSICAL SYNTHESIS

The controversial attempts to reconcile Keynesian and neoclassical streams of thought were undertaken in part by "converts" to Keynes's message (or by those who, like Pigou, recanted), who yet remained under the influence of the neoclassical teaching on which they were brought up. In the United States Samuelson was largely instrumental in constructing and propagating the so-called grand neoclassical synthesis (see Modigliani 1980; Klein 1966; Tobin 1971; Hicks 1977). In a sense the germ of the synthesis can be found in a controversial passage by Keynes:[5]

> If our central controls succeed in establishing an aggregate volume of output corresponding to full employment as nearly as is practicable, the classical theory comes into its own again from this point onwards. If we suppose the volume of output to be given, *i.e.* to be determined by forces outside the classical scheme of thought, then there is no objection to be raised against the classical analysis of the manner in which private self-interest will determine what in particular is produced, in what proportions the factors of production will be combined to produce it, and how the value of the final product will be distributed between them. [Keynes 1936, pp. 378–79][6]

In view of the controversial nature of the subject, the shifting conceptions in time, and its dominance over postwar American mainstream economics, it is advisable to glean the essence of the synthesis from Samuelson's 1951 statement:

> My viewpoint is that of a general neoclassical theory that incorporates into the classical tradition whatever parts of the Keynesian and neo-Keynesian analysis that seem to possess descriptive validity for the present-day economy. In its general outlines, I think this is the viewpoint that Marshall, Walras, and Wicksell would subscribe to if they were alive today; and I am inclined to think that Adam Smith himself would claim an important share in its formulation. [Samuelson 1966, p. 1271].

In the early 1950s he described the synthesis as something of a "compromise doctrine," which emerges from the marriage of classical, neoclassical, and Keynesian analysis:

A legitimate and convenient name for this common core is, I suggest, "neo-classical." Neoclassical analysis permits a fully stable *under*employment equilibrium only on the assumption of either frictions or a peculiar concatenation of wealth-liquidity-interest elasticities; and this is in a sense a negation of the more dramatic claims of the Keynesian revolution. On the other hand, this neoclassical doctrine is a far cry from the old notion that unemployment is simply the consequence of imposing too high real wages along a sloping aggregate marginal productivity demand schedule for labor: it goes far beyond the primitive notions that by definition of a Walrasian system, equilibrium must be at full employment; and beyond the view that the same analysis which demonstrates a drop in price will equate supply and demand in any small partial equilibrium market will also suffice to prove that a drop in general wages must clear the labor market. It rejects the question-begging gobbledy-gook of Say's law of markets. . . . [Samuelson 1966, p. 1581]

Later (in 1967) he pointed out that

once we introduce systematically into a post-Keynesian system treatment of stocks of assets, monetary and real, and take into account fluctuating levels of real unemployment, there remain no inconsistencies between the classical system and the Keynesian system. The synthesis of common content emerges with an eclectic position on the interplay of real and monetary factors in determining the structure and levels of interest rates. [Samuelson 1972, p. 559]

To grasp the essence of Samuelson's perception of the reconstructed neoclassical theory, it is of some interest to note what he claimed (in a 1972 discussion with Don Patinkin on the neoclassical dichotomy) it has no need of, namely: (1) equation of exchange formulations; (2) assertion that the velocity of circulation is independent of the interest rates; (3) use of aggregate price level concepts; (4) explicit use of a "real balance" variable; and (5) the crude quantity theory of money in the real world of fluctuating output (Samuelson 1977, pp. 780–89; see Patinkin 1972).

What is generally perceived as the crux of the neoclassical synthesis was summarized by Samuelson with shifting emphasis in the successive editions of his textbook. The neoclassical synthesis was given great prominence in the third edition (1955, p. vi), where he promised that "it heals the breach between aggregative macroeconomics and traditional microeconomics and brings them into complementing unity." Thus, the neoclassical synthesis means that "if modern economics does its task well so that unemployment and inflation are substantially banished from democratic societies, then its importance will wither away and the traditional economics (whose concern is *wise* allocation of fully employed resources) will really come into its own — almost for the first time" (ibid., p. 11; see pp. 40, 212, 360, 569–70, 579, 624, 659, 666, 676, 709, and 733).

In the mid-1960s Samuelson still maintained that "mastery of the modern analysis of income determination genuinely validates the basic classical pricing principles; and the economist is now justified in saying that the broad cleavage between microeconomics and macroeconomics has been closed" (1964, p. 361; see pp. 590 and 592). He concluded:

Modern economic analysis does provide us with a "neoclassical synthesis" that combines the essentials of the theory of aggregative income determination with the older classical theories of relative prices and of microeconomics. In a well-running system, with monetary and fiscal policies operating to validate the high-employment assumption postulated by the classical theory, that classical theory comes back into its own, and the economist feels he can state with renewed conviction the classic truths and principles of social economy. [Samuelson 1964, pp. 908–10]

In the later editions the neoclassical synthesis has been fading away. In the eleventh edition it does not appear in the index; it is not called so by name, but its notion is present in a much weaker form (see Samuelson 1980a, p. 322).

THE POLICY IMPLICATIONS OF THE NEOCLASSICAL SYNTHESIS

While theoretically there are a large number of possible combinations of ways and means to full employment, in reality opportunities to design and implement alternative policies are much more circumscribed. Naturally, the problem is selecting not only an "optimal" policy mix, but also one that is both effective and politically acceptable.

In the early 1950s Samuelson attempted to formulate certain policy implications of the neoclassical synthesis. Full employment, in his view, should be regarded as only one of many goals and pursued only to the extent that the benefits exceed the costs. With maintained "high employment" the old questions of scarcity and costs come into their own:

We all wish for men to be employed rather than idle; but we also wish for them to be employed at useful tasks and under conditions of personal freedom. We wish for our parents to enjoy old-age security beyond that enjoyed by our grandparents. . . . Attacks on the rights of property and on gross inequality in the distribution of wealth and income seem to elicit resonant responses in modern democracies; at the same time, our mixed system of private and public enterprise does require incentives to elicit human efforts and it does still depend upon pecuniary profits and losses to organize the bulk of economic activity. [Samuelson 1966, p. 1291]

A community can have full employment, can at the same time have the rate of capital formation it wants, and can accomplish all this compatibly with the degree of income-redistributing taxation it ethically desires. [Ibid., p. 1330]

Clearly efficiency does matter, for a more efficacious husbandry of resources enables the economy to achieve a higher realization of ends. But this is not equivalent to realization of given ends with fewer resources (unemployment). Samuelson was adamant that modern neoclassical welfare economics does not consider waste of resources in unemployment as optimal:

Sound economic bookkeeping tells us that in real terms people can now (1) afford to have more private consumption goods, including leisure; and *exactly the same considerations* tell us that they can now (2) also afford to have more public or governmental goods and services. How they choose to apportion the extra released resources between the private and public categories must rationally depend on the shapes of their preference patterns ("indifference contours") between public and private goods. [Samuelson 1966, p. 1273]

To accomplish the first a tax transfer adjustment is required. For the second increased government spending is needed. Therefore, just as there are family budget spending patterns, there are similar income patterns for public and private services. "The effective quantitative pattern of these income-relations will depend upon peoples' tastes, upon the distribution of incomes and democratic voting power, and a host of such institutional factors" (ibid.).

Given alternative ways of yielding a desirable pattern of wants fulfillment, efficient output entails such a combination of available resources for producing the maximum product mix that the various buyers, as individual and interdependent democratic citizens, really want. Scarcity entails choice among opportunities available, reckoning all consequences when weighing alternative actions. At all times public services should be viewed as vying with each other as well as with private demand for consumption and investment for the limited resources available. Undertaking public works cannot be justified by needs of stabilization policy alone. The only justifiable reason for undertaking them (or any other policy) is as dictated by individual and social choices.

Samuelson felt very strongly that the neoclassical reformulation

need involve (1) no relaxation of vigilance over inefficiency in government, (2) no relaxation of vigilance against invasion by government of private consumption and personal liberty, (3) no acceptance of boon-doggling as a necessary evil at any time, and (4) no minimization of the strategic problems in programming either public expenditure or tax legislation. [Samuelson 1966, p. 1274]

The implication is that expansion or contraction of each activity of the governmental sector is to be subjected to a cost-benefit analysis in terms of utilizing resources that could be better utilized elsewhere. This does not mean opposition to government expansion that does meet the test.

Samuelson strongly criticized setting up rules of fiscal policy in a dynamic system (see Stein 1969; Buchanan and Wagner 1977):

> No one can predict with certainty whether fluctuations in autonomous private investment will be sharp or mild in the years ahead or whether non-fiscal programs can be counted on to reduce their residual fluctuation down to a broad or narrow range; thus the neoclassical doctrine does not tell us whether the indicated optimal pattern of cyclical fluctuation of government expenditure will be sharp or mild. [Samuelson 1966, p. 1281]

He felt that it would be well-nigh impossible to predict the composition of full employment income for the years ahead:

> There are no stable investment propensities, nor consumption propensities either for that matter, that, together with any general notions about the electorate's preferences between private goods and public services, tell us much about what the proper level of government expenditure should be. Our problem has been rephrased and not answered. As rapidly as private investment demand fluctuates in its total, as rapidly as the electorate changes its mind as to its rate of indifference between ordinary consumption and ordinary public services, as rapidly as the polls show reversals in sentiment with respect to economy-mindedness among the voters, as rapidly as the exigencies of the cold war and the foreign situation change, then so too must government expenditure change — and all this regardless of any stabilization motivation in government programs. [Samuelson 1966, pp. 1283–84]

Taxes shift resources from private to public uses. Samuelson (1966, pp. 1223–39) formulated a unifying theory of optimal resource allocation to public goods and optimal distribution of tax burdens. Fiscal and monetary policies may have qualitatively and quantitatively divergent effects. Thus the optimal mix of policies needs to be determined flexibly so as to best suit the given situation and the desired ends (ibid., pp. 1288–89, 1323, 1361).

Theoretically, full employment can be achieved with widely differing compositions of output, patterns of investment and consumption, and mixes of public and private sectors. In the 1950s Samuelson contended (ibid., p. 1321) that once near-full employment has been ensured by appropriate stabilization policies, the "purely classical" question may be asked: "How much of current national income ought to be saved, and how fast a rate of progress should be our goal?" Scientific economics cannot resolve the question about the "desired" rate of capital formation, nor that of the economy's ability to achieve a postulated rate of investment. "With proper fiscal and monetary policies, our economy can have full employment and whatever rate of capital formation and growth it wants" (ibid., p. 1329).

Of course, it is accumulation of capital and technical (economic) dynamism — and the two cannot be entirely separated — that matter for economic growth. Samuelson stressed (ibid., p. 1317) that if, throughout its history, the American economy "had saved only one-twentieth of its income instead of roughly one-eighth" and if a larger portion of the saving had gone to scientific research, "we should today enjoy even larger levels of output than we now do."

Samuelson strongly advocated (ibid., pp. 1725–26) that in order to enhance the rate of capital formation and thereby the growth rate of potential GNP, the government can supplement "private thrift by public thrift." It can do so by making credit more available and cheaper to investors and by making fiscal policies more austere, thus sacrificing current consumption for future benefits. He concentrated on the interplay of fiscal and monetary policies with private thrift in determining alternative combinations of investment and consumption at full employment and thus the rate of growth. In order to achieve a relatively higher investment rate and lower consumption, one would resort to a full employment policy generated by restrictive fiscal policy and expansionary monetary policy. He reminded his students of two problems:

> The neoclassical synthesis can banish the paradoxical possibility of thrift becoming abortive and can in this sense validate the classical notions concerning capital formation and productivity. On the other hand, modern societies necessarily are pursuing monetary and fiscal policies — and it is these policies that shape the resulting pattern of high-employment consumption and investment. [Samuelson 1955, pp. 570–71]

According to standard neoclassical theory, as the rate of interest is reduced, even in the absence of technical progress, previously unprofitable techniques may now be adopted, resulting in increased output and productivity. And with technical advancement the stimulus to growth is reinforced by induced capital deepening. The objective of growth acceleration, in Samuelson's view, can be achieved primarily by means of (conventional and unconventional) monetary policy constructed so as to promote long-term deepening of capital. Samuelson pointed out (1966, p. 1288) that we can bank on monetary policies and debt management to markedly influence private investment, which is palpably responsive to the rate of interest. In short, such a growth-oriented program would involve a mix of low interest rates and easy credit with restrictive fiscal policies entailing sufficiently large budget surpluses to neutralize excessive demand-pull inflationary pressures. Aside from its questionable empirical assumptions, one of the limits of such a policy is adverse balance-of-payments repercussions in view of the mobility of funds from the domestic to foreign money markets in search of higher interest rates.

The restrictive fiscal policy entails increasing tax rates relative to required government spending, which would reduce personal and corporate incomes and thus restrain consumption sufficiently to allow the scarce resources, in the postulated full-employment economy, to be reallocated to the investment effort (ibid., p. 1726). *Par contre,* a habitually expansionary fiscal policy with austere monetary policy — resulting in interest rates sufficiently high to restrain investment and consumer spending so as to reduce demand-pull inflation — will result in investment lower than that which would otherwise have prevailed. This assumes that full employment is maintained and cost-push inflation is absent. In the mixed economy, with downward wage-price stickiness and persisting varied rates of unemployment and idle capacity, different monetary policies can result in varied rates of resource use.

> Expansionary monetary policies that keep investment spending higher than would otherwise be the case lead initially to lower money rates of interest and ultimately to lower real-productivity yields on the enhanced stock of physical capital equipment. But they achieve this not at all at the expense of current consumption, for consumption too is higher than would otherwise be the case. Both capital formation and consumption can be increased by utilizing resources that would otherwise be dissipated in mass unemployment and industrial excess capacity. [Samuelson 1972, p. 558]

Serious misgivings have been expressed about the possibility of deepening of capital, not only by the Cambridge-on-the-Cam Keynesians but also by some American Keynesians (see Robinson 1962, Chap. 5; Kalecki 1945; Harrod 1973; Eisner 1958, 1975). Although Samuelson has not given in to the critics, he admitted in 1962 (1966, p. 1727) that "events have been working out in a way that these critics might have expected." Furthermore, "governors of the Federal Reserve System find themselves acting out the role of inflation fighters of last resort: fiscal ease voted by the people is used to offset monetary tightness contrived by the Central Bank" (1978, p. 25; see Tobin, 1980b, pp. 52–53). And herein is the kernel of this "Greek tragedy" as Samuelson sees it.

Samuelson stressed that "it is in the realm of monetary policy that a mixed enterprise system like ours can do the most to slow down or step up its rate of growth" (1966, p. 1400; see Negishi 1979, p. 148). But as a good eclectic he considered it only "right that fiscal policy should receive much emphasis" (1966, p. 1399; see Blinder and Solow 1973, 1974; Musgrave 1978). However, he contended that "basic reform of our tax system must be determined essentially on grounds of ethics and morality, not — as recent discussions would lead one to believe — as a vital contribution to economic growth" (1966, p. 1725). Here are *some* of his views on this subject (see Break 1976; Aaron and Boskin 1980; Pechman 1980; B. M. Friedman 1978).

Accelerated depreciation spurs growth, but policies (such as in West Germany and Sweden) that allow for a sizable share of the assets' historical costs to be written off in one or two years are nothing but "deliberate bribes to coax out faster growth," as was in fact the Kennedy tax investment credit. In order to promote investment in real assets (rather than hoarding money), assets could be depreciated on a base adjusted for the rate of inflation. Lenient taxation of capital gains has not only the merit of encouraging investment risk, but also the demerit of promoting unsavory speculation. Tax averaging can help to promote risk taking. If it were feasible to switch from a progressive income tax to a graduated tax on consumption and wealth, this would not sacrifice equity and would be the single most effective growth-promoting device, for only windfall gains that were spent or hoarded would be taxed. Contrary to popular belief, high marginal rates of taxation are not a disincentive to investment in view of the more lenient capital gains taxes. Reduction of the corporate tax rate *might* stimulate investment, but much depends on the incidence of that tax. A shift to preponderantly ungraduated consumption taxation would promote saving out of full-employment income, but it would be counterproductive if such parsimony would not be translated into investment (Samuelson 1966, pp. 1394–99).

Samuelson also saw an important role for government in promoting capital formation and technical dynamism by means of more extensive and intensive investment in research, education, and health. He expressed a guarded interest in indicative planning, but "the matter is a controversial one in the American political scene" (ibid., p. 1721; see Tobin 1980b, p. 37).

There is a long-standing argument that inequality of incomes is a necessary component of rapid growth. Samuelson does not believe that philosophically "the argument stands up that a free people, gathering together to set up the rules and laws for a good society, will agree on a social compact that leaves intact the inequality meted out by the market.

Instead people subject to the same vicissitudes of life are likely to opt by overwhelming majority to establish a network of graduated or progressive tax rates based upon what is conceived to be ability to pay" (1976, p. 82). Moreover, postwar experience also shows that reducing inequality is not a handicap to growth. The percentage share of the United States in world GNP was dropping steadily. "Egalitarian Sweden has now surpassed us in real per capita GNP and probably Switzerland and West Germany have also" (1973b, p. 84). Furthermore, in terms of after-tax income equality, eleven countries were ranked as follows: Netherlands, Sweden, Norway, United Kingdom, Japan, Canada, Australia, West Germany, United States, Spain, and France. If nations well ahead of the United States in this list record vigorous growth rates, why should inequality be regarded as a growth promoter? (1976, p. 82; see Feldstein 1977; Thurow 1980).

In John Stuart Mill's tradition, Samuelson maintained (1966, p. 1445) that distribution cannot be regarded as fundamental datum, but can be changed by public policy. But there is strong resistance to any policy that has redistributional effects. A reformer may be well advised to reflect on the implications of the well-entrenched inequality that cannot be easily dislodged (see Kalecki 1971; Dobb 1973; Tinbergen 1975):

> The weight of evidence suggests to me that there are deep-seated causes for the Lorentz-Pareto distributions of actual income. They can be changed (for good and evil) by government policies and by trade-union and other collusions. But they do stubbornly resist such changes in their *real* magnitudes, and their laws of motion over time seem to me to be best understood and forecasted in terms of hypotheses about relative factor supplies, the nature of technological invention and innovation, and (to a lesser degree) in terms of changes in the degree of imperfection of competition in commodity and factor markets. [Samuelson 1977a, p. 121]

For a variety of reasons, to some of which I have alluded previously, the aspiration goal of the early 1940s of maintenance of full employment (Samuelson 1966, p. 1429) has been scaled down to the stabilization of the so-called high employment, and the focus has shifted to tradeoffs. Already in 1953 Samuelson alluded to the cruel tradeoff between unemployment and inflation. He speculated (ibid., p. 1307) on the possibility that "a very small degree of unemployment in the labor market might serve to persuade or to force unions from asking and getting increases in their money wages greater than productivity changes. If so, we are lucky and the wage-price dilemma does not exist."

Understandably, the economists who had a vivid memory of the Great

Depression tended to underemphasize inflation. At the outset of World War II, when the economy shifted from insufficient demand to excess demand, the demand-pull inflation was conspicuous. In the postwar period different sources of inflation began to emerge, with different configurations and force over time. But the problems became really serious only in the latter 1960s and alarming in the 1970s and gave rise to clashing analyses of the nature of inflation and proposed remedies, more about which later.

The famous "45° Keynes cross" diagram popularized by Samuelson is, of course, a crude approximation. Flexibly interpreted, the "Keynesian notion" is that the rate of increase of prices depends on the state of the economy and that the degree of resource utilization determines the shape of the aggregate supply curve. Thus, with an increase of effective demand, the primary effect is on output, but as the economy approaches nearer to the difficult-to-define neighborhood of full employment, the price increases become more steep, and once the threshold of full employment is passed, the effect is primarily on prices. One of the crucial issues is how changes in spending will be distributed between changes in real output and the price level. This depends, inter alia, "upon how much or how little labor and capital remains unused to be drawn on, and upon how strong or weak are the cost-push upward pressures that come from the institutional supply conditions of organized labor, or oligopolistic price administrators and more perfectly competitive enterprises" (Samuelson 1966, p. 1371).

A. W. Phillips's findings of the inverse relationship between the rate of unemployment (a real magnitude) and the growth rate of wages (a monetary magnitude) over just a century in British industry implied that the lower the level of aggregate economic activity, the weaker are the wage pressures, and that reduced unemployment entails stronger wage demands (with the inference that wage inflation means price inflation; it is wages minus gains in productivity that are among the key determinants of prices)[7] (Phillips 1958; Lipsey 1960).

In 1960 Samuelson and Solow gathered American data in an attempt to analyze to what extent this relationship held for the United States. For earlier periods in their long time series, the results were quite dissimilar, but for 1946 to 1958 the points did cluster along a curve that was not unlike one that could have been derived from Phillips's data. Hence they concluded that for the American economy, a 2 percent annual wage increase (corresponding to the average productivity growth) would correspond to a 5–6 percent unemployment rate, and that at the "desirable goal" of 3 percent unemployment, inflation would advance by 4–5 percent annually. Thus these were the derived tradeoffs between price stability and unemployment on the one hand, and "near-full employment" and inflation, on the other (Samuelson 1966, pp. 1346–51; see Tobin 1972).

Solow subsequently extended the series and admitted that though the data for 1960–1969 were not too far off from their previous findings, those for 1970–1977 were quite contrary. He found that for 1970–1972 the economy continued to move along a Phillips curve that had deteriorated by about two percentage points. But in 1974–1977, when much of the instability was generated by the supply side and "external and special" factors, the data depicted price-employment relationships that were quite at variance with the simplified view of the two-variable Phillips curve. Solow suggested that aside from unprecedented price shocks, there is an upward bias in the economy, with wages and prices becoming increasingly downward sticky, inter alia, because the economic actors expect that the economy will not be subject to extreme booms and busts — and inflation then becomes the price of stabilization (1978b, pp. 11–18; see Baily 1974; Hall 1980; Piore 1979).

The controversial Phillips curve (later augmented by expectations and various interpretations of the level of unemployment and potential output) was considered as a convenient portrayal of choice: The price of lower unemployment is higher inflation, and lower inflation can be bought at the cost of higher unemployment. Fundamentally, it made the target of full employment a variable one, with the implication derived by many that the only "cure" for inflation is contrived deflation and unemployment. But in the early 1970s the tradeoffs became increasingly cruel, and in the latter 1970s, the curve seemed to have disappeared from view. Milton Friedman suggested that a so-called positively sloped Phillips curve appeared (1977, pp. 459ff.). Those who believed in the existence of a Phillips curve (and in a sense some who did not) were struck by the sharp worsening of "tradeoffs" and the unsystematic shifts of the curve. Hence the whole question of improving the "tradeoffs" assumed new dimensions (see Samuelson 1980a, p. 777; Klein 1977, 1978a; Okun and Perry 1978).

Of interest here is Lawrence Klein's position. He negates the need to go back to the drawing boards. Contemporary macroeconomic theory can explain recent events. It is only necessary to use it appropriately to fit the new configuration of circumstances. Klein argues (1977, p. 411) that "the Phillips Curve is being misunderstood and that proper analysis of full system properties can lead to the generating of rising prices and rising unemployment in a model that is based on received doctrine, including acceptance of the hypothesis underlying the Phillips Curve."

Similarly, Alan Blinder (1979) contends that there is a perfectly coherent, mainstream Keynesian explanation of what happened in the sorry 1970s. To grasp why the obituaries of the tradeoff were premature and that it is "alive and well and living," it is necessary to distinguish between the tradeoff itself and the Phillips curve as an empirical regularity. The Phillips curve relations work well only as long as macroeconomic fluctuations originate on the demand side. The disintegration of the Phillips curve in the 1970s was primarily due to adverse shifts in aggregate supply as the predominant source of economic instability. Policymakers can still exploit the tradeoff between inflation and real output. Their ability to influence the macroeconomy is largely limited to the demand side, for they do not yet know how to shift the aggregate supply curve:

> . . . regardless of what type of statistical Phillips curve the data for the years 1980–2000 actually produce, the policymakers' trade-off between inflation and unemployment will persist until someone finds a reliable way to manipulate aggregate supply. The limited capability of policy to influence supply poses a particularly vexing problem in a stagflationary world since any stabilization policy adopted in response to stagflation is bound to aggravate one of the problems even as it helps cure the other. Such is the policy dilemma of stagflation. [Blinder 1979, pp. 20–21]

THE REVIVAL OF THE ANTI-KEYNESIAN MOVEMENT

The policies pursued in the United States since World War II, and especially in the 1960s, came to be identified with the mainstream economics of the neoclassical Keynesians. The failures of policies to cope with the new configuration of problems (stagflation) in the 1970s have to some extent influenced the disaffection of economists from the mainstream and the gain of adherents by the critics who, besides the other Keynesian schools and the left, are chiefly represented by economists in the first group. In the latter form we are witnessing the resurrection of anti-Keynesian economics in new guises.

The Keynesian revolution has always been under attack from many quarters. Here I should like to single out economists in the first group, under the leadership in the United States of the libertarian Chicago school, founded by Henry Simon, led by the famous Frank Knight, who was scornful of the post–New Deal world, and enhanced by the articulate and scintillating Milton Friedman, the high priest of "capitalism and freedom" and of monetarism (the new form of quantity theory of money). What Friedman called the monetary counterrevolution challenged not only the Keynesian techniques of achieving full employment, but also the basic philosophy that such a state and the society to which it gives rise are desirable. Monetarism has evolved into splinter groups. The distinctive new development here is the emergence of a younger generation of mathematical economists of what may be called the "new classical school" or "new monetarism" (including Robert Lucas, Thomas Sargent, Neil Wallace, the "born-again" Robert Barro, and Bennett McCallum), whose criticism is directed not only explicitly against the Keynesians, but also implicitly against the "old monetarism" of Friedman. The fundamentally libertarian approach and conservative ideology appear in many other forms, of which the disciples of Friedrich von Hayek and James Buchanan are among the recognized modern varieties. In addition, there is a heterogenous group of pragmatic neoconservatives (including Martin Feldstein, Michael Boskin, and Robert Hall) and the evangelists of the supply side (particularly Arthur Laffer, Jude Wanniski, Paul Craig Roberts, and Michael Evans).

Economists in the first group seek a remedy to the present quandaries in reliance on the market mechanism. The postwar stabilization policies are considered to be based on spurious, unfounded, or misguided economic theory and misperception of economic processes. With important differences discussed below, these economists tend to attribute the retrogression in economic performance (particularly stagflation and growing instabilities) to the expanded role of government and its misguided policies. Government regulation is also blamed as a major cause of decreasing productivity growth and for effecting the decline of the birthrate. Existing tax rules, welfare-oriented spending, and transfer payments are blamed for the falling rates of saving and capital formation. The stress is on inflation, and not unemployment, as the cardinal problem of the American economy (see Feldstein 1980). In broad contours, the difference here between the new and old monetarism (and other conservative economists who share its economic philosophy) is that the former (to be discussed at greater length later) concentrates on the impotence of systematic macropolicies, while the latter focuses on the limitations of stabilization policies, on their adverse effects, and, more generally, on the harmful effects of government intervention.

The concern with the economy's productive capacity, and hence with the factors that promote or inhibit its expansion and utilization, is an economic problem par excellence. It is a distortion to claim that the problem was disregarded by the Keynesians. The currently faddish supply-siders focus on tax and other government-created disincentives to saving (which they erroneously equate with investment), work, entrepreneurship, productivity, and efficiency (see Laffer and Seymour 1979; Boskin 1980). Their assumptions seem to be based on spurious quantitative relationships. They anticipate benefits without actually knowing how to elicit them. The redistributive measures that they favor are likely to intensify social strife, without producing the desired effect on capital formation and productivity. They exaggerate the inhibiting role of government and underrate the quantitative weight and multiplicity of other factors affecting productive capacity. They view the economy as if it were not subject to business cycles and trends. This, of course, needs to be contrasted with a generalized supply and demand model in the Keynesian tradition, which is admirably pursued by Lawrence R. Klein in Chapter 15, this volume. As Samuelson quipped, God gave economists two eyes, one to watch supply and the other to watch demand. And, in a sense, a "one-eyed economist" is as bad as a "one-armed economist."

In matters of macro policy, the "Chicago school" (old monetarism) is characterized primarily by a distrust of government intervention; a trust in the intrinsic stability of the private economy; a reliance on the rule of monetary growth and on the stock of money as the policy target; and a dominant preoccupation with inflation, rather than with unemployment. The policy prescription of this school, reduced to its bare essentials, is to chart an unvarying monetary course, undisturbed by either economic conditions or prospects, with the understanding that the economy will adjust itself to this steady course. Where such an adjustment takes place will be the "best" possible solution, no matter what the rate of unemployment will be.

The essential tenets of monetarism are subject to dispute.[8] For our purposes we may single out two basic tenets: (1) that change in the money supply (M) is the only systematic factor governing the level of aggregate nominal income (PQ), but M affects PQ only with long and variable lags and imperfectly; thus (2) the monetary rule. The incompatibility of the Keynesian approach with the monetarist — the essence of the dispute over money, which "besides being the root of all evil is the source of much bad temper among economists" (Samuelson 1972, p. 744) — was ably summarized by Samuelson. He maintained (1977a, p. 765) that, according to the Keynesian perception, even when the money supply is held constant: (1) significant shifts in propensities to consume and save would affect the nominal value of current production and affect either or both average prices and total output; (2) an outbreak of investment opportunities or "animal spirits" on the part of investors would systematically affect total output; and (3) increased public spending or reduced taxes (and even the former offset by increased taxes) would systematically affect total output. "It is natural that a Keynesian should resent monetarism as not doing justice to the richness of reality. A good neoclassical post-Keynesian should feel equally resentful" (ibid., p. 768).

Samuelson admitted that in his earlier writings he tended to understate the role of money and the potency of monetary policy. But he does not agree with those "who think that monetary policy by itself is the sole or principal mechanism for controlling the aggregative behavior of a modern economy. I believe such a view to be factually wrong or irrelevant; and would add that, even if monetary policies truly had this exaggerated degree of potency, I would not deem it optimal social policy to rely exclusively or primarily upon that weapon alone" (1966, p. 1361). Surely money does matter, but not alone, and the debate goes on.

In another fundamental sense the disagreement is about the danger of setting up arbitrary rules that would place a dynamic economy, subject to exogenous shocks and endogenous shifts, in a straightjacket:

> In principle, the choice has never been between discretionary and nondiscretionary action: for when men set up a definitive mechanism which is to run forever afterward by itself, that involves a single act of discretion which transcends, in both its arrogance and its capacity for potential harm, any repeated acts of foolish discretion that can be imagined. [Samuelson 1966, p. 1362]

One implication of the monetarist perception is that *"inflation is always* and *everywhere a monetary phenomenon* in the sense that it is and can be produced only by a more rapid increase in the quantity of money than in output" (Friedman 1970b, p. 24). Hence the problem of cost-push inflation does not exist. The quantity theory of money does not provide a theory of inflation, for it begs the question of "the determinants of the determinants," the forces that make the Fed misbehave, and how the economy would be affected if the Fed did obey the monetary rule. A policy to contain macroeconomic instabilities that assumes a competitive pricing model and that explains inflation by monistic demand-pull is seriously inhibited. It is ineffective because it lacks plausible notions of how prices and wages are determined and changed in the real world of market power and of the varieties and sources of inflation.

There are several varieties and sources of inflation (real, monetary, and institutional). There is no single cause (inordinate money supply, budget deficit, union wage push, oligopolistic pricing, OPEC, and so on), nor is there a single cure. The eclectic attitude is not caused by intellectual indecision or uncertainty, but because the multipatterned experience requires a bold mixture of causations.

In the present world, price escalation in one sector is not usually offset by deescalation in another; it tends to upset the entire price structure and raise its average level. Existing institutional arrangements are conducive to price-wage leapfrogging in the face of a major microeconomic inflation. The dynamics and transmission mechanism of inflation are conditioned by the strong dependence of current wage and price changes on recent and past movements and expectations of future movements. These factors are reinforced, inter alia, by management's desire to have a relatively stable and content work force and the possibility of passing on cost increases to consumers in sometimes even higher prices than those warranted by high wage settlements. Monetary expansion is not the cause but the result of sustained general inflation because central bankers must be accommodative in order to avoid deteriorating economic activity in the short run. Most electorates desire and insist on high employment levels, which naturally makes stable prices a difficult goal to achieve. Also, the present-day mixed economy does not tolerate suffering and starvation. Hence the changes in attitudes and institutions make prices and wages increasingly downward rigid, which, together with the exogenous price shocks, are a source of stagflation (see Samuelson 1977, pp. 802–04).

Samuelson is very pessimistic about price stability. "I wish there were some new 'supply-side economics' that could be relied on to tame stagflation. There is not." Although the United States still has the potential for positive growth, "I doubt we shall live up to that potential between now and 1985" (1980d, p. 69; see Blinder 1979; Gramlich 1979).

Friedman claims that there is really no policy choice, for we might as well reconcile ourselves to the dismal prospect of having more unemployment now or later. Friedman's concept of the "natural rate of unemployment" — a term he coined to parallel Knut Wicksell's "natural rate of interest" — is a throwback to pre-Keynesian economics. It rejects the possibility of a permanent tradeoff between price stability and full employment; unemployment above the "natural rate" would decelerate inflation, and below the "natural rate" would accelerate inflation — but these are only transitory phenomena. The "natural rate" deals essentially with the elusive and difficult to model expectations and expectational errors, and relates variations in unemployment rates to incorrect inflationary expectations because "what matters is not inflation per se, but unanticipated inflation; there is no stable tradeoff between inflation and unemployment; there is a 'natural rate of unemployment' . . . which is consistent with the real forces and with accurate perceptions; unemployment can be kept below that level only by an accelerating inflation; or above it only by accelerating deflation" (Friedman 1977, p. 458).

On technical grounds alone the natural-rate hypothesis is very imprecise because no one really knows where the elusive "natural rate of unemployment" resides (see Lerner 1975, pp. 5–6). The concept leaves unexplained the determinants of the inflation rate at the natural level. Further, if there really is such a level, why does it vary so dramatically from period to period in any one country and from country to country in any one period (Kahn 1975, p. 1170)? Aside from the insuperable difficulty of fathoming the natural rate, it cannot be defended on welfare criteria (indeed, it can only be strongly attacked on such grounds). No matter what its size, it is definitely larger than the rate representing frictional, structural, or voluntary unemployment (see Tobin 1974, p. 94). Some of the policy implications are that to reduce the "natural rate" we should repeal the minimum wage law and remove union and other restrictions on the labor market.

"There is no sight in the world more awful than that of an old-time economist foam-flecked at the mouth and hell-bent to cure inflation by monetary discipline" (Samuelson 1973a, p. 55). Unfortunately we are witnessing his rebirth.

The "made-in-Washington" 1975 and 1980 recessions could be criticized by conservative economists as only chicken-hearted attempts at curing inflation. The policymakers hoped that "cooling off" the economy would restrain inflation. The error lay in the nature of the tradeoff—in not realizing that to appreciably reduce inflation would at those junctures have required catastrophic rates of unemployment (Samuelson 1977a, pp. 794–95). Conservative economists are quite aware that a mild recession (or a sharp, short-lived one) will not do the trick. They believe that the government has to declare firmly that it will sanction any rate of unemployment required to usher in price stability and to prove that it will uphold this decision in the face of politically unpopular unemployment, plant idleness, and reduced profits (see Samuelson 1980c, p. 69; Feldstein 1979; Fellner 1976).

Can we experiment with the welfare of the nation by attempting unemployment rates of 10, 15, or X percent? How high is the cost of price stability? Samuelson answers:

> I am not persuaded by the force of theoretical argument, or by the statistical and historical data so far available for different mixed economies, that even in the longest run the benefits to be derived from militant anti-inflationary polices don't carry excessive costs as far as average levels of unemployment and growth are concerned. And even if the benefits did decisively outweigh the costs in the longest run, history is a onetime thing and mankind at this stage of the game can ill afford to make irreversible academic experiments whose outcomes are necessarily doubtful and whose execution could put

strains on the already-strained political consensus of modern nations. [Samuelson 1977a, p. 807]

The militant anti-inflationary policies are likely to damage for a long time the fabric of the economy and society by lowering the aspirations, expectations, and performance of economic actors and by inhibiting investment and technical and economic dynamism. The long-term loss of output and retrogression in the progress of the human condition seem to be far more nefarious consequences than the evils of inflation. Also, in a slump various groups intensify their pressures for favors, which often results in an increase in inefficiency, monopolistic or monopsonistic power or trade union excesses, and protectionism, which obstructs further the protracted process of adjustment.

Samuelson is convinced that even with the prevailing conservative trend, *realpolitik* is such that the conservative economists will not get the opportunity for the harsh experiment they desire (1980c, p. 69). However, we can expect slower growth in the future partly due to the surge of oil prices and depletion of all natural resources. Also, growing affluence makes for slacker effort and discipline. And the process of innovation and technical change is also subject to oscillations (1980b, pp. 30–32). With good reason he views stagflation as an inherent characteristic of the present and future mixed economy. "The bell I fear to be hearing tolls for the most affluent countries" (ibid., p. 27; see Abramovitz 1981).

The currently fashionable and technically sophisticated "new classical macroeconomics" attributes much stronger perpetual market-clearing properties to our economy than do the earlier monetarists and even denies that there is a tradeoff to anticipated monetary policy in the short run. This school perceives the economy as normally in or near equilibrium, unimprovable by policy interventions. The theory is based on two crucial postulates: (1) all markets clear all the time instantaneously and (2) rational economic actors exhibit optimizing behavior. (Bob Solow has noted [1978a, p. 204] that the proponents of this theory "regard the postulate of optimizing behavior as self-evident and the postulate of market-clearing behavior as essentially meaningless. I think they are too optimistic, since the one that they think is self-evident I regard as meaningless and the one that they think is meaningless, I regard as false.") Departure from equilibrium is due to expectations of future economic events subject to significant errors, which tend to be transient. Money is neutral, and systematic monetary and fiscal countercyclical policies tend to have no significant effects on the real economy because the outcomes of the policies are informed predictions of anticipated and understood economic events and will be fully accounted for and offset in decision-makers' rational expectations. Macroeconomic policy can succeed only if policymakers are able to persistently bamboozle the micro agents. Supposedly, economic actors are fast learners who use and revise efficiently all available information (which renders the policymakers' behavior a crucial determinant in forming expectations) and who succeed in eliminating expectational misconceptions. The school places the foremost stress on unsystematic (i.e., unanticipated) monetary-fiscal shocks (policy surprises, entailing expectational distortions) in the fluctuation-generating mechanism, underrating real economic disturbances that occur in the process of economic growth and change (Lucas and Sargent 1978, pp. 49–72; Muth 1961, pp. 299–306; "Rational Expectations" 1980).

The test of theory is relevance for reality and, whatever the "new classical macroeconomics'" other great shortcomings, its empirical foundations are flimsy.[9] The content of "rational expectations" is questionable, for it does not explain how these expectations are formed, the learning process by which the actors discover, acquire, and interpret the information, and the use they make of it (see Simon 1979, p. 505; B. M. Friedman 1979). The theory rests on such untenable postulates as conventional competitive "supply equals demand" and the inordinate importance attached to the price-clearing mechanism and flexibility of industrial prices in both directions. Thus disequilibrium is promptly and smoothly eliminated by the forces of excess supply or demand. The impediments to the dynamic adjustment process and the difficulties, efforts, and costs involved are underrated or ignored. It is particularly debatable whether the alleged self-stabilizing and self-correcting economic mechanism is sufficiently forceful when the vulnerability of the economic system to external or random disturbances is considered. Usually the dynamic system can be moved toward equilibrium by some forces while others push it away. Nor is such an equilibrium necessarily desirable.

Classical economics is superior to its present-day version in that it perceived competition as part of a growth process and conceived the allocation problem within the context of a dynamic economy with changing endowment of resources, techniques, and tastes. Its present-day version concentrates unduly on the government as a source of economic instability. Its approach is based on a distorted vision of economic processes and abstracts from the salient features of the realities of modern capitalism. Such a version could be "seriously advanced only by persons with extravagant faith in their own abstract models and with historical amnesia'' (Tobin 1980a, p. 46; see Akerlof 1979; Buiter 1980; Hahn 1980). This version seems to be a stronger and shorter-run perception than that of earlier monetarists like Milton Friedman of the classical concept of neutrality of money and the long-run dichotomy between real and monetary phenomena (which says that the latter determines only the absolute price level and can have only short-run, transient real consequences). The "new classical macroeconomics" seems to be a retrogression from the classical view and subsequent neoclassical theorizing on the dynamics of transitional states of stable equilibrium and the dynamic modifications of the crude classical system (see Samuelson 1972, p. 558). In his presidential address to the American Economic Association, Franco Modigliani quipped that if the theory of rational expectations were valid, the analysis of the Great Depression could be reduced to a severe attack of laziness and the *General Theory* would never have been written (1977, p. 6). He concluded:

> We must . . . categorically reject the monetarist appeal to turn back the clock forty years by discarding the basic message of *The General Theory*. We should instead concentrate our efforts in an endeavor to make stabilization policies even more effective in the future than they have been in the past. [Modigliani 1977, p. 18]

A "KEYNESIAN" CRITIQUE OF THE NEOCLASSICAL SYNTHESIS

The neoclassical synthesis has been under attack from various quarters and for different reasons — not only for the details of its construction, but for its very foundations. In the previous section we have perused some of the anti-Keynesian critiques. Here I can do no more than sketch some of the "family quarrels."

First, it is of some interest to note Samuelson's own ambivalent attitude to neoclassical price theory. As Kenneth Arrow pointed out (1967, p. 733), "a careful examination of the papers both on theory and on policy yields only the most oblique suggestions that neoclassical price theory is descriptive of the real world. Of course, there is no flat denial, but Samuelson's attitude is clearly guarded and agnostic." Indeed, the neoclassical synthesis has not provided us with the macro-micro integration that it was purported to have done:

> Samuelson has not addressed himself to one of the major scandals of current price theory, the relation between microeconomics and macroeconomics.

Neoclassical microeconomic equilibrium with fully flexible prices presents a beautiful picture of the mutual articulations of a complex structure, full employment being one of its major elements. What is the relation between this world and either the real world with its recurrent tendencies to unemployment of labor, and indeed of capital goods, or the Keynesian world of an underemployment equilibrium? [Arrow 1967, p. 734]

And Arrow points out further that

the recurrent periods of unemployment which have characterized the history of capitalism are scarcely compatible with a neoclassical model of market equilibrium. A post-Keynesian world in which unemployment is avoided or kept at tolerable levels by recurrent alterations in fiscal or monetary policy is no more explicable by neoclassical axioms, though the falsification is not as conspicuous. [Arrow 1974, p. 2]

Furthermore, Arrow (1967, p. 734) sees two additional "major scandals" of the neoclassical general equilibrium theory, which fails to (1) take seriously, capture the essence of, and integrate imperfect competition into the system and (2) account for costs of transaction and of obtaining information, thus of running the market resource allocation process itself.[10]

In the standard and authoritative study on general equilibrium analysis, Arrow and Hahn point out (1971, p. 361) that in a world "with a past as well as a future and in which contracts are made in terms of money, no equilibrium may exist." In the real world the bulk of economic activity is oriented toward an uncertain future, and only sparse forward markets exist. Arrow and Hahn perceive that "the Keynesian revolution cannot be understood if proper account is not taken of the powerful influence exerted by the future and past on the present and by the large modifications that must be introduced into both value theory and stability analysis, if the requisite futures markets are missing" (ibid., p. 369).

Partly as a result of "self-criticism," general equilibrium theorists have attempted to remedy the "scandals" and to refine the theory. After almost conquering mainstream theory and accomplishing many feats, the "mature" general equilibrium theory is in a state of disarray. Even its protagonists admit that the results are far less illuminating than the aspirations. Even the questions posed are too restrictive and often lack relevance to the real world. One of the problems is that the modern economies are far more centralized than the model envisages. Furthermore, the model neglects economic power, historical setting, institutional specificities, and social class as an explanatory variable. "This lack of contact between the economic theory and sociological reality may well be the most damaging criticism of the neo-classical construction'' (Hahn 1972, p. 2; see Hahn 1977).

Some general equilibrium theorists feel that it would be a denigration to call the neo-Walrasian Arrow-Debreu model a ''microfoundation for macroeconomics,'' for ''it is not a bridge between two distinct bodies of knowledge. It is in fact coextensive with both micro and macro, each being a particularization by way of different *ceteris paribus* statements'' (Weintraub 1979, p. 71). They claim that general equilibrium theory is the applicable investigative logic to approach the problems of compatibility between microeconomics and macroeconomics. If some macroeconomic problems cannot be investigated within the Arrow-Debreu framework, then this framework should be modified or widened — a commendable endeavor whose fruitfulness is yet in question (ibid., pp. 73–74 and 89–162; see Hicks 1979, pp. 1451–54; Samuels 1979).

In this context a significant addition to the literature is the provocative set of lectures by Edmond Malinvaud, who elucidated the modifications required for general equilibrium theory to deal effectively with the Keynesian problem of unemployment. Malinvaud (1977) aims at reconciling the differences between economists concerned with unemployment and those working on price theory, which arise from the former's suspicion that the latter will tend to advance a Walrasian competitive theory explanation of unemployment. There is also the noteworthy attempt by Takashi Negishi (1979) to build a new, non-Walrasian economic theory capable of explaining microeconomics of a Keynesian ''fixprice'' macroeconomic equilibrium with involuntary unemployment.[11]

Understandably, the reaction is mixed. Those unsympathetic to the general equilibrium approach, like Lord Kahn (1977), claim that the attempt to reconcile Walrasian and Keynesian modes of analysis and perceptions is a mésalliance. Even some mainstream neoclassical Keynesians point to the difficulty, if not undesirability, of making macroeconomic models look like the abstract and elegant general equilibrium constructs without emptying them of ''the aggregative simplicity, institutional content, and definiteness of conclusion which are their *raison d'être*'' (Tobin 1980a, p. x; see Samuelson 1980a, p. 773; Harcourt 1977, pp. 372–96; Negishi 1979, p. 195). Moreover, one cannot analyze market behavior and relations without a perception of the macro setting in which they operate. Hence microeconomics also needs a macrofoundation (see Robinson 1977, p. 1320; Solow 1979, p. 354).

Another stream of criticism is that implied in Sir John Hicks's recantation of his former position. The ''Hicksian Walrasianism'' and its by-product IS-LM are classics in more than one sense (see Clower 1975).

This framework was instrumental in teaching so-called Keynesian economics — criticized by Joan Robinson (1978, p. xiv) for confusing and reducing "the General Theory to a version of static equilibrium" (see Weintraub 1977, p. 45; Harcourt 1977, p. 5). In his recent change of heart, Hicks admits that his model was a relapse into statics and reduced the General Theory to equilibrium economics. He contends (1977, p. 148) that the *General Theory* "provides a model on which academic economists can comfortably perform their accustomed tricks. Haven't they just? With ISLM I myself fell into the trap. . . . The *General Theory* is a brilliant squeezing of dynamic economics into static habits of thought. The *Treatise* is more genuinely dynamic, and therefore, more human." Hicks sees the neoclassical synthesis as "the colonization of more and more of the *dynamic* territory by 'classical' (if Walrasian was classical) methods. At the height of its success, the colonization seemed to be complete; 'Keynes' had been pushed right over the edge. The quarry of the hunt had just disappeared" (1979, p. 1452).

The view reappears, ever more frequently, that in the synthesis of Keynesian and pre-Keynesian economics, it is the latter that has been gaining preeminence, preempting the former (see Minsky 1975, p. ix; S. Weintraub 1977, pp. 45–66; Harcourt 1977, p. 392):

> Despite its name, the neoclassical synthesis was not really a synthesis of neoclassical with Keynesian ideas . . . but merely the reassertion of the neoclassical framework with the addition of some Keynesian "macro" terminology. The flavor of some of Keynes' specific policy recommendations was retained, but the essential *logic* of Keynes' economic theory was discarded. Thus the neoclassical synthesis had the result that the fundamental Keynesian revolution was aborted. [Davidson 1980, p. 151]

Such statements echo what Joan Robinson has been saying for years. She claims that the neoclassical synthesis has opened the way for the "neoclassical Keynesians" (whom she calls by a less polite name) to pursue "theorems about an ideal free market economy." In this way, "Keynes' work, far from being the starting point for realistic study of the imperfect market economies in which we live, became an excuse for economists to carry on as before" (Robinson and Cripps 1979, p. 140).

Essentially, "behind the esoteric dispute over 'reswitching' or heterogeneity of capital there often lurk contrasting views about fruitful ways of understanding distributional analysis and affecting its content by alternative policy measures" (Samuelson 1977a, p. 113). Joan Robinson militantly attacks (1978, pp. 91ff.) what she calls the "pre-Keynesian theory after Keynes," the treatment of accumulation decisions as governed by the propensity to save of the economy as a whole, and the validity and relevance of neoclassical price and distribution theories. When he formulated the neoclassical synthesis, Samuelson underrated the seriousness of the problem of insufficiency of effective demand and overrated the ability and willingness of the policymaker to stabilize the economy so as to utilize its full potential. The neoclassical synthesis suffers from the separation of long-run growth trends from short-run, demand-determined fluctuations[12] — a controversial and perplexing problem in business cycle theory (see Feiwel 1975, Chap. 5).

One of the differences between the neoclassical Keynesians and the Cambridge-on-the-Cam Keynesians is that the latter assign greater weight to the objective of maintaining full employment and its content and equity, and a lower weight to efficiency considerations.[13] This does not mean that both approaches do not attach importance to both considerations, but that they assign relatively different weights to them.

Joan Robinson perceives the essence of the Keynesian revolution to lie in placing the analysis in historical time and stressing the pervasive influence of uncertainty — concepts that fell into neglect with the rise of the neoclassical synthesis, but that, as we have seen, are increasingly recognized, though the intrinsic difficulties of modeling have yet prevented their effective incorporation into mainstream analysis. In her 1971 Ely lecture, she reiterated eloquently her position:

> Consider what was the point of the Keynesian revolution on the plane of theory and on the plane of policy. On the plane of theory, the main point of the *General Theory* was to break out of the cocoon of equilibrium and consider the nature of life lived in time — the difference between yesterday and tomorrow. Here and now, the past is irrevocable and the future is unknown.

Uncertainty was the very essence of Keynes's problem (see Robinson 1980, 1979; Kahn 1977):

> In the new macro-micro theory, this point is lost. By one simple device, the whole of Keynes' argument is put to sleep. Work out what saving *would be* at full employment in the present short-period situation, with the present distribution of wealth and the present hierarchy of rates of earnings for different occupations, and arrange to have enough investment to absorb the level of saving that this distribution of income brings about. Then hey presto! we are back in the world of equilibrium where saving governs investment and micro theory can slip into the old grooves again. [Robinson 1978, pp. 4–5]

The Cambridge-on-the-Cam Keynesians stress that a key element in Keynes's theory is that the industrial price level is determined by the level of costs, which depends mainly on the relation of nominal wages to productivity.[14] Thus, aside from such cost-push inflation generated by the increasing prices of primary materials, energy, and foodstuffs, the main propeller of inflation is the labor market (Kahn 1976, 1974, pp. 16–17 and 30; Kaldor 1976). Inflation is deeply rooted in the institutions, market, and noncompetitive arrangements and attitudes in the postwar mixed economies.

In an economy suffering from stagflation, the question of distribution becomes increasingly more acute. And it is in this context that the problem of reconstructing economic theory — to integrate what is valid in the contrasting approaches — begs answer. What follows is suggested as only *one* of the building blocks of a new synthesis — one yet to be designed.

In a review of the influential *On Keynesian Economics and the Economics of Keynes,* Joan Robinson acknowledged that "there is something" to Leijonhufvud's contention "that we who worked with Keynes were saved from the misunderstandings rife in America because we had the benefit of oral teaching which was not made clear in the book." But, she continues, "I think that there are more important explanations. First Kalecki brought to England his own version of the General Theory, which tightened up some loose threads in Keynes' version and brought it into relation with imperfect competition, supplying a missing link in Keynes' theory of prices. To judge by this survey, Kalecki had very little influence on American doctrines" (Robinson 1969, p. 582).

Kalecki's influence on and differences with the Cambridge-on-the-Cam Keynesians are not part of this story, but his ideas are. Kalecki's contributions, even if sometimes not directly identified with him, are especially significant because, as an independent architect of a seemingly overlapping General Theory, he derived profoundly distinct theoretical and policy implications, which are of particular importance, inter alia, because of the modern assaults on the Keynesian revolution and the need to extend and generalize the General Theory and also because his ideas are less amenable to the neoclassical synthesis. What follows is a brief summary of some of the salient differences between Keynes's and Kalecki's constructs (see Kalecki 1971; Feiwel 1975, Part 1).

1. Keynes concentrated his attack on the macroeconomic failures, but did not challenge the established value and distribution theory. The model of perfect competition was foreign to Kalecki, who dealt with imperfect competition and oligopoly. Kalecki's macro model has a more useful microeconomic base. To build a realistic theory, Kalecki explained how industrial prices are formed by markups on costs and distinguished

between "cost-determined" and "demand-determined" prices. The intensity of the "degree of monopoly" (together with other distributional factors) is a key for the determination of macrodistribution. The distributional factors are essentially pertinent to effective demand and to fluctuations in aggregate output and utilization of resources.

2. Kalecki's theory of profits is based on the principle that wage-earners do not save, but spend what they get, and that entrepreneurs get what they spend. Thus entrepreneurs' profits are governed by their propensity to invest and consume and not the other way round. His consumption function analysis is based on social classes rather than on a "fundamental psychological law."

3. Kalecki's model not only describes a wider range of economic phenomena, but also presents the economic process in motion (i.e., how one sequence develops from the preceding ones). The model encompasses long-run dynamics and some supply considerations.

4. Kalecki did not approach the theory of effective demand through the multiplier, but through the theory of the business cycle, where two basic relations are established: (a) the impact of effective demand generated by investment on profits and national income and (b) the investment decision function, where the rate of investment decisions at a given time is roughly determined by the level and the rate of change in economic activity at some earlier time. One of the distinctive properties of his model is the clear separation that Kalecki makes between investment decision and actual implementation. The investment-realization lag explains the cumulative character of expansionary and contractionary processes.

If the current rate of investment surpasses that of the preceding period, the level of current profit will rise, profit expectations will improve, investment demand will increase, and more orders will be placed, followed by an increased rate of investment activity and enlarged income. The income-generating capacity of investment is the source of prosperity and encourages a further rise in investment. But investment has also a capacity-creating effect; every completed investment adds to productive capacity, competes with the stock of equipment of older vintage, and discourages more investment. Sooner or later investment stops rising and so does the level of current profit. The rate of profit falls. The rise in investment is transitory, and the boom cannot endure. A process of cumulative contraction takes place. The growth of national wealth contains the seeds of retardation.

While his earlier writings were clearly influenced by the severity of the Great Depression, in the subsequent development of the argument, he made allowances for the relative weak impact of the capital destruction effect. He introduced a certain "corrective" — a trend factor that shifts investment upward as the cycle continues. In a growing economy investment fluctuates along the long-run trend line. Innovations raise the prospects for profit, thus stimulating investment and engendering an ascending trend. Innovation becomes another weighty factor in the determination of the investment function, together with the change in the rate of profit, the rate of change in the stock of capital, and the "internal" gross savings (depreciation and undistributed profits) of firms. Kalecki sought to develop a theory integrating growth and cyclical processes.

5.   To Kalecki the key prerequisite for becoming an entrepreneur is the ownership of capital. The outside finance that can be secured is largely restricted by the size of the entrepreneurial capital. Moreover, entrepreneurs tend to be unwilling to use their full borrowing potential because risk increases with the amount invested. In case of bad investment, the higher the ratio of borrowing to the entrepreneur's own capital, the greater is the decrease of the entrepreneur's income or the risk of wiping out his equity. These considerations are important for the theory of investment decisions and in the analysis of factors circumscribing the size of the firm. Such decisions are related to the firm's "internal" accumulation of gross savings. These savings allow the firm to make new investments without facing the problems of the limited capital market or "increasing risk."

6.   Kalecki deals with an open system. He treats the rate of export surplus as a promoter of prosperity and the balance-of-payments difficulties that tend to accompany an upswing as a factor limiting expansion.

7.   Whatever the rationale of the *economics* of full employment, the *political* problems are formidable. Kalecki realized that full employment policies could be used to make the system work better and more equitably. He saw the opportunity, but was mindful of the grave political problems and, in 1943, predicted the emergence of the political business cycle. He argued that opposition by the "leaders of industry" to full employment stimulated by government spending may be expected because of the inherent fear of government interference, opposition to the objects of government spending (particularly to public investments and the subsidizing of consumption), fear of inflationary pressures, opposition to sustained full employment (as against mere prevention of deep depressions), and the dislike of the social and economic changes resulting from the maintenance of full employment (including laxity of workers' discipline). He felt that business cycles in milder form than hitherto would

continue and result in some sort of stop-go, where the government would vacillate between combating unemployment and inflation.

The Great Depression shook the capitalist system to its very foundations, but it did not collapse. The first twenty-five postwar years were remarkably prosperous — whatever exceptions one may take to the methods of achieving prosperity, to the content and distribution of the cake, and to the long-term effect on productivity, well-being, and quality of life. While the business cycle was neither dead nor obsolete, sharp depressions were avoided as a result of major interventions of the new actor in the "cycle drama" — the government. For a quarter of a century, capitalism — still fairly far remote from full utilization of resources, but without severe depressions and with relatively mild fluctuations (sometimes generated by the government — the political business cycle) — became a qualitatively new phenomenon.

There occurred a fundamental alteration in the commonly held views about the inevitability of business cycles; the desirable rates of economic activity; and the legitimacy, responsibility, ability, and effectiveness of government's manipulation of the levels of macroeconomic activity. To be sure, popular views about government intervention to promote prosperity have shifted over time. There appears to be a cyclical element in the electorate's demands for and tolerance or disapproval of what is popularly, and not always correctly, identified as "Keynesian policies" and attitudes toward objects of spending.

Interestingly, the postwar success story was followed by retrogression in the 1970s — recovery from which has proven to be extraordinarily difficult and protracted, with a deteriorating long-term trend — that has undermined the conviction that in "post-Keynesian" capitalism a growing and high-employment economy with increasing living standards is the norm. We have gone from an exaggerated view about the potency of the "Keynesian medicine," however misinterpreted and misapplied, to a far-reaching agnosticism. Now the fashion is to deprecate the positive contributions of Keynesian economics. The 1970s saw a questioning of the government's good intentions, for the consequences of the government's actions may be quite the reverse, an increasing questioning of the need for and effectiveness of stabilization policy, and assaults on the Keynesian revolution. The challenge was not devoid of positive developments, for it shook the complacency of some economists and forced them to reexamine and rethink what should, can, and cannot be done. It exposed some weak points and stimulated a search for overcoming the shortcomings. As Solow admitted (1978a, p. 204): "Every orthodoxy, including my own, needs to have a kick in the pants frequently, to prevent it from getting self-indulgent, and applying very lax standards to itself."

There are distinct limitations to public policies in a dynamic, stochastic, and increasingly interdependent world. Exaggeration of either the opportunities or limitations leads to many pitfalls. However, as Samuelson noted (1980b, p. 25), "democratic societies do not adhere to self-denying practices and let the Walrasian game of pure economics play itself out. *The same self-interest that provided the gasoline to make the classical game of markets operate must be expected in today's political sphere to motivate interferences with the laissez faire scenario.*"

It is a legitimate task and duty of democratic governments to design and implement an appropriate economic policy to ensure sustained long-term expansion and full utilization of the economic potential and to raise the standard of living of the entire population over time. Ipso facto, this calls for a unified theory of growth, fluctuations, price, and distribution and for an innovative mix of compatible macroeconomic and microeconomic policies directed at both short-term fluctuations and long-term growth and at overall composition of output and income, employment, capital accumulation, choice of techniques, productivity, and structural imbalances. By implication, under the present circumstances, the conventional fiscal and monetary policies are inadequate; at the very least they need to be reconstructed and dovetailed with prudent supply management and incomes policies. To be effective such policies have to recognize political and institutional realities and account for the fact that political interventions have a timing of their own, while many of our problems require a long-term approach.

This is a tall order and a challenge. But to those of us who perceive the inherent instabilities and failures of the market and see both opportunities and limitations in private and government actions, there hardly seems to be a period in postwar history when active and innovative policy is more imperative.

Looking back and ahead Samuelson mused:

> The neoclassical economists of goodwill had a noble and feasible vision. They advocated redistributive taxation and transfers to reduce the stark inequalities of laissez faire. . . . And the do-gooders like me envisage a role in the mixed economy for democratic policies designed to influence the fraction of high-employment GNP going to capital formation, and envision a measure of democratic planning to deal with externalities and probabilistic problems of the future. [Samuelson 1980b, pp. 26–27]

My dream is to make the mixed economy work better. . . . Is it utopian to retain and promote the *humane* qualities of the *mixed economy* while conserving the *efficiencies* of the market mechanism? Yes, it is utopian. But the rational pursuit of this goal provides our generation of economists with a worthy challenge. [Ibid., p. 35]

NOTES

1. Milton Friedman admits (1976, pp. 10–15) that "it pains" him to concede that Adam Smith provides arguments for government intervention. In particular, he points out that since Smith wrote

> there is hardly an activity which has not been regarded as suitable for governmental intervention on Smith's ground. It is easy to assert, as Smith himself does again and again, that there are "external effects" which place something or other in the "public interest" even though not in the "interest of any individual or small number of individuals." There are no widely accepted objective criteria by which to evaluate such claims, to measure the magnitude of any external effects, to identify the external effects of the governmental actions, and to set them against the external effects of leaving matters in private hands. Superficially scientific cost-benefit analysis erected on Smith's basis has proved a veritable Pandora's box. [Friedman 1976, pp. 14–15]

2. Hicks has pointed out that Don Patinkin's work (which I have not included in my listing) is largely classical in spirit: "The theory which Patinkin sets out, though it owes much to Keynes, is not Keynesian; it is a modernised version of the theory which Keynes called 'classical'" (Hicks 1957, p. 289; see Davidson 1967).

3. The references to each variant can be found in the list of references under its most representative exponents.

4. This subject will be treated at length in my study on the various schools in contemporary economic thought and their policy implications. The same applies to the analyses of contemporary "anti-Keynesians" both left and right.

5. Joan Robinson (1976, p. 9) for one deplores this passage as "ill-considered" and quite contrary to Keynes's main argument.

6. As is well known, Keynes refers to "classical" economics in connection with the problem of neglect of effective demand. He groups under that heading economists from Ricardo to Pigou who are conventionally classified into either the classical or neoclassical schools. When referring to "classical" microeconomics, Samuelson usually means "neoclassical." He uses the term *post-Keynesian* meaning primarily "after Keynes" (influenced by Keynes), but more specifically in reference to the "neoclassical Keynesians."

7. As Solow (1978c) argues, there is little specifically Keynesian (historically or analytically) about the Phillips curve. The monetarists criticized it at an early stage. "Once upon a time economists had believed that there was no durable (I will not insist on permanent) gearing between real things and monetary things. Keynes had disagreed and apparently carried the day. Now it was argued that there could be no durable gearing between real things and the rate of change of monetary things, and some of the arguments sounded very much like the earlier ones" (ibid., p. 147).

8. The vast literature on the subject has been ably summarized by Thomas Mayer (1978). The key propositions of monetarism were outlined by Friedman (1979b). For pros and cons of the debate, see also Johnson 1972; Nobay and Johnson 1977; Stein 1976; Klein 1971, 1977; Hahn 1980; Modigliani 1977; Tobin 1974; Robinson 1962; Kahn 1975; Hicks 1975; Weintraub 1978.

9. On the implausible assumptions of human behavior made by the "new classical macroeconomics" and the dismissal of some economic fads, see Klein, Chapter 15, this volume.

10. See Robert Kuenne, Chapter 17, Takashi Negishi, Chapter 8, and Earl Beach, Chapter 9, this volume.

11. See also Negishi, Chapter 8, this volume.

12. In his reply to recent assaults on Keynesian economics and the fixation with the "supply side," James Tobin remarked (1980b, p. 37): "Journalists love simple dichotomies: the Keynesians ignored supply and even, we are told, thought demand would create its own supply. . . . Far from being wholly demand-oriented, the neoclassical synthesis paid a great deal of attention to the factors determining long-run growth and to policies that might raise the level and slope of the economy's full-employment path."

13. On the problems of efficiency versus equity, see Alan S. Blinder, Chapter 20, this volume.

14. The fundamental role of nominal wages in determining prices, incomes, and all money values stems not only from their function as a cost component, but from the fact that they are largely spent and then constitute part of aggregate nominal demand. Keynes's own analysis of the behavior of nominal wages is unsatisfactory. Understandably, his main preoccupation was not with rising wages, but with certain difficulties of securing falling wages (Kahn 1974, p. 17).

REFERENCES

Aaron, H. J., and M. J. Boskin, eds. 1980. *The Economics of Taxation*. Washington, D.C.: Brookings.

Abramovitz, M. 1981. "Welfare Quandries and Productivity Concerns." *American Economic Review* 71(1):1–17.

Ackley, G. 1978. "The Costs of Inflation." *American Economic Review* 68(2):149–54.

Akerlof, G. 1979. "The Case against Conservative Macroeconomics." *Economica* 46:219–38.

Arrow, K. J. 1967. "Samuelson Collected." *Journal of Political Economy* 75:730–37.

———. 1974. "Limited Knowledge and Economic Ideas." *American Economic Review* 64:1–10.

———, and F. H. Hahn. 1971. *General Competitive Analysis*. San Francisco: Holden-Day.

Azariadis, C. 1975. "Implicit Contracts and Underemployment Equilibria." *Journal of Political Economy* 83:1183–1202.

Baily, M. N. 1974. "Wages and Employment under Uncertain Demand." *Review of Economic Studies* 41:37–50.

Barro, R. J. 1976. "Rational Expectations and the Role of Monetary Policy." *Journal of Monetary Economics* 2:1–32.

———. 1979. "Second Thoughts on Keynesian Economics." *American Economic Review* 69:54–59.

———, and S. Fischer. 1976. "Recent Developments in Monetary Theory." *Journal of Monetary Economics* 2:133–67.

———, and H. Grossman. 1976. *Money, Employment and Inflation*. Cambridge, England: Cambridge University Press.

Baumol, W. J. 1967. *Business Behavior Value and Growth*. New York: Harcourt Brace Jovanovich.

Benassy, J.-P. 1975. "Neo-Keynesian Disequilibrium Theory in a Monetary Economy." *Review of Economic Studies* 42:503–23.

Blinder, A. S. 1979. *Economic Policy and the Great Stagflation*. New York: Academic Press.

———, and R. M. Solow. 1973. "Does Fiscal Policy Matter?" *Journal of Public Economics* 2:319–37.

———, and R. M. Solow. 1974. "Analytical Foundations of Fiscal Policy." In A. Blinder, et al. *The Economics of Public Finance*. Washington, D.C.: Brookings.

Boskin, M. J., ed. 1980. *The Economy in the 1980s*. San Francisco: Institute for Contemporary Study.

Break, G. F. 1976. "The Incidence and Effects of Taxation." In A. Blinder et al. *The Economics of Public Finance*. Washington, D.C.: Brookings.

Bronfenbrenner, M. 1977. "Ten Issues in Distribution Theory." In S. Weintraub, ed. *Modern Economic Thought*. Philadelphia: University of Pennsylvania Press.

Brunner, K., and A. H. Meltzer, eds. 1976a. *Institutions, Policies and Economic Performance*. Amsterdam: North-Holland.

———, and A. H. Meltzer, eds. 1976b. *The Phillips Curve and Labor Markets*. Amsterdam: North-Holland.

Buchanan, J. M., and R. E. Wagner. 1977. *Democracy in Deficit*. New York: Academic Press.

Buiter, W. H. 1980. "The Macroeconomics of Dr. Pangloss: A Critical Survey of the New Classical Macroeconomics." *Economic Journal* 90:34–50.

Cagan, P. 1978. "The Reduction of Inflation by Slack Demand." In William Fellner, ed. *Contemporary Economic Problems*. Washington, D.C.: American Enterprise Institute.

Clower, R. 1965. "The Keynesian Counterrevolution." In F. H. Hahn and F. P. R. Brechling, eds. *The Theory of Interest Rates*. London: Macmillan.

———. 1969. "What Traditional Monetary Theory Really Wasn't?" *Canadian Journal of Economics* 2(2):299–302.

———. 1975. "Reflections on the Keynesian Perplex." *Zeitschrift für Nationalokonomie* 35(1–2):1–24.

Davidson, P. 1967. "A Keynesian View of Patinkin's Theory of Employment." *Economic Journal* 77:559–78.
———. 1978. *Money and the Real World*. London: Macmillan.
———. 1980. "Post Keynesian Economics." *Public Interest*. Special Edition, pp. 151–73.
Denison, E. F. 1979. *Accounting for Slower Growth: The United States in 1970*. Washington, D.C.: Brookings.
Dobb, M. H. 1973. *Theories of Value and Distribution since Adam Smith*. Cambridge, England: Cambridge University Press.
Duggal, V., and L. R. Klein. 1971. "Guidelines in Economic Stabilization." *Wharton Quarterly* (Summer), pp. 20–24.
Eichner, A., and J. Kregel. 1976. "An Essay on Post-Keynesian Theory." *Journal of Economic Literature* 14:34–53.
Eisner, R. 1958. "On Growth Models and the Neo-classical Resurgence." *Economic Journal* 68:707–21.
———. 1975. "The Keynesian Revolution Reconsidered." *American Economic Review* 65(2):189–94.
Feiwel, G. R. 1975. *The Intellectual Capital of Michal Kalecki*. Knoxville: University of Tennessee Press.
Feldstein, M. S. 1977. "Does the United States Save Too Little?" *American Economic Review* 67:116–21.
———. 1979. "The Welfare Cost of Permanent Inflation and Optimal Short-Run Economic Policy." *Journal of Political Economy* 87(4):749–68.
———, ed. 1980. *The American Economy in Transition*. Chicago: University of Chicago Press.
Fellner, W. 1976. *Towards a Reconstruction of Macroeconomics*. Washington, D.C.: American Enterprise Institute.
Fisher, S. 1979. "On Activist Monetary Policy with Rational Expectations." National Bureau of Economic Research, Working Paper No. 341.
Friedman, B. M. 1979. "Optimal Expectations and the Extreme Information Assumptions of 'Rational Expectations' Macromodels." *Journal of Monetary Economics* 5:23–41.
———, ed. 1978. *New Challenges to the Role of Profit*. Lexington, Mass.: Lexington Books.
Friedman, M. 1968. "The Role of Monetary Policy." *American Economic Review* 58:1–17.
———. 1970a. "The Market v. the Bureaucrat." *National Review* 22(19):507–10.
———. 1970b. *The Counter-revolution in Monetary Theory*. London: Institute of Economic Affairs.
———. 1976. *Adam Smith's Relevance for 1976*. Los Angeles: International Institute for Economic Research.
———. 1977. "Nobel Lecture: Inflation and Unemployment." *Journal of Political Economy* 85(3):451–72.
Frisch, H. 1977. "Inflation Theory 1963–1975: A 'Second Generation' Survey." *Journal of Economic Literature* 15:1289–1317.

Goodhart, C. A. E. 1975. *Money, Information and Uncertainty*. London: Macmillan.

Gordon, R. J. 1976. "Recent Developments in the Theory of Inflation and Unemployment." *Journal of Monetary Economics* 2(2):185–219.

——, ed. 1974. *Milton Friedman's Monetary Framework*. Chicago: University of Chicago Press.

Gramlich, E. M. 1979. "Macro Policy Responses to Price Shocks." *Brookings Papers on Economic Activity* 1:125–66.

Grandmont, J.-M., and G. Laroque. 1977. "On Temporary Keynesian Equilibrium." In G. C. Harcourt, ed. *The Microeconomic Foundations of Macroeconomics*. London: Macmillan.

Hahn, F. 1972. *The Share of Wages in National Income*. London: Weidenfeld and Nicholson.

——. 1977. "Keynesian Economics and General Equilibrium Theory: Reflections on Some Current Debates." In G. C. Harcourt, ed. *The Microeconomic Foundations of Macroeconomics*. London: Macmillan.

——. 1980. "Monetarism and Economic Theory." *Economica* 47:1–17.

Hall, R. E. 1974. "The Process of Inflation in the Labor Market." *Brookings Papers on Economic Activity* 2:343–93.

——. 1980. "Employment Fluctuations and Wage Rigidity." *Brookings Papers on Economic Activity* 1:91–142.

Harcourt, G. C., ed. 1977. *The Microeconomic Foundations of Macroeconomics*. London: Macmillan.

Harrod, R. 1973. *Economic Dynamics*. London: Macmillan.

Hicks, J. R. 1957. "A Rehabilitation of 'Classical' Economics?" *Economic Journal*, 67:278–89.

——. 1974. *The Crisis in Keynesian Economics*. New York: Basic Books.

——. 1975. "What Is Wrong with Monetarism?" *Central Bank of Ireland*. Winter Bulletin, pp. 79–93.

——. 1977. *Economic Perspectives*. Oxford: Clarendon Press.

——. 1979. "Review of Weintraub's *Microfoundations*." *Journal of Economic Literature* 17:1451–54.

Jaffe, W. 1980. "Walras's Economics as Others See It." *Journal of Economic Literature* 18:528–49.

Johnson, H. G. 1972. *Inflation and the Monetarist Controversy*. Amsterdam: North-Holland.

——. 1978. *Selected Essays in Monetary Economics*. London: Allen and Unwin.

Kahn, R. 1974. *On Re-reading Keynes*. London: Oxford University Press.

——. 1975. "Monetarism and Incomes Policies." *Banker* 125(596):1167–70.

——. 1976a. "Thoughts on the Behaviour of Wages and Monetarism." *Lloyd's Bank Review* 119:1–5.

——. 1976b. "Keynesian View." In "Symposium on Inflation." *Scottish Journal of Political Economy* 23(1):11–16.

——. 1977. "Malinvaud on Keynes." *Cambridge Journal of Economics* 1:375–78.

Kaldor, N. 1976. "Inflation and Recession in the World Economy." *Economic Journal* 86:703–14.

Kalecki, M. 1944. "Three Ways to Full Employment." In *The Economics of Full Employment.* Oxford: Blackwell.

———. 1945. "Full Employment by Stimulating Private Investment?" *Oxford Economic Papers* 7:83–92.

———. 1971. *Selected Essays on the Dynamics of the Capitalist Economy 1933– 1970.* Cambridge, England: Cambridge University Press.

Keynes, J. M. 1936. *The General Theory of Employment Interest and Money.* London: Macmillan.

Klein, L. R. 1966. *The Keynesian Revolution.* New York: Macmillan.

———. 1971. "Empirical Evidence on Fiscal and Monetary Models." In J. J. Diamond, ed. *Issues in Fiscal and Monetary Policy.* Chicago: DePaul University Press.

———. 1975. "Review of Hicks's *The Crisis of Keynesian Economics.*" *Challenge* (November–December), pp. 65–66.

———. 1977. "The Longevity of Economic Theory." In *Quantitative Wirtschaftsforschung.* Tubingen: Mohr.

———. 1978a. "Disturbances to the International Economy." In *After the Phillips Curve.* Boston: Federal Reserve Bank of Boston.

———. 1978b. "The Supply Side." *American Economic Review* 68:1–7.

Laffer, A. B., and J. P. Seymour, eds. 1979. *The Economics of the Tax Revolt.* New York: Harcourt Brace Jovanovich.

Leijonhufvud, A. 1968. *On Keynesian Economics and the Economics of Keynes.* New York: Oxford University Press.

———. 1981. *Information and Coordination.* New York: Oxford University Press.

Lerner A. P. 1975. "Stagflation." *Intermountain Economic Review* 6(2):1–7.

———. 1977. "From Pre-Keynes to Post-Keynes." *Social Research* 44:387– 415.

———. 1978. "Keynesianism: Alive, if Not So Well, at Forty." In J. M. Buchanan and R. E. Wagner, eds. *Fiscal Responsibility in Constitutional Democracy.* Boston: Martinus Nijhoff.

Lipsey, R. 1960. "The Relation between Unemployment and the Rate of Money Wage Rates in the United Kingdom, 1862–1957: A Further Analysis." *Economica* 27:1–31.

Lucas, R. E. 1975. "An Equilibrium Model of the Business Cycle." *Journal of Political Economy* 83(6):1113–44.

———. 1976. "Econometric Policy Evaluation: A Critique." In K. Brunner and A. H. Metzler, eds. *The Phillips Curve and Labor Markets.* Amsterdam: North-Holland.

———, and T. J. Sargent. 1978. "After Keynesian Macroeconomics." In *After the Phillips Curve.* Boston: Federal Reserve Bank of Boston.

McCullum, B. T. 1979. "The Current State of the Policy Ineffectiveness Debate." *American Economic Review* 69:240–45.

Malinvaud, E. 1977. *The Theory of Unemployment Reconsidered.* Oxford: Blackwell.

——, and Y. Younes. 1977. "Some New Concepts for the Microeconomic Foundations of Macroeconomics." In G. C. Harcourt, ed. *The Microeconomic Foundations of Macroeconomics.* London: Macmillan.

Mayer, T., ed. 1978. *The Structure of Monetarism.* New York: Norton.

Minsky, H. P. 1975. *John Maynard Keynes.* New York: Columbia University Press.

Modigliani, F. 1977. "The Monetarist Controversy or, Should We Forsake Stabilization Policies?" *American Economic Review* 67(2):1–19.

——. 1980. *The Collected Papers of Franco Modigliani,* vol. 1. In A. Abel, ed. *Essays in Macroeconomics.* Cambridge, Mass.: MIT Press.

Morishima, M. 1977. *Walras' Economics: A Pure Theory of Capital and Money.* New York: Cambridge University Press.

Musgrave, R. A. 1978. *The Future of Fiscal Policy.* Leuven: Leuven University Press.

Muth, J. R. 1961. "Rational Expectations and the Theory of Price Movements." *Econometrica* 29(3):299–306.

Negishi, T. 1979. *Microfoundations of Keynesian Macroeconomics.* Amsterdam: North-Holland.

Nobay, R. A., and H. G. Johnson. 1977. "Monetarism." *Journal of Economic Literature* 15:470–85.

Okun, A. M. 1975. "Inflation, Its Mechanics and Welfare Costs." *Brookings Papers on Economic Activity* 2:351–90.

——, and G. L. Perry, eds. 1978. *Curing Chronic Inflation.* Washington, D.C.: Brookings.

Patinkin, D. 1965. *Money, Interest and Prices.* New York: Harper & Row.

——. 1969. "The Chicago Tradition, the Quantity Theory, and Friedman." *Journal of Money, Credit and Banking* 1:46–70.

——. 1972. "Samuelson on the Neoclassical Dichotomy: A Comment." *Canadian Journal of Economics* 5:279–83.

——. 1976. *Keynes' Monetary Thought.* Durham, N.C.: Duke University Press.

——. 1979. "A Study of Keynes' Theory of Effective Demand." *Economic Inquiry* 18:155–76.

Pechman, J. A., ed. 1980. *What Should Be Taxed: Income or Expenditure?* Washington, D.C.: Brookings.

Perry, G. L. 1980. "Inflation Theory and Practice." *Brookings Papers on Economic Activity* 1:207–41.

Phelps, E. S., et al. 1970. *Microeconomic Foundations of Employment and Inflation Theory.* New York: Norton.

Phillips, A. W. 1958. "The Relation between Unemployment and the Rate of Change of Wage Rates in the United Kingdom, 1861–1957." *Economica* 25:283–99.

Pigou, A. C. 1951. *Keynes's "General Theory."* London: Macmillan.

Piore, M. J., ed. 1979. *Unemployment and Inflation: Institutionalist and Structuralist Views.* White Plains, N.Y.: Sharpe.

"Rational Expectations." 1980. *Journal of Money, Credit and Banking* 12(4), Part 2:691–836.

Robinson, J. 1962. *Economic Philosophy.* Chicago: Aldine.

————. 1969. "Review of Leijonhufvud, *On Keynesian Economics and the Economics of Keynes.*" *Economic Journal* 79:581–83.

————. 1976. "The Age of Growth." *Challenge* (May–June), pp. 4–9.

————. 1977. "What Are the Questions?" *Journal of Economic Literature* 15:1318–39.

————. 1978. *Contributions to Modern Economics.* New York: Academic Press.

————. 1979. "Misunderstandings in the Theory of Production." *Greek Economic Review* 1:1–7.

————. 1980. "Time in Economic Theory." *Kyklos* 33(2):219–29.

————, and F. Cripps. 1979. "Keynes Today." *Journal of Post Keynesian Economics* 2:139–44.

Samuels, W. 1979. "Roy Weintraub's *Microfoundations*: The State of High Theory, a Review Article." *Journal of Economic Issues* 13(4):1019–28.

Samuelson, P. A. 1955. *Economics,* 3rd ed. New York: McGraw-Hill.

————. 1964. *Economics,* 6th ed. New York: McGraw-Hill.

————. 1966. *The Collected Scientific Papers of Paul A. Samuelson,* Vol. 2. Ed. by J. E. Stiglitz. Cambridge, Mass.: MIT Press.

————. 1972. *The Collected Scientific Papers of Paul A. Samuelson,* Vol. 3. Ed. by R. C. Merton. Cambridge, Mass.: MIT Press.

————. 1973a. *The Samuelson Sampler.* Glen Ridge, N.J.: Horton.

————. 1973b. "Inequality." *Newsweek,* December 17, p. 84.

————. 1976. "Tax Reform." *Newsweek,* September 27, p. 82.

————. 1977a. *The Collected Scientific Papers of Paul A. Samuelson,* Vol. 4. Ed. by H. Nagatani and K. Crowley. Cambridge, Mass.: MIT Press.

————. 1977b. (Interview with), "Some Dilemmas of Economic Policy." *Challenge* (January–February), pp. 28–35.

————. 1978. "The Role of Profit in a Mixed Economy." In B. M. Friedman, ed. *New Challenges to the Role of Profit.* Lexington, Mass.: Lexington Books.

————. 1980a. *Economics,* 11th ed. New York: McGraw-Hill.

————. 1980b. "The World Economy at Century's End." MIT, mimeographed.

————. 1980c. "Living with Inflation." *Newsweek,* February 25, p. 69.

————. 1980d. "Where the Economy Stands." *Newsweek,* April 28, p. 69.

Sargent, T. J. 1976. "A Classical Macroeconometric Model for the United States." *Journal of Political Economy* 84:207–37.

————, and N. Wallace. 1976. "Rational Expectations and the Theory of Economic Policy." *Journal of Monetary Economics* 83(2):207–37.

Sherman, H. 1976. *Stagflation.* New York: Harper & Row.

Shubik, M. 1975. "The General Equilibrium Model Is Incomplete and Not Adequate for the Reconciliation of Micro and Macroeconomic Theory." *Kyklos* 28(3):545–73.

Simon, H. A. 1979. "Rational Decision Making in Business Organizations." *American Economic Review* 69:493–513.

Solow, R. M. 1978a. In *After the Phillips Curve*. Boston: Federal Reserve Bank of Boston, pp. 203–09.

———. 1978b. "What We Know and Don't Know about Inflation." *Technology Review* 81(3):2–18.

———. 1978c. "Down the Phillips Curve with Gun and Camera." In R. L. Teigen, ed. *Readings in Money, National Income, and Stabilization Policy*. Homewood, Ill.: Irwin.

———. 1979. Alternative Approaches to Macroeconomic Theory: A Partial View." *Canadian Journal of Economics* 12:339–54.

———. 1980. "On Theories of Unemployment." *American Economic Review* 70:1–11.

"Stabilization Policies: Lessons from the '70s and Implications for the '80s." 1980. St. Louis: Center for the Study of American Business, Working Paper No. 53.

Stein, H. 1969. *The Fiscal Revolution in America*. Chicago: University of Chicago Press.

Stein, J. L., ed. 1976. *Monetarism*. Amsterdam: North-Holland.

Streissler, E. 1977. "What Kind of Microeconomic Foundations of Macroeconomics Are Necessary?" In G. C. Harcourt, ed. *The Microeconomic Foundations of Macroeconomics*. London: Macmillan.

Thurow, L. C. 1980. *The Zero-Sum Society: Distribution and the Possibilities for Economic Change*. New York: Basic Books.

Tinbergen, J. 1975. *Income Distribution*. Amsterdam: North-Holland.

Tobin, J. 1971. *Essays in Economics: Macroeconomics*. Chicago: Markham.

———. 1972. "Inflation and Unemployment." *American Economic Review* 62:1–18.

———. 1974. *The New Economics One Decade Older*. Princeton, N.J.: Princeton University Press.

———. 1976. "Hansen and Public Policy." *Quarterly Journal of Economics* 90:32–37.

———. 1977. "How Dead Is Keynes?" *Economic Inquiry* 15:459–68.

———. 1980a. *Asset Accumulation and Economic Activity*. Chicago: University of Chicago Press.

———. 1980b. "Stabilization Policy Ten Years After." *Brookings Papers on Economic Activity* 1:19–71.

Weintraub, E. R. 1979. *Microfoundations*. Cambridge, England: Cambridge University Press.

Weintraub, S. 1977. "Hicksian Keynesianism: Dominance and Decline." In S. Weintraub, ed. *Modern Economic Thought*. Philadelphia: University of Pennsylvania Press.

———. 1978. *Capitalism's Inflation and Unemployment Crisis*. Reading, Mass.: Addison-Wesley.

15 THE NEOCLASSICAL TRADITION OF KEYNESIAN ECONOMICS AND THE GENERALIZED MODEL

Lawrence R. Klein

NEOCLASSICAL ROOTS OF KEYNESIAN ECONOMICS

The introduction of the Keynesian system into economics during the 1930s was, indeed, revolutionary. Almost a half-century later its main structure stands, in spite of claims of counterrevolution. It has, nevertheless, changed, and its future is likely to be evolutionary, in natural extensions of its original base.

In his early classes in Keynesian economics and related subjects, Paul Samuelson consistently emphasized that Keynes was a classical economist schooled in the Cambridge tradition of Marshall and Pigou. More precisely, we should have called him a neoclassical economist. Not only was Keynes a student of the neoclassicists, but he also reasoned in the neoclassical way in developing each block of the structure of his overall macrosystem, as it appeared in the *General Theory of Employment, Interest and Money*.

What do these issues have to do with the original structure of the Keynesian system? Two basic principles of neoclassical economics are (1) the pursuit of optimizing behavior and (2) the clearing of markets. Each piece of the original Keynesian model is based on some form of optimizing behavior. The propensity to consume can be deduced from the theory of consumer behavior, in which a household is viewed as maximizing a utility function subject to a budget constraint. The propensity to invest comes from the schedule of marginal efficiency of capital, in which the equating of the price of an investment to its discounted (marginal) revenue stream is surely an indirect approach to profit maximization by the firm. Finally, the liquidity preference theory of financial asset holding can be readily explained in terms of optimal portfolio choice.

Supply and demand for cash clears the money market in this system, while savings and investment (supply and demand for investment funds) clears the goods market. In the first case the interest rate is presumed to be the equilibrating variable that clears the market, while in the second case it is fluctuating income or output level that clears the saving-investment market.

Behind the three well-known Keynesian functional relationships (propensity to consume, propensity to invest, liquidity preference) lie the supply and demand functions for labor. This is perhaps the only point at which Keynes diverted from a strict neoclassical position. The neoclassical approach would have labor supply and demand at an equilibrium real wage that occurs at full employment. Keynes's principal point was that a full employment equilibrium does not necessarily exist, and that the economy can become locked into an equilibrium position at less than full employment.

Keynes achieved this result by violating neoclassical homogeneity conditions for the supply function of labor, but there are other approaches to the same results. If there is homogeneity in the supply and demand functions — each depending on the real wage — then the market-clearing condition of neoclassical economics would have to be violated in order to achieve the Keynesian result. In any event, Keynes was in the neoclassical tradition for his mode of reasoning and general approach, but he did not become a slave to this point of view in everything he said about the economy of the real world.

Neoclassical theory of behavior deals with micro units, while the corresponding Keynesian concepts refer to macro units — *all* consumers and *all* producers. These two analyses are bridged by the principles of aggregation, which were never carefully explored by Keynes. Among different possible routes to aggregation, one that is straightforward deals with higher moments or parameters of distribution functions. Keynes allowed, in a superficial way, for the effect of income distribution on consumer behavior, but the consequences for his analysis were never carried through. In the case of investment and liquidity preference function, there is practically no consideration of aggregation problems. The same is true of labor supply and demand. In the latter connections the demographic distributions of the labor force are very important and account in a strategic way for shifts in these functions in recent years. These shifts, as will be explained below, have resulted in the most serious criticisms of Keynesian economics as it deals with contemporary issues of full employment, inflation, and instability of the main industrial economies.

KEYNESIAN ECONOMIC POLICY AND CURRENT ECONOMIC PROBLEMS

The neoclassical tradition shows up clearly in the theoretical structure of the Keynesian system. The associated economic policies known as aggregative demand management follow from the structure of the system but are not necessarily neoclassical in ideology or method. If the Keynesian model is accepted as giving a correct interpretation of aggregative behavior and institutional structure, then the fine-tuning approach to economic demand management looks quite reasonable. For many years this policy technique seemed to work quite well, reaching its zenith in the first half of the decade of the 1960s. It fell into disrepute when inflation became more serious and when a number of other socio-politico-economic events occurred — events that do not seem to be well suited for Keynesian aggregative analysis.

The principal characteristic of Keynesian economic policies is not so much that they focus on demand management as that they are strictly macro policies. In that respect they are consistent with the neoclassical tradition, for they do not concern micro choice and do not interfere with the working of the market mechanism. This aspect is often overlooked. They affect general taxes, general spending, and overall money supply. They let the market mechanism deal with allocation problems. The trouble with their present applicability, however, is that some of the contemporary economic problems are not macro. They deal with situations of particular groups, particular processes, particular markets. Overall macro policy may not reach these issues at all or may do so in a highly inefficient way; therefore, alternative policy approaches must be sought, and theoretical support for these new policy thrusts should come from a system that goes beyond Keynesian macroeconomics.

Let us consider some present structural issues that confront economic policy. The most important single thing wrong with the world's industrial economies is that they have simultaneous high inflation and high unemployment. It is not a case of less-than-full employment equilibrium because the system is in a highly unstable state, with inflation rates varying between 5 percent at the best and 20 percent at the worst. In the early 1960s inflation rates were in the neighborhood of 2 percent in some countries, notably the United States, and unemployment rates were between 5 and 6 percent. That combination seems to be almost out of reach now.

The clearing of labor markets, with nominal wage rates changing to adjust supply and demand for labor, has been affected by demographic distributions. The percentage of youths who are unemployed has risen all over the world. This is partly a consequence of high birth rates just after World War II. It is also a racial matter in the United States and a result of changed attitudes of women toward work outside the home. These demographic shifts have made the clearing of labor markets at reasonable values of nominal wage rate very difficult. In the United States the situation is exacerbated by the institutional nature of minimum wage legislation.

Keynesian-type macro policies of demand management are not very helpful in dealing with this situation. The structure of wages, job training for unskilled youths, and some reconsideration of social insurance benefits are some specific policy problems that come to mind. These are outside the purview of aggregative Keynesian models. If they are introduced the models must be extended considerably in order to explain the enlarged set of endogenous variables associated with demographic structure.

Another dimension of present-day problems occurs in the fields of environment, energy, and food. These three are singled out for attention because they have been so critical on several recent occasions, but they are not unique. Environmental problems developed with congestion, pollution (air, water, solid waste, noise), scarring of terrain, elimination of species, exhaustion of water, and other harmful side effects of intense economic activity. The measures of GNP and similar aggregative magnitudes failed to take account of these "bads" together with "goods" in estimating total output. The aggregative measures were main objective or target variables in the Keynesian model. Either costs of production were underestimated or output was overestimated, and GNP-type indicators gave misleading signals. If policies are to be oriented toward dealing with environmental problems in addition to traditional GNP problems, they will have to look beyond conventional Keynesian macroeconomic policies. The policies must be targeted toward the pricing of specific "bads." Taxation of environmental damage or subsidization of environmental protection call for specific structural policies. Examples are requirements for stack scrubbers in electric power production, restriction of aircraft landings and takeoffs, rerouting of traffic, replacement of terrain after strip mining, and so forth. All these policies lead to higher capital costs and, eventually, to a better environment (better quality GNP).

These are real problems. In a sense, they impose constraints on the straightforward application of Keynesian-type macro policies, but in order to know what the constraints are, it is necessary to extend the theoretical model far beyond the simple Keynesian system. Both policy design and system design go hand in hand.

Energy in a very convenient, inexpensive form was accepted as a fact of life during the development of the Keynesian revolution and during the successful implementation of Keynesian policies during the 1950s and 1960s. There should have been a warning to the industrial world, at the time of the closing of Suez in 1956–1957, that abundant and cheap oil supplies from the Middle East would be subject to risk of limitation. This warning was ignored or not properly interpreted, and Keynesian policies that stimulated growth were pursued with little recognition of the required energy needs.

The oil embargo of 1973–1974 and the subsequent escalation of oil prices have made energy issues chief among economic problems of many industrial nations. Keynesian economic theory and macro policy are almost completely uninformative about meeting this problem through measures that jointly induce conservation and enhance supplies. Specific taxes, subsidies, freeing of market restrictions, and many other structural policies are called for. These policies interact closely with magnitudes in Keynesian models — trade balance, inflation rate, aggregate consumer expenditures — and therefore their implementation must be appropriately integrated with the theoretical system of Keynesian economics. It is not satisfactory to ignore them, and it is not satisfactory to try to compartmentalize theory into an overall macro sector and a specific, independent energy sector. Solving the energy problem is undoubtedly one of the biggest factors in solving the inflation problem. Because of this connection the Keynesian model must be extended to include suitable treatment of energy economics.

Just prior to the onset of the major energy issues that surfaced in 1973, there had been enormous food price rises as a result of Soviet harvest failures, the international food procurement processes, and dietary shifts in fast-growing parts of the world. This was not the first time that food problems (starvation, short supplies, price rises) had come to the fore-front of inflationary pressures. Just as the theoretical model showed need for an energy sector, it also showed need for an agricultural sector. Again, it has not been a matter of rejecting the Keynesian macro model, but a matter of extending it to deal with new types of policies — bringing back idle acreages, revamping price support schemes, regulating trading contracts for food exports or imports. In the case of the United States, agricultural exports have become a mainstay of our net external economic position in the face of enormous energy import costs. Ways and means of promoting agricultural exports while maintaining a traditional American role in aiding distressed areas (PL 480) became central policy issues that are far afield from macro fiscal and monetary policy.

To a great extent, the impact of environment, energy, and food on the functioning of the U.S. economy has ultimately manifested itself in declining productivity growth. Keynesian economics is more sympathetic with the relationship

$$\dot{p} = \dot{w} - (\dot{X}/L) \tag{15.1}$$

than with

$$\dot{p} = \dot{M}, \tag{15.2}$$

where $\dot{p}$ = inflation rate $(dlnp/dt)$, $\dot{w}$ = rate of change of unit wage $(dlnw/dt)$, $(\dot{X}/L)$ = rate of change of worker productivity $(dln\,(X/L)/dt)$, and $\dot{M}$ = rate of change of money supply $(dlnM/dt)$.

The first relationship derives from the approximate constancy of labor's share of total production, an implied relationship in many renditions of Keynesian macroeconomics. The second relationship derives from the crude quantity theory of money, assuming full-capacity production. The quantity theory relationship is contradicted by the Keynesian theory of liquidity preference and plays an important role in anti-Keynesian economics.

Productivity growth is a key factor, according to the first relationship, in offsetting wage gains so as to hold prices steady. To a large extent energy shortfalls or high energy costs have hampered productivity growth in application of the usual techniques of production, and energy policy, together with capital investment policy, forms an important approach to dealing, indirectly, with the problem of inflation. The selection of policies to promote investment may be looked upon as part of general aggregative fiscal policy, but it must be made more specific with industry or sectoral targets, and this requires a theory and model that goes far beyond the scope of aggregative Keynesian theory.

What is true of energy in relation to productivity is also true of job training for unskilled youth, for environmental protection, and for agricultural policy. They all have an impact on productivity in complex ways that cannot be seen through the eyes of Keynesian economics alone.

The simple relationships in equations (15.1) and (15.2) are not meant to be directly applicable to economic policy or management. They are simply illustrative of ideas. There is no alternative, in my opinion, to the large-scale system that combines the overall thinking of Keynes with the intersectoral thinking of Leontief. In a sense, this combined model aims to approximate in empirical work the Walrasian ideal. We shall never come very close to the enormity of the scope of that system, but we can produce ever-better approximations that provide an increasing amount of micro detail without sacrificing the ability to sum the micro parts into the main aggregative magnitudes that are standard components of Keynesian economics.

These arguments are built on the specific examples of demography, environment, energy, and food; yet the fundamental problem goes far beyond these areas. These are now recognizable problems, and they may remain as problems for some time to come; yet new crises are sure to arise. The objective should be to have a large-scale model with many sectors so that there will be a compartment where the unanticipated new problem can be placed for, at least, preliminary investigation until a more appropriate system can be designed in an evolutionary way.

The large-scale Wharton Model that combines input-output analysis with Keynesian macroeconomics had modest energy sectors prior to 1973. In fact, at the suggestion of industry specialists, it introduced in baseline projections, for a decade or more ahead, an increasing dependence of the United States on oil imports and a consequent worsening of the trade balance. It did not go so far as to incorporate the breakdown of the Bretton Woods system and devaluation/depreciation of the dollar, and it did not foresee the size of the oil price increase, but it did focus on many of the main policy issues during the period 1971–1973. Also, when the energy problem reached crisis proportions in 1973, the model was instrumental in projecting a consequent recession (November 1973). On the whole, the Keynes-Leontief model gave a far better indication of the ensuing substitution against energy than did engineering-type volumetric projections with fixed proportions, which were frequently cited during 1973–1974.

Following this experience, the basic model became much more energy intensive. Coal, oil, and natural gas were separated from mining as a whole. Electric power production was split from delivery of gas and also by type of fuel. Much more detail for energy policy can now be handled in such models. All this is typical of the evolutionary process.

GENERALIZED MODEL FOR GENERALIZED POLICY

An accounting framework for the Keynes-Leontief system tells a great deal about its equation structure, for the approach is to develop equations to explain the entries in this system of accounts. Chart 15.1 shows the overall structure.

The centerpiece of the chart is the usual input-output system of Leontief. This is true of accounting flows, only. The traditional parameterizing of this system is to treat

$$(X_{ij}/X_j) = a_{ij} \tag{15.3}$$

as a set of technical coefficients, where X_{ij} = flow of real output from sector i to sector j; X_j = total real gross output to sector j (total gross output = total gross input); and a_{ij} = technical coefficient showing requirements of input i per unit of output of j.

Conventional input-output analysis does not treat a_{ij} as strict constants but introduces no systematic way of changing them. There is a resort to technical engineering information in a somewhat informal way. Some formal interpolation schemes, called the RAS method, have been introduced for moving the coefficients a_{ij} through time, but the approach pioneered in the development of Wharton Model is to estimate the a_{ij} as functions of relative prices. The ratio X_{ij}/X_j, like price ratios, simply represents endogenous variables of a large model.

Using Cobb-Douglas theory, the ratios are $X_{ij}/X_{Kj} =$ const. P_K/P_i. Using CES theory, another parameter is introduced.

$$\frac{X_{ij}}{X_{Kj}} = \text{const.} \left(\frac{P_K}{P_i}\right)^{\sigma_j} \tag{15.4}$$

where σ_j = elasticity of substitution in the jth sector. Nested CES functions, multilevel CES functions, and translog functions have also been used in further generalizations.

These relationships thus introduce the neoclassical concepts of cost minimization for efficient production, or the elasticity of substitution concept. Accordingly, the production function is generalized to

$$X_j = F_j(X_{1j}, \ldots, X_{nj}, K_j, L_j, t). \tag{15.5}$$

Both intermediate production flows (the X_{ij}) as well as original factors (K_j and L_j) are used as inputs. This is extremely important for dealing with structural policies, for energy inputs, various argicultural inputs, and other intermediate inputs are direct arguments in the production function. This gives far greater scope to policy assessment than does the traditional two-factor relationship

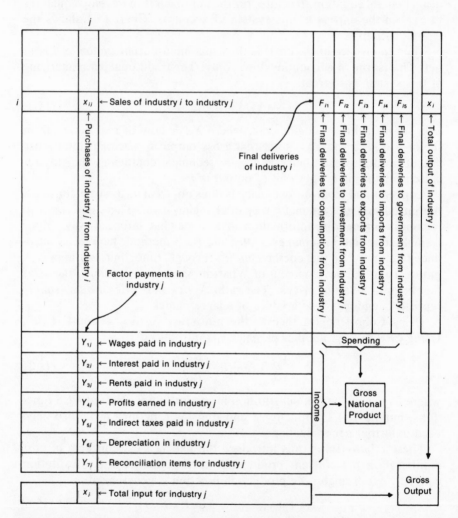

Chart 15.1. Relationship between Interindustry Transactions, Final Demand, and Factor Payments

$$\text{GNP} = F\ (K,L,t) \tag{15.6}$$

in Keynesian models. Gross output of a sector rather than value added is now used as the basic output variable, and intermediate inputs are given explicit consideration.

The two remaining parts of the layout in Chart 15.1 deal with final demand (the right-hand rectangle) and income payments, or value added (the lower rectangle). The deliveries to final demand by each producing sector make up the elements of the final demand matrix. They are the elements of F from the fundamental input-output relationship

$$(I - A)X = F. \tag{15.7}$$

F is a column vector, each element of which is the sum of deliveries to specific kinds of final demand:

$$F = \begin{pmatrix} F_1 \\ F_2 \\ \vdots \\ F_n \end{pmatrix}$$

$$F_j = f_{j1} + f_{j2} + \cdots + f_{jn}. \tag{15.8}$$

The final demand types are the elements of GNP. In the simplest form they are

$$C_j + I_j + G_j + E_j - M_j, \tag{15.9}$$

which could be interpreted as deliveries by sector j to private consumption, to private capital formation, to government purchases, to net exports (exports minus imports). These are simply a limited number of indicative entries. In reality, there would be many types of consumption, capital formation, public spending, and foreign trade. The number should be suited to the size and complexity of the input-output system.

From an accounting point of view, the important thing to recognize is that the column sums of F form a row whose elements sum to GNP. A macro model explains the column sums directly, as well as their total. Some of the matrix entries in the right-hand rectangle would also be generated directly in a macro model, but rarely would the whole matrix of elements be estimated directly. For this purpose, another matrix expression is constructed:

$$F = CG. \tag{15.10}$$

The elements of C are the entries in the right-hand matrix divided by their column sums:

$$C_{ij} = f_{ij} \bigg/ \sum_{i=1}^{n} f_{ij}. \qquad (15.11)$$

The elements of G are the components of GNP that are explicitly modeled in the macro system.

Within a column, the entries below the input-output system in the bottom rectangle are components of value added in a sector. These are wages, capital rental costs, profits, and indirect taxes (less subsidies). The Keynesian system typically models aggregate income payments as well as final demand. In a complete supply-side analysis, however, the factor payments within a sector are modeled, sector by sector. This means including factor-demand relationships and determination of unit factor costs — wage rates, interest rates, depreciation rates, and tax rates. Profits are residuals. Prices in this system are determined at the industry level and then transformed into final demand prices.

These relations between final demand and industry output or between prices by sector and final demand deflators are

$$(I - A)X = CG. \qquad (15.12)$$

The relationship between gross output (X) and value added (Y) is

$$X_j - \sum_{i=1}^{n} X_{ij} = Y_j = \text{value added } (j)$$

$$X_j - \sum_{i=1}^{n} a_{ij}X_j = Y_j$$

$$Y_j/X_j = (1 - \sum_{i=1}^{n} a_{ij})$$

$$Y = BX$$

$$B = \begin{pmatrix} 1 - \Sigma a_{i1} & 0 & \ldots \ldots & 0 \\ 0 & 1 - \Sigma a_{i2} & \ldots & 0 \\ \vdots & & \ddots & \vdots \\ 0 & 0 & \ldots & 1 - \Sigma a_{in} \end{pmatrix}$$

$$(I - A)B^{-1}Y = CG$$

$$Y = B(I - A)^{-1}CG. \qquad (15.13)$$

This *row* relationship converts the elements of G into elements of Y or components of GNP into the vector of value added by sector. From the relation between Y and X, we can obtain gross output.

The *column* relationship is

$$q'Y = d'G. \qquad (15.14)$$

The vector q is the price deflator of value added, while d is the vector of deflators of GNP components. The relationship

$$q' B(I - A)^{-1}C G = d'G \qquad (15.15)$$

shows how the elements of the vector d are obtained as column-weighted sums of the elements of q. This relationship is obtained by equating, term by term, the coefficients of elements of G in both sides of the above equation. The matrix equation is

$$d = C'(I - A)^{-1}Bq. \qquad (15.16)$$

Corresponding to the transformation of q into d, we have a transformation of p into d:

$$p = A'p + Bq$$
$$q = B^{-1}(I - A')p$$
$$d = C' (I - A)^{-1}B \, B^{-1} (I - A')p$$
$$d = C' (I - A)^{-1} (I - A')p. \qquad (15.17)$$

The sector production functions, wage determination equations, interest rate equations, indirect tax equations, and factor demand functions enable us to complete the explanation of the national income (value added) by sector.

Two further groups of relationships must be added to this system for completion. They are demographic relationships underlying population and labor supply, and flow-of-funds relationships underlying the determination of interest rates, exchange rates, and monetary aggregates.

This is an enormously large model with both supply-side and demand-side content. It is a truly interrelated model in the sense that macro details of the national income and product accounts cannot be determined independently of the structure of production through the input-output system. Conversely, interindustry flows cannot be determined independently of the Keynesian-type explanation of final demand and national income payments. It is neoclassical in spirit; it is a feasible model and has, in fact, been estimated in different variants. It is the system underpinning for contemporary policy. Just as the system is tied together by interdependence, so should policy be so tied together. Macro policy cannot be intelligently set without structural policy, and structural policy needs macro policy. The goals of full employment without inflation cannot be reached by macro policy alone, but, given adequate time, a feasible combination of macro and structural policies can achieve this goal, according to the underlying model, which is long-term in concept.

THE DISMISSAL OF SOME FADS

The American economy has clearly come into troubled times. We flooded world markets with dollars in supporting the war in Vietnam; we failed to tax properly to finance the war; we suffered price explosions in world commodity markets during the late 1960s and early 1970s; we sold enormous amounts of grain at unfavorable prices after the Soviet harvest failure of 1972; we suffered the oil embargo and price explosions in oil markets. These and other events cumulatively induced an era of inflation with deteriorating growth, rising unemployment, and declining improvement in productivity. Does this sequence of events invalidate Keynesian economic policy of demand management?

It is fair to say that Keynesian thinking and Keynesian policy were inadequate for dealing with these and other major disturbances, but it should not be said that demand management is wrong where it is needed, and it should not be said that an extended model, built around a Keynesian core and integrated with appropriate supply-side relations, cannot cope with the intricacies of the new situation. The theory and model for the 1980s is clearly different from that for the era 1930–1965, but I shall argue that the Keynes-Leontief model is the type needed and not the counterrevolutionary models recently being proposed.

It is not unnatural that when the economy is in trouble, people should seek some fresh ideas, but it is by no means clear that the new ideas need be replacement of a system of thought rather than appropriate revisions and extensions of mainstream thinking. An immediate reaction by some — almost "knee-jerk" in character — might be to seek a new high correlation for a single relationship that appears to explain a great deal in one fell swoop.

This was the approach of the monetarists who, in 1970, with the help of a new U.S. administration that appeared to be sympathetic, rediscovered a high correlation between nominal national income and money supply (in a lag distribution). The graveyard of economic ideas is filled with sudden discoveries or rediscoveries of high correlations that seem to work beautifully in a fairly short sample period and fall apart disastrously when relied on for projection into the future. The simple monetarist formula broke down in the face of the disturbances of the early 1970s. It had no revealing information about commodity or energy prices, nor about harvest conditions or floating currency rates that were governing the overall course of events. In addition to breaking down in the face of disturbances, it was plagued by inherently noisy information in the main monetary aggregates. There have been successions of data revisions because of reporting errors, conceptual errors, and technical progress in the working of financial markets. There has been practically no attempt to model these intricate details adequately in order to rely on the monetarist approach, and there has been inadequate attention to the choice of monetary aggregates ranging all the way from M_1 to M_7 and on to total credit. The more relevant the magnitude, the more difficult it is to control it; thus the monetarist approach may be empty from the viewpoint of policy.

There is no easy way out of the difficult situation into which the United States and other industrial economies have lapsed. The single-equation and single-minded approach of monetarism will not work any better than in the early 1970s, when the St. Louis Model operators had to admit that their system was not suited for short-range forecasting and when it was shown that mainstream, large-scale econometric models outperformed the purely monetarist approach (see Anderson and Carlson 1976; McNees 1973a, 1973b).

There has been a beneficial spinoff from the debate with the monetarists. Model builders of comprehensive systems have been induced to pay far more attention to the careful modeling of the financial sector. It is often found that large-scale models of a distinctly nonmonetarist slant, based on the Keynesian concept of liquidity preference, do, indeed, have steady-state solutions that indicate long-run proportionality between money stock and nominal total output value, but this is a *result* for the ratio of two endogenous variables and is not *causal*. It is not suitable for the formation of long-run policy (see Klein 1978).

Monetarism was reintroduced as a theoretical point of view in order to justify a certain economic policy. The policy recommendation is to propose strict targets for one or more monetary aggregates, to use central banking policy to try to keep within target ranges, as fixed rules, disregarding the consequences for other market characteristics, mainly interest rates, and to let the rest of the economy be as free as possible, with reductions in the amount of government economic activity. A similar point of view has been behind another new fad in macroeconomics — namely, the idea of rational expectations. The promulgators of this viewpoint maintain that economic decision making by households and firms is based on their perceptions of the present and future course of the economy. Their perceptions form the basis for forming expectations of decision variables, such as market prices and income flows. The agents of economic decision making are assumed to have the same information as public authorities, and decision units have already taken account of possible intervention by authorities to improve the economic situation; therefore, public policy actions are fully anticipated in expectations and can do no good.

Generally speaking, the promoters of this fad argue that activist public policy to improve the economy will be in vain. They are not arguing against the use of formal models as much as they are arguing against the pursuit of policy in general. Yet they have specific arguments against the use of econometric models for the formation of policy. In the general model for the economy as a whole,

$$F(Y'_t, Y'_{t-1}, \ldots, X'_t, \Theta') = e_t, \tag{15.18}$$

where F is a vector of functions, Y is a vector of endogenous variables, X is a vector of exogenous variables, Θ is a vector of parameters, and e_t is an error vector. The proponents of rational expectations argue that elements of Θ are not constant but depend on the policy instruments in X.

$$\Theta = \Theta(X) \tag{15.19}$$

such that when policy changes are introduced through changes in X, the values of Θ will change by amounts that will just offset the effects of the policy changes.

This is a highly stylized model, based on implausible assumptions about human behavior. Information is very unevenly spread throughout the population of economic decision units. The information flows available to different private citizens are strongly dispersed, and not randomly so. The information sets available to public authorities are quite different in scope, timing, and accuracy. Different people use information in very different ways. The parameters of economic models are not necessarily constant, but they are very unlikely to depend primarily on X and in just such a way as to nullify public policy actions. In short, it appears to be a contrived theory and to arrive at a no-action outcome. It is hardly intuitive or operational. This approach offers little by way of positive findings and is hardly consistent with evidence that past economic policy moves have affected the economy. The use of expectations is a time-honored activity in economic theorizing and has been used in specific forms in many instances of econometric model building. A body of data on stated expectations already exists, and much of it is built into models that are being used. These data cover investment expectations, consumer purchase expectations, and business expectations about economic activity. These data bases will surely expand in the future and find increasing applicability in econometric model construction. A fruitful research path is to go to expectations material directly and rely less on surrogate variables. There is, however, nothing in existing models that use direct measurement to suggest that activist policy is futile.

The prevalent use of econometric models for the formulation of economic policy is to search for improved economic performance by considering alternative policy simulations or scenarios. This approach is criticized as being inefficient and likely to fall short of potential for the economy. The concept of *optimal control* has been suggested as a more systematic method of searching for the *best* policy combination.

Let us regroup the variables of the general economic model into the following subgroups:

$$Y_1, Y_2, \ldots, Y_{n_1} = \text{target endogenous variables;}$$

$$W_{n_1+1}, W_{n_1+2}, \ldots, W_n = \text{nontarget endogenous variables;}$$

$$X_1, X_2, \ldots, X_{m_1} = \text{instrumental exogenous variables;}$$

$$Z_{m_1+1}, Z_{m_1+2}, \ldots, Z_m = \text{noninstrumental exogenous variables.}$$

Policymakers are assumed to control instruments (X) in order to achieve (as closely as possible) targets (Y).

The policy-making body should optimize a criterion function — maximize gain or minimize loss — subject to the system constraint. The optimization should be implemented over a policy horizon. The procedure would follow the implications of:

$$L((Y_{11} - Y_{11}^*), \ldots, (Y_{n_1h} - Y_{n_1h}^*),$$
$$(X_{11} - X_{11}^*), \ldots, (X_{m_1h} - X_{m_1h}^*)) = \min, \qquad (15.20)$$

subject to

$$F(Y_t', W_t', Y_{t-1}', W_{t-1}', \ldots, X_t', Z_t', \hat{\Theta}) = 0 \qquad t = 1, 2, \ldots, h.$$

The loss function is written as L; the target variables are Y^*; and the instruments are X. The horizon length is h, and the sample estimate of Θ is $\hat{\Theta}$. This formulation is nonstochastic, with point estimates being used for Θ and $E(e_t) = 0$.

This problem formulation and solution looks good on paper. It does not take into account the politics and time delays of policy implementation, the possibility of using policy to alter the constraint system, the uncertainty of model performance, the uncertainty on the objective function, or the complicated nature of the problem when both n_1 and m_1 are large. It does not appear that public authorities are disposed to let policy formulation be automatic or to give up the prerogatives for altering F. There is little evidence that enormous gains could be realized by going for the "optimum" rather than continuing to make intelligently inspired simulation searches.

Optimal control theory and application teach a great deal about policy methods and about estimated system properties, but they do not stand ready to transform the economic policy problem to a higher plane of achievement at this time. There is no evidence that it has the power to lead us from the present state of stagflation (see Ball 1978; Hirsch, Hymans, and Shapiro 1978). This field of scholarly investigation in economics is not a fad, but the notion that it can provide a policy breakthrough is faddish. The approach is, however, system free and is not tied to any particular specification of economic behavior.

Supply-side economics is right in line with the evolutionary nature of the Keynesian system. The Keynes-Leontief model is inspired by the potentials of supply-side economics, and it has a great deal of supply-side content that has already been built into the presently used group of Wharton Models. There is, however, a national preoccupation with one supply-side behavioral characteristic in certain recent policy recommendations for large-scale tax cuts. It is asserted that labor supply is very sensitive to tax reductions. A neoclassical labor supply function could be written as

$$L^s = f\left(\frac{w-t}{p}\right), \tag{15.21}$$

where w = nominal wage rate before tax, t = marginal tax yield (on an extra hour's pay), and p = price level. This is typically an upward-sloping function, so the lower the rate of taxation, the greater the supply of labor. It is claimed that if workers could retain a larger amount of each unit of gross wage (or other) income, they would be motivated to work harder.

Another tax effect comes from the denominator of the real wage, p. This is the deflator of output at market prices and, therefore, includes the rate of indirect taxation, sales tax, and the like. It also includes the rate of payroll taxation resulting from employer contributions for social insurance because many employers mark up final prices on the basis of total costs, including payroll tax costs. The higher the rate of indirect taxation, the lower the real wage rate.

Models already account for the rate of indirect taxation. The Wharton Model, for example, includes a positive association between labor supply and the real wage rate, before direct taxes are deducted — that is, (w/p) is the included variable instead of $((w - t)/p)$. But the rate of direct taxation, represented by personal income tax, is accounted for by including real disposable income per worker as another variable in the labor supply equation. The striking point, however, is that the sign of the marginal effect is negative!

This result occurs because there are two possible effects of direct taxes, or of take-home pay, in the labor supply function. There is a positive incentive effect, but there is also a negative "target" effect. The closer that workers get to their target levels of income, or the more that they surpass present aspirations, the less they have to work and the more they can enjoy leisure. The work-leisure tradeoff gives rise to a well-known and long-accepted concept of labor economics, called the *backward-bending supply curve of labor*. It was frequently cited during World War II as a cause of worker absenteeism in high-wage defense plants. The proponents of massive tax cuts, across the board, must risk having the negative–work incentive effect outweigh the positive effect. The Wharton Model results suggest that the negative effects do outweigh the positive, even though they do not prove this in a definitive sense. The work-leisure tradeoff leans heavily toward leisure in our affluent community, and the burden of proof is certainly on the shoulders of the specialized brand of supply-side economics. Rather than rest the case on a priori reasoning by assertion or even by crude regression analysis, it would seem much more convincing to examine factory records on absenteeism, associated wage changes, deductions from gross pay, and the use of leisure-time activities. It hardly seems possible that subjective motivations resulting from incentives can be discovered without personal interview surveys by sampling techniques. Until more careful investigations are made, it is not reasonable to accept the claims by the supply-side enthusiasts that large and protracted personal income tax cuts will overcome the present stagflation problem.

Another variable in the labor supply function of the Wharton Model, and one that also has strong credentials among labor market economists, is the discouraged worker hypothesis. This idea suggests an inverse correlation between labor supply and unemployment. When labor markets are tight (unemployment low), it is relatively easy to find jobs, and workers are encouraged to be in the market for positions. In periods of high unemployment, the reverse happens, and many potential job seekers are discouraged from looking for work. As taxes are reduced the unemployment rate should fall and labor supply should rise, thus cushioning the inflationary impact of expansion. This aspect of labor market behavior is already built into mainstream models, where careful simulation analysis indicates that massive tax cuts, across the board, are not adequate by themselves to correct stagflation. This fad provides no adequate basis for overturning received macroeconomic doctrine.

There may be grains of truth in the policies of tax cuts, but they cannot be trusted to do the wonders that their backers claim lie in store for the economy. There is no visible alternative to patient extension of the basic model to include the supply-side fundamentals of the Keynesian-Leontief system and to press steadily for policies that stimulate capital formation, raise the fraction of GNP saved (and invested), improve energy balance, deal with the environment, and ultimately raise the growth rate of productivity improvement. This is a more firmly established policy mix, which eventually leads to improvement of the inflation-unemployment tradeoff, according to simulation exercises with estimates of the Keynes-Leontief system (see New York Stock Exchange 1979).

REFERENCES

Anderson, L., and K. Carlson. 1976. "St. Louis Model Revisited." In L. R. Klein and S. Burmeister, eds. *Econometric Model Performance*. Philadelphia: University of Pennsylvania Press.

Ball, R. J. 1978. *Report of the Committee on Policy Optimisation*. London: HMSO.

Hirsch, A. A., S. H. Hymans, and H. T. Shapiro. 1978. "Econometric Review of Alternative Fiscal and Monetary Policy, 1971–75." *Review of Economics and Statistics* 60:334–45.

Klein, L. R. 1978. "Money in a General Equilibrium System: Empirical Aspects of the Quantity Theory." *Economie Appliquée* 31(1–2):5–14.

McNees, S. K. 1973a. "The Predictive Accuracy of Econometric Forecasts." *New England Economic Review* (September/October):3–27.

———. 1973b. "A Comparison of the GNP Forecasting Accuracy of the Fair and St. Louis Econometric Models." *New England Economic Review* (September/October):29–34.

New York Stock Exchange. 1979. *Building a Better Future*. New York: NYSE.

16 SAMUELSON AND TRENDS IN MONETARY POLICY

Henry C. Wallich

POSTWAR DEVELOPMENT OF MONETARY POLICY

At the beginning of the spring term of 1941, it became known among Harvard graduate students that Paul Samuelson would offer a Saturday morning seminar on Keynes's General Theory. Several of us made the weekly trip from Harvard Square to MIT. We had all had a grounding in Keynes from Alvin Hansen and John Williams. Hansen was very much the advocate, stressing fiscal policy and minimizing the potential of monetary policy. Williams remained skeptical, but his defense of monetary policy conceded much to the prevailing disenchantment. Both dealt with Keynes in literary rather than analytical terms.

Samuelson clarified the Keynesian system for us by casting it in a rigorous, even though not yet mathematical, mold. What had previously been presented as somewhat vague tendencies became hard relationships. To his credit he resisted the temptation of the times to drop the interest rate altogether from the analytical framework because of its alleged unimportance. But to him, as to all of us, monetary policy appeared as by far the junior member of the fiscal-monetary team.

These widely held views and attitudes of the profession had, if anything, hardened by the end of World War II. The economy had emerged from the war with an enormous increase in liquidity from the already very high levels reached at the end of the 1930s. M_1 velocity had dropped from 3.93 in 1929 to 2.86 in 1933, 2.61 in 1939, and 1.94 in 1946. The essential experience had been that velocity was in no sense constant. In addition, corporations and households had acquired a large volume of highly liquid government securities. The main concern of the Treasury and Federal Reserve was to avoid disturbing the public debt, and the Federal Reserve continued, albeit with increasing reluctance, to peg government security prices. Monetary policy seemed to offer little potential for restraining inflation, which in any event loomed less large in public concerns than did the fear of the great postwar depression.

The mainstream orthodoxy of the times was well expressed in the closing passage of the chapter on "Federal Reserve Monetary Policy" in the first edition of Samuelson's textbook:

> Partly as a result of the need of the Treasury and the banking system to keep up government bond prices and keep down interest rates, and partly as a result of the demonstrated weaknesses of monetary control policies from 1929 to 1941, the trend of modern thinking seems to be away from central banking money and interest-rate policy toward . . . fiscal policies. . . . [Samuelson 1948, p. 356]

Very similar sentiments were voiced during Joint Economic Committee hearings, the "Douglas Hearings" of 1949, and the "Patman Hearings" of 1951 (*Monetary Credit and Fiscal Policies,* 1950; *Questions on General Credit Control,* 1951). Probably a majority of the economists testifying or responding to questions followed this line. Nevertheless, there was also a growing number of economists who, without attributing great strength to monetary policy, were concerned with the inflationary implications of continued pegging of the debt, from which a gradual withdrawal had begun on March 4, 1951.

Defenders of the potency of monetary policy were at pains to make plausible how the very modest interest rate movements that they thought appropriate could have a significant restraining effect in the face of still-abundant liquidity. They placed increasing emphasis on the channel of transmission running to lenders rather than to borrowers and stressed availability effects, reluctance to accept losses on securities, and the resultant lock-in of funds. They sought to dispel the notion that small changes in interest rates were ineffective, while large changes would threaten collapse.

From these unpromising beginnings the impressional estimation of the potency of monetary policy — althought not, I might add, the estimation of the competence of its practitioners — has come a long way. The transition from "virtually impotent" to "the most powerful single instrument" over the last thirty to forty years does not represent a shift from error to truth. Contemporary views seem to have oddly reflected the truths of their times. It is the times that have changed, and with them the appropriate interpretations of economic behavior and policy. Truth, at least in fields so tied to historic conditions as monetary policy making, seems to be relative. Error lies in trying to generalize at too low a level of generality.

While this reevaluation of the potential of monetary policy was progressing glacially in the United States, it had moved much faster in many foreign countries. The difference seemed to be in direct proportion to the extent to which Keynesian doctrines had permeated economic thinking. In continental Europe hard money policies revived early. In the United Kingdom and Scandinavia, the mainstream of thought seemed to parallel that in the United States.

After the Treasury-Federal Reserve "Accord" of 1951, the Federal Reserve was initially engaged in exploring and redefining its monetary policy techniques. The "bills only" (more correctly "bills preferably") doctrine was implemented as a means of encouraging a self-sustaining, medium- and long-term government securities market and of moving away as far as possible from the pegging which the system had abjured. The analysis of monetary and credit developments began where it had left off in the 1920s. Emphasis was on the tone and feel of the money market, with the concept of easing and tightening tied firmly to changes in interest rates. The volume of bank credit received recognition, but the money supply still played only a minor role. Until 1960 the Federal Reserve did not publish any single series reflecting or naming the concept "money supply." The intent of monetary policy was anticyclical in terms of interest rates, with great emphasis on catching upper and lower turning points. Whether or not policy was anticyclical in terms of quantity indicators does not seem to have been a primary concern. The British Radcliffe Report, while it probably went further than mainstream American thinking in stressing liquidity and deemphasizing money as a unique asset, probably was representative of an important segment of U.S. monetary policy thinking during the late 1950s.

Monetary policy making received a thoroughgoing review at the hands of the Commission on Money and Credit, whose work began in 1958. The publications of the commission covered a wide range, including such monetarist contributions as that by Friedman and Meiselman, which

asserted the superior stability of velocity as compared with the investment multiplier. But the principal focus was in traditional terms, with
emphasis on the impact of monetary policy on particular sectors, the
duration of lags, and the timing of monetary policy changes. The strong
impact on housing that developed during the 1960s as a result of the
processes of disintermediation and reintermediation triggered by interest
rate ceilings under Regulation Q had not yet become as dominant a
feature of the monetary policy transmission mechanism as it did during
the later 1960s.

The 1960s also brought the flowering of the "New Economics." With
the tax cut of 1964, fiscal policy achieved a new high in professional and
public esteem. These policies were the product of policy planning in
which Paul Samuelson, as adviser to candidate and later President Kennedy had an important role. It was widely reported that he had an
opportunity to preside over their implementation as chairman of the
Council of Economic Advisers but preferred not to sacrifice his academic
role. In today's context of "supply-side economics," it is worth noting
that the fiscal policies of the early 1960s were not exclusively demand
oriented. They contained a portion of supply-side economics in the efforts
to stimulate business investment through accelerated depreciation and
investment tax credits. Monetary policy, it was widely thought, played
a useful, but only supporting, role by maintaining an environment of low
interest rates. One of the more deliberate efforts to achieve a particular
monetary effect by seeking to tilt the term structure of interest rates
("Operation Twist") amounted to less than what was assumed in the
profession and was subsequently found to have had only very minor
effects.

CRITIQUES OF THE FEDERAL RESERVE AND
ASCENDENCY OF MONETARISM

Throughout this period monetarism was progressing. The policy criteria
of the Federal Reserve were severely criticized. These criteria had increasingly come to focus on the concept of net free reserves (i.e., the
positive or negative differences between borrowings from the Federal
Reserve and excess reserves). These were believed to provide a quantitative measure of money market conditions, which continued to be the
Federal Reserve's principal focus. It was made plausible, by Friedman,
Meigs, Dewald, and Brunner and Meltzer, that net free reserves did not
provide the Federal Reserve with an exogenous handle on monetary

conditions, but implied very different consequences depending on whether the economy was expanding or contracting.

The key feature of monetarist analysis was to define monetary policy in terms of the money supply, in contrast with the Keynesian emphasis on interest rates. Because of the close relationship that was asserted to exist between money and nominal GNP, this monetarist emphasis was bound to lead to a reweighting of the relative effectiveness of monetary and fiscal policy in favor of monetary policy. Seen in this light, the relative roles of fiscal and monetary policy in the expansion of the 1960s looked very different than they did to the New Economics. The economy expanded because the money supply was expanding, not because the government was running a deficit. In Keynesian terms the maintenance of relatively low and fairly stable interest rates had appeared as a neutral monetary policy. In monetarist terms it was seen as a powerfully expansionist policy because the money supply was rising. Had the money supply not increased, the deficit would have pushed up interest rates, private borrowers would have been crowded out, and there would have been little increase in GNP. On the other hand, if the government had maintained a balanced budget, the same increase in the money supply moving through other channels would have produced approximately the same rise in income. It was the reassertion of a quantity theory world, as against the Keynesian world of underemployment equilibrium, but with monetary policy capable of affecting real activity in the short run, as against a Keynesian world where fiscal actions represented the predominant channel of policy influence on the economy.

Some sort of test of the alternative views was provided by the surcharge on the personal and corporate income tax and the expenditure ceilings, largely ignored later, that were enacted in June 1968 as antiinflation measures. The Federal Reserve was concerned about the danger of overkill and adopted interest rate policies that allowed the money supply to expand rapidly. Acceleration of the money supply won out over the surcharge; the economy and prices accelerated.

The move into a continuously inflationary environment further helped to put monetarism in the saddle. In Chairman Martin's last FOMC meeting in January 1970, a shift was initiated that gradually moved policy focus from an interest rate target, accompanied by a money supply and bank credit proviso, to a money supply target accompanied by an interest rate proviso. The earlier technique had used bank credit only as a check on the appropriateness of the federal funds rate targeted. (Under the procedures in effect before 1970, the federal funds rate was one of several dimensions of money market conditions that the FOMC took into account. The others included member bank borrowings, member bank net reserve positions [net free reserves], and the three-month Treasury bill rate.) Beginning in 1970 the procedure was reversed.

In principle this procedure would have permitted a fairly rigorous control of the monetary aggregates, provided the FOMC was prepared to move short-term rates to whatever levels could be expected to generate the desired money supply. The relationships of interest rates, income, and money supply had been shown econometrically to be fairly stable, which indeed was the basic tenet of monetarism. In practice, however, the Federal Reserve was reluctant to move short-term rates as vigorously as might have been necessary. As a result the procedure involved the risk that the aggregates might move off track and become procyclical, as they had been so often in the past. The Federal Reserve's evident concern about interest rates caused the market to look very closely at every movement of the federal funds rate as a possible tip-off to policy changes. That caused the entire short-term interest rate structure to become firmly linked to the funds rate, which in turn made the Federal Reserve even more cautious in moving that rate.

The reliability of the money supply as a monetary policy target was sharply called in question, moreover, by the massive shift in the money demand function that occurred in 1974–1977 and again in 1978–1979. By the end of 1979, the Federal Reserve Board's money demand equation, fitted through mid-1974, overpredicted the amount of money demanded at a given level of interest rates and nominal GNP by some $40 billion. This meant that the Federal Reserve's money supply (M_1) targets, of 5 to 7.5 percent M_1 growth in 1975, and 4 to 7 percent in 1976, were actually excessively easy. That this did not lead to even more inflation than actually occurred is probably attributable to the fact that the targets indicated would have been severely restraining had the earlier relationships of income, interest rates, and money continued to prevail.

As the inflation progressed, still another of monetarism's tenets gained wider acceptance: Emphasis on a stable policy, manifested by money supply growth, displaced earlier emphasis on anticyclical "fine tuning." Thus, while in one sense events had exalted the power of monetary policy, in another its ambitions seemed to become more modest. Subsequent experience, however, indicated that a stable money supply policy, rigorously implemented, is by no means cyclically neutral; cyclical increases and declines in the demand for money and credit, meeting a stably growing money supply, may produce wider swings in interest rates than Keynesian fine tuning would have ever dared to institute. Such a policy can be called cyclically neutral only in a very specific and limited sense.

Monetarist criticism of the Federal Reserve has ignored this peculiarity of the money supply targets and has instead focused on such aspects as the instability of monetary control, the use of the funds rate as the instrument of control, the use of lagged reserve requirements, and the "loophole" of the discount window. The Federal Reserve, meanwhile, has eliminated the second of these points of criticism — the federal funds rate technique — and has moved to a reserve strategy in controlling the aggregates. This has had the effect expected by the Federal Reserve of making interest rates more volatile without, so far, better control of the aggregates, perhaps owing to the sharp cyclical movements of the economy during the year following introduction of the new technique and to the effects of imposing and removing credit controls.

Keynesian criticism of the Federal Reserve, in which Paul Samuelson occasionally joined, has typically stressed concern with supposedly excessive monetary restraint and has quite frequently recommended a return to interest rate targets. This criticism, which at key points in the 1970s sometimes became severe, has been muted by the experience of high rates of inflation and, more fundamentally, by acceptance of the fact that there seems to be no durable Phillips curve tradeoff between inflation and unemployment.

For the Federal Reserve, criticism from opposing sides is often helpful. Both sides cannot be right at the same time, and the middle position may be the best. Great dangers for monetary policy could arise, however, from acceptance of the view, now increasingly widely heard, that sees a stable money supply policy as the only weapon needed against inflation and failure to implement such a policy as the sole cause of inflation. Once fiscal policy, regulatory policy, and private wage- and pricesetters are freed from any sense of responsibility for achieving price stability, the outlook becomes very dim.

SAMUELSON AND MONETARY POLICY DISCUSSIONS

In the debates associated with the development of ideas in the light of changing circumstances, Paul Samuelson has been a leading participant. The professional scene in the United States is flexible enough to provide full scope to a man whose creative abilities reach all the way from mathematical theory to the details of policy formulation. Ever since his initial role in the Kennedy administration, Samuelson has been a leading member of policy advisory groups operating in Washington, such as that initiated by Seymour Harris at the Treasury, the rotating group chaired by G. L. Bach at the Federal Reserve, and others. Through contributions to foreign newspapers, and particularly through his column in *Newsweek* magazine since 1966, his views on a wide range of policy topics have always been before the public. His readers have not only been educated, but have also enjoyed the distinctly nonacademic tone of most of these discussions.

Samuelson's views have moved with the times. As I noted earlier, the very pronounced change in the doctrinal climate from underemployment Keynesianism to the quantity theory world of monetarism has been less a movement from error to truth than an adaptation of theory to changing reality. The views of the 1930s and 1940s and the views of 1980 probably are equidistant from the truth of their day. The permanent truths of economics, if they exist, must be sought at a higher level of generality. It is in this area, of course, beyond the shifting sands of daily policy formulation, that Samuelson's principal contributions lie.

REFERENCES

Samuelson, P. A. 1948. *Economics*. New York: McGraw-Hill.
U.S., Congress, Joint Committee on the Economic Report. 1950. *Monetary Credit and Fiscal Policies,* Hearings before the Subcommittee on Monetary, Credit, and Fiscal Policies, 81st Cong., 1st Session. Washington, D.C.: Government Printing Office.
————. 1951. *Questions on General Credit Control and Debt Management.* Subcommittee on General Credit Control and Debt Management. Washington, D.C.: Government Printing Office.

17 OLIGOPOLY THEORY IN A RIVALROUS CONSONANCE FRAMEWORK:
The Case for Lessened Generality
Robert E. Kuenne

Cromwell, I charge thee, fling away ambition:
By that sin fell the angels.

— Shakespeare, *Henry VIII*

It is the thesis of this brief paper that the terrain of economic theory is littered with fallen angels and that the rate of tumbling has become torrential in the last thirty years. The theorist, encumbered by an increasingly complex mathematical apparatus that presses him to seek unambiguous results at all costs in terms of reality, searches for hypotheses that permit him to evaluate deduced expressions in qualitative dimensions. The methodology itself places a great premium on crisp results and universal truths purchased at the expense of hypothesizing pure competition, concave or convex objective functions, single-objective decision making, complete, zero-sum, loggerheads rivalry, or, at the other extreme, joint-profit maximization and a host of other convenient if distorting instrumental postulates.

In an important sense mathematical methodology has become an end rather than a means and has led otherwise balanced theorists into such sterile talmudism as to ponder whether this or that excess demand correspondence is or is not upper semicontinuous in a never-never land of their own creation. The futile search for the ambitious, universally applicable, unambiguous theorem in an economic world of imprecision, structural diversity, and multiobjective strivings, where the mores and folkways of one or more subcultures may be meaningful in shaping results, must be turned to goals at once less intellectually grandiose and more fruitful.

I suggest that economic theory has neglected a direction that Samuelson pioneered: the adaptation of programming frameworks to the development of more powerful *theoretical* techniques. In his well-known work on spatial theory (Samuelson 1952) and his classic collaboration with Dorfman and Solow (1958) on the general theoretical uses of linear programming, Samuelson pointed to methods of deriving realistic insights that less-operational theoretical techniques could not yield and that were capable of close tailoring to specific problems.

No area of economic theory stands in greater need of development today than oligopoly theory, particularly in manners that permit it to be incorporated in a general equilibrium framework. Until general equilibrium theory develops frameworks that permit the spectrum of realistic rivalrous behavior to be captured, it will remain the tiresome pedantry it has become today. In what follows I suggest a simple approach that offers hope of successful fitting to actual industrial or cartel behavior.[1] It has been applied in an experimental study of OPEC's pricing behavior (Kuenne 1979a, 1979b).

RIVALROUS CONSONANCE AND CRIPPLED OPTIMIZATION

The theories of oligopoly that we have are overly rigid in their overarching goal of achieving general explanatory significance. Game-theoretic matrices, dominant-firm leadership, Cournot behavior, joint-profit maximization, Stackelberg leadership-followership, and the rest are rather narrowly restrictive and yield at best insights with occasional applicability. I suggest, however, that if we drop the tempting but impossible goal of finding "the" or "a" theory of oligopolistic behavior under collusive or noncollusive conditions, we can make progress in getting leverage over realistic firm behavior, at the negligible cost of "general" but irrelevant theorems.

Mature oligopolistic industries form environments that are mixtures of the rivalrous and the cooperative in proportions that vary with the nature of the product, the history of the industry's development, the personalities of its leaders, and, in a general sense, its "political-sociological" matrix. Pure "loggerheads" rivalry in the sense of two-person, war-of-survival game theory or pure joint-profit maximization cooperation do not capture the realistic "rivalrous consonance" of interests that rules among oligopolistic firms in the real world. Power structures characterize the sociology of such sectors, but they are neither completely anarchic as Cournot behavior postulates, nor thoroughly democratic as joint-profit maximization implies, nor as authoritarian as dominant-firm variants presume. Degrees of rivalry, collusion, and power possession combine to form a continuous spectrum of potential patterns for realistic oligopolistic decision making.

Sadly for useful results, extreme behavior patterns are generally advantageous in yielding unambiguous — if irrelevant — general theorems. I urge that we must investigate the less general cases of industrial structure, whose essence can be captured only in numerical specification in their theoretical depiction. We must become interested in formalizing the analysis of specific industries and their relations to other specific industries, in defining their specific mixtures of rivalry and cooperation within their communities, and in mapping their specific power relationships as they rule among their members. Manipulating such frameworks in "simulative" theorizing may yield insights only into a single industry or group of industries, but those insights at least have the potential of realistic relevance. It profits us not at all to derive general theorems about a generalized oligopolistic behavior that has no existential being.

Further, firms in realistic oligopoly are not unidimensional goal seekers. They may strive to maximize profits in some sense, but they or their fellow rivals may *alternatively* seek a target rate of return, or a satisficing level of net revenue, or to stay within some bounds of the leaders' price or prices. *Simultaneously* with any of these (or other) primary goals, the firm may wish to accommodate other goals, such as obtaining minimum or maximum market share, keeping price change within a period between certain bounds, meeting or exceeding a minimum rate of growth in sales, and so forth. The typical realistic oligopoly is a *multiobjective* decision-maker, perhaps implicitly or explicitly arranging such possibly conflicting aims in a hierarchy of priorities. Again, no pattern of objectives can be abstracted as a "general" case, and the theorist must ground his choice in the specifics of the firms and industry.

The perceived interdependence of firms in realistic oligopoly implies that goals must be sought in the light of rivals' goals. If the firm optimizes in its goal seeking, that optimization is "crippled" by its need to aid in, acquiesce in, or fight against the optimizing behavior of its rivals. The degree and type of collusion will reflect the power structure within the industry. Power may simply be the ability of a rival to punish a firm for uncooperative behavior, or, more subtly, it may blend into a genuine live-and-let-live feeling of community among firms.

In the light of these considerations, I suggest that one manner of incorporating the general equilibrium, mutually interdependent, multiobjective nature of oligopolistic decision making in a theoretical model specification is through nonlinear, goal-programming frameworks that incorporate power structures. In modeling OPEC, for example, I have used the following framework for members $i = 1, 2, \ldots, 11$.[2] Member i's objective function is to maximize own-profit plus the sum of profits of all other rivals when those other-profits have been discounted by "consonance factors." Formally, firm i seeks to maximize

$$Z_i = x_i p_i - x_i c_i + \sum_{j \neq i} \Theta_{ij}(x_j p_j - x_j c_j), \qquad (17.1)$$

where x_k is the sales function of member k, defined and fitted as

$$x_k = a_k - b_{kk} p_k + \sum_{j \neq k} b_{kj} p_j + b_{ky} y + b_{kr} r, \qquad (17.2)$$

with y an index of world economic activity and r an index of tanker transportation rates. Further, in (17.1), c_i is (constant) lifting cost for a barrel of member i's crude oil, and Θ_{ij} is the valuation member i places upon \$1 of member j's profit in equivalent amounts of member i's profit. Hence, if $\Theta_{ij} = .25$, member i treats \$1 of member j's profit as the equivalent of \$.25 of its own and in its pricing decisions will value any loss inflicted on member j in those terms. The matrix $\Theta = [\Theta_{ij}]$ with $\Theta_{ii} \equiv 1$, defines the perceived power structure of the oligopoly in rivalrous consonance interpreted within a crippled optimization framework.[3]

Each firm maximizes its Z_i subject to a set of constraints that reflects its secondary goals. For example, in my model of OPEC I specified two constraints for each member i, which set upper and lower bounds on sales:

$$x_i - U_i \leq 0 \qquad (17.3)$$

$$L_i - x_i \leq 0, \qquad (17.4)$$

with the nonnegativity constraint,

$$x_i \geq 0. \qquad (17.5)$$

In principle and in practice it is possible to design a specific set of constraints that captures each member's subordinate goals, even though they are quite different from the goals of its rivals.

Iterative solutions to the nonlinear optimization problem (17.1)–(17.5) for each nation, holding all other rivals' prices constant at each step of the solution process, are obtained through the use of a modified SUMT (Sequential Unconstrained Minimization Technique) algorithm. The cartel members, taken singly, maximize their profits in a crippled fashion through the need to consider the impacts of their pricing decisions on all other members' profits. The rivalrous consonance is captured in their begrudged need, by virtue of the power structure, to take these impacts into explicit account in their price decisions, with each binary relation of member i to member j specified in a Θ_{ij}. Further, this crippled optimization on the part of each nation is, at every step of the solution, constrained by the whole of the nation's own constraint set.

Interestingly, if all Θ_{ij}, $i \neq j$, are set equal to 0 (Θ_{ii} are identically 1), the cartel prices in a generalized Cournot environment, myopically ignoring its impacts upon its rivals. Further, when all Θ_{ij} are set equal to 1, cartel prices are determined by joint-profit maximization. Hence, it is quite possible to interpret industry behavior at these extremes. More important, however, by setting the Θ_{ij} at intermediate levels between 0 and 1 (negative levels would depict price warfare and values above 1 would represent unrealistic altruism), we can incorporate power structure patterns that more closely approximate reality. It is possible to treat the Θ_{ij} as variables and to generalize the Stackelberg solution as a Nash equilibrium (see Kuenne 1980).

When the algorithm has converged to a price solution for the oligopoly (if price is the decision variable), under conditions of product differentiation each nation's price is determined. If the Z_i are not concave in own-prices, p_i, the problem solved will not be convex and only local maxima will be attained. Further, of course, if any of the constraints are not convex in p_i, global maxima will not be guaranteed. But in this respect also we break away from the rigidities in our thinking induced by methodologies that seek to warp reality to their purposes. I find that it is all but impossible to convince students that realistic optimization problems may not be convex and that the solutions obtained by oligopolies in the real world may be merely good rather than the very best in some sense. If a model cannot be convexified, they reject it not because it is unrealistic, but because it does not yield the neat solutions their methodologies comfortingly assure them *should* rule!

What the framework developed above and illustrated in the specifics of OPEC does offer hope of capturing are the nongeneralizable specifics of an oligopoly's decision making:

1. Each firm may be programmed to set prices or outputs, depending on management's perceived strategy;
2. That strategy may be a multiobjective strategy in any number of dimensions;
3. The power structure of the oligopoly is explicitly included in an operational manner and in a manner that preserves each firm's binary relation to every other;
4. As we have illustrated the framework, the major objective of firms involves profit maximization, but other objectives may be incorporated instead; for example, target rates of return, price leadership, or satisficing can be depicted and, indeed, each firm may be treated as having a different major objective.

Further, by incorporating supplier-customer relations among firms between oligopolistic industries, a general oligopolistic equilibrium framework can be produced and a major desideratum achieved.

Hence, the structure is a flexible and a powerful one that permits tailoring to goal patterns and power structures unique unto themselves. This implies that it can be manipulated parametrically to derive theorems that are relevant only to the operation of that industry, rather than to some misconceived general structure termed "oligopoly." Our theoretical ambitions are properly compromised, driven as they should be by the problems we face.

In the present state of our analytical capability, the derivation of operational theorems will require in most instances the use of numerical data relating to the industry. I have called this "simulative theorizing" — that is, the derivation of insights into the performance of a system when that derivation is linked directly to and limited by the quantitative values of parameters. The need to abandon the search for qualitative theorems that can be unambiguously evaluated on the basis of qualitative knowledge of the system alone should not be considered a sacrifice imposed by our framework. Rather, that necessity is apparent in the field of large-scale economic theorizing. We are saturated with nice, cleanly proven qualitative theorems whose existence hinges on unrealistic instrumental hypotheses that seriously endanger the realistic applicability of the insights asserted. Simulative theorizing is a general direction demanded by the hugely interdependent causal patterns of economic phenomena, not by rivalrous consonance theory specifically.

CONCLUSION

I have argued for a variety of insufficiently tried directions in economic theory, all of which, typically, have been pointed to directly or indirectly by Samuelson's work. No one has demonstrated more clearly the limitations of qualitative theorem derivation in economics than the Samuelson of the *Foundations* (1947). Although he has not revealed strong preferences for oligopoly theory in his writings — one hesitates to write this, for is there *anything* in economics he has not treated somewhere? — his early interests in programming frameworks and their potential for economic theory certainly point in the directions of crippled optimization frameworks.

NOTES

1. For a more detailed analysis in a general equilibrium context, see Kuenne 1974b, 1978, and, in more formal fashion, 1974a.
2. Ecuador and Gabon were excluded because of data insufficiencies.
3. For the estimation of OPEC's Θ, see Kuenne 1979b.

REFERENCES

Dorfman, R., P. A. Samuelson, and R. M. Solow. 1958. *Linear Programming and Economic Analysis.* New York: McGraw-Hill.

Kuenne, R. E. 1974a. "Toward a Usable General Theory of Oligopoly." *De Economist* 122:471–502.

———. 1974b. "Towards an Operational General Equilibrium Theory with Oligopoly: Some Experimental Results and Conjectures." *Kyklos* 27:792–820.

———. 1978. "General Oligopolistic Equilibrium: A Crippled-Optimization Approach." In T. Bagiotti and G. Franco, eds. *Pioneering Economics.* Padua: Cedam.

———. 1979a. "A Short-Run Demand Analysis of the OPEC Cartel." In P. N. Nemetz, ed. *Energy Policy — The Global Challenge.* Toronto: Butterworth.

———. 1979b. "Rivalrous Consonance and the Power Structure of OPEC." *Kyklos* 32:695–717.

————. 1980. "Duopoly Reaction Functions under Crippled Optimization Regimes." *Oxford Economic Papers* 32:224–40.

Samuelson, P. A. 1948. *Foundations of Economic Analysis*. Cambridge, Mass.: Harvard University Press.

————. 1952. "Spatial Price Equilibrium and Linear Programming." *American Economic Review* 42:283–303.

18 UNDERSTANDING THE MARXIAN NOTION OF EXPLOITATION: *The "Number One Issue"*

Edward J. Nell

According to Samuelson, "The Number One Issue in Appraising Karl Marx's Theoretical Innovations" is "what Marx claimed as most originally his . . . namely [his] way of handling 'surplus value'" (1977, p. 250).[1] "It is precisely Marx's models in Volumes I and II of equalized-rates-of-positive-surplus-value-markups-on-direct-wages-alone that have seemed bizarre to most non-Marxian economists," who have therefore joined in a "near-universal rejection . . . of these . . . paradigms as a) gratuitously unrealistic, b) an unnecessary *detour* from which Marx in Volume III had to beat a return, even though . . . he was too stubborn or too unperceptive or too unscientific to admit [it]" (ibid.).

This, he repeats, "has been the Number One issue in the debates about Marxian economics throughout the years of [his] professional life." He gives his own opinion:

> Save as only an admitted first approximation, justifiable for dramatic emphasis and hortatory persuasiveness or defended because of its obvious greater simplicity of algebraic structure, the paradigm of equalized-rates-of-surplus-values

I am grateful to Ulrich Krause, Heinz Kurz, and Anwar Shaikh for detailed comments and criticism.

279

is an unnecessary detour from the alternative paradigm of equalized-rate-of-profit that Marx and mainstream economists inherited from Ricardo and earlier writers. The digressing Marxian alternative paradigm not only lacks empirical realism as applied to competitive arbitrage governing capital flows among industries and competitive price relations of different goods and services, but also is a detour and a digression to the would-be student of monopolistic and imperfect competition, to the would-be student of socialism, to the would-be student of the modern mixed economy and its laws of motion, to the would-be student of the historic laws of motion of historic capitalism. [Samuelson 1977, p. 251]

Lest there be any doubt, he later states "for dogmatic clarity" the position he thinks serious economists, Marxian and non-Marxian, will ultimately agree on:

1. *No* new analytical insight is given, statically or dynamically, by Marx's own novelties of theoretical analysis that involve — *macro*economically or *micro*economically — the concept of the "rate of surplus-value," either in the form of s_j/v_j or of S_j/V_j, $\Sigma s_j/\Sigma v_j$ or $\Sigma S_j/\Sigma V_j$

(a) into the explanation of the distribution of income between labor wages and property capital return, or

(b) into the determination of society's general profit rate (or total of profit return), or

(c) into the microeconomic empirical configuration of goods and prices in a system of perfect or imperfect competition (or of imperfect knowledge, or of stochastic exogenous disturbance) or

(d) into the realities of the class struggle or the understanding of power relations between groups and governments, internationally or nationally, or

(e) into the ethical nature of "exploitation" and inequality of income. [Samuelson 1977, pp. 295–96]

(To this he adds three qualifications: The algebra of the surplus value regime is easier to handle, so it might have expository uses; if labor intensities in different sectors are similar, labor values might be useful approximations to prices; and blind alleys may be interesting or suggestive, even though blind.)

Samuelson, in effect, poses two questions:

1. What insight do we get from the study of the rate of surplus value that we do not get from a study of the rate of profit?
2. Why and how does the rate of surplus value "explain" the rate of profit in a way that the rate of profit does not equally "explain" the rate of surplus value?

His answer to the first is that there is no such insight and to the second that there is no such explanatory power.

EXPLAINING EXCHANGE VALUE

Samuelson's argument has concentrated almost exclusively on the comparison, for given (single-product) physical input and labor coefficient matrices, of the different accounting regimes of labor values, with a uniform rate of surplus value, and prices of production, with a uniform rate of profit. As is well known now (since Sraffa and known to mathematically inclined students of the subject before), the labor-value accounting regime corresponds to the intercept of the wage rate–rate of profit frontier at which the rate of profit is zero. (All that is necessary is to convert labor values into ratios.) Hence the two regimes are connected by a one-to-one mapping. (Samuelson's "eraser theorem" amounts to saying that if an economy is at one point on the wage-profit frontier it is not at some other point.) The analysis of the "transformation problem" is simply an examination of the properties of this mapping and can tell one no more, or less, than what these are, given the various possible properties of the matrix, whether wages are advanced or not, the durability of capital and nature of depreciation, and so forth.

The question of what are the economically relevant mathematical characteristics of the price system can best be answered by examining the price system itself. However, these characteristics will all have a mapping into the value system, so one could look for them there (though they might not be so readily recognizable). But neither system provides any "explanation" for the other; they are simply connected by a one-to-one mapping.

If this were the only issue, it would be hard to see what all the fuss has been about. But it is certainly not the issue that chiefly interested Marx. Indeed, the properties of the price system, of paramount concern to neoclassical economists, were located by Marx at a different level of theory altogether. (Chaps. 6–12, and 42, 43, and 45 of Vol. III analyze the working of the price system; Chap. 50, "Illusions Created by Competition," concerns its interpretation. The price system is a surface phenomenon; the theory of value concerns the deep structure.) The main question for Marx, one not usually raised by modern mainstream economists (in spite of its obvious importance in Third World countries today and in economic history generally), is why there is such a thing as value-in-exchange at all. This question has two parts. There is, first of all, the logical question of what social conditions must exist for there to be, and to continue to be, value-in-exchange and second, the historical question of how and when these social conditions came into existence (and, of course, how they are developing over time).

This question may be neglected by modern economists, but it was not always so. Walras, for example, devotes a good deal of attention to the logical question (1954, Lessons, 3, 5, and 10; see especially p. 101, "Rareté, the cause of value-in-exchange"), and so does Wicksell. Samuelson himself discusses the "law of scarcity" in the early pages of his famous textbook and uses it to explain why there are few, if any, "free goods" (i.e., why everything has a price), the modern equivalent of explaining the existence of value-in-exchange.

The neoclassical or mainstream answer is cast in terms of scarcity and individual preferences, the necessity of "economizing" or "making choices" in a world with not enough to go around. The Marxian tradition has always rejected this answer as inadequate to the question. The issue is not, "Why do we have to make choices?" (to which a correct, though unilluminating, answer is surely, "Because there isn't enough, given all that we want"), but "Why are the choices we face of this kind, given what we have?" And this leads to a wholly different perspective.

The reason we face the kinds of choices we do is that we live under the kind of social arrangements that we have. "Choices" are not made in the abstract; choices are necessarily between these commodities and those, this job and that, one investment or another, and they are made by persons occupying specific social roles with definite obligations and responsibilities — housewives or heads of households, managers or directors of firms. The array of choices that people face depends on the system of production and the distribution of claims to the product. These social arrangements, in turn, must be supported and reproduced. It is in this context in which value arises and must be defined.

To put it with dogmatic clarity, value arises not because choices have to be made, but because a surplus has to be brought into existence and appropriated. Moreover, this surplus is produced by workers working with means of production that they use up; the workers must be supported and the means of production replaced at the same time that the surplus is appropriated. This leads to a special and important peculiarity of capitalism: Replacement and appropriation are both accomplished at the same time, through the market — that is, by means of exchange. Yet an exchange, in equilibrium, is always an exchange of equivalents. How, then, can a *surplus* be appropriated, in value terms, through exchange?

In Marx's analysis this is the key question, and the answer lies in the nature of the commodity, labor. The buying and selling of labor power is the fulcrum on which the entire theory of value turns. It explains the origin of the surplus, the nature of exploitation, and the inherent connection between exploitation and value.

The General Labor Theory of Value

This connection between exploitation and value simply does not exist in neoclassical economics, so it might be wise to examine it more closely. At a general level Marx argues that the fact that commodities "have value" is to be explained by the fact and only by the fact that they are products of wage labor, which is to say, exploited labor. To "have value" is to be exchangeable in a regular way for a universal equivalent. For a universal equivalent to exist, exchange ratios between any two commodities must be consistent with the exchange ratios of either with any third. The ultimate insight of the LTV in its most general form is that value as a societywide phenomenon, expressed in universal equivalence with money ("everything has its price"), can arise only in social circumstances of class conflict. If commodities exist, if things have exchange value, then there must be exploited labor. No "harmony" is possible through the market, for value and commodity exchange, and so class conflict, are preconditions for markets.

Let's call this general doctrine the GLTV and take a closer look at the claim that value is the reflection of class conflict in the mirror of economics. All activities that can be privately organized are, or produce, commodities and so have value; the key condition for this arrangement is that labor be exploited, which in turn implies a division of society into owners of means of production and workers who "own" only their capacity to work. This is a large claim, and it is not the way everyone has read Marx. For instance, it has become commonplace to remark, and to lament, that Marx simply took over Ricardo's position[2] on the LTV, in the process, of course, both developing it and placing it in a social and historical perspective. In that case Marx's theory would still be substantially that of Ricardo; embodied labor would explain exchange value and so prices, while the level of wages in relation to total output would explain profits. The central questions would be those Samuelson tackles on the working of the price system.

But in fact the first nine chapters of *Capital,* Volume I, are devoted to a set of issues completely different from those that interest Samuelson. Prices and the rate of profits figure neither as the targets of the inquiry, nor among the explanatory concepts. When Marx finally does set about to determine a quantitative concept, it is not the rate of profit, but the rate of surplus value (rate of exploitation), and this comes only in Chapter 9. Are the first eight chapters just a prelude, presenting the social and historical background? *That certainly is not what Marx thought.*

Capital begins with a discussion of commodities and money, moves on to the transformation of money into capital, and then shows that the production of surplus value in the labor process is the foundation of the earning power of capital. The entire discussion, although illuminated by examples drawn from history, moves on the plane of theory. It is *not* a presentation of socio-historical background; it is the central core of Marx's theory, leading up to the determination of the rate of surplus value.

Commodities, the form in which the wealth of capitalist societies presents itself, have two aspects, use value and exchange value. These in turn correspond to two aspects of the labor that produces them: concrete specific labor, which produces use value, and abstract labor, which generates exchange value.[3] Concrete labor is the practical work of producing use values; abstract labor is the condition of being exploited, measured as the amount of time in simple labor equivalents spent working in that status.

Marx next enters on a long and detailed examination of the forms of exchange value, culminating in the general form of value that ". . . results from the joint action of the whole world of commodities. . . . A commodity can acquire a general expression of its value only by all other commodities, simultaneously with it, expressing their values in the same equivalent . . ." (1967, p. 66). The general form of value requires some commodity to act as universal equivalent. But insofar as the commodity does so, it cannot be used as means of production or of subsistence or of luxury consumption. It is no longer the use value it once was; it is money. "The difficulty lies, not in comprehending that money is a commodity, but in discovering how, why, and by what means a commodity becomes money" (ibid., p. 92).

The commodity that becomes money already has value.[4] For general commodity production to exist, there must be fully developed exchange, and for Marx that *requires* that exchange values be expressed (and compared) in universal equivalent form and carried out by means of circulating money.

If money is the universal medium by which commodities are exchanged, then capital will have to circulate in money form. The capitalist advances money for commodities, then sells commodities for money.

But this makes no sense. Selling commodities for money, and then buying commodities again, is practical enough. The exchange value of the two sets of commodities may be the same, but the use value of the second set to the owner will be higher.[5] In contrast, buying commodities for a sum of money and selling them again for that same sum is a complete waste of time. (Marx is assuming that all commodities sell for their cost of production and that all exchanges are fair and equal; no agents in the market have any special privileges.) To assume that on resale, commodities can fetch more than they cost, *in general,* is contradictory.[6] "Circulation, or the exchange of commodities, begets no value" (ibid., p. 163).

At this point Marx states exactly what he is up to:

> The conversion of money into capital has to be explained on the basis of the laws that regulate the exchange of commodities, in such a way that the starting-point is the exchange of equivalents. Our friend, Moneybags, who as yet is only an embryo capitalist, must buy his commodities at their value, must sell them at their value, and yet at the end of the process must withdraw more value from circulation than he threw into it at starting. His development into a full-grown capitalist must take place, both within the sphere of circulation and without it. These are the conditions of the problem. Hic Rhodus, hic salta![7] [Marx 1967, p. 166]

We began from universal commodity production; all activities are commodities, so human work will be also. The solution lies in the buying and selling of labor power. The seller pays its cost of production, the (socially determined) subsistence wage, but obtains its use value — namely, the workers' capacity to work for a period of time. What the worker *does* in this time depends on what the buyer of labor power can get out of him. Workers work; work means changing the form of materials, cutting, shaping, processing, and so on. The faster, or harder, or longer hours a worker works for a day's subsistence pay, the more material input he will convert into output. Marx analyzes the labor process with great care, and his chapter on "The Working Day" has never been surpassed for controlled outrage in exposing injustice. Material input, wear and tear of machinery, and so on, summed up, form the "constant" capital that must be advanced. Such capital is simply converted into output, adding its own value, but no more. The wage bill, however, is "variable" capital; it is spent on the purchase of labor power, which, if coerced or cajoled suitably, *can produce in a day more than the value needed to pay its subsistence.* The ratio between the time worked "for the capitalist" and the time worked "for himself" (produc-

ing what it would take to buy his subsistence) is the rate of exploitation.[8]
Thus, while buying materials, equipment, and labor power at cost or true
value and selling the goods produced by labor for their cost or true value,
the capitalist is still able to turn a profit.

In short, the first nine chapters of *Capital* are devoted to relating
commodities, values, and free exchange to capital and the exploitation
of labor; the latter explains the earning power of capital, which, in turn,
explains the driving force of its circulation, the motivation that runs the
whole system. This, then, is the general answer to the question why we
face the kinds of choices we do. It is the *general* form of the labor theory
of value.

Samuelson's Interpretation

Given that Marx devoted the first nine chapters of *Capital,* Volume I, to
the discussion of the issues just summarized, why does Samuelson ignore
this and assume that Marx's object in proposing a "labor theory of
value" was to explain prices? If that had been his purpose, he was not
only incorrect, but *he himself knew it,* since Volume III was drafted
before Volume I was written in final form! Why does Samuelson think
he would put forth an incorrect theory of prices when he had already
worked out (albeit imperfectly) many of the aspects of a correct theory?
Samuelson's answer appears to be that Marx was committed, for ideological reasons, to the LTV and was reluctant to admit that he had to
give it up. But this does not account for the discussion just examined,
which has nothing to do with explaining prices or profits and focuses
wholly on connecting universal value-in-exchange with the exploitation
of labor in a class society.

Marx's argument can be separated into three stages. The first and
most fundamental is that the exchange accomplishes two things simultaneously — exchanging the replacement goods to permit reproduction
and appropriating the surplus. It must be shown how this can be done
consistently with exchange as the exchange of value equivalents. The
key to this is the unique nature of labor power, which in turn sets the
stage for the examination of the labor process as the source of surplus
value. Labor is hired and paid a wage for a given time. But the work it
does in that time depends on what the capitalist can cajole or coerce out
of it. This is the conflict at the point of production. If labor works
sufficiently slowly, there will be no surplus. If it works faster or harder,
there will be. But capital directs the work and can replace lazy or rebel-

lious workers with others who are more energetic or more compliant. Finally, the competition of capitalists establishes a uniform rate of profits and thereby sets the prices of production for the commodities so produced.[9]

Samuelson, wedded to the theory that value derives from utility in conditions of scarcity, simply ignores the first two stages of Marx's argument. Not surprisingly, he then finds that the third stage doesn't seem to make sense. Let's look at his discussion more closely.

He starts with a no-surplus model. Exchange value is determinate, but there is nothing left over for profits or for taxes. Then, " . . . perhaps because of an invention that makes venison more digestible, the minimum needed wage drops . . ." (1971, p. 406). The appeal to an unexplained invention to account for the surplus is no accident; it crops up again a few pages later. For Marx, of course, the surplus arises because it is *produced*; workers produce it because capitalists make them *work* long enough hours, or hard enough in given hours, in order to generate it. Exploitation is a matter of structural coercion. Circumstances are so arranged that a large mass of people must agree to do as they are told by others in order to support themselves and their families. Samuelson completely ignores this.

Moreover, he also misses the fact that once a surplus exists, exchange accomplishes two objects at once — replacement and appropriation. He not only has no answer to how this can be done consistently with exchange as the trade of value equivalents — he is apparently not even aware of the question.

Having "invented" a surplus, Samuelson's next move is to discuss how Malthusian population pressure combined with growth resulting from savings out of profits would determine the real wage and therefore the rate of profit. He himself, evidently, does not feel that this is an adequate approach to long-run questions, but he argues that Marx was mistaken, in terms of his own model, to dismiss bourgeois economics. Insofar as the model is valid, it could be as legitimately claimed by neoclassicists as by Marxists. Marx, of course, discusses accumulation, wages, and the growth of the labor force in Chapter 25 of Volume I, "The General Law of Capitalist Accumulation," to which Samuelson does not refer. The analysis of accumulation, absolutely basic in Marx, takes place at a *different level of abstraction* than does the analysis of value and exploitation. The GLTV exhibits the central relationship of the capitalist mode of production. The GLCA states the basic "law of motion" of the capitalist system; the latter, therefore, presupposes and builds on the former.

Thus, Samuelson's discussion should have remained at the same level of abstraction as Marx's and should have directed itself to the same question — the explanation of value-in-exchange in conditions in which a surplus is produced under capitalist relations of production. By shifting levels — and ignoring Marx's and later Marxist discussions of GLCA — he makes it seem that modern growth analysis can answer questions in Marxian value theory. By ignoring the first two stages — and the real purpose — of Marx's inquiry, he makes it seem that Marx simply had two theories of prices, a bad one to which he was ideologically committed and a good one, which was insufficiently worked out.

So, to understand the Marxian notion of exploitation, the best course is to do what Samuelson should have done — that is, set up a simple model of production and exchange and analyze it, according to the various prevailing theories. I will consider three treatments of the question of exchange value: the standard Marxian, the neoclassical, and what has been termed the neo-Ricardian system. Since value is perhaps the most fundamental concept of economics, a theory of value should be able to handle all plausible and simple cases. The model we will now examine, however, though simple and plausible, presents serious problems for each of the three approaches just mentioned. However, a Marxian analysis, based on the first nine chapters of Volume I, handles the matter easily and shows exactly how the rate of exploitation determines both the rate of profit and prices.

A SIMPLIFIED MODEL

Consider the following simplified economy. There are two producing institutions. Each uses the other's product as means of production, but *workers in each consume only their own product*. We begin with "simple commodity production," assuming that workers in each sector own their own means of production.

Let the two goods be n and m. The producer or producers of M work l_m days using n_m means of production to produce 1 unit of m output. The producer or producers of n work l_n days using m_n for this unit of output. The two (sets of) workers both do different kinds of work, since they work up different means of production, and have completely different consumption patterns. Taking the price of n as unity, we have for exchange equations:

$$n_m + w_m p_m l_m = p_m \tag{18.1}$$

$$m_n p_m + w_n l_n = 1 \tag{18.2}$$

where w_m is the "wage" of the m-producers and w_n the "wage" of the n-producers. (Even though both sets of workers are paid in "real" terms, in the form of the respective producer's consumption good, both must be expressed in *value* since that good must be traded for means of production.)

Eliminating p_m yields w_m in terms of w_n:

$$w_m = \frac{n_m m_n + w_n l_n - 1}{l_m(w_n l_n - 1)} = \frac{1}{l_m}\left(1 + \frac{n_m m_n}{w_n l_n - 1}\right) \tag{18.3}$$

and, clearly,

$$\frac{dw_m}{dw_n} = \frac{-n_m m_n l_n l_m}{[l_m(w_n l_n - 1)]^2} < 0. \tag{18.4}$$

By substituting (18.3) into (18.1), we obtain p_m in terms of w_n:

$$p_m = \frac{1 - w_n l_n}{m_n}, \text{ and } \frac{dp_m}{dw_n} = -\frac{l_n}{m_n}. \tag{18.5}$$

So we see that p_m varies continuously and monotonically with the division of the gains between the parties. The real wage will be uniform for the two producers (even though paid in different commodities) when $w_n = w_m p_m$. In this case the original system reduces to two equations in two unknowns, the price and the uniform real wage. But in *general* the exchange ratio of the products, the price system, is indeterminate until the *division of gain,* or *the relative worth of the two different lines of work,* has been settled.

No analogous problem arises in the pure exchange economy. It is not just a matter of relative pay scales; it is an issue of direct confrontation, for what one gains the other loses. The difficulty of reducing all labor to simple, abstract labor receiving a common wage is now in plain view; different lines of work are not only wholly different, they are also interdependent, as a consequence of which the gain of one is the other's loss.

Continuing with the model, we write the quantity equations for the two parties:

$$q_m = m_n + c_m q_m l_m \tag{18.6}$$

$$1 = n_m q_m + c_n l_n \tag{18.7}$$

Here q_m stands for the *relative* quantity of m to n — the number of wheelbarrows per hundredweight of apples needed in equilibrium. The scale of the system will not be fixed until we know the amount of labor.

Solving (18.6) and (18.7) we can obtain the same relation between c_m and c_n that we found before between w_m and w_n:

$$c_m = \frac{n_m m_n + c_n l_n - 1}{l_m(c_n l_n - 1)} . \tag{18.8}$$

Using this and solving for q_m, we obtain:

$$q_m = \frac{1 - c_n l_n}{n_m} , \text{ and } \frac{dq_m}{dc_n} - \frac{l_n}{n_m} . \tag{18.9}$$

Equations (18.5) and (18.9) together imply:

$$p_m = \frac{n_m}{m_n} q_m, \tag{18.10}$$

provided that $w_m = c_m$ and $w_n = c_n$.

This result can be obtained another way, by multiplying, first, equations (18.1) and (18.2) by the quantities, q_m and 1, and then equations (18.6) and (18.7) by the prices, p_m and 1. The resulting equations are respectively equal to each other; comparing them, we see that either (18.1) and (18.6) or (18.2) and (18.7) yield $p_m m_n = q_m n_m$, provided that $w_m = c_m$ (which from (18.8) and (18.3) implies $w_n = c_n$). Notice that this is the same relationship between prices and quantities that would follow from a *uniform* ratio of net earnings to direct labor (absorbing the whole surplus), which equaled the *uniform* rate of consumption per head, with the entire surplus consisting of the consumer goods in the proportions in which they are consumed in the aggregate.

The provision in (18.10) amounts to assuming that conditions are stationary and that each producer consumes only one of the goods. These assumptions, though at the cost of some complexity, can easily be relaxed. Equation (18.10) clearly yields a straight line when graphed (Figure 18.1). For later, we will want the relationship between w_m and q_m.

From (18.3) we have:

$$w_n = \frac{1 - m_n p_m}{l_n} .$$

Hence:

$$w_m = \frac{1}{l_m} \left(1 - \frac{n_m}{p_m} \right) . \tag{18.11}$$

Clearly,

$$\frac{dw_m}{dp_m} = \frac{n_m}{l_m} p_m^{-2} > 0, \text{ and } \frac{d^2 w_m}{dp_m^2} = -2 \frac{n_m}{l_m} p_m^{-3} < 0.$$

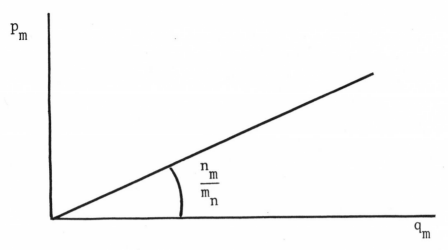

Figure 18.1

Substituting from (18.10):

$$w_m = \frac{1}{l_m}\left(1 - \frac{m_n}{q_m}\right),\tag{18.12}$$

which obviously has the same shape — namely, that of a hyperbola that approaches $-$infinity when $w_m = 0$, and $1/l_m$ when p_m approaches infinity. When $w_m = 0$ the curve cuts the horizontal axis at $p_m = n_m$ (Figure 18.2).

Standard Marxism and Neo-Ricardian Theory

The difficulties this simple model poses for the three approaches to the theory of value are readily seen. Standard treatments of Marxism, for example, face a serious problem interpreting the concept of labor time. Workers in the two sectors perform different tasks, presumably using different skills and facing different problems and dangers. An hour of labor time, therefore, does not mean the same thing in the two production processes. A common way of circumventing the issue is to interpret labor as the product of the consumption that supports it. Two different lines of work are comparable even though the jobs performed and skills employed are different because the labor time is supported by the same consumption. But this avenue is closed here, since the two sets of workers consume different commodities. If labor time has no meaning, how-

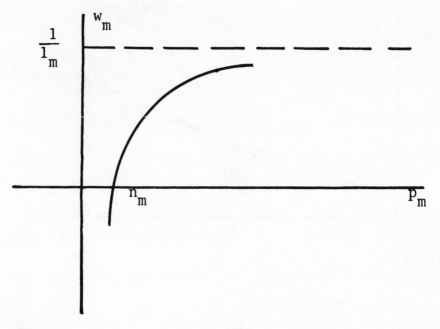

Figure 18.2

ever, standard Marxism is in serious trouble. Since c, v, and s are all expressed in labor time, no analysis is possible without a well-defined basic labor unit.

The concept of simple commodity production also comes to grief. Interpret each sector as a guild, owned by its workers and operating at a stationary level (no growth). Each guild consumes its own product and trades with the other for means of production. According to the traditional doctrine, each set of workers should obtain the same net earning per unit of direct labor. This would suggest equilibrium at the point, $w_n = w_m p_m$. But there is absolutely no reason for this. There is no unit of direct labor; there are *two* kinds of direct labor with no connection between them until their relative value is established. Simple commodity production is indeterminate in this case.

Neo-Ricardian models customarily write a vector of labor times in the different sectors. This is invalid in the present model for the same reasons. Hence these models, too, cannot handle this case. Of course, this need not bother proponents of such an approach, since once a rate of profit is introduced, prices can be determined. Since neo-Ricardians are opposed to the labor theory of value as an account of prices, this would appear simply as a special case supporting their general position.

However, the flaw in neo-Ricardian models lies in the fact that they have no explanation of the surplus. It is simply there — by postulate. The matrix of "input coefficients" is assumed to be "productive." Like Samuelson they rely on exogenous "inventions" that have somehow taken place in the past. However it happened, it has already taken place and has nothing to do with the analysis of exchange value and reproduction. We shall return to this point in a moment; first, there is the question of how a neoclassical approach would handle this model.

Neoclassical Theory

There are two possibilities, a short-run or stationary-state analysis in terms of the disutility of labor, and a long-run approach, which adds consideration of the rate of profit and time preference. According to conventional theory, the amount of labor performed will depend on the disutility of additional labor as compared with the utility yielded by the reward in consumption. This can be illustrated by a simple diagram (Figure 18.3) in which we measure the quantity of output on one axis and the amount of consumption on the other. Iso-utility curves then show the amount of consumption that would be required to compensate for the disutility of the labor involved in producing given amounts of output[10] (remembering that production coefficients are fixed).

If Q is measured on the vertical axis, then a definite amount of consumption, $C = \overline{C}$, will be required to compensate for the disutility of producing any Q at all, and as Q increases more and more C will be needed to compensate additional Q. Next, add a line from the origin, representing the "wage" obtained by producing the output. Since there are constant returns, this will be a straight line rising from left to right. The point where this line is tangent to an iso-utility curve gives the absolute quantity the producer will produce and the corresponding total consumption he will obtain at that wage.

We can draw the diagrams for different assumptions about the shape of the utility functions. For example, assume that for C_m, a rise in the real wage (a downward swing of the line) will call forth more labor — that is, Q_m increases. But in the case of Q_n, let a rise in the real wage result in a diminished willingness to work, so Q_n decreases. Put two diagrams together by flipping the second one over on its side and plotting C_n along the Q_m axis (Figure 18.4). Then join up the points on the

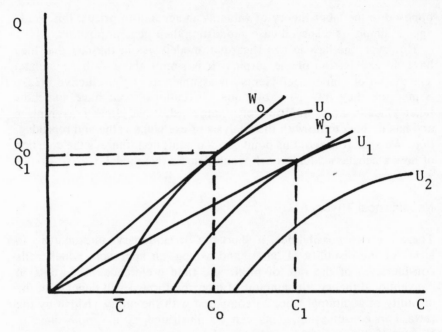

Figure 18.3. A rise in the wage, from W_0 to W_1, leads to a higher level of consumption, C_1, and a higher leve of utility, U_1, but to a lower output, Q_1.

respective Q axes that correspond to a given wage pair. Thus to $(w_m w_n)$ there corresponds the line $q_1 q_1$, the slope of which gives the *relative* quantities produced. When w_m falls and w_n rises, there will be a new relative quantity line, $q_2 q_2$. We can thus read off the relationships between w_m and q_m; they will depend on the assumed shapes of the indifference curves. Starting from $w_m = 0$, no m will be offered; w_n will be at its maximum, so $Q_n > 0$, but will be low. Then as w_m rises and w_n falls, *after a point* Q_m will rise, while Q_n will also increase. If

$$\left|\frac{dQ_m}{dw_m}\right| > \left|\frac{dQ_n}{dw_n}\right|,$$

the curve will have a steep positive slope; otherwise it will be shallow. If the two are equal, then relative quantities will be constant.

Suppose, however, that both producers have regular labor-consumption indifference maps. Then as w_m rises, after a point Q_m rises, and as w_n falls, Q_n falls; hence both effects will cause Q_m to rise with w_m. Suppose both producers have perverse indifference maps. Then as w_m

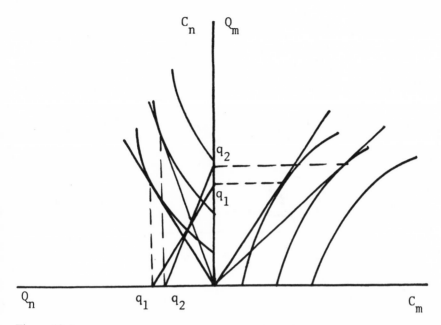

Figure 18.4

rises, Q_m, initially positive, falls, and as w_n falls, Q_n rises up to a point. Hence the relative quantities will fall as w_m rises.

Since these cases are all expressed as functional relationships between w_m and q_m, we can graph them on the diagram of equation (18.12), which expresses the structural relationship between w_m and q_m. (We are assuming that initial supplies are suitable.) However, the resulting graph is not a conventional supply and demand diagram. The structural equation is not analogous to either a supply or demand curve; it shows the pairs, w_m and q_m, that *can and must occur together* if the structural assumptions of our simple context are fulfilled. The behavioral relationships, on the other hand, show the w_m necessary to call forth or, more precisely, to compensate for the disutility of producing a certain q_m. An intersection of the two curves, then, is a point at which the chosen (or acceptable) balance between work and consumption is compatible with the structural possibilities and constraints.

Figure 18.5 illustrates four plausible cases; many others can easily be imagined. SS is the structural curve, and the others represent different possible behavioral curves corresponding to different assumptions about the indifference curves. Curve I represents the case in which both are

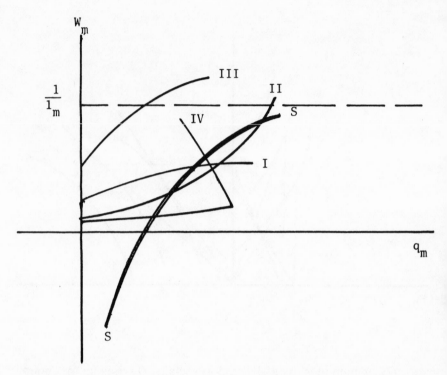

Figure 18.5

regular and the minimal wage for the m-producer is feasible. A small rise in w_m will cause a large increase in q_m, and we can expect a single intersection. Curve II represents the case in which the indifference curves of the m-producer are perverse and those of the n-producer regular, with the minimal wage feasible. Initially the rise in w_m will, after a point, call forth more m-production, while the fall in w_n will reduce n-production. But then the perverse effect takes over, and the curve turns sharply up. Two intersections are therefore likely (though there would be none or a tangency point, if the perverse effect took over very early). Curve III is the reverse case, in which the m-producer has regular, and the n-producer perverse, indifference curves. In this case the curve first rises steeply and then flattens when the perverse effect takes over. Unless this is quite early there will be no intersection; otherwise, one. Finally, curve IV represents the case in which both producers have perverse indifference maps. The curve begins from a positive w_m intercept and at first rises with a shallow slope, exactly like curve I. But when the perverse effects take over, the curve bends sharply back, now rising from right to left (i.e., the slope becomes *negative*), so that there will be two intersections, unless the perverse effects occur very early.

Stability questions have not been defined for this simple context, so it would be inappropriate to analyze such matters here, beyond remarking that just below the upper of the two intersections of curve II, more w_m is available than is required to call forth that q_m, while the reverse is true just below the lower of these two intersections. However the parties react to out-of-equilibrium situations, this kind of consideration will eventually play a determining role.

The Initial Endowments

The initial endowments clearly pose a problem. Assuming an equilibrium exists, the structural equations determine the *relative* outputs, and the behavioral equations determine the *absolute* levels. Hence if the initial endowments of means of production are to be fully and exactly utilized and are to be reproduced regularly, then one and only one set will be compatible with any given equilibrium, since only one set of initial inputs could yield the equilibrium outputs while being fully utilized.

If either or both of the endowments are too small, the equilibrium outputs cannot be produced. But if either or both were too big, equilibrium could be established simply by not using a portion of the endowment. The part not used, however, would then be kept for means of production next period, thus reducing replacement demand, or would be traded for the consumption good, thus reducing current consumer demand. Or, finally, it could be used for some combination of both.

Assume first that one endowent is too big and the other just right, for equilibrium. In terms of Figure 18.5 it is easy to see how the excess endowment could be used to permit the system to end up with the equilibrium output, so that when the excess endowment is used up, the system would be able regularly to reproduce the correct endowments. Suppose that there is excess endowment of m. It might seem, then, that a portion of the excess m should be kept by the n-producers as means of production for next period. This would effectively reduce the coefficient, m_n, to a lower value, m'_n, shifting the structural curve inward and making the curvature more pronounced. If the remainder of the excess m went to consumption, then more m could be produced for any given utility map. This would shift the behavioral curve outward. If the excess endowment were divided so that these two shifts exactly offset one another, this would leave the intersection of the behavioral and structural curves at the same point on the relative quantity axis. The resulting behavior would use up the excess endowment but reproduce the proper relative quantities for the following period, when the curves would return to the positions corresponding to the actual coefficients.

In cases like IV, where the curves have opposite slopes, these two movements are clearly offsetting, and the division that will preserve the equilibrium quantities can easily be calculated. But a difficulty arises in cases like I and II, where the curves have the same slopes, for then both movements tend in the same direction.

The above is necessary to reach the correct relative quantities for reproduction, but it is inconsistent with the price system. The endowment of m is given to the producer of n; hence the producer of n will retain part of his excess endowment, or additional means of production, and will trade the rest to the producer of m, who is also the consumer of m. But the producer of m has to trade m for n at the correct price, $p_m = (n_m/m_n')(q_m)$; to increase the consumption of m, the producer of n would have to take that much less m in exchange for the n required as means of production for m. The correct price follows from the (revised) coefficients and the quantities alone; to reduce the amount of m exchanged any further would raise its price above the proper level, in effect making a gift of the excess m. In other words, with an excess endowment of only one good, transactions leading to the equilibrium cannot take place consistently with the postulates of scarcity and value, in conjunction with the price equations.[11]

Completing the Model

So far we have treated only part of the neoclassical analysis. To develop a complete model we should have to include an examination of time preference and the rate of profit. But it will not actually be necessary to enter into a detailed discussion of such a model, for two striking facts immediately confront us. The first is that the theory of time preference and the rate of return is an *additional* consideration; it does not supplant the theory of the disutility of labor. Hence the difficulties uncovered above still stand. For instance, once we introduce the rate of profit, the equations read:

$$(1 + r)n_m + w_m p_m l_m = p_m. \tag{18.13}$$

$$(1 + r)m_n p_m + w_n l_n = 1. \tag{18.14}$$

These must now be interpreted as representing specifically capitalist institutional arrangements. We have left simple commodity production behind. Assuming that all profits are invested and all wages consumed:

$$(1 + g)m_n + c_m q_m l_m = q_m. \tag{18.15}$$

$$(1 + g)n_m q_m + c_n l_n = 1. \tag{18.16}$$

Eliminating p_m yields,

$$w_m = \frac{1}{l_m} \left[1 + \frac{(1 + r)^2 n_m m_n}{(w_n l_n - 1)} \right] ; \tag{18.17}$$

so that, given r, w_n is determined as a hyperbolic function of w_m. Thus, if capitalists' time preference determines a level of the rate of profit, an analysis similar to that just examined will be needed to determine w_m and q_m and thus w_n. As we have just seen, there is no reason to suppose that any solution exists or, if it does, that it will be unique. Hence, a long-run neoclassical approach is beset with the same difficulties that afflict the short-run stationary version.

Worse is to come. The model has no concept of labor-in-general. It can be argued that even though existing workers are specialized both as to skills and consumption, so that they will not shift employment, new entrants or potential new entrants to the labor force are not so restricted. Hence, once we are considering the long-run position of the economy, we must introduce some concept of a real wage made uniform by competitive pressures.[12]

Perhaps surprisingly, this is not at all difficult. We define ω in analogy with the rate of profit, as the percent of extra consumption — or real wages — over the level socially necessary and normal for subsistence. Thus we must introduce a socio-historical subsistence norm; but once we take this as defined, the competitive pressures generated by potential new entrants to the labor force will see that the percentage by which the actual wage exceeds this is kept the same in the two sectors. The equations are now:

$$(1 + r)n_m + \omega w_m p_m l_m = p_m. \tag{18.18}$$

$$(1 + r)m_n p_m + \omega w_n l_n = 1, \tag{18.19}$$

where w_m and w_n are now taken as fixed. Eliminating p_m gives r in terms of ω:

$$1 + r = [1 - \omega(w_n l_n + w_m l_m) + \omega^2(w_n l_n w_m l_m)]^{1/2}. \tag{18.20}$$

No neoclassical economist could object to this. Of course, competition can be expected to establish a uniform wage as well as a uniform profit rate, even when both jobs and consumption patterns are different, but the effect of this is to undermine the neoclassical approach completely. The decision of how much work to offer will still be made by workers in each sector on utility grounds, and the decision of how much capital to offer will be made by capitalists on time-preference grounds. So we have two independent equations with which to complete the system, but the system has only one degree of freedom. (The workers' calculation, in conjunction with the structural equation, supposedly determines the wage rate, relative sectoral sizes, and the scale of the system — the amount of labor. We have seen the difficulties in this determination. But added to these is the further problem that the rate of profit capitalists would require, on the basis of their time preferences, to supply the capital corresponding to the scale and relative sizes of the sectors determined above need not be the rate that follows from the wage-profit equation, when the equilibrium wage is inserted into it.) The neoclassical approach, therefore, ends in inconsistency, unless the two kinds of decisions are both made by the same agents and so are coordinated. In that case we would have *only one social class*; capitalists and workers would be the same people. Thus neoclassicism faces a dilemma: Either it is inconsistent, or it cannot describe class society.

Our matchbox-size model has now created something of an impasse. Both standard Marxist and orthodox neoclassical approaches to value theory fail. Neo-Ricardians (in which we can include Samuelson as regards his writing on Marx) can, of course, solve the equations, but they have no way of accounting for the surplus. Samuelson assumes a Malthusian supply-and-demand theory of the real wage and imagines "inventions" that create the surplus. But why do workers have to work? Presumably because their grandfathers did not save enough. Why don't they borrow capital and set up in business for themselves? The neo-Ricardian scheme assumes the existence of two classes, but does not explain how this distinction is itself maintained and reproduced.

These are the questions that the GLTV addresses. The surplus arises from the pressure of employers to make workers work. Exploitation *creates* the surplus; competition necessitates the sharp dealing that ensures that exchange value is universal, and that surplus value is appropriated by capital. Whether the surplus is appropriated in the form of interest or of profit is a secondary question. The important points are the pressure on workers to produce the surplus and the fact that exchange accomplishes replacement and distribution together.

THE MARXIAN SOLUTION

The surplus emerges because employers make workers do more work in a given time than is needed to reproduce the goods they consume during that time. This must now be shown in the equations. We introduce a variable, t, to indicate the speed of production, the number of times input is converted into output during the period for which wages are paid. Since each sector uses the other's output as means of production, the two sectors must coordinate the timing of production. If one sector finished before the other, it would not be able to sell its product since the other would not yet be in a position to buy. If the faster-producing sector nevertheless kept its workers on, at make-work jobs, it would lose the advantages of speeding up. But if it laid its workers off while waiting for the other sector to finish, it would confirm workers in the belief that working harder or faster just leads to unemployment.[13] With a uniform t, then, we have

$$(1 + r)tn_m + \omega w_m p_m l_m = tp_m. \tag{18.21}$$

$$(1 + r)tm_n p_m + \omega w_n l_n = t. \tag{18.22}$$

We define these variables so that when

$$t = \omega = 1, r = 0; \tag{18.23}$$

(i.e., the economy can just support and reproduce itself). A positive rate of profit will emerge when $t > \omega \geq 1$. For $\omega = 1$, the subsistence wage, t therefore represents the rate of exploitation. When $t > 1$, $\omega = 1$, a surplus will be produced. Aggregate gross production will be in the same proportions as in the simple reproduction case ($t = 1$). Hence aggregate *net* production will be in the same ratio as the subsistence wage bills. The surplus, in other words, will consist of quantities of the two consumer goods, in the same ratio they are required for subsistence. The ratio of this composite surplus product to the aggregate means of subsistence does not depend on prices; it is a pure quantity ratio, which reflects the intensity of work.[14] Since the quantities in the numerator and denominator consist of the composite subsistence good, the ratio measures "unpaid labor" to "paid labor"; it is precisely Marx's rate of exploitation. It in no way implies that relative prices equal ratios of direct plus indirect embodied labor times. On the contrary, we can see from the equations that prices will depend on the rate of profits. The rate of profit, however, depends on t, the measure of the rate of exploitation. Hence *exploitation explains both prices and the rate of profit, even when labor is fully heterogeneous.*

This can be seen by solving the equations for r in terms of t:

$$r = [(t - \omega w_n l_n)(t - \omega w_m l_m)]^{1/2}[t^2 m_n n_m]^{-1/2} - 1; \qquad (18.24)$$

and for p_m in terms of t:

$$p_m = [(t - \omega w_n l_n)t n_m]^{1/2}[(t - \omega w_m l_m)t m_n]^{-1/2}. \qquad (18.25)$$

Differentiating and rearranging yields:

$$\frac{dr}{dt} = \frac{1}{(t^2 m_n n_m)^{1/2}} \left[\frac{1/2[(t - \omega w_n l_n) + (t - \omega w_m l_m)]}{(t - \omega w_n l_n)(t - \omega w_m l_m)} \right.$$

$$\left. - \frac{(t - \omega w_n l_n)(t - \omega w_m l_m)}{t} \right]. \qquad (18.26)$$

So dr/dt will be positive if the expression in brackets is positive. Let $X = \omega w_n l_n$ and $Y = \omega w_m l_m$. Then cross-multiply and rearrange:

$$\frac{dr}{dt} > 0 \text{ iff } t > \frac{(t - X)(t - Y)}{t - \dfrac{X + Y}{2}}. \qquad (18.27)$$

If $X = Y$, $t - X = t - (X+Y)/2$, so these cancel and $t > t - Y$. If $X \neq Y$, choose the larger, say $X > Y$. Then $t - X < t - (X + Y)/2$, so $(t - X)/[t - (X + Y)/2] = a < 1$. Then $t > a(t - Y)$, and $(dr)/(dt)$ always > 0, Q.E.D.

Differentiating and rearranging the price equation yields:

$$\frac{dp_m}{dt} = \frac{1}{2} \left[\frac{(2t - X)n_m}{[(t - Y)t m_n]^{1/2}[(t - X)t n_m]^{1/2}} \right.$$

$$\left. - \frac{(2t - Y)m_n[(t - X)t n_m]^{1/2}}{[(t - Y)t m_n]^{3/2}} \right], \qquad (18.28)$$

where X and Y are as defined above. Again to determine whether $dp_m/dt \gtrless 0$, cross-multiply the expression in brackets. Cancelling and rearranging, we get

$$\frac{dp_m}{dt} \gtrless 0 \text{ iff } \frac{2t - X}{2t - Y} \gtrless \frac{t - X}{t - Y}, \qquad (18.29)$$

which reduces to

$$\frac{dp_m}{dt} \gtrless 0 \text{ iff } X \gtrless Y. \qquad (18.30)$$

The movement of prices with changes in the rate of exploitation depends on the ratio of the labor coefficients in the two sectors. The rate of exploitation therefore determines both prices and the rate of profits.[15] The preceding, of course, has taken ω as fixed. Note that if ω can vary, then if $dt/t = d\omega/\omega$, $dr = 0$; more generally $dr \gtreqless 0$, according to whether $dt/t \gtreqless d\omega/\omega$.

But what determines t? Surely a neoclassicist could reply that as long as t reflects the increasing disutility of additional effort, balanced against the diminishing returns from such extra effort, the calculation of how hard to work in a given time will be made in good neoclassical optimizing fashion. Then if pay is proportional to the marginal intensity of work (i.e., compensating marginal disutility), we have a perfectly acceptable neoclassical situation.[16]

This, of course, is the giveaway. *Any* situation can be interpreted in neoclassical terms, given a little imagination and Humpty Dumpty's approach to words. "'When I use a word,' Humpty Dumpty said, in a rather scornful tone, 'it means just what I choose it to mean — neither more nor less'" (Lewis Carroll, *Through the Looking Glass,* Chap. 6). *Any action whatever* will be carried to a certain point and stopped (necessarily, since we don't do one and only one thing all day, forever) and so can be interpreted as the result of the interaction of forces favoring the action but declining in intensity, with those unfavorable to it constant or gaining in strength. The question is not, therefore, whether such an interpretation can be given, but whether it makes any sense. And the answer, of course, is no. The central point of Marx's theory is the conflict between workers and the capitalist firms that employ them. Thus there is no question of "diminishing returns" or "increasing disutility"; it is a matter of *dominance* and *subordination*. Can the employer effectively exact obedience? Will the workers submit to authority? What Marx saw is that this is not an either/or question. It is a matter of degree, and t, or, perhaps, t/ω, is the measure of the success of the employers. Thus t is not determined by choices; it is settled through continuing, day-to-day conflict over the rules and practices and expectations governing everyday life on the job.

Changes of Technique

There is an apparently serious objection to the preceding argument. Suppose there are several "techniques" of production for some or all of the commodities. The choice of technique that maximizes the rate of exploitation (notoriously) need not be the same as that which maximizes the rate of profits. In this case the rate of exploitation is not only irrelevant; it would also be misleading. Put another way, a given rate of exploitation implies different profit rates in different techniques. Since the techniques will be adopted on the grounds that they maximize the rate of profit, we have to know the rate of profit to know the technique in order to calculate the corresponding rate of exploitation. Our theorem connecting t and r has it just the wrong way around.

There are serious problems here. First (unlike the "method of physical quantities" generally), the choice-of-techniques problematic, borrowed from neoclassical production function theory, is genuinely asocial and ahistorical, as Joan Robinson never tires of stressing. Second, the choice-of-techniques argument moves on a different level of abstraction than does the claim that the rate of exploitation explains the rate of profit. And, third, the argument, once it is set in historical time, *does* require a specification of the rate of exploitation. These three points are closely related.

A set of techniques, one for each commodity, makes up a technology, according to modern theory. At any moment there will normally be known a number of different ways of producing at least some commodities, so the different techniques can be grouped together in different technologies. In a technology, then, a given level of the real wage will imply a set of prices and the rate of profit. The technology *chosen* will be that one that maximizes the rate of profit. To keep the diagram simple, assume *either,* with Marx, that all the techniques in each technology have the same organic composition of capital, *or,* with Sraffa, that all technologies are in standard proportions. Then the real wage-rate of profit-tradeoff is a downward-sloping straight line. The vertical axis represents output of consumer goods, so the real wage can be marked out on it. The horizontal axis represents the rate of profits. The slope of each line, then, is the capital-labor ratio for that technology.

At any given time an actual technology will be in place. Social systems do not rise full blown, like Venus from the waves. For this actual system the rate of exploitation will be determinate. In each sector an actual labor force is employed under established working conditions, and between them and their employers there will be a modus vivendi. Both sides will be constantly pushing to change this — employers to increase productivity and reduce costs, employees to raise wages and improve working conditions — but it is surely legitimate to "freeze" the balance of forces in the workplace and analyze the working of the system for a given level of productivity and real wages. The currently existing technology can be represented in Figure 18.6 by line AB, where OA measures output per worker and OW the wage, so OA/OW is the rate of exploitation. OB is

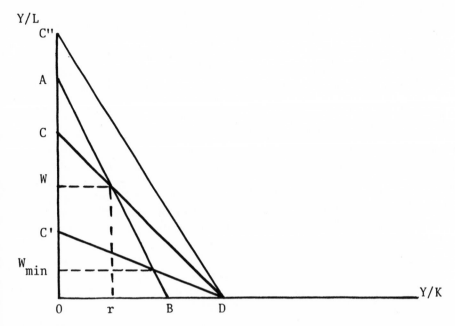

Figure 18.6

output over capital and Or, profits over capital, and OA/OB is the capital-labor ratio.

Consider the technology represented by CD, which has a lower capital-labor ratio. At any wage below W it will give a higher rate of profit, so, according to modern thinking, it will be "chosen"; it is simply and unambiguously "superior" at these levels of the real wage.[17]

Technology CD does not yet exist. (It may, of course, include many of the same industries now in place, but at least some must be new.) The present real wage may carry over in the new situation; that presumably depends on the labor market. New technology creates a new workplace situation; new jobs will have to be defined, new factories built. Relations in these new work situations cannot be "frozen"; no one knows what they will be. Of course, assumptions about work intensity can — and must — be made, but *until* they are made, the *position* of line CD is indeterminate. Productivity may be OC, or OC′, or OC″; which it is depends on how long, how hard, and with what care and attention workers will work.[18] In fact, even the physical coefficients of input depend on this; if workers are careless and wasteful because they dislike the new setup, then material and machine inputs per unit of output will be higher, and the rate of profit corresponding to a given real wage line will be lower, than otherwise. Put this to one side; let us suppose the engineers can say, reasonably accurately, what these material inputs per unit of output should be. The number of workers required to operate the technology is also known; finally, the wage required to sustain a worker for a given period of time is known. This is enough to tell us the horizontal intercept of the wage-profit frontier, for whatever the speed at which workers work, the input per unit of output remains the same. However, it does not give us the frontier's vertical intercept nor, consequently, the slope. For that we have to know how much work — processing input into output — workers will do in a given amount of time. And that is simply asking, in Marx's sense, what the rate of exploitation is. Until we know the answer to that, we do not know whether the second technology is superior to AB at some, all, or no levels of the real wage.

Thus the choice-of-technique arguments fail. The analysis moved at too abstract a plane; it was developed without regard for the fact that any change of technology involves moving from one concrete actual situation, in which the balance of forces in the workplace can (often) reasonably be taken as known and "frozen," to a new, as yet untried situation, in which it can only be estimated. More important, the "balance of class forces" — and therefore the position of the wage-profit frontier — depends on factors different in kind from those determining material input into output. Social and political questions predominate in the former, engineering in the latter. Marx sought precisely to separate, and then relate, these two categories of influences on the rate of profits.

SUMMARY

Samuelson claims that the labor theory of value is totally without use value. No new insights are provided by any of its concepts. The rate of surplus value does not explain the rate of profits, and labor values provide an incorrect account of prices. Marx simply followed a blind alley when he developed the argument of Volume I.

But Samuelson failed to look at the structure of Marx's argument. Marx provided an account of value-in-exchange and showed this to depend on the conditions in which labor is exploited and compelled to produce a surplus, which capital appropriates through the exchange mechanism. Marx's approach proved able to handle a simple but significant model in which Marxist, neoclassical, and neo-Ricardian analyses all came to grief. Exchange accomplishes both replacement and distribution, exploitation explains the production of the surplus, and the rate of exploitation explains both prices and the rate of profit. Far from following a detour, Marx's route lay right along the turnpike. Neoclassical theory pictures value-in-exchange as arising from the interaction of relative preferences and relative scarcity, given some postulate of insatiable wants. In contrast, Marx sees value as the expression of the exploitation of labor; exchange accomplishes at one and the same time both the allocation necessary for reproduction and the appropriation of the surplus, while understanding the buying and selling of labor power provides the key to grasping the origin of the surplus. The neoclassical picture leads one to analyze markets in terms of harmony and optimization. Marx's approach takes one beneath the surface to class conflict at the point of production and relates this to the circulation of capital (the turnover between money-form and commodity-form), the interdependence of sectors, and the appropriation of the surplus in the form of profits. This provides the foundation for a *political* analysis of economic relationships.

NOTES

1. Though this paper is critical of Samuelson, it should be said at the outset that his work on Marx is admirable both for its vigor and its clarity. It marks a milestone in the serious reevaluation of Marx.

2. As Ricardo recognized, however, embodied labor won't do under free competitive conditions, except in the special case, assumed by Marx in Volume I, in which all industries or departments have equal organic compositions of capital. Capital will flow to where rates of return are highest, thus establishing a uniform rate of profits, and the resulting prices will not reflect direct embodied labor, although, as we shall see, they will vary with changes in the productivity of labor.

3. Concrete labor is easy to understand, abstract labor more difficult. The distinction between them must not be confused with the distinction between simple and skilled labor, both of which are concrete. The reduction of skilled labor to simple is, for Marx, largely a matter of history and custom, including the ability (or lack of it) of groups to entrench themselves and enhance their status. It "rests in part on pure illusion, or to say the least, on distinctions that have long since ceased to be real, and that survive only by virtue of a traditional convention, in part on the helpless condition of some groups of the working class." (Marx 1967, Vol. I, p. 192, no. 1).

4. "When it steps into circulation as money, its value is already given. . . . This value is determined by the labor-time required for its production" (Marx 1967, p. 92). [Exchange requires not only a universal equivalent, but a fit and proper one. "The truth of the proposition that, 'although gold and silver are not by nature money, money is by nature gold and silver,' is shown by the fitness of the physical properties of these metals for the

functions of money" (ibid., p. 89)]. When Marx's theory determines the money wage, it also fixes the real wage. Hence, though Marx's insistence that money is an essential moment in the turnover of capital, so that exchange value *must* be expressed in money terms, is fundamental to understanding both effective demand and accumulation in Marxian terms, the theory of exploitation can make use of the neo-Ricardian equation systems.

5. "So far as regards use-value, it is clear that both parties may gain some advantage. Both part with goods that, as use-values, are of no service to them, and receive others that they can make use of. . . . With reference, then, to use-value, there is good ground for saying that exchange is a transaction by which both sides gain. It is otherwise with exchange-value" (Marx 1967, p. 157).

6. "Suppose, then, that by some inexplicable privilege" a seller is able to sell at some percentage above what he previously paid. He seems to pocket a gain. Then he goes to buy and finds all other sellers now offering only at the higher prices. Or suppose one capitalist is clever enough to take advantage of another; what the one gains, the other loses. The total amount of value in circulation is unaltered. "If equivalents are exchanged, no surplus-value results, and if non-equivalents are exchanged, still no surplus-value" (Marx 1967, p. 160).

7. Marx attached an important footnote to this passage, which explains why he insisted on assuming the SLTV throughout Volume I. ". . . . the formation of capital must be possible even though the price and value of a commodity be the same; for its formation cannot be attributed to any deviation of the one from the other" (1967, p. 166). He knew perfectly well that, in general, prices deviate from value — Volume III was drafted before Volume I was written — but he wanted to forestall the notion that the existence of profit could be explained by a systematic discrepancy between price and value. Hence "to explain profit at all, it must first be explained on the assumption that prices equal values." Dobb made this point long ago (1972, Chapter I).

8. It should be evident that this argument does not depend on whether the true values of goods are measured by ratios of embodied labor times or by prices. The subsistence goods support labor for a given time; whatever their prices are, the real wage is thus the equivalent of a certain amount of labor time. Hence the rate of exploitation can be expressed in terms of the division of the working day. Samuelson and other critics are surely right on this point.

9. These are, of course, not separate stages *in reality*; they are separated *methodologically* for the purposes of analysis. The first part of Volume I examines the first stage; later parts of Volume I take up the second stage. (The section on "Primitive [*original* — a mistranslation] Accumulation" indicates some of the ways by which society became divided into a class of owners and a mass of propertyless workers). Volume III then (not altogether adequately) shows how a rate of profit and prices of production will be formed on the basis of the surplus value so produced.

10. Recall our strong assumption that each group of workers consumes only its own product. Here "tastes" are pronounced and uncompromising; no doubt if the two groups of workers were willing to consume each other's goods baskets, at suitable tradeoffs, neoclassical theory would fare better. But that is admitting that orthodox theory cannot handle strong differences in tastes, even while it celebrates individual variety. The argument is designed to show that none of the three usual approaches can handle "heterogeneous labor," while Marx's theory can. To assume that both set of workers have the same or similar utility functions violates the terms of the problem.

11. Suppose there were excess endowments of both goods. An intuitive argument suggests that, in general, there can be no presumption that equilibrium can be reached, using

all of both endowments. Start with the division of m between consumption and means of production (assuming the best case, that the curves are shaped so that the shifts are offsetting) on the hypothesis that all excess n is used for means of production. The formula $p_m = (n'_m/m'_n)q_m$ then gives the price at which m and n must exchange, and the problem will be that the portion of m consumed causes the actual exchange ratio to diverge from this. By allocating a suitable part of the excess n to consumption, however, this would be remedied; the m-producer could trade excess n to the n-producer for his excess m, and all will be well if this consumption trade takes place at the same exchange ratio, p_m, that prevails in the trade for means of production. But any allocation of n to consumption will shift the function expressing the willingness to produce n for a given wage w_n. Hence an allocation of excess n to consumption must be matched by a corresponding allocation of m, to keep the relative amounts in the equilibrium ratio, q_m. It is clear that these changes need not lead to the desired pattern of exchange, for as the allocation of excess n to consumption is increased, the allocation of excess m to consumption will also increase, and for exactly the same reason both "effective coefficients" will move in the same direction. Hence, while cases may well exist in which the trade of excess endowment for consumption purposes will take place at the price that prevails in the exchange of means of production, there can be no general presumption that such an all-around exchange ratio exists.

12. Notice that this is not a way open to simple commodity production. According to that scheme, workers own their own means of production. Hence new entrants would inherit a position from retiring workers, so would enter *already specialized*. No competitive pressures would be generated.

13. Of course, inventories could be carried, but at a cost that would have to be compared to the costs of finishing up and waiting. *Given* an inventory policy, however, the slowest producer sets the pace; no one can produce at a faster clip than that, apart from the inventory leeway.

14. The dual of this, however, will be found at the point on the wage-profit frontier where $r = 0$ and $\omega = \omega_{max}$. The prices associated with this point will equal ratios of embodied labor time, and ω_{max} will equal the rate of exploitation just defined. (For further analysis, see Nell 1964, pp. 155–221.)

15. Ulrich Krause has pointed out in private correspondence that these results neatly generalize. For an earlier treatment of exploitation and work intensity, extended to heterogeneous labor, see Nell 1964.

16. Accepting neoclassical theory's proposed determination of t or t/ω would just get it out of the frying pan into the fire. By the same token we should have to accept a time preference determination of the rate of profit. As we noted earlier, that means adding two equations, one for t/ω and one for r, to a system that has only one degree of freedom. (Since t/ω is a ratio of intensity of effort to pay, it is the appropriate variable for utility theory to determine.)

17. If we relax the either/or assumption above — equal capital-labor ratios in all sectors, or being in the standard proportions — then the wage rate–profit rate frontiers will no longer be straight lines, and they may intersect several times. This is significant for the critique of neoclassical theory, but has no bearing on the present argument.

18. The argument and the diagram are presented, for simplicity, on the un-Marxian assumption that profit is not figured on advanced wages. If wages were advanced as part of capital, then changes in the intensity of work would change not only the vertical intercept but also the horizontal one of the wage-profit frontier. A speedup, for example, would increase output for a given wage bill, raising the rate of exploitation and profits in the same

proportion, but only part of capital, constant capital, would be raised in that proportion. Hence the maximum rate of profit would be raised.

REFERENCES

Dobb, M. 1972. *The Political Economy and Capitalism: Some Essays in Economic Tradition.* Westport, Conn.: Greenwood Press.

Krause, U. 1981. "Heterogeneous Labour and the Fundamental Marxian Theorem." *Review of Economic Studies* 48:173–78.

Marx, K. 1967. *Capital.* 3 vols. New York: International Publishers.

Nell, E. J. 1964. "Models of Behavior with Special Reference to Certain Economic Theories." B.Litt., Oxford.

———. 1980. "Value and Capital in Marxian Economics." *Public Interest*, Fifteenth Anniversary Issue: "The Crisis in Economic Theory."

Samuelson, P. A. 1971. "Understanding the Marxian Notion of Exploitation: A Summary of the So-Called Transformation Problem between Marxian Values and Competitive Prices." *Journal of Economic Literature* 9(2):399–431.

———. 1977. *The Collected Scientific Papers of Paul A. Samuelson*, Vol. 4. Ed. by H. Nagatani and K. Crowley. Cambridge, Mass.: MIT Press.

Walras, L. 1954. *Elements of Pure Economics.* Ed. by W. Jaffe. London: Allen and Unwin.

19 POLITICAL ECONOMY AND INSTITUTIONAL VERSUS CONVENTIONAL ECONOMICS

Gunnar Myrdal

We all know that the academic discipline now commonly referred to as "economics" a couple of generations ago was equally commonly called "political economy." The first chair I held at the University of Stockholm, in 1933, as successor to Gustav Cassel, was named "Political Economy and Financial Science."

What did economists in earlier time mean by inserting the adjective *political*? And why was it dropped? Was the change meant to be only a rationalizing abridgement without logical significance? Or was the change motivated by a deeper significance?

As an idiomatic alteration of term, the change from *political economy* to *economics*, when it gradually occurred, was seldom if ever discussed as a problem or even noted as signifying an important change in the emphasis or direction of our work. Looking backward, however, it seems to me to have been important as a sign of a change in the pursuit of our work. It pertained to a fundamental difference in approach in studying the economy.

INSTITUTIONAL ECONOMICS

I will try to give a more systematic account of what I mean by institutional economics. The borderline is somewhat blurred, as some economists of the conventional school sometimes venture to take a broader approach to practical problems. The conscious and systematic institutionalists are, however, in a tiny minority. I will now formulate in logical terms the reasons for the broader approach.

The most fundamental thought that holds institutional economists together, however different they otherwise are, is our recognition that even if we focus attention on specific economic problems, our study must take account of the entire social system, including everything else of importance for what happens in the economic field: foremost, among other things, distribution of power in society, and, generally, economic, social, and political stratification, and indeed all institutions and attitudes. To this we have to add, as an exogenous set of factors, induced policy measures applied with the purpose of changing one or several of these endogenous factors.

The dynamics of this social system are determined by the fact that among all the endogenous conditions there is *circular causation,* which implies that, if there is change in one condition, others will change in response. Those secondary changes in their turn will cause new changes all around, even reaching back to the condition, the change of which we assumed initiated the process, and so on in further rounds.

So the whole system will be moving in one direction or another, and it may even be turning around its axis. There is no one basic factor, but everything causes everything else. This implies *interdependence* within the whole social process. And there is generally no equilibrium in sight.

One important aspect of this process is that most often, though not always, changes that are reactions to a more primary change tend to go in the same direction. To give an abstract example: Improved nutrition among poverty-stricken masses in an underdeveloped country will raise productivity of labor, which, in turn, will increase the opportunity to improve production and nutrition further. This is why circular causation normally will have *cumulative effects.* Through feedbacks regularly causing more primary changes to have repercussions *in the same direction,* the results, for good or ill, may after some time be quite out of proportion to the initial impulse of change of one or several conditions.

Those initial changes — that is, the *policy interventions* — which in this model are defined as exogenous, are, in a wider perspective, also dependent on the endogenous conditions and their changes, to which they are reactions and which also in many ways constrict and influence their scope and direction. We keep them separate in this model of circular causation with cumulative effects in order to preserve a degree of freedom for an analysis in terms of planning (i.e., policy deliberations and decisions conceived of as not entirely restricted and determined by the existing conditions and ongoing changes).

As the system is moving, partly under the influence of policy measures, the *coefficients of interrelations* among the various conditions in circular causation are ordinarily not known with quantitative precision. Elements of inertia, time lags, and, in extreme cases, the total nonresponsiveness of one or several conditions to changes in some set of other conditions raise problems about which precise knowledge is seldom available. This is largely true even in developed countries with their more complete accounting for all social conditions and their more perfected statistical services. But it is particularly true in underdeveloped countries.

Consequently, our analysis of development problems must often end in tentative generalizations and mere plausible hypotheses, built upon limited observations, discernment, and conjectural judgments. Even in developed countries the widening of the perspective, implied in this institutional approach, will regularly destroy the neat simplicity of both analysis and conclusions in conventional economics.

Our endeavor, of course, must be to develop concepts that more adequately grasp real conditions and their interrelations and to direct empirical study to ascertain the quantitative coefficients of those interrelations. But we should be aware of the huge area of less reliable, complete, and precise knowledge.

These remarks are offered as hints at the master model of institutional economics, which must be holistic even when focused on particular economic problems. I believe institutional economists all have in common in the back of their minds the master-model of the movement of the whole social system, within which there is causal interdependence. While studying an economic problem, they will, therefore, come to include in their economic analysis noneconomic factors, selected by the criterion of relevance for what happens.

A CRITIQUE OF CONVENTIONAL ECONOMICS

In calling the holistic approach the fundamental principle of institutional economics, I imply that our main criticism of conventional economists is that they work with narrowly closed models, which limit the analysis to too few conditions. These are traditionally chosen from conditions called "economic factors," which regularly are more susceptible to quantification, even though this quality too is often opportunistically exaggerated, and not only in regard to underdeveloped countries.

Holding down the variables to only a few that can be quantified makes possible the use of impressive mathematical models. They regularly presuppose a sharp restriction of vision; almost the entire social system is kept out of sight. This should at least require a clear *statement of assumptions* with respect to conditions and determinants that are not considered. Such an account of what is left out is usually not given. Most of the time it is not even consciously perceived.

I should add that when in recent decades some economists, but more often sociologists, have actually attempted to account for, besides the "economic factors," the importance of one or another condition that they can measure — for instance, a vital index — it has most often been done in a similarly restricted way in regard to all other conditions in the social system. And again it has been done without spelling out in clear terms of assumptions all that has not been considered, and still less have they attempted to integrate their findings into a broader framework. In our journals we are getting a crop of ever more minute studies, which lack even attempts toward the integration into a view of the whole social system that is the demand of the institutionalists. I find them therefore irrelevant and uninteresting.

The institutional economists will so regularly stretch out their analyses into fields where, for reasons already hinted at, quantitative precision is not yet possible. This easily leads to a facile characterization of much of our research as qualitative instead of quantitative. But we are equally, or more, intent on reaching quantitative knowledge as soon and as widely as possible. We are in fundamental agreement with Jevons's old dictum that more perfect knowledge is attainable only when we can measure conditions and changes of conditions.

Seemingly greater precision in conventional economic analysis is attained only by leaving out a whole world of relevant things. But as we institutionalists have become accustomed and trained to treat matters that, though relevant, cannot be easily represented by figures, we have generally developed a more critical scrutiny of statistics. Particularly when conventional economists turn to a discussion of practical and political problems, but also in their abstract models, they too are often using aggregate figures for gross national product or unemployment or other economic matters within their view with great carelessness. In regard to their dealing with figures, conventional economists don't show the same urge for clear concepts and the same concern for estimating uncertainty of measurements as, for instance, has always been standard in demographic research.

I should add that when institutional economists have to be critical about the closed models of their conventional colleagues, this does not, of course, imply that we are hostile to models and theories. But we want the models and theories — regularly conceived by us as systems of questions that are logically integrated to the empirical reality around us — to be more adequate to this reality.

I should, at last, point out that institutional economists generally are, at the same time, political economists. For all of us, as far as I know, economics is a ''moral science'' in Mill's meaning of the term. While conventional economists, like most other social scientists, are what in the history of philosophy is known as naive empiricists, having convinced themselves that they are simply dealing with observable facts, we institutionalists have been involved in the problem of how to account for the role of human valuations in research.

We are all utterly sceptical about the welfare theory of conventional economists. As we cannot accept as a valuational basis for our research the outmoded moral philosophy and hedonistic psychology of our classical and neoclassical predecessors, we have to account for what other valuational basis we have for our research.

We have thus generally had our eyes open for prevailing biases in research when valuational assumptions are concealed, while the very idea of that type of opportunistic distortion is an almost forbidden thought in conventional economics. Studies of how influences from the surrounding society have conditioned economic research are almost missing in the writings of conventional economists. Looking back, these influences are more apparent. I suspect the unwillingness to be aware of the problem of prevalent and systematic biases in economic research may be one of the explanations for the disinterest in the history of economics. One common bias among most conventional economists is the more-or-less explicit assumption of market rationality and optimality, while actual markets are becoming less and less perfect and in some areas are disappearing altogether.

I have so far been attempting to argue the case for political and institutional economics in terms of logic. While, however, I believe that in the near future it is destined to gain ground at the expense of conventional economics, it is not primarily because of the strength of its logic but because it will be needed for dealing in an effective way with the practical and political problems that are now towering and threatening to overwhelm us. Much of present establishment economics, and in particular those very abstract theoretical constructs that up till now have enjoyed highest prestige among economists, will, I believe, be left by the wayside as irrelevant and uninteresting.

20 ON MAKING THE TRADEOFF BETWEEN EQUALITY AND EFFICIENCY OPERATIONAL

Alan S. Blinder

THE TRADEOFF BETWEEN EQUALITY AND EFFICIENCY

I want to begin by proposing an empirical experiment, the outcome of which I think every professional economist knows. Take all the pages of all the economic journals of the past twenty-five years that have dealt primarily with microeconomic topics. Determine what fraction of the total pages had to do with issues of efficiency rather than with issues of equity and income distribution. (Admittedly, some arbitrary decisions would have to be made here.) Next, take all the pages devoted to microeconomic issues in all the newspapers, magazines, and the *Congressional Record* (excluding the testimony of economists!) of the past twenty-five years and compute the same fraction. I will give odds that this experiment will show that the public is *far* more concerned with equity relative to efficiency than are economists.

Let us take it for granted that things turn out this way. What are we

My research on income distribution has been supported by the National Science Foundation. A. B. Atkinson, Charles Beach, and Hugo Sonnenschein offered useful suggestions on an earlier draft. Finally, I am proud to be a student of Paul Samuelson, in both the narrow and broad senses.

to make of this "fact"? There are two possible conclusions, each no doubt having some validity, but the two have radically different implications for our profession.

The first possibility is that the public simply has no understanding of the meaning and importance of economic efficiency. Under this interpretation, if people did have this understanding, they would care much more about efficiency than they now do. In this case the job of the economist is to be a missionary, carrying what he knows about Pareto optimality to the farthest corners of the nation, even to darkest Washington.

This, I suggest, is the dominant view in the profession today; and surely Paul Samuelson has done enough good work to guarantee himself a place in heaven. To be sure, the missionary view has a certain amount of validity. It seems clear that neither the public nor our politicians have much appreciation of economic efficiency, and I am prepared to believe that, if they knew what it was all about, they might care about it more than they now do. The Pareto criterion is, after all, terribly appealing.

However, let me consider the other possible interpretation of the evidence: that it is the neoclassical economists, heedless of many warnings from Samuelson and others, who are wearing the blinders. Suppose, as one of my colleagues has put it (Baumol 1978, p. 8), that "the most persistent reason for non-economists' resistance to our most cherished policy recommendations is our determined disregard of their implications for distributive justice." And suppose further that the public, even if it had a full understanding of economic efficiency, simply would believe that the distributional consequences of economic policy are far more important. What then? Since economists normally believe that individual preferences ought to be respected, regardless of what they are, it seems that we should cease being missionaries and try instead to redirect economic thinking away from efficiency and more toward equity and equality.

Now, as I said, both views probably have some validity. Consider the following example.[1] A survey of British economists and members of Parliament solicited opinions on the advisability of peak-load pricing for buses and subways. Of the ninety-five economists who answered the question, ninety favored higher fares in rush hour while only one favored lower fares. (Who was he?) This is a remarkable degree of consensus, and I have no doubt that most economists would have voted the same way. But the eighty-eight MP's who answered the question saw things quite differently. More than half of them (forty-six) favored equal fares (the "fair" fare?), and a substantial minority of twenty-one even favored *lower* fares during the rush hour. Only twenty four, barely more than 25 percent, favored higher fares in the peak period. No wonder that fares, in practice, are equal!

The contrast here is startling, and it raises the following question: If all the MP's were taught to appreciate the efficiency gains of peak-load pricing, how many votes would be changed? To hold the prevailing view of the economists' mission, we must believe that an overwhelming majority would throw their support to peak-load pricing. I myself am not persuaded that this would occur.

This little example suggests to me that economists and the public at large have something to learn from each other. We still have some missionary work to do, because the important principles of economic efficiency are not well understood. But we must also end our head-in-the-sand attitude about equity and equality, especially in areas in which the distributional consequences of public policy decisions are much more important than they are in the peak-load pricing example.

The trained economist, weaned on Samuelson's elementary textbook and schooled in his *Foundations of Economic Analysis,* will, of course, counter that the choice that I pose need not be made at all. There is, as we all know, a *tradeoff between equality and efficiency.* Furthermore, as the late Arthur Okun put it:

> Anyone who has passed a course in elementary economics can spout the right formal rule: promote equality up to the point where the added benefits of more equality are just matched by the added costs of greater inefficiency. [Okun 1975, p. 90]

Because of this tradeoff, there is no reason to choose between worrying about efficiency and worrying about equality. Like a Jewish mother, we can blissfully worry about everything at the same time!

Equipped with a set of social indifference curves between equality[2] and efficiency, we can balance our concern for the two conflicting goals by finding the point of tangency of a social indifference curve with a mythical tradeoff frontier. Very neat and very pat! However, I doubt that this analysis has ever been of much use in practice. The purpose of this brief paper is to explore what economists must do to make the tradeoff more operational than it now is.

HOW LEAKY IS THE BUCKET?

I turn first to the shape of the tradeoff locus between equality and efficiency. Just how might we go about finding out what it looks like?

To rephrase the question a bit, let us recall a very apt analogy made by Okun (1975, pp. 91–92). In his well-known book, *Equality and Efficiency: The Big Tradeoff,* he posed the following question: Suppose a plan is devised to transfer money from the richest 5 percent of the income distribution to the poorest 20 percent. But the transfers can be made only with a leaky bucket, so that for every dollar that we take away from the rich, a fraction b is lost and only the remaining $1 - b$ actually reaches the poor. How large a leak, Okun asked, would you tolerate and still want to make the transfer?

The answer clearly depends both on personal value judgments and on the parameter b, which is related to the slope of the tradeoff function. I shall return to the issue of value judgments in the next section, where I shall relate Okun's leaky bucket to the standard social welfare function approach pioneered by Bergson and Samuelson. But much can be learned just by estimating the parameter b for alternative redistributive policies. For example, one policy may simply dominate another in the sense that its bucket is less leaky *globally*. In this case it is clear that we can *choose the superior redistributive policy* (but not decide how vigorously to pursue it) without knowing anything about social preferences.[3]

How, then, might we obtain quantitative knowledge about the leakiness of the bucket? First, we must consider what it is that is leaking out. To an economist the obvious things to measure are the real resources lost in the process of making the transfers: the sum of the deadweight losses and the administrative costs of the program. This, in turn, suggests to me that we must develop something analogous to a macroeconometric model that incorporates the best knowledge we have about the deadweight losses of various taxes and other programs.

What might such a model look like? Several general characteristics quickly come to mind. First, much as I have long preferred the life-cycle perspective (Blinder 1974), it is clear that we will have to settle for a model based on *annual* variables. If our objective is to make the tradeoff operational, we must recognize that we have neither the data, nor the estimated empirical equations, nor even the necessary incidence theory, to make a life-cycle approach feasible. This improvement is probably a generation or more away.

Second, once again to my personal chagrin,[4] we shall probably have to make the model a full-employment model because we lack the theory of tax incidence that is necessary to isolate and measure the relevant deadweight losses when markets do not clear. Third, the available data dictate that the income distribution will have to be characterized by the Current Population Survey time series on quintile or decile shares. Call these $d_1, \ldots, d_n$ (n = 5 for quintiles, n = 10 for deciles). These data fall short of perfection[5] and also offer us only about thirty-two annual observations. So it is clear that the equations we estimate cannot be too elaborate.

To make things spuriously concrete, suppose we stick to linear models and estimate the following structural model to explain the distribution of income:

$$d = Ay + Bg + u, \qquad (20.1)$$

where $d = (d_1, \ldots, d_n)$ is a vector of income shares, $y = (y_1, \ldots, y_m)$ is a vector of macroeconomic variables such as GNP, wages, profits, interest rates, and so on; $g = (g_1, \ldots, g_q)$ is a vector of government policy instruments; u is a vector of stochastic errors; and A and B are matrices of estimated coefficients. These equations would tell us how the income shares of each group depend upon various (endogenous) aggregate variables and various (exogenous) policy decisions.

System (20.1) has much in common with models built by Charles Metcalf (1972) and Charles Beach (1976), who related group-specific income items (wages, interest, and so on) to the corresponding economy-wide aggregates (and to other variables as well) through a series of identities and behavioral equations. However, the model I have in mind would have to be quite different from those of Metcalf and Beach because: (1) They used the unemployment rate as a principal explanatory variable. I am envisioning here a full employment model that abstracts from the business cycle. (2) Dynamic elements, such as saving and capital accumulation, must be incorporated in the model because questions involving such things as the corporate income tax and a tax on interest income cannot be addressed without them.

To complete the model, we need a macro model to determine the aggregate variables:

$$y = Cy + Dg + v, \qquad (20.2)$$

where C and D are more matrices of coefficients and v is another error vector; I have assumed that research will show that the *direct* influence of the distributional variables (though certainly *not* of the policy variables that affect the distribution) is nil.[6] It is important to note that system (20.2) will look very different from our current econometric models. These models focus on the determination of aggregate demand, employment, and the price level and are generally based on Keynesian macroeconomic theory. The model I have in mind in (20.2) will determine the size of GNP at full employment (i.e., full first-best potential GNP less the sum of all efficiency losses), relative factor shares, various relative prices and rates of return, and things of this sort. It will probably take the form of a general equilibrium system with a demand function, a supply function, and an equilibrium (market-clearing) condition for each of k markets. (I am thinking here of k on the order of 5 to 15 rather than 100 to 200.) Its theoretical underpinning, which would guide the specification of the equations, would be incidence theory. It seems closest in spirit to the general equilibrium algorithmic approach to public finance questions first pioneered by Shoven and Whalley (1972), but a stronger empirical base would be required.

Equation systems (20.1) and (20.2) — $n + m$ linear equations in $n + m$ unknowns — can be solved for their reduced form, which I write:

$$d = Fg + u^* \tag{20.3}$$

$$y = Gg + v^*, \tag{20.4}$$

where matrices F and G are straightforward transformations of the estimated structural parameters in (20.1) and (20.2). To go from these equations to the necessary tradeoff, we need a scalar measure of equality (call it e) and a scalar measure of efficiency (call it f). Suppose these are:

$$e = e(d) \tag{20.5}$$

$$f = f(y). \tag{20.6}$$

For the function $f(\cdot)$ I have an obvious and simple suggestion:

$$f(y_1, y_2, \ldots, y_m) = y_1,$$

where y_1 is the GNP that is actually obtained (first-best potential GNP less all deadweight losses). That is, we define maximal efficiency as minimal deadweight loss. The definition of the function $e(\cdot)$ is more complex, as Atkinson (1970) has taught us, and I will have more to say about it in the next section.

We now have the ingredients to construct a tradeoff function for *each* policy instrument. Consider instrument g_i (for example, the corporate income tax rate, the payroll tax rate, and so on). The effect of a small change in g_i on efficiency is, if $f(y) \equiv y_1$,

$$\frac{\partial f}{\partial g_i} = \frac{\partial y_1}{\partial g_i} = G_{1i},$$

a constant given the assumed linear structure of (20.1) and (20.2). The corresponding effect on equality is:

$$\frac{\partial e}{\partial g_i} = \sum_j \frac{\partial e}{\partial d_j} \frac{\partial d_j}{\partial g_i} = \sum_j e_j(d) F_{ji},$$

a variable that depends on d [unless $e(\cdot)$ happens to be linear]. The slope of the tradeoff function *for this policy instrument* is, of course, the ratio of these two. If, as we usually suspect, policies that promote equality harm efficiency, the two will be of opposite sign, so the tradeoff will be negatively sloped. Furthermore, if, as we also normally expect, a given dose of g_i has less and less of an effect on equality as equality increases, then the slope will also get steeper as e rises; the tradeoff function will be concave.

This formalism, of course, is meant only to be suggestive of the kind of empirical analysis that will have to be undertaken in order to make the tradeoff operational. The important point to note is that a good deal of this work has already been done in the context of standard macro models, in empirical studies of particular markets, and in research on specific questions of tax incidence. What is needed is a major research effort to pull these disparate strands of research together, refine and develop them where necessary, and fill in some missing pieces. It is a big job, but not an insuperable one. It strikes me as somewhat comparable to putting together a large-scale macroeconometric model.

QUANTIFYING OUR PREFERENCES

I mentioned earlier that some policy issues might be settled strictly from quantitative knowledge of the relevant tradeoffs. But for most important decisions, we will surely have to quantify our preferences as well. Where one policy does not dominate another, which policy is "better" truly depends on social preferences.

Okun's leaky bucket gives us a convenient way to learn what we need to know about our social welfare function. Recall that Okun's question is this. Income is to be transferred from income class 2, with average income y_2, to income class 1, with average income $y_1 < y_2$. But for every dollar that we take away from group 2, we succeed in giving only $1 - b$ dollars to group 1. Okun's question is: How large a value of b can you tolerate and still want to make the transfer?

People will obviously differ in their answer to Okun's question because their attitudes toward equality differ, and the answer will also depend upon how much larger y_2 is than y_1. Let me introduce the following assumption:

HOMOGENEITY ASSUMPTION. *For each individual, whatever his tastes for equality, the answer to Okun's leaky bucket question depends only on these tastes and on the ratio y_2/y_1.*

This means, for example, that if a person answers $b = 0.5$ when $y_2 = \$50,000$ and $y_1 = \$5,000$, then he must also answer $b = 0.5$ when $y_2 = \$100,000$ and $y_1 = \$10,000$. It is a homogeneity postulate in that it means that our taste for equality is independent of average income, so that as the economy grows richer we become neither more nor less egalitarian.

This assumption is of course, not entirely unobjectionable. But I hope it is reasonable, for with it I can prove the following very powerful theorem.

THEOREM. *If the social welfare function is additive across individuals, and if the homogeneity assumption holds, then the social welfare function must be:*

$$\sum_{j=1}^{n} \left(A_j + B_j \frac{y_j^{1-\epsilon}}{1-\epsilon} \right). \tag{20.7}$$

To call this a "theorem" is probably an abuse of language, for it is a transparent corollary of the work of Atkinson (1970) and others on the measurement of inequality.[7]

The proof is fairly simple. An additive social welfare function takes the form:

$$W = \sum_{j=1}^{n} \phi_j(y_j).$$

If we are just willing to make a transfer from group 2 to group 1 when the marginal leakage is b, then b is defined by:

$$-\phi_2'(y_2) + (1 - b)\, \phi_1'(y_1) = 0$$

or

$$\frac{\phi_1'(y_1)}{\phi_2'(y_2)} = \frac{1}{1-b}. \tag{20.8}$$

Under the homogeneity assumption, the chosen b will depend *only* on the ratio y_2/y_1, so:

$$\frac{\phi_1'(y_1)}{\phi_2'(y_2)} = h\left(\frac{y_2}{y_1}\right) \tag{20.9}$$

for some function $h\,(\cdot)$. The question is: What functional form(s) satisfy (20.9)? Differentiate (20.9) first with respect to y_1 then with respect to y_2 and then divide the two results. After some simplification, this results in:

$$\frac{y_1 \phi_1''(y_1)}{\phi_1'(y_1)} = \frac{y_2 \phi_2''(y_2)}{\phi_2'(y_2)}. \tag{20.10}$$

If we fix y_1, since this must hold for *every* choice of y_2, we see that $\phi_2'(y_2)$ must be a constant elasticity function. A similar argument implies that $\phi_1'(y_1)$ is a constant elasticity function. Then by (20.10) the two elasticities must be the same, which completes the proof.

The importance of this theorem is that it gives us a constructive way to identify the social welfare function from knowledge of the Okun leaky bucket parameter, b.[8] To see this, look at (20.7). The A_j are inessential, and might as well all be set to zero. The B_j are weighting factors and, if we work with groups of equal size — such as deciles or quintiles — it seems reasonable to set all the B_js to unity.[9] In this case the social welfare function has only a single parameter, ϵ, and we can identify it by using (20.8), which can be written:

$$\frac{y_1^{-\epsilon}}{y_2^{-\epsilon}} = \frac{1}{1 - b} .$$

Thus:

$$\epsilon = \frac{\log \left[1/(1 - b)\right]}{\log (y_2/y_1)} .$$

As an example, let us compute Okun's personal social welfare function. He told us (1975, p. 94) that $b = 0.6$ when $y_2/y_1 = 9$. From these values his implied ϵ was .42. Table 20.1 gives a wide variety of b values corresponding to different social welfare functions (the parameter ϵ) and different possible redistributions (the ratio y_2/y_1). It is interesting to note, as a sidelight, how extraordinarily egalitarian is Atkinson's (1970) suggestion that ϵ is probably between 1.0 and 2.0. Atkinson would, for example, redistribute income when $y_2/y_1 = 10$, even if 90 to 99 percent of the contents of the bucket leaked out. Okun, it would seem, was far less egalitarian than this. Introspection tells me that the U.S. electorate is less egalitarian than Okun. If $.2 \le b \le .4$ is a plausible range for the median voter when $y_2/y_1 = 10$, then ϵ is only around .1 or .2.[10]

Table 20.1. The Value of $b = 1 - (y_1/y_2)^\epsilon$

ϵ	y_2/y_1	2	3	4	5	10	25
.10		.07	.10	.13	.15	.21	.28
.20		.13	.20	.24	.28	.37	.48
.40		.24	.36	.43	.48	.60	.72
1.00		.50	.67	.75	.80	.90	.96
2.00		.75	.89	.94	.96	.99	.998

We have now almost made our social preferences operational. Only two questions remain. How will we determine the value of ϵ in practice? And how will we use this to construct an aggregate measure of inequality for use in equation (20.5)?

For the first question, I will unabashedly claim that the tolerable level of b is precisely the sort of datum that politicians ought to be able to provide for us — battling it out in committee rooms in the same way they battle out other issues. If we knew what the tradeoff function really looked like, economists could tell legislators the b's that correspond to various transfers from y_2 to y_1 and ask the politicians whether the proposed transfers are advisable or inadvisable. From the answers to a series of such questions, we could infer Congress's value of ϵ.[11]

As to the measurement of inequality, once we have accepted the homogeneity assumption and measured the parameter, ϵ, it seems only natural to use Atkinson's measure of inequality:

$$e = 1 - \frac{x}{\bar{y}},$$

where $\bar{y}$ is mean income, and x is the "equally distributed equivalent" defined from the social welfare function as:

$$\sum_{j=1}^{n} \frac{y_j^{1-\epsilon}}{1 - \epsilon} = n \left(\frac{x^{1-\epsilon}}{1 - \epsilon} \right).$$

Thus equation (20.5) would be:

$$e = 1 - \left\{ \frac{1}{n} \sum_{j=1}^{n} d_j^{1-\epsilon} \right\}^{1-\epsilon},$$

since $y_j = d_j \bar{y}$.

IN CONCLUSION

I have argued here that Okun's leaky bucket holds the key to making the tradeoff between equality and efficiency operational. I have proposed a research agenda that would probably take several economist-years of labor. The approach is very different from, and indeed almost diametrically opposed to, any of my own previous research on income distribution (which shows how much foresight I have). It would bring together empirical macroeconomists, general equilibrium theorists who are interested in becoming general equilibrium practitioners, labor economists, and, most especially, public finance specialists. A project like this would have been infeasible just a few years ago, but the time may now be ripe.

If we decide to follow this route, we can probably learn a lot about research strategy from the development of macroeconometric models. These models started out very simple and naive. They did not wait for the relevant theory to be "perfected" before trying to give it empirical content. The best models were developed by teams of researchers at universities, in government, and even in the for-profit sector. Many mistakes have been made along the way, and the models keep changing as errors or misconceptions are discovered and as the nature of the economy's problems changes. While it seems to be a popular sport to criticize and even ridicule these models, I myself have little doubt that they rank alongside input-output analysis as one of the two greatest achievements of empirical economics. This is, therefore, not a bad tradition to emulate.

We should not be embarrassed if our first attempts are clumsy or simplistic and are soon abandoned in favor of new and superior models. What I am calling for, in a word, is a model that does for the tradeoff between equality and efficiency what the Klein Model I did for macroeconomics. And if we build such a model, economics will be well on its way toward becoming a much more operational discipline than it is today — a goal that Paul Samuelson set for us decades ago.

NOTES

1. The figures came from Brittan 1973, p. 93.
2. Hereafter, I shall speak of *equality* rather than *equity* as the alternative goal to efficiency. While the two are not the same, my goal here is to make the tradeoff operational, and equality has the advantage of being measureable (with due apologies to A. B. Atkinson). Regarding *equity*, rather than equality, see Baumol 1978.
3. Lest this possibility seem fanciful, I would suggest that most economists view the negative income tax as dominating our current hodgepodge of welfare programs in this sense.
4. See Blinder and Esaki (1978), where the effect of unemployment on the distribution of income is stressed.
5. See, for example, Blinder 1980.
6. See, for example, Blinder 1975 or Metcalf 1972. If this supposition proves wrong, a term Ed will have to be added.
7. Which is, in turn, a corollary of a more general result. See, for example, Katzner 1970, p. 31.
8. The basic idea appears in Atkinson 1975, p. 49.
9. With groups of equal size, B_js different from unity would be a way of expressing explicit preferences for one group's utility over another's.
10. If I am right about this, Americans are remarkably inegalitarian. An $\epsilon = .15$ implies

that the marginal utility of a rich person with income ten times as large as that of a poor person is 71 percent as high as that of the poor person.

11. We may, of course, encounter inconsistencies. I have only one empirical observation to make on this point. Okun (1975, p. 95) gave a second example in which $y_2/y_1 = 1.8$ and reported that $b = .15$ for him. This implies $\epsilon = .28$, which is not too terribly different from .42, but is not equal either.

REFERENCES

Atkinson, A. B. 1970. "On the Measurement of Inequality." *Journal of Economic Theory* 2:244–63.

———. 1975. *The Economics of Inequality*. London: Oxford University Press.

Baumol, W. J. 1978. "Equity vs. Allocative Efficiency: Toward a Theory of Distributive Justice." *Atlantic Economic Journal* 6(1):8–16.

Beach, C. M. 1976. "Cyclical Impacts on the Personal Distribution of Income." *Annals of Economic and Social Measurement* 5:29–52.

Blinder, A. S. 1974. *Toward an Economic Theory of Income Distribution*. Cambridge, Mass.: MIT Press.

———. 1975. "Distribution Effects and the Aggregate Consumption Function." *Journal of Political Economy* 83:447–75.

———. 1980. "The Level and Distribution of Economic Well-Being." Cambridge, Mass.: National Bureau of Economic Research.

———, and H. Y. Esaki. 1978. "Macroeconomic Activity and Income Distribution in the Postwar United States." *Review of Economics and Statistics* 60(4):604–09.

Brittan, S. 1973. *Is There an Economic Consensus?* London: Macmillan.

Katzner, D. W. 1970. *Static Demand Theory*. New York: Macmillan.

Metcalf, C. E. 1972. *An Econometric Model of the Income Distribution*. Chicago: Markham.

Okun, A. M. 1975. *Equality and Efficiency: The Big Tradeoff*. Washington, D.C.: Brookings.

Shoven, J. B., and J. Whalley. 1972. "A General Equilibrium Calculation of the Effects of Differential Taxation of Income from Capital in the U.S." *Journal of Public Economics* 1:201–321.

IV VIGNETTES OF THE MAN AND THE SCHOLAR

21 PAUL A. SAMUELSON: *The Harvard Days*

Abram Bergson

I first met Paul Samuelson after he came to Harvard in September 1935. He had just completed his undergraduate studies in Chicago. Having been awarded a Social Science Research Council Fellowship to do graduate work in economics, he had considered going to Columbia. Lest Harvard pride be unduly inflated by his decision in its favor, I must add that his decision cannot really be taken to attest to Harvard's superior academic merit. As Paul (I have called him that for over four decades and must do so here) has explained, the impelling considerations were nonscholarly: essentially, the desire to be at a New England institution with "green ivy" (Samuelson 1977, pp. 887–88).

It is intriguing to speculate on what might have become of Paul, Columbia, Harvard, and contemporary economics if his decision had been otherwise. Certainly the Harvard of the latter thirties would not have been as exciting a place to do graduate work in economics as it turned out to be.

I myself had become a graduate student in economics at Harvard in September 1933. It already says something about the pace of Paul's development in economics that I first got to know him in an advanced seminar that we attended together in the academic year 1935–36, that being his first and my third year of graduate work.

The seminar was Economics 18: "Price Theory and Price Analysis." Under that heading, the then Assistant Professor Wassily W. Leontief offered a rigorous and amazingly lucid mathematical exposition of core aspects of microeconomics: consumer demand theory, theory of the firm, and so forth.

Paul, I seem to recall, came into the course somewhat after it had begun, but before meeting him there I had already heard about the brilliant new arrival from Chicago. Paul was an auditor rather than a credit student in the course, but, apart from an auditor's being relieved of formal requirements such as a paper, the distinction is not apt to be meaningful in a Harvard economics seminar. It hardly was so for Paul in Economics 18.

The seminar was a small one (besides me, only three students were enrolled for credit), and Leontief conducted it informally, so that we could readily participate in discussion when that seemed in order. Paul certainly participated. Should anyone else falter in his analysis, Paul was almost always able to repair the deficiency promptly.

But that is only to say that Paul already manifested then what has since become proverbial: his capacity to perceive almost instantaneously the interrelated essentials of a complex analytic matter. I have particular reason to recall his early aptitude in that regard, for in the second term of 1935–36, I decided to do a paper for the seminar on the subject of Frisch's "new methods" of measuring marginal utility of real income. A cardinal question that I should have to explore, it soon emerged, concerned the implications of Frisch's underlying assumption of "expenditure proportionality" for the household utility function. I still recall discussing the matter with Paul and his conjecturing that expenditure proportionality must imply a household indifference map of a sort that has since come to be called "homothetic." As it turned out, that was the case, though I had to exert some effort to demonstrate the fact.

I recall subsequently presenting some interim results of my work on Frisch, at an ad hoc session of the seminar, to an encouragingly appreciative audience of two: Leontief and Samuelson. My seminar paper, incidentally, was subsequently published in the *Review of Economic Studies* (October 1936).

Whatever claim to fame I may have as an economist seems to derive to a marked degree from another paper that I wrote when I was a graduate student at Harvard: the essay on the foundations of welfare economics that was published in the *Quarterly Journal of Economics* in

February 1938. In turning to welfare economics at the time, I vaguely remember desiring, among other things, to clarify my thoughts about optimal resource allocation in a planned economy. I was then beginning to get into the subject of socialist economic planning, which was later to become a major preoccupation for me.

I wrote the welfare economics article on my own, rather than for a course, and must have done practically all of my work on it in the year after I took the Leontief seminar — that is, during 1936–37. It was only natural, though, that as my work progressed I should discuss it with Paul. He was, I think, the first person to whom I presented my idea of introducing a social welfare function into the analysis and using it to demonstrate the value judgments underlying previous formulations.

In that way I benefited not only from Paul's helpful suggestions but from his manifest interest. That was especially to the good since welfare economics enjoyed little favor at Harvard at the time. Among faculty who were inclined to formal analysis, Haberler was almost alone in being particularly attentive to work in welfare economics. For Schumpeter, that branch of economics held no interest to speak of. Leontief seemed rather ambivalent regarding it.

At the risk of digressing, though, I must note that Taussig too manifested an interest in welfare economics. I had taken his theory course in my first year at Harvard, and we did spend some time there on Pigou's *Economics of Welfare*. I still remember that, in accordance with his famous Socratic method, Taussig one day initiated a discussion of Pigou by turning to me and asking: "What is social welfare?" Happily, I do not remember my probably not very coherent answer.

I found Taussig a rather awesome but still sympathetic teacher, and when I completed my essay on welfare economics, I turned to him for advice as to what to do with it. I was, needless to say, delighted to hear from him that he would publish it in the *Quarterly Journal of Economics*, of which he was then editor.

But that was in the spring of 1937, and Taussig, already at the end of a long tenure, soon retired as editor, to be succeeded by A. E. Monroe. To complete the story, Monroe in due course balked at publishing a piece such as mine, which was replete with mathematical symbols. At least, he urged, I should put the mathematics, including the social welfare function, in an appendix. As might be inferred from the essay as it finally appeared, I somehow successfully resisted Monroe's pressure.

In recording the foregoing experience here, I have wandered from my theme, but have not really abandoned it, for it happens that, among the Harvard economics faculty of the time, Monroe was by no means alone in being something less than enamoured of mathematical economics. True, two one-semester courses were offered in mathematical economics, one for undergraduates, by Leontief, and the other for graduates, by E. B. Wilson, of the School of Public Health (Paul took the latter course and has referred to Wilson as his "revered teacher"). True, too, Leontief himself, of course, freely employed mathematics in his research, and Schumpeter, as everyone knows, was an enthusiastic, though not always deeply understanding, champion of the use of mathematical techniques. Haberler was also favorably disposed, and some others were similarly inclined, or at least not opposed.

The fact remains, however, that a good many of the senior faculty were more or less hostile to mathematical economics. According to a legend that has circulated too long and widely to be unfounded, the then department chairman promptly dismissed a graduate student teaching fellow when he learned that the latter had used some mathematical notation in a section of the introductory economics course that he gave. In the circumstances, if some graduate students nevertheless found the Harvard milieu hospitable to the use of mathematical methods, Paul's own active commitment to, and creative use of, such procedures was not the least of the reasons.

But, to repeat, some of the senior faculty were favorably inclined to the use of mathematical techniques, and one place where one was free to employ them was an informal faculty–graduate student seminar on economic theory that met periodically. The seminar was probably most active in the late thirties. Schumpeter, Haberler, and Leontief were among the faculty attending. It goes without saying that Paul, by that time no ordinary graduate student but a prestigious Junior Fellow,[1] was an outstanding participant. I still recall vividly some of the exchanges in which he took part. Providing as it did an opportunity to a participant to present for close scrutiny any of his current analytic work that might be of general interest and to learn at an early date of the ongoing work of others, the seminar probably was for many students a high point of their stay at Harvard.

While we were at Harvard together, Paul not only contributed to my education in economics, but seemingly also had a profound impact on my personal life. It appears that, as one of a group of celebrants of Paul's marriage in July 1938 to Marion Crawford (now lamentably deceased), I was so much impressed with the clearly felicitous turn of events for him that I vowed on the spot to abandon bachelorhood at an early opportunity — or so I have been told — and it is said that Shigeto Tsuru, the future president of Hitotsubashi University, who was then likewise a fellow graduate student, was spurred to make the same commitment. At any rate, in the following fall both of us duly appeared in Cambridge with newly acquired wives!

My graduate school days came to end in June 1940 when, on receiving my doctorate, I accepted an appointment at the University of Texas. Paul himself left Harvard soon after to join the MIT faculty.[2]

Impressive as Paul was as a graduate student, I must admit that I hardly anticipated the extraordinary eminence that he would attain. But, then, who could have known that the young author of a number of profound and original papers in mathematical economic theory would not only continually create similarly fundamental analytical works but also produce a pedagogical masterpiece that was to become one of the most successful and influential economics texts of all time? And who could possibly have apprehended that the very same person was a future advisor of American presidents and the future author of a widely read column in a popular newsmagazine? Still again, who could have foretold — but enough said. Let's face it. Paul's achievements have not only been beyond any plausible expectation. They are incredible even now.

NOTES

1. And thus a member of the newly established Society of Fellows. Appointed for a term of years, the Junior Fellow had no academic duties.

2. The circumstances of Paul's departure from Harvard have often been a subject of speculation. In a forthcoming essay on the history of Harvard economics instruction, Edward S. Mason sheds some further light on that matter. At the conclusion of Paul's term as Junior Fellow, he was recommended for an instructorship at Harvard, but Paul opted instead for an appointment at MIT that he had reason to consider more attractive. In order to counter the MIT offer, a majority of the economics department at Harvard voted to recommend Paul for an assistant professorship, but, according to Mason, "so large a negative vote was registered that the recommendation failed."

REFERENCE

Samuelson, P. A. 1977. *The Collected Scientific Papers of Paul A. Samuelson*, Vol. 4. Ed. by H. Nagatani and K. Crowley. Cambridge, Mass.: MIT Press.

22 PAUL A. SAMUELSON:
A Personal Tribute and a Few Reflections
George A. Akerlof

Sköl, Paul Samuelson! If my feelings are typical, this volume will give many people, in addition to myself, great pleasure in providing an opportunity to thank you for many deeds of unusual kindness over many years. Your contribution to MIT, economics, and America has not been just a technical contribution; it has been, as well, a moral one — always standing on the generous side of the economic and political issues.

Since this is a personal tribute, it accordingly seems appropriate to mention this generosity as it affected my own life as a graduate student at MIT from 1962 to 1966. The students of my time remarked frequently on the benign character of the "institutions" of the MIT economics department. This ranged from serious concerns, such as those of classroom teaching, examinations, and financial support, to the less serious concerns of the arrangements and social functions of graduate student life. Although seemingly unimportant, these last had a great effect on our learning, since MIT students of the time were particularly close and learned a great deal from each other.

Even in the midst of all his activities in the early 1960s, as researcher, textbook writer, columnist, government adviser, sometime commodity speculator, and teacher, Samuelson was still, in my memory, always free to see any student any time. It was the theory of my cohort of graduate students that his leadership was responsible for the general benign character of MIT. Who is ever thanked personally for good institutions? I am sure that no one ever thanked him for his efforts — but I also know that each of us is still personally grateful.

The purpose of this volume is to assess Samuelson's achievements in economics. The works that are in writing are easy to assess. The public has them, most of them collected in four large, easily accessible volumes. Other essays in this volume will undoubtedly mention all the major written contributions contained in these four volumes. There is, in addition, a side to Samuelson known only to people with whom he has had close contact — the unwritten Samuelson, that great fund of witticism and wisdom who has been a delight and joy, even if sometimes a puzzlement, to all who have known him.

First, a mention of the witticisms. I never eat a banana without remembering that Milton Friedman learned how to spell the word banana but did not know where to stop (i.e., Friedman knows standard economics but not its limitations). I never cross the country without realizing that diminishing returns prevent all the world's wheat from being grown in a flower pot. When I visited the Louvre, I remembered that Samuelson had challenged my fellow graduate student Richard Auster to put a production possibility frontier on the back of the Mona Lisa (although in this case I could not recall why he wanted it there).

Behind these witticisms there was almost always a point of some deep meaning. Let me mention two serious examples from his classes.

The early 1960s were the days of standard Keynesian economics (as taught in the Samuelson textbooks). The Phillips curve and Kennedy-Heller-Samuelson economics were in their prime. I remember, however, a few disturbing remarks at the beginning of one theory class. Raymond Saulnier had argued that if people added inflationary expectations to their wage demands, at low unemployment inflation would not remain constant, according to the prevailing Phillips-curve theory of the time, but would, on the contrary, rise steadily. Samuelson then traced out in a few brief sentences what is now known as the Phelps-Friedman natural rate theory. Then he mused over whether or not the Saulnier argument should be taken seriously. If Saulnier was wrong, knowledge of the argument would lead to much unemployment; on the other hand, if Saulnier was right, the government had few degrees of freedom, and knowledge of the argument, although correct, would do little good. Econometric evidence was too ambiguous to discriminate such a subtle hypothesis. In these few sentences at the beginning of a class Samuelson not only presaged the new macroeconomics of the next fifteen years, but at the same time his modesty about the limitations of economics was, I am convinced, now as then, exactly right.

Having been away from MIT for fifteen years, I now know that his courses aimed at giving us doubts about the utilitarian basis for economics. First there was the story of the dread General Butler with 30,000 men. He said that he would prefer that each of them die a horrible death than that he should receive a pinprick to a single finger! There is probably no MIT student of my time who is not still in some small degree in awe of the terrible General Butler. Samuelson repeated the story more than once, yet it has taken me some time to appreciate his fascination with this story. The next year, at the beginning of another class, he mentioned that, according to Dennis Robertson, economists had nothing to say about love. I now see that this is the Butler story in another guise. For Butler, despite his perversity, was nevertheless the economic man. Samuelson, like Dennis Robertson, was deeply disturbed by the failure of economic models to represent some of the fundamentals of human behavior — love, passion, hate, greed, vengeance.

These issues in utilitarian theory are now beginning to come into the center stage of economics. For example, Amartya Sen is writing about nonutilitarian views of social welfare in the *Economic Journal* and Gary Becker has just finished a book on altruism. Assumptions, such as those of utilitarianism, which may be innocent when plotting the demand for cheese, are not necessarily innocent when demands or supplies that encompass emotional issues — such as the supply of labor or the demand for discrimination — are involved. It remains to be seen whether the next ten years will bring these problems further into the forefront of economic theory. At the minimum, Samuelson was looking for answers to these questions and urging his students to do so fifteen years ago.

The two examples I have just given are meant to illustrate that his classes not only taught economics from the textbook, but that his scattering of remarks foresaw how the textbooks were (and still are) yet to be written. Even more remarkable, as the person of his generation who made the greatest contribution to standard economics, he not only taught us this economics but also tried to instill in us proper modesty about its use. His aim was not only to teach us how to spell "banana," but also to know where to stop.

23 THE CONTRIBUTIONS OF PAUL A. SAMUELSON TO ECONOMIC ANALYSIS:
A Revealed Preference Approach
Michael D. Intriligator

One of Paul Samuelson's important contributions to economic theory is the revealed preference approach to consumer demand, under which underlying and unobservable preferences are revealed by actual market choices. The purpose of this note is to apply a similar approach to evaluate Samuelson's own contributions to economic analysis. Just as consumers make market choices in purchasing certain goods and not others at certain prices, economic theorists make choices in citing certain articles and not others in their publications. Thus a simple tabulation of frequently cited articles would reveal which works have had the greatest impact, with the number of times cited a crude measure of the degree of their impact. Fortunately, the *Social Science Citation Index* can be used to obtain such a tabulation.

Samuelson's most frequently cited articles during the period 1966–1979, in order of number of times cited, are as follows:

Rank	Article	Number of Citations 1966–1979
1	"Prices of Factors and Goods in General Equilibrium," *Review of Economic Studies* 21 (1953):1–20.	289
2	"The Pure Theory of Public Expenditure," *Review of Economics and Statistics* 36 (1954):387–89.	246
3	"Diagrammatic Exposition of a Theory of Public Expenditure," *Review of Economics and Statistics* 37 (1955):350–56.	150
4	"Social Indifference Curves," *Quarterly Journal of Economics* 70 (1956):1–22.	117
5	"Parable and Realism in Capital Theory: The Surrogate Production Function," *Review of Economic Studies* 29 (1962):193–206.	110
6	"An Exact Consumption-Loan Model of Interest with or without the Social Contrivance of Money," *Journal of Political Economy* 66 (1958):467–82.	102
7	"Lifetime Portfolio Selection by Dynamic Stochastic Programming," *Review of Economics and Statistics* 51 (1969):239–46.	94
8	"Spatial Price Equilibrium and Linear Programming," *American Economic Review* 42 (1952):283–303.	86
9	"Proof that Properly Anticipated Prices Fluctuate Randomly," *Industrial Management Review* 6 (1965):41–49.	83
10	(with F. Modigliani), "The Pasinetti Paradox in Neoclassical and More General Models," *Review of Economic Studies* 33 (1966):269–301.	78
11	"General Proof that Diversification Pays," *Journal of Financial and Quantitative Analysis* 2 (1967):1–13.	77
12	(with R. M. Solow), "Analytical Aspects of Anti-Inflation Policy," *American Economic Review* 50 (1960):177–94.	75

This tabulation includes only articles cited at least fifty times during this fourteen-year period. Four other points should be made about this tabulation. First, it is based only on citations appearing in articles published during the period 1966–1979, so Samuelson articles of a much earlier period would be expected to be cited relatively less frequently than those of the immediately preceding and contemporaneous period. Second, the reprinting of Samuelson's papers in *The Collected Scientific Papers of Paul A. Samuelson,* starting in 1966, led to citations to articles in the reprinted volumes rather than to the original journal publication, and these citations are not included. Third, some of Samuelson's most important contributions appeared in books, especially his *Foundations of Economic Analysis,* which are not included in this tabulation. Fourth, Samuelson has had a profound effect on both economic analysis and the teaching of economics through his text, *Economics, An Introductory Analysis,* which since 1948 has been one of the most widely used principles texts.

The tabulation does lead to some conclusions concerning the revealed preference of economists for Samuelson's work. In terms of number of citations, it appears that Samuelson's three most important contributions to economic analysis were his development of factor price equalization, his analysis of the concept of public goods, and his work in portfolio and finance theory. A fourth major contribution is Samuelson's development of revealed preference theory.

Samuelson's analysis of the concept of public goods and his development of a pure theory of public expenditure appears in articles ranked 2, 3, and 13, which were cited a combined total of 465 times. He studied public goods, which, in contrast to private goods, are goods for which more consumption by one individual does not mean less consumption by another individual. Examples include national defense and radio and television broadcasts. Samuelson obtained the conditions required for optimality of public expenditure when there exist public as well as private goods.

Samuelson's second major contribution, his development of factor price equalization, appears in articles ranked 1, 16, and 20, which were cited a combined total of 402 times. According to the basic factor price equalization theorem, free trade will equalize factor prices internationally among countries having identical constant-returns-to-scale production functions assuming perfect competition, no specialization (each country produces some of each good), and no factor-intensity reversals. Under these conditions rewards to productive factors will be equalized even if factors are perfectly immobile domestically, so that given product prices, factor prices are determined independently of factor supply. This theorem was proved by showing that there is a unique mapping from product prices, which are set internationally, to factor prices. This result has been of fundamental significance not only for international trade theory but also for general equilibrium theory and the mathematical theory of global univalence of mappings.

Samuelson's third major contribution, his work in portfolio and finance theory, appears in articles ranked 7, 9, 11, 17, and 21, which were cited a combined total of 363 times. He has made several important contributions in this area. He has developed a model of lifetime portfolio selection, proved that diversification pays, proved that properly anticipated prices fluctuate randomly, and studied warrant pricing.

Samuelson's fourth major contribution is his development of revealed preference theory. This work, which appears in the article ranked 15, was cited sixty-two times, but it must be included in any list of Samuelson's most important contributions. This area did not generate as many citations as the ones previously discussed, since the article was published many years ago and it is reprinted in *The Collected Scientific Papers of Paul A. Samuelson.* In addition, this area was further explored in Samuelson's *Foundations of Economic Analysis,* which is very frequently cited. In this area Samuelson made the fundamental contribution of developing the theory of revealed preference, according to which market choices can be used to infer preferences. This theory has been applied to the evaluation of real national income and the construction of index numbers in the article ranked 19.

Among Samuelson's other contributions, his treatment of social indifference curves, which appears in the article ranked 4, was cited 117 times. He showed in this article that there exist nonintersecting contours in output space corresponding to the contours of the social welfare function in utility space, provided income is optimally redistributed among households. Samuelson's development of the surrogate production function and the factor price frontier appeared in an article ranked 5, which was cited 110 times. In this article Samuelson proved that for a constant-returns-to-scale production function using capital and labor, there exists a technical relationship between the factor prices of the rental and the wage. The (negative) slope of this relationship is the ratio of the factor inputs, the capital-labor ratio, so the elasticity of this relationship at any point is the relative share. Samuelson's development of the overlapping-generations model appeared in an article ranked 6, which was cited 102 times. In this article Samuelson explored the implications of a dynamic model in which the intertemporal issues are intergenerational, with each consumer living two periods. One implication is a biological social rate of discount, equal to the rate of growth of population.

This note has attempted to summarize some of Samuelson's more influential contributions in article form. It has underscored the fact that, even omitting his extremely influential books, Samuelson has had a major sustained impact in many areas of economic analysis, particularly, in recent years, in the areas of public goods, factor price equalization, and portfolio and finance theory.

24 ON THE SUPERLATIVE IN SAMUELSON

Martin Bronfenbrenner

I was once assigned, as an undergraduate student of English literature, a paper, "On the Superlative in Shakespeare." As I recall my sophomoric effort of a generation and a half ago, it was long enough and conventional enough for an excellent grade. Shakespeare, I said with no claim to originality, was a master of tragic, comic, and historical drama all three, and likewise of the sonnet cycle in poetry. He was not an innovator in matters of form, but a superb practitioner of the conventional forms of his own era. In other ages he might have mastered the eighteenth-century novel, the Homeric epic, or the Wagnerian music-drama, although he would hardly have invented any of these. Furthermore, I realized, Shakespeare's historical dramas were now considered badly flawed and biased as history, while the wit and humor of his comic genius were now comprehensible, if at all, only darkly through the glasses of commentary and footnote. Finally, in my opinion, Shakespeare burned himself out early, accomplishing nothing of note after the age of 45 and dying at 52. I nevertheless claimed that English literature had not yet seen his equal for the range of his several excellencies.

In the case of Paul Samuelson as a contemporary economist, I am tempted to dust off and reapply my Shakespearian analogy on a smaller

345

scale. As my choice of title for this essay implies, I have not resisted temptation.

Over and beyond the four hefty volumes of Samuelson's *Collected Scientific Papers*, of which more later, three major works stand out: *Foundations of Economic Analysis, Economics* in its several (currently eleven) editions, and *Linear Programming and Economic Analysis* (with Robert Dorfman and Robert Solow). The earliest of these, *Foundations*, subjects received economic theory to the harrow of the logical-positivist movement in the philosophy of science. It has also done more than any other single publication to lift mathematical economics as mathematics out of the rut of "a little potted calculus" in which it had languished for most of its previous life. The second major work, *Economics, An Introductory Analysis*, was *the* standard elementary textbook for a generation of professionals and intelligent laymen in English-speaking countries. (Translations into other tongues exist in multiplicity, but have been less influential.) Samuelson's *Economics* embodied the "new economics" and "neoclassical synthesis" of 1945–1970, compounded of essentially fiscalist Keynesian macroeconomics and essentially Marshallian microeconomics, with an overlay of imperfect competition. Samuelson's third major work, *Linear Programming*, spearheaded a temporary near-takeover of economic dynamics by a programming approach exemplified by the various turnpike theorems of development planning. The takeover, never completed, seems subsequently to have lessened, and turnpike theorems seem a little passé, although fashions in scholarship, as in dress, are known to reverse themselves on occasion.

In addition to these three volumes and the *Collected Scientific Papers*, any estimate of Samuelson's work and its significance must include the public Samuelson of frequent congressional testimony and of frequent policy statements in *Newsweek* magazine and elsewhere. These have been, and remain, influential in "neo-New Deal," "compassionate liberal," and antimonetarist directions. But at the same time Samuelson has remained an academician. He has refrained not only from retiring to live on his investments and textbook royalties, but also from formal membership on the Council of Economic Advisers or acceptance of other equally responsible official positions. These public service opportunities could have been his for the asking, at least in the Kennedy administration. I think Samuelson's resistance to the siren song of "mattering" in Washington was a wise one. Samuelson is not at his best in rough-and-tumble debate. He does not always avoid the appearance of arrogance, authoritarianism, and superciliousness in elementary presentations to those political types formerly known as "sons of the wild jackass," those financiering types known as "wizards" for however long they evade both jail and bankruptcy, and those journalistic types whose appetite for alcohol exceeds their appetite for learning.

Such is the body of work and professional activity that I submit to be "superlative" in Samuelson among contemporary Anglo-American economists, although hardly among economists generally (or social scientists generally) of all times and places. Others in Samuelson's age group, perhaps, have equaled or even surpassed him in rigor or in vigor, but hardly in both. Others, perhaps, have made roughly equivalent or even superior contributions in one or another of the fields touched on in this introduction, but who among them, I wonder, has equaled Samuelson across the board? I consider Friedman and Hicks, Myrdal and Mrs. Robinson, and reluctantly shake my head, although others may well disagree. One must go back one generation, to the generation of Keynes and Schumpeter, or so it seems to me, to find Samuelson's equal among economists at once generalist and specialist in so many fields. Which conclusion may be damning my generation as much or more than it praises Samuelson!

INITIAL IMPRESSIONS

It is difficult to estimate one's most illustrious contemporaries fairly in brief compass, either orally or in writing. Professional politicos and critics, I know, bungle the attempt every day, usually showing themselves, in Dryden's terms:

> . . . so over-violent or over-civil
> That every man to them is God or Devil.

The favorable estimate falls naturally under suspicion of being a plea for crumbs from its subject's table of disposable influence. The unfavorable estimate falls under even greater suspicion of being a spiteful concoction of jealousy and envy — only this and nothing more. (Should not some part of the subject's prizes and honors and appointments have gone in all justice to the critic, or to the critic's friends?) On both counts I plead as great a degree of disinterest as I can muster and hope against hope that some considerable fraction of my readers will believe me most of the time.

I first met Samuelson in the fall of 1934, on the verge of his wunderkind days. His wunderkind status was recognized within the economics department at the University of Chicago, but hardly anywhere else. He was then 19, a senior undergraduate who knew more economics than did any of the incoming graduate students — in particular, more than I did. Rumor had it that he could already pass the dreaded doctoral "prelims" without studying and before taking his bachelor's degree; also, that he had already read everything worth reading by every economist worth reading, and a good many other pieces by a good many other economists as well. As the academic year 1934–35 progressed, I found no reason to disbelieve either rumor. Personally, Samuelson was a completely sober and earnest young man. He talked verbal mathematics by preference when he talked at all, which was seldom — at least by the gabby standards of Chicago. The ready Samuelson wit and humor and the graceful Samuelson hand with English prose were there, if at all, only in embryo; perhaps Harvard encourages such embellishments better than Chicago does. Three little tales, of absolutely no significance in themselves, will indicate the wunderkind quality of Samuelson's undergraduate mind.

First, budding Chicago economists of those years trembled in the presence of the ferocious Jacob Viner. Viner could (and did) end careers by ejecting some aspirant "not ready" for his required theory course, "Econ. 301," as when said aspirant could not "go to the board and draw *that*" (meaning some confused nonsense said aspirant had just fumbled forth). Selected Chicago undergraduates were also permitted exposure to this treatment. Samuelson was one of these in 1935, but I too had been a selected undergraduate the previous year at Washington University, and his admission meant less to me than it should have done. What brought me around was Samuelson's temerity in Viner's presence. While most of us were escaping at top speed after class, saved by the bell, Samuelson would approach the dreaded "Jake" politely but firmly: "Professor Viner, in today's lecture I think you made the following mistakes . . . ," usually mathematical ones, since Samuelson already knew more mathematics than Viner did. (I give Viner credit for admitting his mistakes when he was wrong, as he sometimes was, and not trying to roar or bluff or bully his way out as pedagogues have done throughout the ages in similar situations.)

Second, I was impressed by the Cobb-Douglas function, but Samuelson had already fitted, on his own, a linear alternative function to Paul Douglas's data on output, capital, and labor. Not only that, but this Samuelson alternative (which ruled out diminishing returns altogether) fit the facts as well as Douglas's better-behaved logarithmic form of the production function. I have gone ahead to do Cobb-Douglas function work of various sorts, but have never shaken off the skeptical doubts implanted so early by Samuelson.

Third, I took the first graduate course in international trade; Samuelson did not. Instead, Samuelson wrote papers on the subject. If I remember the manuscript he showed me, it purported to prove rigorously that any country with monopoly power over one or more of its exports, or with monopsony power over one or more of its imports, could always do better for itself (achieve greater gains from trade) by utilizing such power than by adherence to free trade. Perhaps I was seeing an early draft of Samuelson's short *A.E.R.* paper of 1938 on "Welfare Economics and International Trade."

So much for the shock of encountering Samuelson as colleague, classmate, and competitor — a shock few graduate students ever encounter. I shall always be grateful for Paul Douglas's kindly reassurances that one really need not be another Samuelson to pass muster as an economist!

FOUNDATIONS AND ECONOMICS

Other contributors to this symposium will presumably concentrate on Samuelson's *Foundations* and his *Economics,* especially the earlier work. My own remarks can therefore be safely brief and superficial.

Foundations, or at least some of its chapters, was not only written in draft form but circulated among the elect as early as 1937–1938, before Sir John Hicks's *Value and Capital* had crossed the Atlantic. *Foundations* represents, therefore, an alternative solution to Hicks's problem of "the operational significance of economic theory," and not merely a gloss or appendix. (It took real courage to plow ahead after the appearance of Hicks's great book!) To me at least, the principal advances of Samuelson over Hicks were two in number. One was the greater concentration on applications; I am thinking particularly of Chapter 8 on welfare economics. The other advance is the correspondence principle articulating the stability properties of comparative statics on the one hand and dynamics on the other.

At the same time, Samuelson has stopped just short of a really thoroughgoing application of logical positivism to economic analysis. Such an analysis, in my view, must include what Samuelson omitted from *Foundations* and later denounced explicitly as an F- (for "Friedman") twist (i.e., the irrelevance of the "realism" or plausibility of whatever initial assumptions underlie one's theoretical model). It is all very well to be aware, and to point out to readers, that the use of unrealistic assumptions does not itself deny the reality of the real world. It is likewise very well to have faith that, in the medium run before we are all

dead, some future theory with more realistic assumptions than Theory
T will outperform (outpredict) Theory T. But if Theory T, assuming
moons made of green cheese and rational behavior of leaves on trees,
clearly outperforms any current alternative, our best policy is to accept
it "irregardless," at least provisionally.

The early editions of Samuelson's *Economics* textbook swept their
field and enriched their author. It included by far the best macroeconomic
(i.e., Keynesian) material then available at the "principles" level and
placed this material in the foreground in place of "supply and demand,"
economic history, or institutional matters. It was also aimed at intellectually alive returning veterans at MIT and the Ivy League rather than at
Raternity Row or Playboy College. Having seized this market in the mid-
1940s, Samuelson's *Economics* in its later editions has retained much of
it ever since.

To gain and hold an appreciable share of the expanding, but increasingly segmented and trendy, textbook market has required secular expansion of Samuelson's *Economics* in several directions, and I think for
three main reasons.

In the first place, as the Raternity Row-Playboy College segment has
regained some of its pre-1930 importance, the text has been simplified.
The more demanding and less descriptive parts of the argument have
been hidden away in notes and appendices, at the cost of some repetition
and duplication.

In the second place, and more important, these notes and appendices
have themselves tended to burgeon and expand, producing a split-level
effect comparable to Marshall's *Principles of Economics*. A new and
probably unanticipated market segment has appeared; graduate students
and practicing economists use Samuelson, uniquely among the elementary texts, as a vehicle for ready reference, as a cram book for advanced
examinations, as a guide to progress in one or more aspects of their
subject, and as a remedy for quantitative and qualitative gaps in their
previous training.

And in the third place, space has been provided, a chapter or two per
edition, for most of the postwar novelties (fads?) in economic teaching
— both new *problems* and new *viewpoints*. Despite periodic efforts to
slim down, there have not been corresponding reductions elsewhere in
the book.

The result of this net expansion can be criticized as offering, not
indeed all things to all men, but many things to many men. In economic
jargon, size may have reached the point of negative returns. In Aesop's

fables, the sad tale of the merchant, his son, and the ass may be the point.

COLLECTED SCIENTIFIC PAPERS

Few economists other than Samuelson himself can read widely and understandingly in the *Collected Scientific Papers*. This means merely that few can match Samuelson in the depth-cum-breadth of their interests in economics and related fields. The casual reader samples papers in his specialties, but writes off much of the rest, where advanced methods are powerfully employed, as finger exercises, showpieces, or virtuoso displays of technique for technique's sake. I may have been as guilty of these sins of sour grapes as have most of my colleagues and therefore welcome this opportunity for open repentance. And furthermore, technical exercises can themselves become simultaneously works of art; witness, in music, Bach's *Anna Magdalena Buch* and the études of Chopin. Why not, in economics, the études of Samuelson?

The particular groups of papers from which I claim personally to have profited most have been in four fields: (1) macrodynamic fluctuations, particularly multiple-accelerator interactions; (2) international trade, particularly the papers leading to and expositing the factor-price equalization theorem; (3) modeling the work of primarily literary economists of past centuries in both general and monetary theory; and (4) economic methodology, particularly the "realism of assumptions" debate. This is not to call myself a devoted Samuelsonian on any or all of these topics, but only to admit that when I differ from him I do so diffidently and with a dangerously large chance of being wrong for reasons of technique, of scholarship, or both.

SINCE 1965

Most of the papers first mentioned, and likewise the early editions of the major works mentioned earlier, date from the period 1935–1960. Since 1965, however, an "anti-Samuelson" and "hate Samuelson" reaction has set in, centering domestically in the Union for Radical Political Economics (URPE).

This reaction arises partially against Samuelsonian technical virtuosity, interpreted as issue dodging or as reducing economics to a lesser branch of applied mathematics. It arises more significantly from dissatisfaction with the allegedly complacent policy stand associated with Samuelson. This is the "new economics" or "neoclassical synthesis" of *Economics* — basically Keynesian macroeconomics, we have said, plus Marshallian microeconomics with a dash of imperfect competition sauce. Doubts arose early about the internal consistency of this convenient and attractive synthesis of Marshall and Keynes. (How can a macroeconomy in Keynesian underemployment equilibrium be the sum of a number of microeconomies, including labor markets, for which the equality of supply and demand is the fundamental equilibrium condition? This is a so-called microfoundations of macroeconomics problem, but such problems are too abstract and arcane to fuel any public reaction.)

Let us accept the Samuelson "neoclassical synthesis" as a latter-day thesis and ignore any lingering doubts resulting from microfoundations difficulties. We find nevertheless a number of antitheses that have arisen and flourished since the early 1960s, both right and left (but mostly left) of Samuelson's *Economics* in political implications. Here is a partial list: monetarism; libertarianism; environmentalism; the Sraffa or neo-Cambridge revolution in capital and distribution theory; a Marxist revival; the New Left and the associated "radical economics"; in international economics, the doctrines of "unequal exchange" and *dependencia,* culminating in a call for an entire new international economic order. These are by no means independent of each other, as witness strong Marxist components in New Left economics, in neo-Cambridge, in unequal exchange, and in *dependencia.* Many of them, moreover, go out of their way to attack Samuelson personally, if only as a symbol of establishment economics or as a spokesman for a genteel version of American imperialism. Samuelson, on his part, has replied to only a few of these antitheses and has reconciled himself to still fewer. He has not, however, been a party to any "conspiracy of silence" to ignore any of them, as the economic "establishment" of 1867 apparently ignored Karl Marx's *Capital.*

One could hardly expect one man, even one man with Samuelson's superlative breadth of knowledge and interest, to take stands on all the points stressed in all the above heresies. Samuelson has, however, done the second-best thing. He has acknowledged their existence; he has treated them with as much judicious objectivity as he could muster (given strong built-in biases against the Herbert Spencer–Friedrich Hayek–Milton Friedman positions on his political right); and by these reactions he has shown all who will listen that conventional economics in its higher reaches does indeed show (belated) concern for and pay (belated) attention to many matters and arguments that it is widely accused of sweeping under the rug.

So far so good, and Samuelson has gone much further on at least three of the fronts — or barricades, if you prefer. In each instance he has defended his own position, often by counterattacking the opposition. He has sought to reduce monetarism to an erroneous and hard-hearted ex-huming of pre-Keynesian error, centering about the quantity theory of money. He has sought to reduce the Sraffa revolution to old wine in new bottles. He has sought to reduce Karl Marx (as an economist) to the position of ''a minor post-Ricardian''; insofar as this estimate is justified, it makes fools of that large segment of radical economics that derives its intellectual baggage primarily from Marx via Lenin, Trotsky, Mao, Cas-tro, or other professed followers.

On the first and third of these positions, I find myself more nearly in agreement with the rebels against Samuelson's ''neoclassical synthesis'' than with Samuelson himself, for reasons that cannot be exposited fully in so brief an essay as this one. On the second front, which relates to Sraffa and to neo-Cambridge, Samuelson and I concur. Samuelson, fur-thermore, has made two separate attempts to prove himself (and me) correct, and Sraffa and company wrong, on a technical level well beyond my (but not beyond his) comprehension. His approach was abstractly mathematical — in the event, unfortunately, less rigorous than he had hoped.

Samuelson proposed to prove that, even if Sraffa and disciples were correct in their picture of the world, that picture would hardly differ from the standard or conventional picture. In capital theory, the intellectual nub of the controversy, Samuelson's contention was that, in Sraffian as in conventional theory, a rise (fall) in the rate of interest on capital would under any but ''pathological'' conditions lead to a less (more) capital-intensive method of production, and this regardless of the way in which we chose to define *capital*. Consider two alternative techniques, Alpha and Beta, for producing a standardized commodity. Suppose Alpha to be more efficient and more profitable than Beta at rates of interest slightly higher than r, but vice versa at rates slightly lower than r. Also suppose the rate to fall — never mind why — from above r to below r, so that the optimal technique shifts from Alpha to Beta. Suppose further that the rate continues to fall; can we be sure that there will be no ''reswitching,'' that Alpha will not replace Beta once more? In conventional economics, the answer is yes, but the Sraffians profess complete agnosticism.

Samuelson made two attempts to derive conventional results from

Sraffian assumptions. The first employed a "surrogate" production function, the consequence of a large number (not merely two) of alternative techniques. The second used the so-called Samuelson-Levhari theorem. But neither attempt succeeded. Critics showed that Samuelson's surrogate production function was itself based implicitly on highly specialized assumptions, akin to a labor theory of value with capital goods reduced to indirect labor. The proof of the Samuelson-Levhari theory was faulty, as the authors themselves admitted when counterexamples were generated by the critics. Even today no one has derived economically meaningful conditions under which reswitching can be ruled out; at the same time, real-world examples of reswitching have been extraordinarily hard to come by. And here, I think, the matter rests.

Not failure but low aim is crime, and Samuelson's contributions are not to be discounted, let alone sneezed at. But, of course, they are unsuccessful, and they do not compare with Samuelson's earlier meteoric rise to preeminence among American Keynesians during his wunderkind period twenty-five to thirty years earlier.

IN CONCLUSION

Should Samuelson retire tomorrow from professional activity, he would surely be remembered in both the short and the long run. The two sets of memories might, however, be very different. My hope in this summary is to compare in advance the two sets of memories. How would Samuelson's short-run and long-run reputations compare?

Samuelson's academic stock has sustained a declining market since approximately 1965. Bears to the right of him, bears to the left of him, volleying and thundering — such is the argument of our last section. It is no longer even as true as it once was that American undergraduates learn their economics from Samuelson, if they learn it at all. One can hardly imagine Samuelson's retirement helping matters, ceteris paribus — barring external events to elicit sympathy for the man and for his views. The picture of Samuelson as pure technician and superestablishmentarian is therefore apt to retain its prominence even outside such ideological bastions as the Union for Radical Political Economics (URPE). It is fostered by a generation jealous, envious, and resentful of Samuelson as a father figure, or, perhaps more aptly, a wicked-uncle figure. And so he may remain for a time in our professional repute merely an extraordinarily gifted economic gymnast, ballerina, trained seal, or perhaps Paganini, performing for, it not kept by, the less-overtly reactionary half of the capitalist-imperialist establishment. To put the matter in other words, Samuelson's name may well become mud for a while, meaning by "mud" some combination of technician *gratia* technique and confinement of ideas within a safe and permissible range.

A Samuelson-baiter would let matters stand here, but the most interesting part of the story is yet to come. I think we can anticipate an eventual reversal of the market for Samuelson academic stock, which will lead to a substantial recovery in Samuelson's reputation. Let us see why this reversal may occur.

In the first place, the jealous and envious elements of the post-Samuelson generation will themselves attain mandarin status in their turn. They will then be subject in their turn to the jealousy and envy of the following generation. Jealousy and envy of father figures is often accompanied by revived respect and affection for grandfather figures. So it has been with, for example, Malthus and Mill in economics; so it appears to be with Irving Fisher in monetary and capital theory; so it may well be with Samuelson.

In the second place, we may come to take a more relative and historical viewpoint in estimating Samuelson. We may judge his contributions primarily on the basis of the state of economics during his wunderkind years, rather than on the basis of its present state after so many others have refined, extended, and otherwise improved on his own work.

And finally, a great deal depends on the success or failure of the several antiestablishment movements since 1965, which were also anti-Samuelson movements. If monetarism, Sraffaism, neo-Marxism, or some sociological economics appropriate to what Boulding has called the "fuzzy borderland" between economics and the behavioral sciences, should achieve great success in theory and practice, Samuelson will be left moldering in his grave. He may represent a last gasp of orthodox/scholastic economics, corresponding to Duns Scotus, that other *doctor subtilis,* in orthodox scholastic philosophy. But if things turn out otherwise, as they very well may, Samuelson will profit from the consequent counterrevolution much as Ricardo did from the counterrevolution against German historicism.

While all this is both vague and imprecise, I suggest that a lower bound can be set to Samuelson's longer-run place in the history of economic thought. My analogy is Camille Saint-Saëns (1835–1921) in the history of music. Saint-Saëns, a Frenchman, was both a brilliant pianist and a fertile and versatile composer. He is remembered for one opera (*Samson and Delilah*), one symphony, two or three concertos for various instruments, and a few shorter pieces (*Carnival of the Animals, Algerian*

Suite). His symphonic poems, widely admired by his contemporaries, are seldom played. Saint-Saëns has been called the greatest composer of his age — who was not also a genius!

This is surely the least that one can say of Samuelson, the lower limit of his repute. He has been surely the greatest economist of his time who is not also a genius. And if we can say more for Samuelson — if future ages adjudge him a genius — his fame will have surpassed its lower bound.

LIST OF CONTRIBUTORS

GEORGE A. AKERLOF, Professor of Economics, University of California, Berkeley

EARL F. BEACH, Bronfman Professor of Economics, McGill University

ABRAM BERGSON, George F. Baker Professor of Economics, Harvard University

ALAN S. BLINDER, Professor of Economics, Princeton University, and Research Associate, National Bureau of Economic Research

MARTIN BRONFENBRENNER, Kenan Professor of Economics, Duke University

JOHN S. CHIPMAN, Professor of Economics, University of Minnesota

GEORGE R. FEIWEL, Alumni Distinguished Service Professor, University of Tennessee

357

MICHAEL D. INTRILIGATOR, Professor of Economics, University of California, Los Angeles

MURRAY C. KEMP, Research Professor of Economics, University of New South Wales

LAWRENCE R. KLEIN, Nobel Laureate (1980), Benjamin Franklin Professor of Economics, University of Pennsylvania

WILHELM KRELLE, Professor of Economics, University of Bonn, and Director, Institut für Gesellschafts- und Wirtschaftswissenschaften

ROBERT E. KUENNE, Professor of Economics and Director, General Economic Systems Project, Princeton University

LAWRENCE J. LAU, Professor of Economics, Stanford University

NGO VAN LONG, Senior Lecturer in Economics, Australian National University

ANDREU MAS-COLELL, Professor of Economics, University of California, Berkeley, and Harvard University

GUNNAR MYRDAL, Nobel Laureate (1974), Professor Emeritus, University of Stockholm

TAKASHI NEGISHI, Professor of Economics, Tokyo University

EDWARD J. NELL, Professor of Economics, New School for Social Research

JOAN ROBINSON, Professor Emeritus, Cambridge University

JAN TINBERGEN, Nobel Laureate (1969), Professor Emeritus, Erasmus University

HENRY C. WALLICH, Member, Board of Governors, Federal Reserve System

HENRY Y. WAN, JR., Professor of Economics, Cornell University